Manual of Reformed Stoicism

Piotr Stankiewicz

Series in Philosophy

Vernon Press

Copyright © 2020 Vernon Press, an imprint of Vernon Art and Science Inc, on behalf of the author.

All rights reserved. No part of this publication may be reproduced, stored in a retrieval system, or transmitted in any form or by any means, electronic, mechanical, photocopying, recording, or otherwise, without the prior permission of Vernon Art and Science Inc.

www.vernonpress.com

In the Americas:
Vernon Press
1000 N West Street,
Suite 1200, Wilmington,
Delaware 19801
United States

In the rest of the world:
Vernon Press
C/Sancti Espiritu 17,
Malaga, 29006
Spain

Series in Philosophy

Library of Congress Control Number: 2019957903

ISBN: 978-1-64889-032-1

Also available: 978-1-62273-648-5 [Hardback]; 978-1-62273-944-8 [PDF, E-Book]

DISCLAIMER
This is a philosophical book – it's purpose is to educate. It is not intended as a substitute for psychological counseling. If you need help, please do not hesitate to see a mental health professional. The author and publisher disclaim any responsibility or liability resulting from the actions advocated or discussed in this book. The purchaser of this book assumes the responsibility for the decisions they take during and/or after reading the book, based on the information in the book.

Product and company names mentioned in this work are the trademarks of their respective owners. While every care has been taken in preparing this work, neither the authors nor Vernon Art and Science Inc. may be held responsible for any loss or damage caused or alleged to be caused directly or indirectly by the information contained in it.

Every effort has been made to trace all copyright holders, but if any have been inadvertently overlooked the publisher will be pleased to include any necessary credits in any subsequent reprint or edition.

to Olga and Natalia

Table of contents

	Introduction	ix
	Part one. Prime matters	*1*
Chapter 1	**It's all about narratives**	3
Chapter 2	**Get rid of useless narratives**	17
Chapter 3	**Things within and not within our power**	31
Chapter 4	**Focus on things within your power**	47
	Part two. Here and now or the principles of conduct	*67*
Chapter 5	**Act deliberately**	69
Chapter 6	**Live the present day**	81
Chapter 7	**Focus on the present action**	91
Chapter 8	**Your lifetime will suffice**	103
Chapter 9	**Define proper alternatives**	111
	Part three. Do not be afraid!	*121*
Chapter 10	**Anticipate mishap**	123
Chapter 11	**Don't dwell on counterfactual scenarios**	135
Chapter 12	**Don't desire acclaim**	147
Chapter 13	**Adversities are challenges**	161
Chapter 14	**Beware of treacherous constancy**	173
Chapter 15	**You are never alone**	183

	Part four. You in this playground	*195*
Chapter 16	**There is no point in flouting the rules of a game**	197
Chapter 17	**There are other games to play**	213
	Part five. Others in this playground	*223*
Chapter 18	**Be autonomous**	225
Chapter 19	**To each their own mistakes**	241
Chapter 20	**Don't ascribe intent**	249
	Part six. All else matters	*261*
Chapter 21	**Whatever the world is like – be a Stoic**	263
Chapter 22	**Follow good examples**	273
Chapter 23	**Practice regularly**	285
Chapter 24	**Be happy – it's simple**	297
	Conclusions and discussions	*311*
	Endnotes	*333*
	Bibliography	*335*
	Index	*337*

It is interesting [...] to imagine what might have happened if Stoicism had had a continuous twenty-three-hundred-year history; if Stoics had had to confront Bacon and Descartes, Newton and Locke, [...] Hume and Kant, Darwin and Marx, and the vicissitudes of ethics in the twentieth century.[i]

Lawrence C. Becker

Introduction

The ancients have found out proper remedies, for the several maladies of the mind, but how they are to be applied, and when, it is the business of the party concerned to enquire.

Seneca, *Epistles*, 64.8[ii]

Try at least: the [...] attempt is not disgraceful.

Epictetus, *Discourses*, IV.1.177

We, reformed Stoics, have a plain but ambitious goal. We want to learn together how to live well and happily. We live today so we don't merely recount ancient Stoicism. Instead, we offer a reformed version for the modern times.

This book is a manifesto of reformed Stoicism. It's intended to be a practical and positive manual, one which is accessible to everyone. It requires nothing from the reader but an open mind. No academic or philosophical background is needed. Besides a few remarks in this Introduction and a fuller outline in Conclusions and Discussions, this book contains no vague theory and no abstractions. Reformed Stoicism is about practice and real action. Also, this book contains no jargon. Reformed Stoicism is clear and comprehensible. It has nothing to do with verbal abracadabra and terminological muddle. It's a philosophy of life and a way of life.

Stoicism was originally developed around 300 BC in ancient Greece. From day one, it has had its distinct features. First of all, it's available to everyone. There are no bounds. Everybody can become a Stoic and live happily by its precepts, regardless of their gender, age, race, sexuality, nationality, intelligence, education, worldview and sense of humor. Second, it can make us happy no matter what our situation is. In these ways, it is universal. It never fails us and it proves helpful in every turn of events. Third, it's easy. It's easy to learn the Stoic way of life and the Stoic happiness is always within our grasp.

Reformed Stoicism is about enjoying and exercising our agency. It's about the flow of making autonomous and right decisions, and about celebrating our ability to make them. The ability to go with this flow (the ancients called it "virtue"), if properly understood, endows us with an almost godlike power which can be put to use in almost all instances of life. This universally available human agency is the best contemporary translation of the ancient Stoic idea of a divine spark present in every human. Its universal availability accounts for the Stoic emphasis on egalitarianism and cosmopolitanism (this part of Stoicism is more important today than ever). The awareness that even in the most difficult situation, we are always capable of making autonomous and right decisions is the Stoic key to happiness.

To these ends, Stoicism offers an impressive and comprehensive system for living a life. Highly original, it was not only one of the first such systems that Western philosophy yielded, but also, in my profound conviction, it is the most fruitful and coherent one. Stoicism is focused on finding the most adroit and most fortunate way of dealing with worldly affairs, all-things-considered[iii] and given the resources available. Stoicism insists that a right way to deal with life can always be found: both when the resources abound and when they are scarce. The latter case translates into the famous Stoic promise that happiness is independent from the external world and that it can be achieved no matter the circumstances.

Why *reformed* Stoicism? Because it is time, in short, for a new generation of Stoics: new Stoics to cope with new problems and seize new opportunities. Human eyes now look into the new millennium and beyond: into a new world of breathtaking change, unprecedented challenge and unfathomable advancement. For these reasons and according to the founding doctrines of our school, our quest for progress and our pursuit of happiness require us to evolve. Our time, in short, calls for a fresh interpretation of Stoicism.

Thus, contrary to our venerable predecessors, we no longer bind our decision-making capabilities to any pre-ordained cosmological order. We don't associate ourselves with any cosmic element, and we don't appeal to any higher power. We neither trust nor rely on "nature" (be it purposive or not), and we don't count on rationality of the universe. We don't shackle ourselves to any metaphysical point of view and we don't root our principles in any speculative insight.

Instead, we place emphasis on human autonomy. We rely on the usefulness rather than on the truth value of narratives. We dismiss the overtly conservative as well as the overtly ascetic misinterpretations of Stoicism. We don't summon the vanity argument. We appeal neither to alleged worthlessness and transience of worldly affairs, nor to the alleged glory and harmony of the universe. Ethically, we don't provide ready-made guidelines for conduct. We accept the burden of individual responsibility instead. We detest the stereotype of "a Stoic" pictured as a lifeless and ice-blooded figure, whose entire ambition amounts to "accepting fate." We prove the dictionary use of the word "stoical" wrong. We advance an interpretation of Stoicism as a philosophy of living an *active* life, understood as a practice of action and discipline of thought. For these reasons, a considerable number of

Introduction

traditional Stoic terms are not employed in this book. There is no reference to "following nature," "conformity to reason," providence or eternal return. The Conclusions and Discussions section provides some more theoretical backing for any interested reader.[1]

The structure of the book is this: in 24 chapters I present 24 Stoic principles *aka* exercises. They are tools which we can use to organize our life, secure happiness and combat mishap. I strove to present each tool as clearly and precisely as possible and I've illustrated them with plain examples from daily life. Each chapter starts off with a brief "in a nutshell" section, which provides the essence of a given principle. The body of each chapter contains a selection of quotes by the ancient Stoics and each quote is followed by my extensive commentary.

This specific structure serves a few purposes. **First**, it introduces a wide array of principles. You can pick and choose whatever you think is best for you. I don't insist that I hold the only correct interpretation. There are many ways to take Stoicism on and everyone should draw what they please. **Second**, as Seneca said, "though one might think that neither of these [precepts] alone were able to [work] [...] yet it must be confessed that when combined they have great power."[iv] **Third**, this book can be used in several manners. One can read it cover to cover and page by page, treating it as a comprehensive handbook of reformed Stoicism. One can also read it piecemeal, whenever and wherever the mood strikes. The "in a nutshell" section can be used as a lifeline to momentarily refresh Stoic ideas. Chapters can be read in any order that seems suitable at the moment. **Fourth**, as reformed Stoics, we divert freely from the original doctrine wherever necessary. On the other hand – we still stick to many points of it. Extended use of the words of the ancient Stoics is the expression of our allegiance to them. **Fifth**, voicing our own argument in the form of commentaries to their works opens up an interpretive space between the original text and its modern meaning. My intention was that the process of thinking up the commentaries may somehow "repeat" itself in the reading process. My wish is that this book can be treated as an open body of writing, an invitation to a joint (author's and reader's) examination of the Stoic curriculum. I hope that whenever you read and re-read this book, the inquiry into the meaning of the Stoic formulas will be repeated and it will become a Stoic exercise in itself.

---

[1] And so does my other Stoic book. See: Stankiewicz, *Does Happiness Write Blank Pages? On Stoicism and Artistic Creativity*.

Finally, a few personal remarks. I wrote this book with the understanding that teaching others is the best way to teach oneself. I can sincerely say that thanks to having written it, I've made one more step towards becoming a better Stoic. If reading it has a similar effect on you, dear reader, I will be nothing but happy. If you find something vague or incomprehensible on these pages – the fault is entirely my own, not the Stoics'. And if you feel overcome by doubt – please remember that you are not the first. Stoicism is not for those who have never fallen, but for those who want to stand up. This is not a book for those who already live perfect lives and have no second thoughts. This is a book for those who want to improve. This is a book that proposes that we go up this path – together. Let's go then.

Part one.
Prime matters

How to look at things

Chapter 1

It's all about narratives

What tortures us, therefore, is an idea. Now every evil is just as great as we consider it to be.

Seneca, *Of Consolation. To Marcia*, 19.1

In a nutshell: The world we live in is not a world of facts, things and events, but a world of our narratives about facts, things and events. We won't live well and we won't be happy unless we understand that our life and happiness hinge on our narratives and nothing else.

***

Our life consists not in facts, but in our narratives (fragment I). Narratives mediate our perception of the world, they insulate us from it (II). Most importantly, our happiness and misery depend on our narratives (III). Narratives mirror our language and *vice versa*: we create narratives by using specific words (IV). All happiness and all misery is caused by our narratives, not by the external world (V). How do we know this? Because, if it was the other way around, everyone would react in the same way to the same facts (VI) and because we often fear things before they actually happen (VII). We are responsible for forming and nourishing our narratives (VIII). Thus, we can't allow our thoughts to be careless and we mustn't forget that we ourselves are the source of everything that concerns us (IX). Stoicism doesn't hold the hardcore position that physical pain doesn't exist and that it's just a narrative (X). Yet, luxuries themselves are not the root of envy and greed, but rather our narratives about luxuries are (XI).

Fragment I

Such as are your habitual thoughts [i.e. narratives], *such also will be the character of your mind. For the soul is dyed by the thoughts.*

Marcus Aurelius, *Meditations*, 5.16

Commentary: This core idea opens not only our first chapter but also the whole Stoic story. The way we live and the way we deal with the world depends on how we think, that is, on our narratives. To be more precise: our every interaction with the world (for example doing something or making a decision) is always preceded by an *act of thought* (which is more or less conscious). In other words, it all starts with us thinking in a certain way about facts, events and errands. At the beginning, we pass a judgment and form an opinion about things. We do it all the time, wittingly and unwittingly, and thus we construct narratives for ourselves. Narratives make up that voice in our head that explains and comments on all things, all day long, 24/7. These narratives constitute all our experiences. This is one of the ground rules of Stoicism: we don't live in the world itself, we live in the world of our narratives.

Does it mean that all the well-known phenomena of common experience, like trees on the earth, like stars in the sky, like waves on the sea, like gossip and splendor, like recognition and oblivion are not there? Not so. These things exist undeniably, but at a distance from us. They don't have an immediate impact on us. We are separated and insulated from them by a soft cocoon of narratives which envelopes us and which mediates our contact with the world. We have direct, real contact with our narratives and with nothing else.

[margin: Kantian?]

It sounds a bit like a paradox. Let's imagine that it's a beautiful summer day and we are driving out of town for the weekend. We feel the pleasant touch of the sun on our skin, we see the blue sky, we enjoy the prospect of having two days off work. How are we *separated* from that? Where are the narratives which envelop us? How is our experience of these things "mediated?"

The Stoic answer is this. Indeed, we can feel the sun and enjoy the prospect, we can see the sky and take in the great weather. But these sensations aren't the source of our bliss themselves. What's the source then? Our narratives about them. Let's take another example: a grim December morning. It's still dark outdoors, but we have to wake up, get dressed, and depart into the cold and snow. We are "used to" thinking about such a situation in quite unpleasant terms. And that's the entire point. It's not the darkness and low temperature that make us unhappy, it's the way we think about it. It's the narrative we have.

Facts, things and events don't define our narratives. We do that ourselves. Fact, things and events, all the outside conditions and circumstances are impotent to form any concrete narrative in our mind. All they can do is offer some bullet points around which we ourselves develop a narrative. Let's go back to the cold weather situation. It's our decision whether we narrate it as unpleasant and difficult, or maybe the contrary: as advantageous to our health or to our exercise regimen. The crucial point is that the narratives make it all possible. Between us and the summer road trip, as well as between us and the dreadful morning, there's a sphere of narratives which enables us to experience both situations in whatever way we like.

Let's take another angle and let's imagine now that we are in pain. Let's imagine that we have a toothache. If there was no difference between the pain itself and our narrative about it, how could we even discuss the possibility of a good life independent of circumstances? A toothache would automatically tarnish any possibility for happiness. Yet, this is not the case. It may be difficult but it's definitely *possible* to be happy despite a toothache. We know this for sure, since even if we can't do it ourselves, there are people who manage to do it. This is because there is the space of our human freedom between external stimulus and our reaction to it. This freedom consists in our narratives which are the buffer between us and the world. This idea is the foundation of the whole Stoic edifice explored in this book.

Fragment II

Things stand outside of us, themselves by themselves, neither knowing naught of themselves, nor expressing any judgment.

Marcus Aurelius, *Meditations*, 9.15

Commentary: The sphere of narratives enfolds us closely. Outside of it, there is an ocean of facts and events from which we are safely separated. Marcus Aurelius pictures it the following way: we reside in a neat and comfortable house and cohabit with nothing but our narratives. All that is outdoors is detached from us, cordoned, fenced off. No outside din can reach us, no turmoil can disturb us. Facts and events are mute. They cannot speak for themselves. They will never say anything unless we give them the floor.

This "house" may be so comfortable because there are no unwanted guests in it. We personally invite and take in all the narratives we live with. Our home is our castle and our own world is our own governance. No visitor is ever a surprise: we personally court, invite and introduce all of our narratives.

The big question that arises now is which narratives should we invite? Which of them should we live with in order to live happily? Which of them should we foster? Which of them should we combat? The book you are holding right now is one big answer to these questions. Read on!

Fragment III

It is not uncommon for the mind, even when there is no apparent sign of distress, to afflict itself with vain imaginations [or] *to make the worst interpretation of some doubtful word.*

Seneca, *Epistles*, 13.12

Commentary: Marcus Aurelius talked about the soul "dyed" with thoughts and about a door that keeps them at bay. Seneca paints another picture, one of a mind which conjures false shapes. He then lays out how these false shapes, i.e. useless narratives, originate. Let's have a closer look at this.

Many important issues tend to float for a long time in vague indeterminacy. Only a small minority of things gives us the pleasant certainty about how they will unfold. Some smaller or greater incertitude is the norm in human life, not an exception. The crucial role of narratives can be seen the easiest here, in the shady area of penumbras, shaky predictions and motley guesstimates. Let's take an example: we've had an important medical exam and we are about to get our diagnosis. Before we put our hands on it, we don't know what our condition is. Yet, the very thought that it may be cancer already makes us sick at heart. Notice though, that for the time being, nothing has happened yet. Something will – maybe – happen soon and we'll have to deal with that. But for the present moment, no adversity is around. There is just our narrative that adversity is looming. The envelope with the diagnosis is still in the doctor's drawer – the only thing that is already with us is our narrative about its content.

Seneca also speaks of "making the worst interpretation of some doubtful word" and this can be read in two ways. First, it may be "a doubtful word," or a grudge that someone holds against us. Second, it may be a grudge that *we* bear against someone. Let's start with the former case.

We can do a disservice to another human in a plethora of ways. We can do it on purpose, we can do it by accident. Sometimes it can be avoided, sometimes it can't. We can inadvertently jab someone when jostling in a crowd or we can do well in an interview and get a job someone else coveted. Yet, all these situations have one thing in common: we never know for sure how others take them. We never know in advance how they understand the situation and we never know what they think about it and about us. They might feel gravely insulted but, just as likely, they might not notice at all. The point is that even though we are never sure, we always make immediate interpretations based on scraps and shreds of impressions. It perpetually happens to us all, round the clock, night and day. We try to guess other people's thoughts based on doubtful traces, equivocal gestures and vague hints. Moreover, we overthink and overinterpret all the time. Someone barely notices but we construct an entire narrative on how and why they feel extremely offended. It's once again all about narratives. It's the very same pattern: our well-being is not a function of external factors, facts and events, but of our narratives of them.

On the other hand, we may be the ones harmed. The difference is that when someone harms or insults *us*, there is no outside measure of grudge. This time we make no reference to an inaccessible judgment locked in someone else's brain. Now we are both the ones affected and the ones who assess. For this reason, it may seem that this situation is somehow easier and more coherent. But it isn't. It's very easy to let our narratives go completely astray and to let our reactions get blown out of proportion. We can exaggerate or we can totally misread the course of events, but the point is always the same: our narratives about facts are more important than the facts themselves.

Fragment IV

> *What shall we say of the fact that the greater part of the things which enrage us are insults, not injuries?*

Seneca, *Of Anger*, III.28.4

Commentary: Language matters. Our narratives and the way we speak mirror each other. Our choice of words has consequences when it comes to developing narratives. Let's discuss this on the following example: we say that "we got angry *because* we got robbed." This assumes that there is a causal relation between robbery and anger. This relation, however, is just an illusion. According to Stoicism, the very fact of illegal removal of property is incapable of forcing us into a specific emotional state. The robbery isn't the cause of our anger, but our narrative about the robbery is. In other words, we are angry not because we were robbed but because, in the wake of the robbery, we – consciously or unconsciously – developed a narrative that the robbery is bad. In other words, we ourselves decided that we become angry. *The language reveals nonstoics and language can make us nonstoics.*

No external fact (like a robbery) is the cause of anger. The cause of anger is that we call some external facts causes for anger. In other words, the robbery in itself isn't a *harm*. Harm doesn't emerge until after we call something a harm. Anger emerges only in response to such thoughts. This can be put even more strongly: harm cannot be the cause of anger because harm in itself doesn't exist. Why is that? Notice: no external fact is a harm *per se*. Harm can be present in our narratives, but it doesn't appear there unless we willingly consent. There is no other harm to us but our own willingness to harm ourselves. And as long as we don't harm ourselves through our own narratives, we will be free of harm and we will have no cause for anger.

This was a "strong" interpretation of Seneca's words.[2] A "weak" interpretation is also possible. The weak interpretation doesn't employ the paradoxical claim that "harm doesn't exist." Instead, it goes as follows. To call a robbery "a harm" and to get angry as a result amounts to a voluntary dismissal of proportionality between cause and effect. This is similar to what happens in court. We prefer to put our fate in the hands of an experienced and rationally-minded judge rather than in the hands of a bloodthirsty mob. For the same crime for which the judge might merely grant parole, the mob might crucify us. Once we let the furious mob get a hold of us, we should expect no commensurability between the deed and reaction to it.

The same happens in our case. If we label the facts and events wrongly, we abdicate reason and abandon logic. We assent that we are angry and miserable *because* we were robbed? We thus resign from being the masters and commanders of our thought. We simply place ourselves at the mercy of an angry mob which uses no logic and errs only to our detriment. Or even worse than that, since (we may add in Seneca's style) the frenzy of haphazard and foolish narratives is far more perilous than what an angry mob can offer. Either way, we are doomed.

In order to avoid this, it's very important to choose our words carefully. We shouldn't say – or even think! – that we are miserable *because* this or that happened. We should say instead that we are miserable because we decided to be miserable in the wake of this or that happening. "We decided" – by developing such-and-such narratives about what happened.

It's clear that a world of difference emerges between these two phrasings. This difference is exactly where the sphere of our freedom is located and it is the root of all Stoicism. Once we grasp this difference, we will easily see that there is no necessity in our reactions to outside events. It's always our own responsibility to answer to whatever happens with whatever narratives we like and deem useful.

Fragment V

> *We have different opinions about the cause of our evils. Someone thinks that they are sick. Not so however, but the fact is that they do not adapt the preconceptions* [i.e. narratives] *right. Someone thinks that they are poor.*

---

[2] Strong but not the strongest possible. Theoretically, we can go further and interpret Stoicism with no reference to facts at all, or even within a framework which assumes that facts themselves don't exist. I don't intend on going that far, however.

Someone that they have a severe father or mother, and another again that Caesar is not favorable to them. But all this is one and only one thing, the not knowing how to adapt the preconceptions [narratives].

Epictetus, *Discourses*, IV.1.42-43

Commentary: The source of human misery lies in the confusion of facts with our narratives about facts. This is what disturbs our internal harmony and cripples our spiritual equilibrium. Some people think that they are prevented from living well by feeble health, lack of money, poor relationships with their family members or low social standing. Stoicism bluntly negates all this. All these views are thoroughly misguided. Poverty and disease aren't the root of evil: our narratives about them are.

Epictetus points out that the very habit of seeking explanations in facts instead of in narratives is a mistake. It distracts us, it focuses our attention in the wrong place. It's a habit that should be kicked, it's a reflex that should be eradicated. We must always remember that "things stand outside our doors," safely cordoned off and with no right to pass. We shouldn't reach out to them and we shouldn't provoke them. We shouldn't even wonder whether they are able to stir our soul. They aren't, unless we let them. If, for any reason, we feel uncomfortable, disturbed or distressed, we should immediately look inside ourselves, into our narratives. An outward glance should never come first.

Fragment VI

People are disturbed not by the things which happen, but by the opinions [i.e. narratives] *about the things. For example, death is nothing terrible, for if it were, it would have seemed so to Socrates.*[3] [But] *the opinion* [narrative] *about death, that it is terrible, is the terrible thing.*

Epictetus, *Encheiridion*, 5

Commentary: We've discussed the precedence of narratives over facts, things and events, but we haven't justified it yet. Let's now try to nail down *why* it's all about narratives.

---

[3] Socrates (~470 – 399 BC) was a Greek philosopher, opponent of the sophists and the teacher of, among others, Plato. He is widely considered to be the founder of classical Greek philosophy and of Western philosophy in general. He was put on trial for alleged godlessness and sentenced to death by a court in Athens. Unwilling to disobey the law, he declined an opportunity to escape from prison provided to him by his disciples.

Epictetus puts forward the following argument: if death was dreadful "in itself," then everyone, without exception, would fear it. If dreadfulness was an inseparable and indelible quality of death, then everyone would dread it. But this is not the case. Some people (e.g. Socrates) weren't afraid of death and thus it follows that death isn't dreadful in itself. Death, which is the same for every human, is not the source of dread. Dread is rooted in our narratives about death, narratives which we create individually and on our own account.

Someone may object here by saying that most people do in fact fear death while only extraordinary individuals don't. In other words, fear of death is an organic and common reaction. Overcoming it is an exception, not the rule, so it doesn't prove anything.

It's not about statistics, though. It's irrelevant whether a great or small part of the human population takes this or that side. What is relevant is that it's possible to get on the safe side. There were individuals who didn't fear death. Therefore, it's possible. That's all. This is enough evidence, this is what suffices for us. All that matters is that there is no necessary determination here. There *is* freedom of choice and freedom of judgment, and the narrative about death is something different from death itself. It doesn't matter that most people don't handle their thoughts. It matters that whoever wants to handle them – can do so.

Another possible objection comes our way: fearlessness doesn't have to be based on the conviction that "death in itself isn't dreadful." Quite the contrary, someone may be unafraid of death *despite* their conviction that death is dreadful. Such a person didn't stop to perceive death as something frightful, but they instead learned how to overcome that fright. In other words, a critic may say that the whole story about narratives is redundant and not necessary to explain the problem. The fear of death can be combated simply by someone's sheer courage or bravery. Doesn't it undermine the Stoic view?

No. Bravery in facing death can be explained in many ways, but on each of them, we pass a point where the idea that death is *per se* dreadful is overcome. How we get there is not that important, at least within this chapter. It doesn't matter if someone gets there by reading this book, by the strength of their experience or by their innate fearlessness. However, one gets there, they are proof that there is no necessary association between death and fear of death. And this is what it's all about.

This reasoning, demonstrated here with the example of death, can be rehashed for virtually everything else. Lack of money isn't bad in itself because not everybody sees it as evil. There are people who can thrive despite limited funds or even live happily in poverty. In the same vein, health issues aren't evil in themselves, because there are people who don't fear illness and don't give in to it. Slander and disrespect aren't evil in themselves because they don't trouble us all: there are folks who don't care about them. Examples can be multiplied. In a word, different people react differently to the same facts, things and events. This is one of the proofs that our life is not about these facts, things and events, but about our narratives.

Fragment VII

> *There are more things, Lucilius, that frighten, than which press hard upon us: and we are often more disturbed from opinion* [narrative]*, than in reality.* [...] *I only require this of you, that you would not anticipate misery since the devils, you dread as coming upon you, may perhaps never reach you, at least they are not yet come. Thus some things torture us more than they ought, some before they ought, and some which ought never to torture us at all. We heighten our pain either by presupposing a cause or anticipation.*
>
> Seneca, Epistles, 13.4-5

Commentary: Another argument for the superiority of narratives over facts, things and events is based on the time order. Let's imagine that something is expected to unfold for good or bad sometime soon. Consider again the medical exam we talked of previously. We started feeling bad, went to see a doctor, did the exam, and now we are waiting for the diagnosis. It's a common reaction to feel anxious, particularly if some serious illness is a possibility. But if the diagnosis or the medical condition itself were the cause of anxiety, then how could we possibly be anxious *before* learning what it was? If facts were the cause of anxiety, then we would expect no one to get anxious until after these facts emerged. But of course, this is not how things work. It's commonplace that we worry in advance and that we anticipate upcoming events with anxiety. This is further proof that the chain of events doesn't affect us directly but through the medium of our narratives.

Let's now discuss something which is bound to happen certainly and unavoidably. Let's imagine that we are in prison[4] or even that we are death row inmates awaiting execution. All means of appeal have been exhausted, all means of help have failed and all means of escape are unworkable. We are absolutely sure that we will die (aren't we all?) but we still have some time left to live. Let's say the execution is set for tomorrow. If life was just about facts,

---

[4] Keeping in mind of course what Walter White said in the immortal wrong-guy-other-bench scene: "There is more than one kind of prison."

then we should be able to rest easily and spend our last night in peace. We aren't dying now, we are dying tomorrow, aren't we? Yet we know that in real-life scenarios most people have trouble sleeping like babies on such a last night. The reason is that it's all about narratives: anticipating the execution is actually more disturbing than the execution itself. A narrative about tomorrow's fact can well destroy our peace of mind today. If we let it.

Fragment VIII

Things themselves have no natural power to form our judgments [i.e. narratives].

Marcus Aurelius, *Meditations*, 6.52

Commentary: Facts, things and events not only "have no natural power" to create a specific narrative in our mind, but in fact they are unable to create *any* narrative. Why is that? And how does it relate to the death row example? Above all, if "things themselves" don't create narratives, who does? The answer is plain: we do. We are the only ones responsible for our own narratives.

This is the crucial thesis of Stoicism: our narratives originate within us. We ourselves develop them and we have no one and nothing but ourselves to blame. We have absolute authority over our own narratives. No narrative ever emerges in our mind without our consent.[5] We are the cause, source and root of them all. Nothing and no one can ever force us to think something we don't want to think. Nothing and no one can ever force us to see things in a different way than we want to see. The logic is rigid and immutable. No matter where, when and in what circumstances, we create all our narratives ourselves.

We can use another picture here. Let's imagine two continents separated by a strait. One continent epitomizes the outside world, populated with facts, things and events. The other one is our mind, populated with narratives. The strait is under our strict control and nothing can cross unless we consent. Anything that wants to get from the outside world into our mind must, of necessity, ask us to lend a hand. There is no other way to cross the strait, there is no shortcut, there is no way to stow away. Every fact, every thing and every event has to ask *us* for the favor of creating a narrative about them. They can't do it alone.

---

[5] In the formal Stoic parlance the act of consent for the emergence of a specific narrative was called *katalepsis*.

Yet, our authority comes with a great obligation. Since we hold the only means of transportation across that strait, we are responsible for everything that makes it to the other side. Nobody can plant contraband on us, nothing can be smuggled against our will. Everything that gets through is on us. All narratives that are present in our mind are there because of us. We authored them all. We have no one to thank and no one to blame but ourselves.

Fragment IX

> *When then we are impeded or disturbed or grieved, let us never blame others, but ourselves, that is, our opinions* [i.e. narratives].
>
> <div align="right">Epictetus, <i>Encheiridion</i>, 5</div>

Commentary: Despite our absolute control over our narratives, it happens all the time that something unwanted makes it through that strait. We often make up useless narratives that make us miserable, narratives that hurt us. How and why does this happen?

The reason is painfully clear: we are often very negligent in the exercise of our right to control our narratives. Or we even abdicate it altogether. We have the right to govern our own thoughts but we often behave like we don't. Again and again, we try to convince ourselves (and others too) that someone or something else is responsible. Everyone and everything else – but not us. How tempting and how wonderfully exonerating it is to think that our narratives are independent from us! How sweet and easy it is to believe that circumstances, institutions, fellow humans, social situation or historical actualities are responsible for what and how we think! The list of possible excuses is infinite but the stark truth is that this is always on us, even if we deny it. It's always our hand that signs off every single narrative. It's always our hand, even if our head declines to guide it.

And if the head declines to guide us then how can we suppose that our narratives serve our interests? Once we let the narratives grow loose, they likely sabotage our life, they discomfort us, they cause pain, they harm, hamper and hinder us. Thus, the central point of Stoicism (and the central point of this book) is that it is our obligation and duty to take responsibility for them. This is the obligation we mustn't disregard and the duty we mustn't neglect. In a word, *Stoicism is a platform for properly managing our narratives.* Stoicism is all about how to think in order to thrive. It's founded on the idea that, first of all, happiness, good life and all earthly flourishing hinge on nothing other than on what we think. Next, there is the idea that what we think is our own doing. Our thoughts (i.e. narratives) are independent from the outside world, they are up to us only. We have to embrace these ground rules. The whole Stoic philosophy rests on them. In this view, Stoicism is nothing other than an organized system of *how* specifically we should shape our narratives in order to live well.

Everyone who abdicates responsibility for their thoughts is miserable. It's an ironclad rule that seeking external causes of misery brings misery upon us. One who doesn't accept that we are our own cause of anxiety will always be anxious. The root of all evil is one and the same for us all. It's the loss of control of our own narratives.

Whenever we feel miserable, we need to look for the cause in our own narratives. Never in the outside world, always in ourselves. Are we angry that we were robbed? Let's remember: some property unlawfully changing owner is not the real cause of anger. The real cause is the useless narrative saying "you should be angry if property changed owner." Let's nail down this narrative, let's pin down the nonstoic assumption that robbery "causes" anger. Let's realize that something has slipped into our soul that should not have slipped. We consented to it but we didn't have to.

Fragment X

> *The pain is light, when not aggravated by fancy or opinion. If you can be persuaded to comfort yourself with saying, "It is nothing, or in effect very little, let us bear it patiently," it will be soon at an end, or this very thought will make it easy and tolerable. All things depend upon opinion* [i.e. narrative]: *not only ambition but even luxury and avarice refer to it. Pain also is proportioned to opinion.*

Seneca, *Epistles*, 78.13-14

Commentary: This is the grist to the mill of the unconvinced. "How is that, dear Stoics? We suffer 'proportionally to opinion?' You claim that pain can be managed with narratives? You dare to say that mere *thinking* in a certain way can alleviate physical pain or even make it disappear whatsoever? Is this what you mean? If so, then either you were never in real pain or worse, your philosophy is trash! Or, presumably, both. A tooth won't stop hurting if I *think* that it doesn't hurt. Sure, I can think it, I can say it a million times. I can even try to believe it. But the pain won't stop – because (alas) it's not subject to our thoughts."

What's the Stoic answer to this? The problem of coping with suffering and physical pain is frequently associated with Stoicism. It will pop up several times in this book and I will try to shed light on it from a few different perspectives. One possible take is this. The quoted words of Seneca can be misread easily and can lead to a common misunderstanding of Stoicism. This misunderstanding equates the whole Stoic notion to mere verbal negation of suffering. "It hurts, but I'll say to myself that pain is not an evil," or "It hurts, but I'll think that it doesn't". Indeed, if this was the Stoic advice, this philosophy and this book would be worthless.

The real thing is much more subtle. The statement "pain is light, when not aggravated by fancy or opinion" doesn't mean that pain is an illusion. It means that the greatest part of our suffering isn't caused by external factors but by the addendum produced by our own mind. In other words, external causes bring about only a small part (let's say it's 20 percent) of our suffering. This 20 percent can't be eradicated or alleviated by any mental procedure. It's just a stone-cold fact. But most of the suffering, the other 80 percent, is our own addition. It's our own doing, self-pity, our own wallowing and exaggeration. It's our narratives that blow suffering out of proportion and it's our narratives that hurt us most.

It's not that pain doesn't exist or that it doesn't affect us. Sure enough, it does. The problem, though, is that we have an unhealthy habit of spicing up suffering with our own seasoning. It goes without saying that we do it needlessly. "Pain is light" doesn't mean that suffering is an illusion, but rather that physical pain makes a slight contribution to the overall balance of our misery. Yes, it's sadly true that even a minor physical ailment can be a negative life-changer and can make us profoundly unhappy. Yet not the ailment itself is at fault here, but the narratives we build on it. The ailment itself is far less painful than all the additions that we masochistically, voluntarily and pointlessly append to it. We are not sure whether an adversity can defeat us? Why don't we help it out by sending reinforcements that will fight against us! These "reinforcements" are, obviously, our own narratives, which we supply our enemies with.

Fragment XI

And how long did Eriphyle live with Amphiaraus, and was the mother of children and of many? But a necklace came between them: and what is a necklace? It is the opinion [narrative] *about such things.*

Epictetus, *Discourses*, II.22.32-33

Commentary: Amphiaraus, as the story goes, was a ruler of ancient Argos. He didn't want to take part in an expedition against Thebes because, by his gift of clairvoyance, he knew in advance that it would end in defeat. However, the party supporting the war managed to buy off his wife, Eriphyle, and had her had him change his mind. She succeeded and Amphiaraus took off against

Thebes. Just as predicted, the expedition was a failure. Most warriors got killed while Amphiaraus was taken alive to the underworld by Zeus himself. All of this happened because of an expensive gift that Eriphyle received: a beautiful necklace, handcrafted by Hephaestus.

Just as it did in antiquity (and in mythology!), the narrative that there is some kind of an inescapable necessity in praising and desiring luxury still ruins lives and relationships today. It haunts us, it deprives and degenerates us, it erodes our political virtues and social responsibilities. It poses a danger to our personal life, it sets us up for conflict and betrayal. Just as it did in antiquity, the narrative that social recognition is valuable in itself still turns our lives upside down. The narrative that the opinion of others is binding and incontrovertible still yields a great deal of pointless suffering. And this is exactly what Stoicism fights with! This is exactly the Stoic line of attack: the goal is to break the deadly loop of seeming causality between facts and narratives. We must break free from this, we must restore control over our narratives and over our life. All the chapters to follow will discuss *how* to achieve this purpose.

Chapter 2

Get rid of useless narratives

In the first place be not hurried away by the rapidity of the appearance [i.e. narrative].

Epictetus, *Discourses*, II.18.28

In a nutshell: Some narratives are useful and other are useless. The latter prevent us from living well and happily. They either tacitly inhibit us from enjoying our lives or they openly bring about suffering and misery. We must learn how to identify the useless narratives and how to get rid of them.

***

We won't be able to be happy unless we get rid of useless narratives. Erasing them is the only way. We can't flee from them, for they will chase us wherever we go (fragment I). Useless narratives originate from our carelessness. They spring up when we don't pay enough attention to what's happening to us (II). Generating a useless narrative amounts to generating misery for ourselves (III). We have to transform the way we think and we have to embrace the Stoic way of thinking (IV). Stoicism proposes five methods for fighting useless narratives. First, we shouldn't be fooled by appearances and we should try to comprehend all issues in their full complexity (V). Second, we should trust the carefully crafted narratives rather than those which emerge spontaneously (VI). Third, the sooner we stand up to useless narratives the better (VII). Fourth, if, however, we don't manage to avoid developing a useless narrative, we should isolate it and suppress its toxic influence (VIII). Fifth, we should divide and conquer: we can use some narratives to fight others (IX). A charming story from Epictetus' own life (X) reminds us that we should never rest on our laurels and we should work hard to prevent any new useless narratives from reappearing.

Fragment I

The causes of solicitude and trouble [follow us] *even beyond the seas. What so secret place is there,* [that] *excludes the fear of the death? What place of rest so well guarded as to be raised above the dread of pain and grief? Wherever you hide yourself, human miseries will alarm you.*

Seneca, *Epistles*, 82.4

Commentary: Our narratives are always with us. We carry them wherever we go, they are present whatever we do. We cannot put them on a shelf and we can't take them off like a useless piece of clothing. They are our second skin: we must live with them and we can't run away from them. Wherever we go, our narratives go with us.

Moving is no remedy for misery or any other disturbance caused by useless narratives. If our clothes are too tight or if they chafe us, there is no point in running away – only changing cloths can help. The same holds for our narratives. If they irritate us, if they vex or hurt us, then the only possible solution is to replace them. We won't be able to move forward unless we abandon the fallacious framework that external facts, things and events can somehow override our narratives. If we don't take this crucial step, we don't avoid the fate of one emperor. As the tale has it, he couldn't drown out his pangs of conscience even though he had an orchestra play fortissimo day and night.

Let's continue with Seneca's example. Let's imagine that fear of death haunts us and shakes our peace of mind. What should we do? It's more clear than ever that no escape will help us: we can't hide from death. It will unmistakably track us down no matter what refuge we hole up in.[6] But here is the alternative. We should dismiss the useless and fear-inducing narrative that death is something terrible. This is the Stoic strategy, this is the key to all that Stoicism allows us to accomplish.

The Stoic road map for a good life doesn't project the changes in the outside world. Quite the contrary. Its central, organizing and overriding principle is to transform our narratives. Let's not bend the world to our crooked thoughts, let's straighten up our thoughts instead. This strategy gives us an irreplaceable and uncompromised power which we can never attain by mere wrestling with the external world. It's always better to control ourselves than to control the world. It's better to get rid of useless narratives about facts than to alter the facts themselves.

Fragment II

> *For as to children masks appear terrible and fearful from inexperience, we also are affected in like manner by events [...] for no other reason than children are by masks.*

Epictetus, *Discourses*, II.1.15

---

[6] See also Marcus Aurelius, *Meditations*, IV.3: "People seek retreats for themselves, houses in the country, sea-shores and mountains [...]. But this is altogether a mark of the most common sort [i.e. not philosophers]."

Get rid of useless narratives

Commentary: Useless narratives originate from facts, things and events for reasons similar to those which make children fear things that adults deem harmless. Kids are newcomers to the world. They haven't learned it yet. They haven't learned that even though certain things seem dreadful at first glance, they needn't be feared. Kids aren't knowledgeable enough to tell the difference between really dangerous and seemingly dangerous things. And since they don't know, they rush into premature judgments and fear some things just in case.

We pointlessly do the same even though we grew out of diapers a long time ago. We fear many things and we don't even bother to verify whether our fear is justified. Let's take an example: someone is badmouthing us. Is this something inherently and intrinsically evil? No, it isn't. For if they are telling the truth, then it's not badmouthing, it's indiscretion at best. On the other hand, if they are telling lies, then it's all the more reason not to care. After all, no truth about us is revealed. The whole situation amounts to someone giving some false statements to someone else. And why should this bother us? Badmouthing won't bring sadness or misery, unless of course we embrace the narrative that it's something sad or miserable.

Nothing is intrinsically good or evil. It's only our narratives that make things, facts and events good or evil. Those narratives don't appear out of the blue. Instead, they are always rooted in an act of thought we commit, either actively thinking something in a certain way or by neglecting our ability to think. The whole Stoic point is that we shouldn't neglect it. This is the core principle: we mustn't ignore our capacity to control our narratives. We mustn't shy away from the effort of developing narratives that are advantageous and useful to us. What does it mean in this specific case? It means that we should perceive badmouthing as a weird habit of envious people. We should understand it as nothing else but proof that these people have some problems with themselves. No more. There is no harm, no hazard, no hindrance in it. Nothing and nobody is a detriment to us unless we mishandle our narratives.

This reasoning holds for all cases. It applies to all situations and all circumstances. It holds for the sentiments we share and the emotions that may carry us away. A baby can assume a "mask" to be scary but he or she may also deem a pink pony to be the most luxurious item in the world and a 9 PM bedtime to be a form of torture. It may seem silly to us but, truth be told, we do just the same thing. Without scruples or second thoughts, we embrace really disastrous narratives. We construct for ourselves all sorts of obnoxious and useless values, goals, endeavors, commitments, desires, aversions, fears, habits, wants and wonts, obsessions and penchants. We don't care whether they are useful or not. We just take whatever narratives come our way. We don't care about their usefulness, we don't care about their relevance. We embrace them not only without a second thought but without any thought at all.

This is a grave mistake, of course. It makes us terrified, anxious and miserable... while we needn't be. We get to love things that are not worth our love and we loathe things that shouldn't be loathed. We get it all wrong because of one simple thing: because we failed to get rid of useless narratives.

Fragment III

Every evil is just as great as we consider it to be.

Seneca, *Of Consolation. To Marcia*, 19.1

Commentary: Picture this: we've accidentally cut a finger with a knife. It hurts, it's bleeding, and Seneca says that every evil is "just as great as we consider it to be." What does that mean? Let's focus on what we can do about this wound. One way to go is to sanitize and dress it, and then try to forget about the incident and move on to more serious matters. We can also sit down though, ruminate on spilled blood and fall down into the dumps. We can start complaining that it hurts too much and that the cut prevents us from work and productivity. We can start thinking that this laceration is not that harmless after all, because we once read on the internet that such cuts may result in sepsis. We can also convince ourselves that such accidents happen only to us and to no one else. Other people don't cut themselves that easily, right? Particularly, only to us it happens at such unfortunate moments, doesn't it? This is the key point. A useless narrative about something is likely developed when we start thinking in terms of "a proof." This cutting of a finger "proves" to us that we are and will always be sloppy, that we are losers. It "proves" that everybody hates us and that everything conspires against us. This is where all the hell breaks loose.

Every single event, even the tiniest one, can easily be blown out of proportion and turned into a cosmic disaster. Useless narratives do just that. The thought that a minor laceration presents us with a risk of gangrene is a useless narrative. The thought that this accidental cut might disempower us to a point where we aren't able to do great things is a useless narrative. The reasoning that this accident proves that we are losers and that the world schemes against us – it is a useless narrative.

In Stoicism, we say that in the very moment that we cut ourselves nothing *evil* actually happens. Instead, a certain fact has occurred and it's now open for us to interpret it. It's up to us how we narrate it. We can call it evil but we don't have to. We can (but we don't have to) start thinking about it as something evil and thus *make* it evil. And this is exactly what we should avoid! This is the very pattern of thinking we should get rid of. There is no use in multiplying evils beyond necessity. Evil consists in useless narratives, not it the facts themselves. It's our responsibility to decide how much evil we allow to emerge and how much of it we embrace. Moreover, we can say that it's useless narratives that actually *are* evil: there is no evil and no misery unless we think them up. A cut is nothing evil, but a useless narrative about a cut is evil. As long as a useless narrative doesn't appear in our mind, there is no evil and no harm. All that is out there is a cut finger. Certainly, it hurts (as all cut fingers do) but the physical pain is – in the Stoic view – our smallest concern.

Fragment IV

Your ship is lost. What has happened? Your ship is lost. Someone has been led to prison. What has happened? They have been led to prison. But that herein they have fared badly, everyone adds from their own opinion.

Epictetus, *Discourses*, III.8.5

Commentary: This is the way of thinking we should shoot at. This is how we think once we got rid of useless narratives. We see bare facts, things and events, we don't add any impromptu interpretations. We see the ship going down but we don't see anything as abstract and awkward as "misery" necessarily attached to it. Misery is something we would have to add to the mix ourselves. But we know we don't have to. So we don't.

A loss of a ship is nothing other than a loss of a ship. Nothing less, but also nothing more. This seeming tautology is very important in Stoicism. Of course, it may seem that some facts just beg for certain narratives and compel us to think about them in a certain way. It would be kind of easy to deem a loss of a ship "misery." But that's just an illusion and a great mistake which we must learn to avoid. Facts don't scream ominous interpretations. We can narrate any given fact, thing or event any way we want. No external thing has the power in it to force us to see misery in it.

Every time we cave into useless narratives, we do so of our own resolve and due to our own laziness. Why of our own resolve? Because developing narratives is always an act of thought. Why due to laziness? Because kicking bad thinking habits is toilsome. In the rest of this chapter, we will discuss *how* we should exercise our mental capabilities and how we can overcome that laziness. In other words, we already know what useless narratives are and now we will learn how to beat them.

Fragment V

Not only from people, but from things the masks must be taken off.

Seneca, *Epistles*, 24.13

Commentary: Our first marching order is this: we should never trust appearances and we should never get fooled or deceived. Facts, things and events wear – figuratively speaking – "masks" and they attempt to sneak into our mind in disguise. They want us to let our guard down, they want to get past our line of defense. Our task is, of course, to thwart that maneuver. We must learn how to analyze narratives and we must learn how to treat them with limited trust.

Let's take the perennial example and let's imagine that we've been in a long-term, serious and happy relationship for a number of years. Everything goes well, we live merrily and happily. But one day we meet someone new: someone who we like on the spot, or... even more than like. Out of the blue, we face an opportunity to have an affair. The temptation starts revving up, the juices start flowing. We jump into thinking that this potential new partner would open a thrilling and refreshing chapter in our life and... and let's pause for a second here. Let's take a closer look on what we've called "a temptation."

Assuming that our life with the present partner is genuinely fulfilling and that we flourish within that commitment, the Stoic breakdown of the situation is simple. The so-called "temptation" is nothing but a cluster of useless narratives. Why are they useless? Because they blindside us. These narratives portray the new potential partner in a hugely distorted way. They make us focus solely on their attractiveness, they make us see only novelty and a sexual adventure in them. We thus become disingenuous to our present partner, to us ourselves and to that new person. We start thinking about them as someone who is endowed with positive traits only. We don't want to see the defects of their character, we don't want to hear if they snore, we don't want to remember that starting an affair implies psychological turmoil. And we don't want to confront the truth of what an affair means to our current relationship. Turning a blind eye to the imperfections of a newly met person, ignoring the thought that sooner or later the novelty wears off and old problems haunt us again – these are great examples of useless narratives.

Importantly, Stoicism doesn't make a case against or in favor of promiscuity. It offers no simple recipe and no ready-to-use answers. Stoicism is not against affairs but against dishonesty and single-mindedness. Seneca's "take off the mask" doesn't mean "open your eyes to the monogamous human nature," but rather "avoid simplified, narrow and naive understanding of what the situation is." We should take off the mask in order to open our eyes, but we won't see any obvious truth. Instead, we must confront the situation in all its complexity. We must remember that an affair is not just the heart rate picking up and the secret get-togethers in motels. It is also – just as importantly – emotional chaos, tears, broken hearts and sometimes broken lives. Getting rid of useless narratives means remembering that nothing is plain, unequivocal and crystal clear. It means never forgetting the other side of the coin. It means remembering that things are never as good or as bad as they may seem at first glance. Yet, they are always more complicated than they seem.

Fragment VI

The difference between the mind of the fool and the mind of a Stoic is that the fool thinks the cruel and harsh things seen by [the] *mind, when it is first struck by them, actually to be what they appear.*

Epictetus, *Fragments*, 9ᵛ

Commentary: The second weapon which helps us get rid of useless narratives is this: we need to pay close attention to the time order in which narratives pop up. Let's take two narratives about the same event. One of them came to our mind immediately, just after the event took place. The other one we have developed after having put some deal of thought into the whole situation. It's thus a product of consideration and some critical analysis. How do the two narratives look like?

It's clear that the former narrative is usually quite useless. Pausing for a moment, taking a deep breath, collecting our thoughts and trying to mull things over – all this helps rather than harms the process of creating a useful narrative. Thinking is usually an advantage – at least it's never a disadvantage. However, we mustn't delude ourselves that sifting narratives through a mindful sieve will be easy or painless. It won't be. There are no free lunches here. This process will always consume a decent chunk of our time and a major part of our energy.

Fragment VII

We ought not to accept an appearance [i.e. narrative] *without examination, but we should say, "Wait, let me see what you are and whence you come," like the watch at night who says "Show me the pass."*

Epictetus, *Discourses*, III.12.15

Commentary: The third weapon in our battle with useless narratives is proper timing. We know already that fighting them always takes effort. Let's discuss now *when* exactly we should exert this effort. The answer is clear: the sooner, the better. We should take the stand against useless narratives before they even appear. The best way to get rid of them is not to harbor them in the first place. Prevention is the most favorable option here: it's best to not let them even start inflicting their ominous influence on us. *Obsta principiis*, as the Romans would say. Nip in the bud.

We should set up a guard. Every narrative-to-be should be carefully scrutinized, scanned and tapped all over. How exactly should we do this? Let's use the passage from Epictetus as a blueprint for examination. The questions we should ask while "interviewing" all the candidates for narratives are: what exactly do you propose? Where do you come from? What good will you do to us?

First off, we won't get anywhere without pinning down the exact *content* of the narrative. Why should we ask about that? Because we often catch ourselves in useless narratives unwittingly just like a fish that can't smell the hook hidden in the bait. In another bad scenario, a useful, sound and reasonable narrative may smuggle a useless one somehow attached to it. For example, there may be a useful narrative that social media is a great way to make new friends. Been there, done that. It doesn't follow, however, that we must envy their allegedly perfect lives they brag about on Facebook. They posted another screen-load of pictures from the Bahamas vacation, hitch-hiking through rural North Korea, yet another newborn baby, or at least a funny cat? Good for them! But does it follow that we need to drop all we do and fly to some tropical island, travel to a dangerous country, conceive a baby or fetch a cat? No, it doesn't follow. The thought that these things are somehow necessary for our happiness (and the thought that posting them online is necessary) is a useless narrative.

Another example: when we meet someone intelligent and attractive, it is a useful narrative to appreciate and acknowledge their talents. It is a useful narrative to try to make friends with them. But does it follow that we should be on the spot swept away with affection for this person? Absolutely not! This is another useless narrative. And there is only one way to put a stop to all this. We must thoroughly scan all the narratives, think thoroughly whether we want to embrace them and inspect whether they are trying to sneak anything useless with them. We should specifically *name* every narrative. We shouldn't whisper, we shouldn't speak in an oblique fashion. We need to use our clear, full sentences. Or even speak out loud. It does miracles.

The next step is to pin down the *source* of the narrative. We must get to know where it came from and how it originated. Let's take another example of a useless narrative: "Watching another episode of a show is more rewarding

Get rid of useless narratives

than the work I've scheduled for today." Notice: the very structure of this sentence suggests that there was some analysis at work, that the ayes and nays have been ordered and the pros and cons weighed. It deludes us into thinking that the urgency of the scheduled duties has been calculated, the attractiveness of the show assessed and some form of a rational judgment has been passed. Needless to say, it's a foolhardy illusion.

Let's just pause for a little second and we will easily see that this erroneous decision is rooted in nothing other than our sloth. This is the bitter threshold the Stoics urge us to pass: let's clench our teeth and let's just do this. Once we cross it, it will get easier. Once we take the first step, we will immediately enter an upward spiral of useless narratives removal. Let's just embrace the initial hard truth: it is laziness that makes us crash on the couch instead of work. It is vainglory, humblebragging and ego-boosting that make us post the next batch of success-story pictures on Facebook. It is a mere need for self-validation that propels us into a new sexual encounter. Once we see this, it all gets much easier. Useless narratives don't just have feet of clay – they are all made of clay. All we must do is learn to see it.

The next step is to ask what good can the proposed narrative do to us. What advantage, what new insight or benefit will it bring about? *How is it useful?* Does it help us get over a cut finger if we believe that it's the ultimate proof that the whole world conspires against us? Will it make us happy if we post a hundred more holiday snaps on Facebook? Will, honestly speaking, procrastinating instead of working really feel that good? Let's remember that's it all about narratives and that narratives are here to make our life easier, not harder. Why, then, willingly put a spoke in our own wheel? Why sabotage our own endeavor? Why embrace useless thoughts? Let's drop this. And in order to drop this: let's think twice about the consequences of every thought before actually thinking it.

Fragment VIII

> *When the appearance* [narrative] *pains you* [...] *contend against it by the aid of reason, conquer it. Do not allow it to gain strength nor to lead you to the consequences by raising images such as it pleases and as it pleases.*
>
> Epictetus, *Discourses*, III.24.108

Commentary: Our fourth piece of artillery against useless narratives is to remember that no one is a perfect Stoic. Despite all our efforts, despite the entire Stoic training, devotion and passion, no matter if we read this book a dozen times or if we think it over a million times, it's still bound to happen that some useless narratives defy our vigilance and sneak in. No matter how hard we try, we must expect this at some point. And then what? No worries, the kingdom is not lost because of one useless narrative. If it emerges, it can be halted. If it takes root in our mind, it can be gotten rid of. It can – and it surely should be.

Once we realize that a useless narrative entered our mind despite our efforts, we must do damage control. We must avoid escalation. Things mustn't get out of hand. We need to prevent this one useless narrative from generating a sequence of others. Alas, it's their habit that they migrate not just in couples but in herds. Thus, our first step must be to isolate it, contain it, and dam its influence. We have come to believe that owning an SUV is an absolute requisite condition of living well? Poor enough. But let's not delude ourselves further into thinking that a Ferrari or a private jet is a necessity. We have given in to a useless narrative that it's better to drink a beer instead of doing the work we are supposed to do? Bad enough. But let's stop right there and let's not go from one beer all the way to a six-pack. Sloth, Netflix and general procrastination have fooled us into watching one too many episodes of a show? Our bad. But let's not watch seven more. Surrendering to one useless narrative doesn't equal surrendering to a score of them.

All of this, however, is just a prerequisite, just a half-measure and an entree to the main course. The main course, of course, is a complete and unconditional elimination of useless narratives. How can we get it done? A good way to start is to erase the *influence* the narrative exerts upon us. We made up our mind that mindless binge-drinking would be the most delectable way to spend the evening? Cool, but let's still force ourselves not to enter the bar. Let's wrestle the useless narrative, let's beat it down, let's strangle it. Let's force ourselves to walk past the bar and go home. Let's force ourselves to sit down to our work. In other words, let's ignore useless narratives. Remember the saying, "dress for the job you want, not for the job you have?" The same here. Let's conduct ourselves as if we had the narratives we want, not as if we had the ones we have. If we press on, they will budge soon.

Useless narratives operate in a very specific way. They tend to give us a strong pushback in the beginning, but they can't stand lasting pressure. If we don't give up, if we push them hard, they will crack. We all know how this works. Once we walk past the bar door and refuse to give in to the temptation, the warm flow of success immediately wells up in us. A flush of mental strength kicks in. Each next step is just easier and easier. Once we stand our ground against useless narratives – they will slide away swiftly. Once we adamantly act against them, once we act as if they weren't there – we make them *actually* disappear. This is a two-way street: not only our narratives influence our behavior but our behavior influences our narratives. And mindful behavior erases useless narratives pronto.

Get rid of useless narratives

Fragment IX

Do not allow the appearance [narrative] *to lead you on and draw lively pictures of the things which will follow; for if you do, it will carry you off wherever it pleases. But rather bring in to oppose it some other beautiful and noble appearance* [narrative] *and cast out this base appearance* [narrative].

Epictetus, Discourses, II.18.25-26

Commentary: Our next weapon against useless narratives is this: just like in judo, we can use our opponent's own strength to defeat them. The power of narratives can work to our benefit. How can we achieve that? Simply, by fighting narratives with narratives.

Let's get back to the friend of ours who posts tons of pictures from their vacation to the Bahamas. They are massively impressive, the likes go through the roof. A desire to follow suit awakens in us. "How come? They went there and we didn't? That's so unjust!" And immediately, a useless narrative follows: "Such a trip must be a marvelous thing! The skies are so overwhelmingly blue, the water seems so tempting. Wow, wow. Actually, why shouldn't we go ourselves? If we squeeze a little, maybe we can afford it...?" The temptation is clear, and so it is clear how this narrative is useless. It's useless because it brings no happiness – quite the contrary, it makes us unhappy on the spot.

How can we use opposite narratives to combat this one? For example, this way: "Yes, the pictures are nice, but actually, such a trip is hugely expensive, isn't it? Actually, it's *too* expensive for me. Not to mention that, truth be told, I never liked the idea of a vacation on a tropical island. I never really enjoyed all the heat and sunbathing. Why would I change my preferences then, just because someone posted something on Facebook?"

Similar tactics can be employed when we are tempted to start an affair. Obviously, useless narratives attack us at gale force, prompting sugarcoated images of wild sex and sweet hugs under the moon. But we don't have to espouse these images. They don't have to be our final word. We can easily call in opposite narratives. Instead of being honey-trapped into thinking about the all-thrills elation of an affair, we can start considering the possibility that after the first night together, it turns out that the new lover snores mercilessly. Or that it turns out after the fifth date that we have nothing interesting to talk about. Or that it turns out in the fifth month that they are just a selfish jerk. In other words, if we don't want to be carried away by narratives of a wild night, we may counter them with narratives of a trivial morning that comes after it.

By thinking this way, we can easily have useless narratives lose their colors and become far less convincing. And this is the whole point. Useless narratives may not disappear instantly, but once we counter them and once we provide a contrasting view, they will lose their seductiveness. Matters will reacquire their subtlety and complexity.

Of course, one may well say that this is an attempt to convince ourselves to some predetermined position, in other words, that it's a process of self-indoctrination. But is it? It's pretty awkward to call "indoctrination" a process the whole purpose of which is to remind ourselves not to be blindsided. We want to see more, not less. Our goal here is to put a multitude of takes on a given problem, not to neglect its complexity.

Also, we need to remember that Stoicism doesn't incite us to avoid all love affairs whatsoever nor does it prevent us from travelling anywhere specifically. It simply reminds us that we have all the right and ability to channel our thoughts in the direction *we* want them to flow. We are the masters and commanders of our narratives. We don't have to rescind this authority because of a Facebook post or because of an attractive would-be-lover. One of the most powerful strategies to retain this authority and control is to deliberately confront one current of thoughts with another one. Let's balkanize our minds. Let's divide and conquer.

The best defense is to go on the offensive. Let's attack useless narratives with other narratives. By doing so, we can either fully accomplish our ultimate goal, i.e., get rid of useless narratives, or we can achieve a partial goal of containing them and slashing their influence. This partial goal is also valuable. And let's keep in mind that this tactic is closely connected to the main principle, i.e., that it's all about narratives. Why? Once we admit that we are surrounded by our narratives, we don't have to surrender to them. They will sooner or later rival and fight with each other (for they are competing for a limited resource, that is the scope of our mind). We need to use that to our advantage. In other words, our goal is to learn the ways and means of proper *management of narratives*, which includes the skill of having them play against each other for our favor. This is the direct way to a good, Stoic life and happiness. Let's remember: we must be the masters of our narratives, not the other way around. Narratives must serve our purposes, not vice versa.

Fragment X

> *Today when I saw a handsome person, I did not say to myself, "I wish I could lie with her," and "Happy is her husband" [...]. Nor do I picture the rest to my mind: the woman present, and stripping herself and lying down by my side. I stroke my head and say, "Well done, Epictetus, you*

> have solved a fine little sophism, much finer than that which is called the master sophism."
>
> Epictetus, *Discourses*, II.18.15-17

Commentary: The story about Epictetus patting his head is a nice recap of the entire discussion of useless narratives. It's a reminder that Stoicism is very practical and that it values concrete action over abstract concepts. In Stoicism, self-aware and efficient struggle against useless narratives is a hundred times more important than solving any number of logical puzzles.

Let's put emphasis on the word "self-aware." Our aim is to organize our narratives to serve our values, our goals and our character. The Epictetus' story is not a cheap sermon condemning casual sex, but a praise of autonomy of choice and kudos for consistent conduct. Neither here nor anywhere else we get any specific commandment like "Avoid casual sex!", "Don't use Facebook!" or "Don't travel to the Bahamas!" It is entirely and solely up to us what kind of love life we want to have and where we wish to spend our holidays. Stoicism is neutral on these matters. What it tells us is *how* to execute – expertly, excellently and efficiently – whatever we set our mind to. Stoic happiness doesn't consist in any specific course of action, or in choosing any specific value, or in pursuing any specific goal. Instead, it inheres in *how* we pursue whatever we choose to pursue. It inheres in self-awareness in defining our goals and values and in perseverance in following them. It rests on a specific approach to our errands, life and ourselves, it rests on a specific discipline of action and thought. But in order to be able to do all this properly, we must start with getting rid of useless narratives. We won't get anywhere unless we unburden ourselves. The golden key to Stoicism is to control the way we think, to override our imagination and make it serve instead of fooling us. We must tame our monkey mind and stop our imagination from producing useless narratives. Useless narratives bring about nothing but misery and lead us astray from the path we have chosen. We must use our narratives to strengthen our resolve – not to doubt ourselves.

Finally, if we successfully get rid of useless narratives, we need to remember that they are swift to come back. Our battle against them is never-ending. It will get easier once we get some experience under our belt but there will never be a lasting truce. We will always have to stay vigilant. We must always defend ourselves against useless narratives (foreign and domestic), which would love to whisper in our ear that some other path of life is more beneficial to us. But no, it isn't. There is only misery out there. Let's remember: the most useless of all narratives is the narrative which presents some non-existent state of affairs as better than the actual state of affairs we live in.

Chapter 3

Things within and not within our power

Remember that division by which your own and not your own are distinguished.

Epictetus, *Discourses*, II.6.24

In a nutshell: All that exists and all that happens can be divided into two domains: that which is within our power and that which is not within our power. Not within our power are things that are external to us and which we cannot change with our sheer will: weather, international politics, the thoughts and actions of other people, our social standing, our wealth, health and life. Within our power are things which are subject to our will only: all that we think, feel and decide, all our judgments, choices and pursuits, all our narratives, the ways we approach the world and attitudes we have towards others and events, all our approvals and disapprovals, all our inclinations and distastes. Above all: within our power are the values we intend to uphold, the goals we set for ourselves and the way we want to develop our character.

***

Accolades, recognition and fame aren't within our power (fragment I), nor is money and our health – for only that is within our power which is completely within our power (II). There is a world of difference between the things that aren't within our power and the things that are within our power (III). Within our power are: our narratives, judgments, decisions, inclinations, aversions, values and goals (IV), i.e., the things that are not subject to external circumstances but solely to our will (V). A musician striving to perform well is a good example to illustrate this (VI). Within our power is all of our spiritual life and all our mental states, including our happiness and misery (VII). Shaping our character is also a thing within our power (VIII). The division into things not within our power and things within our power has a few characteristic features, and between the two sets of things, a specific relation holds (IX).

Fragment I

> *Of things some are in our power, and others are not [...]. Not in our power are the body, property, reputation, offices.*
>
> Epictetus, *Encheiridion*, 1

Commentary: The division into things that are and aren't in our power is the fulcrum of Stoicism. If, in some cataclysm, all we know about Stoic philosophy were to be destroyed, and only a single piece of it passed on to the next generations, which piece would be most informative?[7] It would have to be the one which we are now to discuss: that all worldly issues can be divided into two sets of things, those which aren't and those which are within our power. This idea, combined with the principle of focusing on things within our power and with what was said in the two previous chapters on the narratives constitutes the foundation on which the whole edifice of Stoicism is built.

Let's start – perversely – from the last things Epictetus mentions: reputation and office. Let's picture all these honors that could possibly be conferred upon us, all the offices into which we could possibly enter, all the rewards we could possibly receive. They aren't within our power because they aren't (at all) subjected to our will. Why? Simply because we don't get to decide who receives them. We don't decide whether we become a nation's president or a member of a city council. The voters decide. We don't decide whether we are nominated for Secretary of State or ambassador. Our superiors decide. The same holds for all prizes from an elementary school piano contest to the Nobel Prize. We don't decide who gets them because they are doled out by a jury, which is completely independent from us.

Fame is the same story. Fame is a form of collective recognition for our achievements (or, oftentimes, recognition despite lack of achievement). It's clear that it's not us but other people who grant fame (or don't). We don't decide who becomes famous, other people do. It follows from the very definition of fame that it's not within our power. It's challenging to even try to

---

[7] I borrow this "If, in some cataclysm..." line from Richard Feynman and his famous statement on human knowledge and the atomic hypothesis as the key part of it. A quick aside is that Feynman's quote would concern the ancient Stoics, who, unlike the Epicureans, opposed the atomistic worldview. Fortunately reformed Stoicism doesn't rely on any particular physical theory.

Things within and not within our power

count those who have desired or deserved fame, but it never came their way. The examples are endless.[8]

Fragment II

> *Things not in our power are the body, the parts of the body, possessions, parents, brothers, children, country.*
>
> Epictetus, *Discourses*, I.22.10

Commentary: Another vital example is wealth, that is, in the broad sense, our income, property, possessions, money and all related assets. All these things aren't within our power. Why? Because everything we possess can be taken away in an instant. Our car may be stolen tonight or we may total it tomorrow. Our home may burn down, or a tornado may rip through our back yard. We may lose our jobs, or we may lose a lawsuit and have our bank accounts drained. At any moment and in an infinite number of ways it may turn out that our control over our finances is completely illusory. Stoically speaking, it's not "control" at all because all material goods aren't within our power.

The same holds for our body and health. Our health is not within our power because, at any moment, it can be arbitrarily changed by external causes we have no control over. We can get sick, we can get infected or poisoned, we can slip and break a leg. How can our health be within our power if it's at the mercy of a virus and an icy sidewalk? It's also quite probable that our health will deteriorate with age, and aging is, again, beyond our control. In a word, we can take great pains to stay healthy but a trivial flu is a challenge that our will won't overcome. For no act of sheer will can make the flu disappear. A mere virus has power over us which our will is unable to combat.

This doctrine raises eyebrows, and fairly so. It's clear that it contradicts common sense. The daily experience teaches us after all that we do have some degree of control over our health. "How come?," someone asks, "What about keeping a diet and practicing sport? It improves health, doesn't it?" A similarly structured question could be posed on the issues of money and wealth. The Stoic claim that they aren't within our power seems quite ridiculous. Even more ludicrous may appear the idea that the balance of our bank account is not

---

[8] *The past* is one more, very interesting example of a thing not within our power. Notice that it satisfies the definition more than perfectly: it is not within our nor within anyone else's power to change the past. I will address this issue at length in the chapter "Live the Present Day" (commentary to fragment VI).

within our power *because* thieves can empty it. For – we tend to think – yes, thefts and embezzlement happen from time to time, but they happen rarely, and despite them, we can still manage our financial situation. We can seek a good job to provide a stable income, we can avoid overspending and so on. It's clear that if we work hard at something we are good at, then, under normal circumstances and in most cases, the probability of making a step up on the economic ladder increases rather than decreases.[9] It's also quite clear that this probability dips if we leave all our income at a bar. So, does Stoicism mislead us?

No, it doesn't. It uses the controversial language on purpose. The use of the Stoic phrase "not within our power" is notably different from our conversational use of it. How? In the Stoic language *only that which is completely within our power is within our power*. Only absolute control over something entitles us to claim that it is within our power. This is the crucial divergence from our everyday speech. Our daily talk is softer, more equivocal and it includes more gray area. When – in everyday parlance – we say that our health depends on our lifestyle and diet or that our financial situation depends on how hard we work, we tacitly set aside all the cases which are beyond our control (like epidemics, recession and wars). We accept a certain margin of risk but we don't take it into account. We assume it just won't come to it. We assume that rare occurrences which suspend the commonsensical predictability of life won't happen to us. In Stoicism, we do the otherwise: we don't accept that risk and we make no assumptions. We don't admit of the degrees we talk of when we say that some things are *partially* in our power. In Stoicism, things are either completely within our power or aren't at all.

Fragment III

> [Things not in our power are] *those which are not in our power either to have or not to have, or to have of a certain kind or in a certain manner.*
>
> Epictetus, *Discourses*, IV.I.129-130

Commentary: Only that is within our power which is fully and unconditionally in our power. We can speak of having control over something only if that control is absolute. There is no room for shades of gray and there are no half-tones here. If we have 99 percent control over something and external factors hold on to the remaining 1 percent, then the thing in question

---

[9] What this doesn't take into account is the system we live in, political, social and economic. The lack of interest in the outside system is undeniably one of the downsides of Stoicism.

is not within our power. It's like the weather or the motion of the planets. That 1 percent is enough. The slightest gap that enables fate to stick its foot in the door is enough and the thing in question irrevocably falls into the abyss of things not within our power. Stoicism is into full and total security. It only trusts doors which are shut all the way.

The ancient Romans had a beautiful expression, *ultimam manum imponere*, which literally means "to apply the last hand." It referred to providing the finishing touches to a literary work. To "apply the last hand" meant making that last round of copy-editing, making the final adjustments before sending it off to the world. This phrase may be useful for us.

Let's suppose that we are trying to verify whether a given thing is or isn't within our power. Let's take our health as an example. When we are young, sharp and vibrant, full of zest and energy, we may be eager to say that our health *is* within our power. After all, what's easier and more fun than to live healthily, eat well and work out regularly? Yet, in Stoicism none of this counts. When it comes to health (or in any similar case) only one thing matters: who gets the last word? Who makes the final statement? Who has the right to apply the last hand? If it's us, then the given thing is within our power. If it's any external force, then the given thing is not within our power. It makes no difference what happens earlier in the process or what happens in typical cases. There is only one issue that matters here and this single issue defines it all. So, if something comes up and we want to verify whether it is within our power or not, we just have to determine who applies the last hand: is it we or fate? This defines all and all else follows.

What about our health then? We often believe, or at least we want to believe, that our lifestyle and our behavior have an impact on it. Good food, regular sleep, temperance in drugs and rock'n'roll – we are often told that all this is advantageous to our health. Yet, Stoicism reverses this view and asks the following question: are the mentioned procedures *enough* for us to stay healthy? Do they *guarantee* that our health will be pristine? The answer is obviously: no, they don't. The next question is: do we control *everything* that influences our health? Of course, we don't. It's not enough to not smoke and to swim three miles a day. Some kindness of fortune is also necessary, benevolence of external factors is needed. All genetic disorders and all unpredictable viruses must be courteous and steer clear of us, all icy sidewalks must extend a saving handrail to us, and all epidemics must kindheartedly take place on far-away continents. In a word, if we want good health, then it's not enough that we do well with that which is within our power. A favor from the things that aren't within our power is also indispensable.

The Stoic point is that we simply shouldn't need that favor. We shouldn't be at the mercy of the external things, we shouldn't be waiting for their grace. We shouldn't be bound to anything that may or may not be granted to us. We shouldn't kneel before fate and beg for its kindness, we should be neither petitioners nor suitors. That's the rationale for the specific Stoic definition of "being within our power." Only that which is completely within our power counts as "within our power." Only things over which we have absolute authority and which require neither favor from external circumstances nor approval from others are within our power. Only that is truly ours about which we don't have to ask the world for opinion.

Pursuant to this, health isn't within our power. This should be clear already. One thing which may not be as clear is whether there is anything at all which is within our power. Doesn't the Stoic definition rule out *everything*? And if not, what then *is* within our power?

Fragment IV

> *Have you* [then] *nothing which is in your own power, which depends on yourself only and cannot be taken from you?* [...] *Look at the thing then thus, and examine it. – Is anyone able to make you assent to that which is false? – No one. – In the matter of assent then you are free from hindrance and obstruction. – Granted.* – [...] *Is then the despising of death an act of your own or is it not yours? – It is my act.* – [...] *Who can compel you to desire what you do not wish? – No one* [...] *But they will hinder me when I desire from obtaining what I desire. – If you desire any thing which is your own, and one of the things which cannot be hindered, how will they hinder you? – They cannot in any way.*
>
> Epictetus, Discourses, IV.I.68-75

Commentary: It is within our power to adopt a certain way of understanding the world rather than another one. It is within our power to interpret facts in a certain way rather than another way. It is within power to embrace these narratives rather than different ones. Above all, "the golden triad" is within our power: it is within our power to decide what *values* we aspire to, what *goals* we set for ourselves and how we intend to *develop our character*.

This short list is not exhaustive but it depicts the common denominator: all things that are within our power are our own doing and all of them are located within our mind and soul. Things that are within our power aren't directly connected to the external world or defined by it. They do not belong to the domain of material things. Only that which is located inside our heads is within our power: the thoughts we think, judgments and decisions we make, values we mean to hold up and goals we intend to achieve.

It is within our power to decide to desire something, but it's not within our power to decide whether this desire will be fulfilled or not. We may want to sit behind a desk and write – this is perfectly within our power. But whether we actually manage to sit and write is not within our power, for the physical activity of sitting and writing can be interrupted by someone or something. Similarly with making plans: it is within our power to plan to become accomplished athletes or writers, but whether we actually manage to become them isn't within our power (an injury may destroy our career or it may turn out that no one reads our books). The same holds for the aversion and willingness to avoid something. We may wish to stay away from slugs and we may wish to not get a brain tumor. To wish is within our power. But it's not within our power whether we manage to actually avoid these things. Our backyard may turn into a slug's promised land, not to mention what may happen in the latter case. In a word, all external things and events aren't within our power. But our attitude to them *is* within our power.

There is one more way to picture this distinction. It's a thought experiment. Let's imagine that we are sitting comfortably in an armchair and attempting to change a given thing with our sheer willpower. Can we redefine our values, rearrange our life goals, rethink our preferences and aversions just by an act of will, just by pure thinking, without getting up and without performing any physical action? Yes, we can. This is how this type of things are done and, thus, these things are within our power. On the other hand, can we inflict *any* physical change on the world by our sheer willpower? Can we move any physical objects? (Readers capable of spoon bending can skip this passage). Can we make ourselves five years younger? Can we multiply zeros in our bank account? Can we set a single blade of grass in motion? No, we can't. Thus, these things aren't in our power. Short and clean.

Fragment V

> – It is your own act then also to desire to move towards a thing, or is it not so? – It is my own act. – But to desire to move away from a thing, whose act is that? This also is your act. – What then if I have attempted to walk, suppose another should hinder me. – What part of you do they hinder? Do they hinder the faculty of assent? – No, but my poor body. – Yes, as they would do with a stone. – Granted. – But I no longer walk. – And who told you that walking is your own act free from hindrance?
>
> Epictetus, *Discourses*, IV.I.72-73

Commentary: Let's analyze this example in detail. It is within our power to wish or not to wish to go for a walk. Nobody and nothing can prevent us from (not) wishing. But let's make no mistake: nothing can prevent us from *wishing* – and from wishing only. To wish to go for a walk is within our power but the walk itself is not. External, not-within-our-power factors have a great share in the walk itself: our body and its surroundings, the physical motion in a given direction and so on. It is perfectly possible that these external factors will pose an obstacle to our walk. It could happen for a variety of reasons: we could get sick, a bomb could go off nearby, or the police could cordon off the area where we intended to take the walk. It is within our power to wish or not wish to go for a walk, but it is not within our power whether we actually go.

Being physically prevented from doing something is, of course, the most brutal and plain-sight visualization of the line between things that are and aren't within our power. A random terrorist or a police officer has control over the location of our body, since they are able to physically take it here or there.[10] And yet, *no one has control over what we think* – all our thoughts are within our power only. No one can storm into our heads and make us think something other than what we want to think.

No outside power has influence on what we think, but what about outside persuasion or blackmail? It's clear that our thoughts are not subject to physical force, but what about more subtle means? What if we are sentenced to house arrest and face a heavy fine if we break it? Doesn't that bear some influence on what we wish for?

The Stoics see this the following way: our wish to go for a walk is still completely within our power, but the external circumstances have changed. In making the decision whether we wish to go for a walk, we must take into account that in the present situation, a walk entails an impending financial loss. A walk and a fine are now inseparably bound together. We cannot pass over that, we cannot bury our head in the sand and pretend that the new circumstances don't exist. It is our duty to be aware of the circumstances, to know them, and to know them well and in detail. Our decision as to whether we wish to go for a walk must be made all-things-considered and must be based on the best information available.

Let's consider a more extreme example. It is within our power – and within our power only – to agree that some statement is true or false. But what if someone holds us at gunpoint and asks whether we agree that two and two

---

[10] As Epictetus colorfully puts it: "What system of philosophy could I have made so that, if a stronger fellow should have laid hold of my cloak, I should not be dragged off; that if ten people should have laid hold of me and cast me into prison, I should not be cast in?" (Epictetus, *Discourses*, I.29.23-24)

make five? What happens then? Epictetus seems to be clear on this: "no one can make you assent to what is false." But what would he say if he was looking down the barrel?

Let's begin with the trivial remark that to assent to something out loud is not the same as to assent to something indeed. Our words don't have to mirror our thoughts. We can say something and still think something else. We assent to something out loud but deep in our heart, we hold to our own. For no one can force or blackmail us to *think* what we don't want to think. Words can be subject to pressure but thoughts are free of any pressure.

But is that all? No. Stoicism underscores that just as no one can force us to think something we don't want to think, no one can actually *force* us to say something we don't want to say. Saying something is a complex effort of our tongue and vocal chords, which are subject to us and to no one else. Only we can set them in the specific motion that produces particular words and sentences. Every word we utter is our own autonomous decision. Even someone who holds a pistol to our head doesn't aspire to control our vocal chords. No one can force us to say anything in the sense in which a terrorist *can* force us to go where we wouldn't like to go. If someone forces us into a car's trunk and drives away, then, as a matter of fact, our body is being carried around by other people. But if someone pulls a gun on us and orders us to utter some particular words – we still have a choice. They can't forcibly move our throat and lips – we have to do it ourselves. It turns out that the terrorist in question doesn't *force* us to do anything, but rather she attempts to influence our will by some indirect methods (the direct methods are unavailable to her). In other words, the terrorist changes the external circumstances so that our decision about uttering or not uttering certain words is made in new, radically changed circumstances. And these new circumstances are the following: we either stand firm that two and two make four and we die, or we assent that two and two make five. *The decision is still up to us.* Only the external conditions have changed along with the predicted consequences of our choice. But the right to choose and the autonomy to make the decision are just as within our power as they were before.

In sum, we shouldn't expect the external world to easily give up its attacks. The world, not being able to reach inside our head and penetrate our will directly, relies on its means of indirect influence. Yet, we may remain unruffled. When it comes to our goals, values, choices and thoughts, it's always us and only us who have the right to apply the last hand. It is ours – and ours only – signature on our every thought, every decision and every act of volition. No outside power is able to forge this signature or to force us to sign anything against our will. Thus, on the ocean of things and events that aren't in our power, there is an immovable and impenetrable island of things that are in our power. It consists of our thoughts, judgments and decisions, as well as our values and goals.

Fragment VI

> *Lute players when they are singing by themselves have no anxiety, but when they enter the theatre, they are anxious even if they have good voices and play well on the lute. For they not only wish to sing well, but also to obtain applause: but this is not in their power.*

Epictetus, Discourses, II.13.2-3

Commentary: The division into things that are and aren't in our power is so crucial in Stoicism that the discussion of it merits another example. Let's imagine that the musician Epictetus talks about knows nothing about Stoicism, or even that she is reluctant towards it. And let's imagine that she meets a Stoic and that they start a conversation about what is and isn't in one's power when it comes to music. What would the conversation look like?

First off, the musician might express her desire to be famous. Her goal is to get her name out there and to make people consider her a great musician. But is that within her power? Of course not. She can't force her name directly into people's minds and she can't compel them to respect it. Despite all her talent and effort, there might be no room in the limelight for her. Her music may be not in tune with the fads and expectations of the time, her manager may fail to do a good job promoting her, she may receive little coverage in the media or she may simply lack luck. There is a wide range of possible reasons but the conclusion is always the same: it's not within her power to ensure that she becomes a famous artist.

Our musician might then take a step back and redefine her plan. A slightly less ambitious version of it may go along this line. "OK, if securing fame is not within my power, I will then focus on my performance today. It's not within my power whether millions of people come to love me, so I will focus on being loved by those few who attend tonight's concert. This, after all, is the fabric of every success. I will try to make them enjoy my performance, clap their hands and love me." What does a Stoic reply to this? As follows: "You are heading in the right direction, dear musician, but, alas, it's still not within your power to ensure that you are admired at tonight's performance. You can't step up to every spectator, grab their hands and make them clap. Also, you can't make it into their heads and push the "like" button. You can't force the audience to applaud, because enjoying or not enjoying something is their own sovereign decision. They may want to clap their hands, but they also may not want to.

Thus, ensuring the applause at the concert today, just as ensuring planetary fame, is not within your power."

The artist may now dodge again and state the following. "Fair enough! It's not within my power whether the audience applauds or boos, but it's within my power to perform well. How people react to the work I do isn't within my power, but to do a good job – it is within my power." Does that sound, right?

Not quite, since the situation is not about the good will of the performer only. There are many moving parts in a good concert. There are many factors at play and there are many necessary conditions that a good concert must meet. Most of them aren't within the power of our artist. For instance, the venue must be adequately prepared. The microphones, the sound system, the whole setup must be arranged properly. The sound engineer can't be too stoned to do her job well. Lights must be so kind as not to go out in the middle of the event. The ceiling must do her the solid of not collapsing during the show. So, although it may seem like a bit of a paradox, the quality of her performance is not within the power of the artist.

If that is so, then our artist might try a last-ditch resort. "Yes, everything external can go south and turn against me, but I can still control how well I sing and play. That is, the beauty of my singing and the virtuosity of my lute-playing are within my power." Yet, the Stoic raises an objection again. It isn't within the artist's power to sing clean and play well, since there are still many slips 'twixt her throat and lip. Many hindrances can happen between the act of volition about singing well and actually voicing a certain note. The artist's throat can let her down and, despite her perfect pitch, she can sing unmercifully out of tune. A lute's string may snap or our artist herself may screw up if she uses too much liquid courage beforehand. Her competitors may hire someone to interrupt her performance. Who can promise her that she doesn't get shot and killed in the middle of the concert? More things happen in this business and in this world than the nonstoics dream of.[11]

But where does this leave us? After this argument and after this forcible retreat, we can almost hear our artist saying, in a somewhat bitter voice, "So, you basically claim that *nothing* is within my power! Everything is controlled by dark and inchoate forces which can thwart each and every one of my endeavors and resolves!" And yet, this one is not true. The Stoic point is that after all these reductions and tactical retreats, we are not left in a lurch. There is something we haven't mentioned yet, something which is immune to this

---

[11] E.g. Igor Talkov, Russian singer and song-writer, was fatally shot during his concert in Yubileyny Sports Palace in St. Petersburg, Russia, October 6, 1991.

type of reductive reasoning. What is that? It is within the artist's power *to wish* to perform the best she can and it is within her power to strive to do so. The will itself, the decision to strive for something is within her power.

The very decision to intend to become an artist and not a sportsman, accountant or soldier – this is within our power. It is within our power to decide whether we prefer to go out on stage rather than to count dollar bills in a bank or to write philosophical treatises in a sylvan refuge. It is within our power to decide to pursue one thing rather than another. And finally, of course, the very desire to be famous, or to sing well, is also within our power. It is not within our power whether we achieve something, but it is within our power to define *anything* as our goal and to intend to achieve it and to strive to do our best.

Fragment VII

It is in my power to let no badness be in this soul, nor desire, nor any perturbation at all.

Marcus Aurelius, *Meditations*, VIII.29

Commentary: What's particularly important is that all anxiety, all sorrow, misery and distress are also within our power. It is within our power to experience them and it is within our power to eradicate them. In other words, *if we feel miserable, it's our fault that we feel so*. The origin of all misery is inside us – this is the crucial Stoic proclamation. It's not other people, it's not fate, it's not the circumstances that make us unhappy, but rather we ourselves make us unhappy. We are responsible for our own unhappiness. It's our own doing and it's our own choice to feel miserable. And the remedy is also a matter of our choice.

The lesson here is clear. If the matters of our soul, mind and spirit are within our power, then we can shape them according to our will, intent and need. In our thoughts and feelings, we are not bound by anything external. Furthermore, our ultimate goal, our *happiness, is also within our power*. In other words, it's within our own reach to make ourselves happy. We don't need the world to extend a helping hand here, no kindness of fate is required. No aid from other people and no divine intervention are necessary. This is the core of Stoicism, and this is the source of the great Stoic bliss, strength and freedom. It's completely up to us whether we are happy or not. Thus: yes, we can live happily and live well. The rest of the book elaborates on how exactly to do it.

Fragment VIII

Integrity is your own, virtuous shame is your own. Who then can take these things from you?

Epictetus, *Discourses*, I.25.4

Commentary: Within our power are not only fleeting judgments and ephemeral thoughts but also the traits of our character. It is within our power to decide who we are and what we are like. A decision to try to save a baby from a burning house is, of course, within our power. But our power is not limited to that single decision only: an enduring disposition and readiness to make such decisions is also within our power. Such a disposition is called "courage" and, therefore, it is within our power to be courageous.

Stoicism opposes those who claim that our character is given to us once and for all (by nature, nurture or whatever) and that it is immutable. This idea may be dangerously comfortable, as it allows and warrants us to hide behind a screen of seeming impossibility ("I can't do anything about it, it's just the way I am"), but it is completely wrong. True, it's not within our power to change our genetic code. True, it's not within our power to change the past, particularly the way we have been raised. But it is within our power to resolve to transform our personality. Personality is not immutable, but malleable. We ourselves decide whether we are courageous or chicken-hearted, noble or mean, honest or treacherous. All our virtues and vices are within our power. We *can* become who we want, even though we may be a far cry from the ideal to begin with. Stoicism is not for those who are perfect, it is for those who want to improve. And it is certainly not for those who claim that we cannot improve.

The decision "I will try to save the baby from the fire" is within our power, but it's not within our power whether we actually manage to save the baby. In fact, it's not within our power whether we even manage to get into the building. The very decision is an act of thought, which is the domain of our freedom, while the remaining events take place in the outside world and are subject to all imaginable hindrances. But our character itself cannot be hindered. The decision "I will try to save the baby" relies on nothing external. Consequently, permanent readiness to make brave decisions is also within our power, for it is contained in the realm of our thoughts. Outside factors can't stop us here and they cannot hamper our transformation into courageous humans. Being courageous is not about the results of our actions, but about presenting a certain attitude. That attitude is subject to our will only. Thus, being courageous is within our power.

An ancient anecdote fits here. Once upon a time, a man, who was famous for his ability to tell a person's character by the look of their face, visited Athens. The disciples of Socrates figured to conduct an experiment. They brought the physiognomist to Socrates and asked him to deduct his character. The diagnosis was surprising: Socrates was declared a lazy man with a fondness for liquor and debauchery. The disciples laughed and declared that the physiognomist made a fool of himself. Socrates said though that this description was totally relevant and accurate, for he indeed *had had* all these defects, but he overcame them by his own work and resolve. And even though Socrates was not a Stoic (he lived about a century before the Stoic school emerged), every Stoic would nod at the merit of this story.

Let's remember that sky is the limit when it comes to improving our character. There are no impossibilities here, no insurmountable barriers. There is no restraint in our work on things that are within our power. Our personality is nothing but a set of specific ways of interacting with the world. It is within our power to change these ways. In general, our attitude toward the things not within our power is within our power.

Fragment IX

> *– A father has disinherited a certain son. What do you think of it? – It is a thing beyond the power of the will, not an evil. – Caesar has condemned a person. – It is a thing beyond the power of the will, not an evil. – The person is afflicted at this. – Affliction is a thing which depends on the will: it is an evil. – They have borne the condemnation bravely. – That is a thing within the power of the will: it is a good. – If we train ourselves in this manner, we shall make progress.*
>
> <div align="right">Epictetus, <i>Discourses</i>, III.8.3-5</div>

Commentary: The division into things within and not within our power has a few interesting traits. What are they? First off, it's clear-cut and unequivocal. Every conceivable thing, action or occurrence is either within our power or it is not. Nothing sits on the fence. There is no gray area here, there are no degrees. No thing is *in part* within our power and in part not. The distinction is sharp.

Second, it is fully defined. *Every* thing is either within our power or not within our power. To every single thing, action or occurrence in the world one of these two qualities can be ascribed: either they are within our power or not. Everything can be described using these two notions. We can't come up with a single example that would render this division useless or otherwise crash it. Every imaginable case can be settled as either within our power or not.

Third, the boundary between these two realms may seem surprising. The proportions are not intuitive. It's stunning how many things land in the realm of things not within our power. As we have discussed, this follows from a specific and very strong Stoic understanding of the concept of "within power."

Fourth, notice a fascinating point. We have the two sets of things, clearly separated from one another. Now, let's pick a single element from the set of things that are not within our power, let it be wealth. Wealth in itself is, of course, not within our power. But let's modify it just a bit: let's substitute "our attitude to wealth" for "wealth" and – as if by magic – we fetch a thing which *is* within our power. Obviously, instead of "our attitude to wealth" we can take "our narrative about wealth," "blinding desire to achieve wealth," "indifference to wealth" and so on. All of these are things within our power. In other words: within our power is our narrative about the things not within our power and our attitude to them.[12] In particular, within our power is our *assessment* of things not within our power. It is within our power to decide whether we deem wealth a good or an evil and – above all – it is within our power to decide where we position wealth in the hierarchy of our values and goals.

---

[12] Mathematically speaking: let $S(x)$ be our assessment of, attitude to or a narrative about given x. It holds that *for every x not within our power, $S(x)$ is within our power.* Importantly, this law is just a specific case of a more universal formula: *for every x, $S(x)$ is within our power.* Regardless of whether x is or is not within our power, $S(x)$ is always within our power. This can be iterated as *for every x, $S(S(x))$ is within our power.* In other words, our attitude to our attitude to something is within our power. And a narrative *about* our narratives is ours too.

Chapter 4

Focus on things within your power

To keep [our] *own, not to claim that which* [is not our own].

Epictetus, *Discourses*, II.16.28

In a nutshell: In order to live well and happily, we need to focus on things within our power. All our thoughts, all our capabilities, all our energies and strengths need to be directed to what we control. As for the things not within our power, we should be as indifferent to them as we possibly can. We shouldn't be concerned with them, we shouldn't care for them. We should hold them irrelevant.

***

We should focus on things within our power and be indifferent to things not within our power (fragment I), because to do otherwise is to enter a direct pathway to dissatisfaction and misery (II). Yet, we must make no mistake as to what "being indifferent" means (III). Responsibility for what happens with us is within us – not outside of us (IV). Whatever happens, we need to translate it into the language of things within our power and we should express it in the things-within-our-power conceptual frame (V). We should carry things by the handle that they should be carried by (VI). How can we learn it? We should beware of illusions and specious needs (VII), and we must remember that no single blunder or failed attempt means total defeat (VIII). Why is it all necessary for happiness? Because, first of all, praising things not within our power equals us becoming their slaves (IX). Second, because it's impossible to be consistent and coherent regarding things not within our power (X). Third, because focusing on things within our power not only eradicates roots of distress and unhappiness, but also transfigures them into sources of joyful freedom (XI). On the other hand, we need to take care not to interpret "indifference to things not within our power" in a superficial or ascetic way (XII).

Fragment I

I have learned to see that every thing which happens, if it be independent of my will, is nothing to me.

Epictetus, *Discourses*, I.29.26

Commentary: This single sentence captures the whole gist of the present chapter. *We should focus on things that are within our power and we should be indifferent to things that are not within our power.* All that we are to discuss here is nothing more or less than explanation, justification and discussion of this one plain ground rule. The sole purpose of the preceding chapter was to serve as a stepping stone for the present principle. We will now build on the distinction made there and we will use it to fully establish and define the core rule of focusing on the things within our power.

Everything can be divided into that which is within our power and that which is not within our power. We need to focus on the former and not care about the latter. But what does it mean "to not care"? It means making an honest, serious and lasting decision to concentrate all our energies, endeavors, desires, wishes, resolve and willpower on that which is within our power. This is an over-arching, strategic decision which is the beginning and source of the Stoic life. It is within our power to decide where we focus our strengths and efforts – and we need to focus them on things within our power.

We shouldn't be overly concerned about whether we are or aren't rich, healthy and famous. Instead, we should rather be concerned about whether we are or aren't self-aware and courageous, whether we live harmoniously and think autonomously, whether we are reasonable, reliable and responsible. These things are within our power, and they are the very things we should focus on. They require and they deserve our utmost attention. We are morally obliged to focus on them, to invest in them, and to cherish them, not anything else. They should be of primary importance to us; they should be our first, final and foremost matter of concern.

What about things *not* in our power then? The Stoic message is that we should focus not on things not within our power, like wealth, health and fame, but on our *attitude* to them. As we have discussed earlier, our attitude to all things not within our power – is within our power. It is not within our power whether we are young, rich and in radiant health, but it is within our power what we think about youth, wealth and radiancy. It is within our power to chain ourselves to praising these things but it is just equally within our power to declare that our happiness, prosperity and bliss are independent from them.

Fragment II

If you desire anything which is not in your power, you must be unfortunate.

Epictetus, *Encheiridion*, 2

Commentary: Why should we focus on things within our power instead of things not within our power? The core reason is simple: because doing otherwise makes us miserable. If we set our mind on achieving or on avoiding something which is not within our power, we thus set ourselves up for a possible failure in achieving or avoiding. Thereby, we open ourselves to failure-induced misery. All our desires, wishes and projects may easily come to naught if we define them in external terms. The course of events may easily sway them in a direction we don't want them to go. Stoicism proposes a simple countermeasure: we should reorganize and reformulate all of our goals and values, so that they are expressed in terms of things that are within our power.

Let's take a common case. Imagine we find in ourselves a strong desire to climb the social ladder – we crave to become rock stars, politicians, top-tier CEOs or, at least, acclaimed philosophers. This desire can propel us to various activities: we go to specific schools, we start careers in adequate corporations, we write books which – in our estimation – will land us on the top of the bestsellers lists and bookstore shelves. However, it should be clear by now that it is not within our power to ensure that we actually get there. Since we intend to achieve something that we don't have full control over, it's possible that we don't achieve it – in which case disappointment and sorrow will follow. We may end up with a dead-end, low-pay job somewhere in the backcountry, with a bitter feeling that we deserve "more than that." This is the source of distress and suffering, this is a big hurdle we put on our track to happiness and fulfillment. Sadly enough, we put it up ourselves.

This pattern is repeated with any example: if we wish for something that is not within our power, we simply put our head under a guillotine and just wait for it to fall. The Stoic solution is always the same: the whole secret is to stop using things not within our power to define ourselves, our values and our goals. It is within our power to stop doing so. And once we do that: pain will disappear.

The same argument holds for what we would like to avoid. As long as we consider cancer or poverty a dreadful thing, we will let them distress us and we will live fearfully in their shadow. But we may, at any time, simply stop treating them as something that should be feared and desist from defining our inclinations and antipathies in their terms (and *on* their terms). Once we do so, our discomfort and fear will immediately evaporate. For a while, it is not within our power to ensure that we don't get sick, it is still within our power to avoid defining our life in terms of fear of sickness.

Fragment III

You will think riches the only thing that can make a person happy. Poverty then will be sure to rack you, and (what is most miserable) even false poverty. For though you possess much, yet because another has more, you will think you want at least as much as that wherein they exceed you. Or do you think that happiness consists in honors? How will it torment you to see such a one made consul, and much more to see another rechosen!

Seneca, *Epistles*, 104.9

Commentary: Wealth is a thing not within our power, and it should be treated as such. We may and we should be happy no matter whether we are rich or poor. Our happiness and our good life are a completely different issue than our financial situation. They belong to two completely different discourses, two completely different dimensions of our life. These two variables have completely nothing in common, they are fully independent of each other. Of course, we get easily deluded to think that it is otherwise, and that is why being nonstoic is so widely popular.

Only the distinction between things within our power and things not within our power is real enough, well-defined enough and clear-cut enough to be fully trusted and relied upon. Only this distinction is explicit, sharp and unmistakable enough to be used as a relevant and useful criterion in our decision-making process. In other words, the only reasonable and coherent attitude to money is to hold money itself as something neutral, but, at the same time, to hold our *attitude* to money as a crucial and life-defining issue. In this vein, we should never think "Good life begins at five hundred thousand a year," but rather: "Good life is totally independent from how much I earn." Why is that? Because five hundred grand is just as arbitrary as fifty or fifteen. All non-zero figures will always be totally arbitrary and difficult to justify. If we agree that good life commences at any specific paygrade, we'll immediately get lost, because we won't be able to come to an agreement about the specific number. Any figure will sound like it was pulled out of the hat and the rationale behind it will always seem flimsy. The only coherent and justifiable way to go is to determine that this number is zero dollars a year, that is, in other words, that good life and happiness are attainable no matter what our income is. They are attainable because, simply and straightforwardly, they are completely independent of our income.

Fragment IV

The first difference between a common person and a philosopher is this: the common person says, "Woe to me for my little child, for my brother, for my father." The philosopher, if [...] [is ever] compelled to say, "Woe to and me," stops and says, "but for myself."

Epictetus, *Discourses*, III.19.1

Commentary: It depends only on us whether we perceive our life as a play of outside factors and forces, or whether we understand it as a sequence of our own decisions. In some sense, both interpretations are equally admissible and equally feasible. There is no law of science, there is no logic and no social convention that would prohibit any of them. They are both open for us to choose from. Only we decide how we prefer to see ourselves and the world. Stoicism, of course, insists that we once and for all drop the viewpoint of things not within our power and that we embrace the perspective of things within our power. Only the latter can serve as an adequate lens to see the world, as a proper conceptual grid for our thinking, and as an efficient leverage for action.

The principle of focusing on things within our power and not caring for things not within our power may be also understood as assuming an "inward" direction of thinking. In other words, focusing on things within our power amounts to a habit of seeking responsibility, reasons and answers within ourselves, not in the outside world. The point is that, regardless of all external facts, things and events, regardless of all that happens around us, we can still be responsible for ourselves and we can retain power over ourselves.

Let's imagine that something adverse happens. Let's say that our computer breaks down. What happens then? The principle of focusing on things within our power makes us concentrate our attention on the following issues: have we taken proper care of it? Have we set up a proper anti-virus program? Haven't we visited X-rated websites too much? Haven't we spilt too much coffee on it? Focusing on things within our power will make us think first of all about what past decision or behavior of ours might have led to the present failure, second, it will make us think about what we can possibly do to prevent such problem from happening again, third, it will make us think on if and how we can remedy the problem. This is the direction in which our thoughts will flow. And where won't they flow? They won't flow towards swearing and self-flogging along the lines of "I am the most unlucky one!," or "This shouldn't have happened to me!", or maybe "Why do these things always happen to me and only to me?" We won't get to hate the world and we won't curse the ways of it. In a word, we need to learn to see in all types of events primarily (or even *exclusively*) that which is within our power. All the things that are not within our power should always remain in the background of our consciousness and conscience.

Let's take another example: let's imagine that we were in a car accident. Fortunately, we get away with no injuries and we are able to think about what happened. If we don't aspire to Stoicism, we may well think like this: "That scumbag didn't yield! It's on him!" Or: "This *always* happens to me!" Or: "It's Friday the thirteenth! Coincidence? I don't think so!" Or: "Clearly, the company that built the road is at fault! If they had designed it better and cared more for road safety – there would be no accidents!" These explanations and excuses are frequent among nonstoics. But what would, in turn, a Stoic say? For example, this: "Yay, this is how speeding in the rain must end!" Or: "When I'm at the wheel, I must keep in mind that crazy drivers are around me and that DUI is not uncommon." Or: "Well... When was the last time I actually checked the brakes?" It's hard to believe that these two types of comments refer to the very same fact. But they do. And of course, we need to avoid the second pattern.

It's important to underscore that adopting this line of thinking doesn't mean neglecting or turning a blind eye to external factors and factual causes of the accident. We don't forget them, we don't disregard them. It is indeed true that potholes in the road or our inebriated fellow humans may contribute to an accident. Stoicism doesn't deny that. It just wants to remind us that we have no control over the maintenance of the roads and sobriety of others. Thus, we shouldn't focus our attention there. Every given situation, like a car accident, is a result of a plethora of objective factors and causes, which all pitch in. Yet, we need to pick only those which are within our power – and we need to focus solely on them. This holds for a car accident, this holds for everything. In every conceivable twist and turn of fortune, we have to focus first and foremost on that aspect of it which is within our power.

Fragment V

When you seek what is not your own, you lose that which is your own.

Epictetus, *Discourses*, I.25.4-5

Commentary: How about situations where it seems that we do have *some*, but not absolute, control over the course of events? After all, we can readily agree that it is smarter to focus on shaping our narratives (which is within our power) than on trying to reschedule a solar eclipse (which is not within our power). But how about, for example, the result of a game of tennis we are playing right now? According to the definitions set forth in the previous chapter, it is not within our power to ensure a favorable outcome of the game. Thus, it apparently follows that we shouldn't care about the score. Shouldn't we, though? We intuitively feel that it sounds off mark. Are we supposed to just leave the court and lose by default?

In the quoted passage, Epictetus points out that every bit of attention which we invest in things not within our power deprives things within our power of the very same bit of our attention. Every time we make a hopeless attempt to seize something that is beyond our control, we unavoidably relinquish our grip on the things we may control. Importantly, this happens also the other way around: the best way to exercise influence over the things we can't control is to focus on the things we can control. In other words, we can affect things not within our power *through* focusing on things within our power. Yet, if we focus on things not within our power – we will lose on both fronts.

This argument may seem a little abstract, and it calls for a fitting illustration. So let's turn again to the mentioned tennis match.[vi] Of course, winning the match is the purpose of playing it (among other purposes, like relaxation, workout and so on). But let's now answer one simple question: is it within our power to secure a victory in the match? No, it's not. It is not within our power to say a magical word (or think a thought) and thus determine who wins. No act of our sheer willpower can make our opponent stop returning the ball and make the scoreboard display our name. But does this mean that we should immediately surrender? Of course not! No, it is not within our power to secure our victory. No, it is not within our power to make sure that we perform to the best of our ability (it may always happen that we get injured, feel sick, and so on). But it is within our power *to try* to play well. In other words, *we shouldn't home in on winning, we should home in on striving to play well.*

This is a huge difference in approach. The result of the match is not within our power, but our toil and attempt to play well – is within our power. One and the same phenomenon (a tennis match) can be perceived from two completely different perspectives. Our Stoic task, challenge and obligation is to always adopt the things-within-our-power perspective. Let's notice now that once we focus on striving to play well (thing within our power) instead of focusing on winning (thing not within our power) we actually *increase* the chances of winning. Moreover, the *easier* way to win is to focus on trying to play well (thing within our power) than to focus on trying to win (a thing not within our power). The reasons for this are clear.

Let's say that that match is close to the end and we are a few points behind. If our goal is simply "to win," then we might start getting nervous or lose motivation and thus perform even worse. But if our goal is "to try to play well" then whatever the score is at the moment, our efforts are not hampered. Every moment is just as good to try to play well, isn't it? It doesn't matter whether we are on our way to a landslide victory or if we are an inch away from a crushing defeat – if we wish, we can always try to play well. Needless to say, this attitude boosts our overall chances for a good performance: we won't get nervous or disheartened that easily. Thus, we will also avoid possible mistakes that would aggravate our situation even more. If we keep in mind only the things that are within our power – we simply play better tennis.

This reasoning is valid in every fragment of reality, in every portion of our life, and in every action we possibly may undertake. It illustrates the general precept that in defining our goals in terms of things within our power ("to try to play well," "to do our job," etc.), we not only make these goals easier to reach but we also make the possible failure of meeting them far less painful (we are not worried by a possible defeat anymore, because we are not concerned about any specific result of the match). We get a double gain and we'll get it anytime we successfully express ourselves, our goals and values in the Stoic language of things-within-our-power. So, let's say not "I want to win the game," but rather "I strive to play well." Let's say not that "I wish to become a rock star," but rather "I wish to prepare the best I can for today's concert." Let's say not "I'd love to be healthy," but "I intend to adopt a healthier lifestyle." Let's say not "I wish I could get this book over with", but "I pledge to myself to stick to writing 10 pages a day." All our experiences, endeavors, values, goals, obligations, projects, intentions and commitments should be expressed in the within-our-power language. Stoicism promises us that it can always be done and, moreover, that it will be always to our benefit.

Let's notice now that this argument quashes on the spot the "Stoicism promotes passivity" type of objection that is sometimes raised. This objection is based on a mistaken reading of the principle of focusing on things within our power. This misreading may sound something like this: "If the result of the game is not within my power, then why on earth even enter the contest? What prevents me from just sitting down on the court and wringing my hands? Why don't I just stay the whole day in bed, doing nothing. For so many things around me are not within my power..."

After all, we have said before, it should be clear why this interpretation is misguided. The things within our power can be a wonderful leverage to produce a favorable outcome in the realm of things not within our power. In this vein, we may say that Stoicism is a system for managing things not within our power *through* things within our power. The principle of focusing on things within our power can be in turn rephrased the following way: we make ourselves of necessity unhappy if we try to directly influence things not within our power. The only way to influence them and not to get miserable in the process – is through things within our power.

Fragment VI

> *Every thing has two handles, the one by which it may be borne, the other by which it may not.*
>
> Epictetus, *Encheiridion*, 43

Commentary: "Focus on things within your power" may be rephrased as "translate everything into the language of things within your power,", or "let's do everything that we do through things within our power." We can further explore this idea, along the line sketched by Epictetus in the quoted passage. We need to learn to see two sides in everything: in every fact, thing and event we face, in every value we would like to uphold and in every goal, we would like to achieve. We need to see two sides in all of them – one side within our power, the other not within our power. Thus, the principle "let's focus on things within our power" comes to mean "whatever we undertake, let's approach it from the side which is within our power." This can be applied to everything. It holds for the adversities we face, for the ordinary events we happen upon, and for all of our endeavors.

Let's take a few more examples. Let's imagine that our nation's network of highways is underdeveloped and requires some serious improvement. What is within our power here and what isn't? This actual state of affairs, the very fact that they are now in bad condition, is not within our power to change. We cannot get anywhere near changing it by mere *thinking* change. Our willpower doesn't make any difference here. So what is within our power? It is within our power to decide, when planning a road trip, whether or not we want to take into account that the roads are bad. It is within our power to decide whether or not we want to leave earlier because of this. But that's not all. It is also within our power to resolve to vote for a party which proposes a major overhaul of the road infrastructure. Moreover, if this problem really haunts us, it is within our power to intend to start our own political movement pushing the rebuild-the-roads agenda.

Another example: it may happen (and at some point it will definitely happen) that we get sick. What is within our power in this case and what is not? This actual state of affairs, the actual fact that we are sick and that we feel beat – this is not within our power to change. It is not within our power to get healthy in a heartbeat – our sheer willpower is not enough here. Merely *thinking* recovery won't put us back on our feet. What is within our power, then? It is within our power to decide whether we prefer to lament in vain about the whole thing or try to get over this hurdle as bravely as possible. Take another example: we conclude that there is too much bureaucracy. Again, this very fact is not within our power to change because we can't fix it by simply thinking about fixing it. Also, the realities of daily life compel us to go to various offices sometimes and run some errands there. It is not within our power to avoid this (unless, of course, we live completely off the grid). Yet it surely is within our power to take this fact into account and to – when going to an office – double-check all the paperwork, get to know in advance which room we should get to and so on.

Adopting this view helps us refute another possible misunderstanding. Here is the problem. If we just – simply and straightforwardly – take the entire world and divide all of its phenomena into the two categories of "within our power" and "not within our power", if we then simply apply the principle of focusing solely on the set of things within our power, we will arrive at a surprising and awkward conclusion. An overwhelming majority of conceivable things, including all external objects and all worldly affairs, is not within our power. The distinction is very peculiar: everything outside our mind is not within our power. All the material objects of common knowledge and all of the stuff that people usually talk about, all the issues and business of everyday experience, all that we see and all that happens to us – all that is not within our power. And, consequently, if the principle says that we shouldn't focus on these things, then we may be led to the misguided conclusion that we shouldn't care for the worldly affairs at all, that we should just sit down and wait for fortune to toss us around (we may dub this "the conservative misinterpretation of Stoicism").[13] In other words, this principle – if read superficially – may be seen as encouragement to passivity and resignation. But does Stoicism really encourage us to drop all action?

Of course it doesn't! The Stoic response is this: we need to carry things by the handle they should be carried by. To do so, let's start not with a purely intellectual act of dividing things, facts and events into two abstract sets. Let's start the other way around. Let's first figure out what interests us and what is it that we would like to do. Only *then* let's plan our actions. And let's plan them accordingly. In other words, let's not draw the line until after we decide what we care about, what we intend to cherish and what we want to be responsible for. Only then let's figure out what part of it is within our power and what part of it is not within our power. And only then let's focus on the former.

Now, let's get back to the highways example. It irks us that the highway network is seriously underdeveloped, we don't like being stuck in traffic, we don't like driving on shabby country roads. Yet, the condition of the roads is a thing not within our power – we cannot change it by merely thinking about it. Does this mean that we should never be concerned about it? If this was the conclusion, then Stoicism would really be a philosophy of slavish subordination to the course of events (not to mention that if such Stoicism was universally adopted, then no one would ever actually rebuild those highways). Let's try the better approach: we begin with picking our area of interest and defining our goals and values. Do we want to live a private life, concentrated on our immediate social environment and engaged only in the issues that concern us privately? Or, to the contrary, do we want to run for public office and engage in statecraft? In Stoicism, both ways are equally

---

[13] For more on this see: Stankiewicz, *Does Happiness Write Blank Pages?*, 70-83.

admissible and equally valuable. They are both open to us – we just need to choose between them. We must decide and then we act accordingly. If we opt for a life of an astronomer, lyrical poet, musician, teacher or a professional athlete, then we should think as little as possible about the highways problem, because it doesn't concern us in any within-our-power way. If, on the other hand, we choose the career of a politician, road builder, or social activist, then the highways become one of the problems we should concern ourselves with. At this point (not any sooner!) we need to figure out what about highways is within our power and what is not. What is not within our power? Geography of our country, prices of building materials, and the actual condition of the highways at the moment we turn to this problem. What is within our power? Making plans, thinking about an agenda and timeline for further works, about ways of financing them, about how we intend to lobby for more money to be allocated to road construction. And this is where we should focus.

This approach clarifies one more problem, i.e., the seeming paradox of Stoic attitude to physical suffering and withstanding it. As mentioned before, this is a problem which has been traditionally associated with the Stoics, and it's an example worth revisiting once more. So, let's imagine again that we have a toothache. Is pain within our power? Or, to be more precise, is stopping pain within our power? No, it is not. Does our principle of focusing on things within our power translate into a crude "try to care not about the pain?" No, it does not. The idea of being indifferent to pain surely sounds great, but it cannot fit into any ethical agenda as a valid *principle* of action, not to mention that such phrasing is completely empty: it doesn't tell us anything about *how* to be indifferent to pain. Epictetus' two handles clarify this: yes, pain itself is not within our power, but it is within our power to reach for a phone to make a dentist appointment. The pain will not disappear because of us doing so, possibly it will not even subside. But we will, in a sense, blanket pain with things within our power (like "deciding to take action and call a doctor"). Focusing on them will, in a way (at least logically, if not sensually), move the pain to the background of our mind.

Fragment VII

> *Do not attach yourself to* [things not within our power] *and they will not be necessary. Do not say to yourself that they are necessary, and then they are not necessary.*
>
> Epictetus, Discourses, IV.1.110

Commentary: This passage from Epictetus covers two weighty problems in one sentence. First, we shouldn't try to figure out which things not within our power are "necessary" and which aren't. We shouldn't see it in terms of "necessity" or lack thereof. Doing so courts the danger of another misunderstanding of Stoicism, "the ascetic misinterpretation."[14] This misconception is, so to speak, about disentangling ourselves from the alleged necessities. According to it, we should *reduce* our needs and desires regarding external world. But it is not so. The Stoic way is not about wiping out our needs and endeavors whatsoever, but about defining them through things within our power.

Thus, we won't focus on the "what is necessary versus what is not necessary" part of Epictetus' formula, but rather on the "saying versus not saying to ourselves" part of it. We must remember that we are the ones who define what is necessary, what is required, and what is valuable to us. There are no universal and rigid rules that dictate to us what is important in our life and what is not. It is up to us and us only: we are at liberty to define it at will. Of all things in this world, it is within our power to decide and define what we cherish and what we want to organize our life around. The only legislative power in this respect is vested in our own mind. There is no objective, supreme hierarchy. It is up to us and on us to decide. We define our own values and goals, we are the only ones responsible for our choice. And we are the only ones to blame.

We define and embrace our values and goals all the time – whether we realize it or not. We either do it consciously and – in the best-case scenario – autonomously (and stoically!), or we mindlessly absorb values that just float around and we mimic the goals that other people aim at. There is of course nothing wrong in being aware of what our socio-political context demands from us. We must never forget, though, that the final word is always ours.[15] To rebel is a Stoic thing and to conform is a Stoic thing. The one thing that is nonstoic is to do either mindlessly.

Stoic happiness and Stoic good life consist in embracing and exercising our right to define our value set and list of goals. In particular, Stoicism urges us to remember that we retain this right in a situation (so common in life) when other people and, in general, external influences, pressure us to conform. We all experience that pressure, all the time and in a variety of ways. When we talk to other people, we may get schooled, either in a passive-aggressive or in a plain aggressive way, that our moral duty is to support that one specific political party that our interlocutor happens to root for. Tradition may be another tremendous source of such pressure. We may be reluctant to overeating, but when it comes to a massive meal at a family reunion – we cave in and dig in just to observe the

---

[14] For more on this see: Stankiewicz, *Does Happiness Write Blank Pages?*, 30–41.
[15] With thanks to Dr. Olga Kaczmarek for discussing this problem at length with me.

custom. It may also be the case (this is often the most dangerous and treacherous part) that there is no direct and specific source of influence, but just a kind of an unwritten and unspoken rule, vague but tenable. This is something akin to Heidegger's *das Man* (with a nod here to readers with background in German philosophy), which irresistibly suggests to us that what kinds of things should be pursued and in what way. Overt diligence in following fashions and fads may be an example here. No one officially announces anything, but we still somehow "know" what kind of stuff is "in" this summer. Also, the marketing and advertisement industries have well earned their right to be mentioned here – their key purpose is to transform our needs and desires according to the interest of the advertiser. All told, what else is an ad for, if not to make us think that we need some particular app or car?

Every time we see that someone or something attempts to sneak past our guard and transform the structure of our values and wants, we must immediately snap to attention. We need to never forget that we are the absolute masters of our own will and of all of our intentions. No external influence can ever rescind this power. The clear and present danger is rather to be found in ourselves, not in the outside world. We tend to fool ourselves into holding up totally irrelevant values and pursuing completely useless goals. We frequently fall prey to autosuggestion and we convince ourselves that we need something that we actually don't need. It can happen in many ways, but the main culprit is, as always, our mental sloth. For example, deep down, we know that social acclaim is not necessary for a good life, but we still manage to persuade ourselves that a quiet and unrecognized life will be dull and unsatisfying. Or, another example: deep down we know full well that pursuing our values and goals requires us to do some serious work tonight, but we nonetheless come to a swift and quiet agreement with ourselves that binge-watching Netflix is a better solution. In sum, we often *know* that Stoicism is right about where we should focus and what we should do, but we still back out from commitment and convince ourselves to think and do otherwise. And this is something we must beware of!

Fragment VIII

Whenever you are obliged by circumstances [i.e. by things not within your power] *to be in a way troubled, quickly return to yourself* [i.e. to things within your power].

Marcus Aurelius, *Meditations*, 6.11

Commentary: Even if we most diligently strive to abide by the Stoic principles, it will inevitably happen at some point that we make a mistake and we let things not within our power to sadden, confuse or distress us. This is nothing new under the sun, for no one is born a Stoic – everybody has to become one (if one wants to). Sooner or later, we will all experience this depreciating feeling of being awash in things we wouldn't even like to be in touch with. We all know this feeling all too well. What should we do about it?

There is just one Stoic precept for such a sad occasion. To wit, we should remember that if we get tarnished by things not within our power, if we fall prey to them and if we get honey-trapped into their wickedness, then, no matter how badly we fail, the way to stand up, dust off and move on is always open to us. Stoicism is accessible on equal terms to everybody. It is open to those of us who, for most of their lives, slaved away in the captivity of external things, and it is open to those who have been excellent Stoics for all of their life but failed just this one time. At any given moment of our lives, we are fully able and entitled to focus on things within our power (and let's remember that the past is not within our power, so it doesn't matter for how long we have been nonstoics). No preparatory internship is required in this department. No defeat will be a lasting defeat unless we give up the fight too early. As long as we are willing to take up the gauntlet again and again, no lost battle will mean losing the war.

From every dire strait, from every difficult situation, from every stress, distress and sorrow we may swiftly and easily return to ourselves, i.e., we may turn to things within our power. Nobody and nothing can prevent us from doing so. No external force can reach into our heads and wipe out this refuge of inner security. No outside circumstances can render things not within our power inaccessible to us. They will be handy and easy to reach in any given moment, they will always provide us with a tranquil abode. Let's remember this, and let's make use of this. The very awareness that there is always a place we can run to will boost our strength and overall confidence.

Fragment IX

> *Cease [...] to admire material things* [and all other things not within our power]. *Cease to make yourselves slaves, first of things, then on account of things slaves of those who are able to give them or take them away.*
>
> Epictetus, *Discourses*, III.20.8

Commentary: Let's now consider *why* Stoicism urges us to focus on things within our power. We mentioned at the outset that one of the basic reasons is to avoid the suffering caused by dissatisfaction. If we strive to get or to avoid something that is not within our power, we set ourselves up for failure.

We sign a warrant for ourselves and we can be sure that, sooner or later, it will be executed.

Yet, this rationale is quite defensive, some would even say negative. Fortunately, it's not the only one – other, more proactive ways of thinking are also available. And they are required, because the justification described above will never appeal to us all. It's based on the assumption that it is better to give up some pursuits right off the bat rather than risk disappointment of failure in the future. This logic will never appeal to those of us who prefer risk-flavored ambition over self-contented security. Let's go over some more arguments then.

The most vital one is this. If we admire things not within our power, we make ourselves their slaves. We make ourselves dependent on them and we thus undermine our freedom and capability to decide for ourselves. As long as we focus on things within our power, we are able to take care of ourselves and of everything important in our life. Everything of importance will be located inside us, in our immediate domain, in the sphere of our direct control. All the sources of our life force, all the ways we perceive ourselves, all the patterns of our thinking, all manners of desire and want, of valuing and scorning things will be subjected to our will only. But this blissful state will automatically come to an end the moment we decide that something not within our power is valuable to us. We will cease being autonomous, we will be at mercy of someone or something, we will voluntarily go under someone or something's rule.

Examples are infinite. Let's picture a sexual addict, someone who is in constant, desperate and insatiable need of new partners and uses them for purposes of self-validation. Such a person is shackled in a double way. First off, their unhealthy attitude toward sexual pleasure makes them a slave to the pleasure itself. Second, they are enslaved by any potential new partner, because any partner-to-be is endorsed with the great power of granting or refusing them their freakishly beloved pleasure. Obviously, such a relationship of power puts the sexual addict in a difficult position where they can be easily leveraged into fulfilling their partner's whims and wishes. Twists and turns of amorous life aside, the same mechanism is at work when someone blackmails us, posing a threat to something that is dear to us yet external. One example, which often receives tons of media attention, is about an individual overtly attached to their reputation. Such a person is enslaved primarily to the reputation itself, because it is not within their power to ensure what others think. Furthermore, such a person will be a slave to anyone who intends to blackmail them. For what is easier than to threaten such a person with revealing information (either true or false) that may compromise their good reputation?

Fragment X

Look around [...] upon all mortals: everywhere there is ample and constant reason for weeping. Someone is driven to daily labor by toilsome poverty, another is tormented by never-resting ambition, another fears the very riches that they once wished for, and suffers from the granting of his own prayer. Someone is made wretched by loneliness, another by labor, another by the crowds which always besiege their antechamber. Someone mourns because they have children, someone because they have lost them.

Seneca, Of Consolation. To Polybius, 4.2

Commentary: Another argument is tailored in a somewhat different fashion, so it may suit the taste of those readers who are not satisfied with the hitherto discussion. We will change the approach now. Instead of talking about how and why not focusing on things within our power brings about misery, we will argue that we should focus on them because to do otherwise is simply impossible. Or, more precisely, that it is, in the longer run, non-doable to focus on things not within our power and to remain consequent, coherent and consistent in the process. In other words, if we don't focus on things within our power, we will devolve into arbitrariness and chaos. Thus, if we want to maintain our integrity, we need to focus solely on them. We just can't have it any other way.

There are too many things not within our power and each and every one of them can pull us in a different direction. Also, each and every one of them can arouse a whole diversity of reactions and feelings, frequently contradicting one another. It is just impossible to think all of them through, it is impossible to contain them in the scope of our mind and to produce and sustain a reasonable and coherent attitude to them. The only viable attitude towards things not within our power is to not focus on them. If we try to do anything else, we will eventually slip into a maze of contradictions, confusions and self-inflicted ambiguity.

Let's now turn to the specific examples trotted out by Seneca. There are infinitely many ways in which nonstoics may and will suffer because of their unhealthy relationship with things outside their power. They can be miserable because of poverty, or, to the contrary, they may be kept up at night by fear of losing their assets. They can suffer because of a lack of a job, or, to the contrary, they may be sick of the work they have to do. Solitude may be painful to them, but so may be excessive company. Bad family relationships may cause heartache, but so does the severing of these relationships. The list can drag on indefinitely while the point remains clear. There are too many things not within our power for a human mind to encompass, and the possible reactions to them are way too diverse for us to coherently manage them.

Thus, the only reasonable and productive solution is to dismiss all things not within our power whatsoever and focus solely on things within our power. Every other decision, every other direction, every other line of thinking will inevitably bring failure. Every attempt at hammering out a compromise with things not within our power will be arbitrary and artificial. The only viable solution is to draw a distinct line and focus on things within our power.

Fragment XI

> [If I don't focus on things within my power, I will be] *perturbed, trembling at every piece of news, and having my tranquility depending on the letters of others. Some person has arrived from Rome. "I only hope that there is no harm!" But what harm can happen to you, where you are not? From Greece someone is come. "I hope that there is no harm!" In this way every place may be the cause of misfortune to you.*
>
> Epictetus, Discourses, III.24.24-26

Commentary: If we don't focus on things within our power we'll court everything and everybody in the world to simply come and become a cause of our misery. It's actually even worse than what we talked about in the commentary to fragment IX. We become slaves not only to people and events, but to virtually everything that is out there. We very easily dole out the strings to which our happiness is attached. And let's not fool ourselves. If we do that, the world will pull them.

There is only one way we can prevent this from happening – we need to focus on things within our power. This maneuver not only gives us a safe exit from the dark noose of enslavement by everything and everybody, but it also turns it all around and changes all the liability into an empowering asset. Everything that has been hitherto a potential cause for misery, suffering and disappointment, now, as if touched by a magic wand, transfigures into a source of bliss. This bliss is kindled by the feeling of being finally free and independent. Other people, their errands and opinions, fame, wealth, health, and all that happens daily around the globe, day and night, the whole 24/7 drumbeat of news and developments, all that doesn't foist itself upon us anymore, it doesn't delude us. We can pick any of these things, we can imagine it and examine it in our mind, we can put any angle on it, we can think it through and through, and we will still see that it has no shred of power over us. We are *free* at last and we are free to laugh at all that used to keep us firmly in its grasp.

Fragment XII

> [The things not within our power should be like] *auxiliaries and light-armed troops in a camp. If we make them our servants, not our masters – then and then only are they of value to our minds.*
>
> Seneca, Of a Happy Life, 8.2

Commentary: Before wrapping this chapter up, we need to make one more comment, which may help to clarify a looming problem. It will also shed light on an important tenet of reformed Stoicism. Here is the thing: it doesn't follow from the principle of focusing on things within our power that we are obliged to somehow abandon things not within our power. Reformed Stoicism doesn't require us to live ascetic lives. It doesn't require celibacy and voluntary poverty. It doesn't compel us to give away all our money, to live in seclusion or to stick to a lean diet. *A Stoic is not a monk.* A Stoic doesn't have to abstain from sensual things and doesn't have to withdraw from the worldly affairs. An escape from people, from life and from the world is *not* a Stoic way.[16]

Why is it necessary to include a reminder like this? Because the ascetic misinterpretation of Stoicism is common and it is important to starkly oppose it. The reasoning is this: an overwhelming majority of facts, things and events are not within our power. If we superficially read "not focusing on them" as "abandoning them," we will empty our life of everything or everybody that we could care about. In other words, we wouldn't be able to actually *do* anything. Anything that we possibly get our hands on would be counted as "not within our power" and we would have to drop it. Anyone to whom we may possibly extend our hands to, would be labeled as "not within our power" and thus deemed as "unworthy" of our interest. Our life would be flat and empty, as we would have no motivation, no tool and no purpose for any worldly activity. The only legit task would be to stay still, refrain from any action and just passively contemplate the passage of time. But such a life, with all due respect, surely is not a Stoic life. This is a gross misreading we must beware of.

Needless to say, this caveat doesn't undermine the principle of focusing on things within our power. Quite the contrary! It is its necessary closure and complement, it delineates the boundary and it secures us against false and radical conclusions. Focusing on things within our power doesn't mean that

---

[16] To be precise: a secluded or withdrawn life is not the Stoic way of life in the sense that Stoicism doesn't require it. But it doesn't forbid it either. If someone wants to live that way – they have all their Stoic right to do so.

things not within our power should be discarded or renounced ("Wealth is not within my power, so I will blow all the money I have," or "Health is not within my power, so I won't take care of myself"), but that they should be managed well. We have to be in control of them, not let them be in control of us. We must use them as tools to pursue our goals and hold up our values, and we must not let them lead us astray.

I said earlier that we should create a habit of translating everything into the language of things within our power. The same holds for ourselves: we should view ourselves in the things-within-our-power categories. If we are asked who we are, we should craft the response in the language of things within our power. Our auto-narrative, our story about ourselves must be told in the language of things that within our power. Our identity needs to be defined in this language and everything that is dear and relevant to us must be based on things that are within our power.

Things not within our power should be mere tool for us, mere raw material that we can and should use to produce whatever we want to produce or pursue. We shouldn't (and we can't!) avoid contact with them, but we should be indifferent to them, just as an architect is indifferent to the bricks that will be transformed into a building. Let's keep this idea in mind while we journey through the rest of the book and through the rest of Stoicism.

Part two.
Here and now or the principles of conduct

How to think and act

Chapter 5

Act deliberately

We ought [...] first to examine our own selves, next the business which we propose to transact, next those for whose sake or in whose company we transact it.

Seneca, *Of Peace of Mind*, 6.1

In a nutshell: Stoicism can't do without rationality in thought and logic in action. The two should accompany us at every stage of every endeavor. From choosing what to pursue, through making plans and carrying them out – we must always remember our purpose. We shouldn't waste time and energy on careless and fruitless activities. We shouldn't do things which don't serve our goals or foster our values. Let all our actions be purposeful and deliberate. Let's never act pointlessly and haphazardly.

***

First off, we must consider whether we are able to do what we intend to do and whether we have the proper capabilities and talents (fragment I). Then, we should define our goal and course of action (II), determine what resources we have at our disposal (III) and consider the consequences (IV). When we act, we should never lose sight of the entirety of our plan (V) and we should always remember the goal we pursue (VI). We should always look at what we do from a long-term perspective and from multiple vantage points (VII). Proper deliberation before taking action is our insurance policy against changing circumstances (VIII). Yet, it will never make us perfectly secure and if the circumstances change greatly, we must reconsider (IX).

Fragment I

You must decide whether your disposition is better suited for vigorous action or for tranquil speculation and contemplation, and you must adopt whichever the bent of your genius inclines you for. Isocrates[17] laid

---

[17] Isocrates (436 – 338 BC) was an ancient Greek rhetorician, a disciple of the sophists (Gorgias and Prodicus) and of Socrates. Around 390 BC he established his own school of

hands upon Ephorus[18] and led him away from the forum, thinking that he would be more usefully employed in compiling chronicles.

Seneca, *Of Peace of Mind*, 7.2

Commentary: Before taking action, we must inspect whether the action in question is in alignment with our talents, abilities and set of values. Within the leeway we have, we should avoid undertakings we don't find ourselves able to pursue and properly equipped for. We should also stay away from endeavors which don't dovetail with the values we wish to uphold. Let's not forget that everyone is a distinct and unique individual with their own preferences and range of talents. Whenever we opt for something, we mustn't disregard the constraints of our individuality. Whenever we toil to fulfill the duties imposed upon us by the society and by the world, we should, within the latitude we have, adjust our pursuits to our talents, abilities and purposes.

Anyone can learn the basics of playing the guitar. Even if we are stone-deaf we can get to rattle through a few standards. Yet, it will cost a ton of time and toil and the result will be mediocre at best. Months of practice will land us on a level that a musical prodigy attains in an hour. Let's now also assume that we possess a genuine talent for something else, say, that we are wizards at mathematics. If we turn to maths, we will make a blistering progress, outdoing everyone else. Why then lose a minute for useless strumming if the same minute would provide a staggering outcome if devoted to maths? To act deliberately means, sometimes, bidding adieu to our dearest childhood dreams of becoming rock stars.

A deliberate action always starts with an honest conversation with ourselves. We must take the time to figure out what craft and what type of job is best for us. We must think of what's the best way for us to benefit personally and to contribute to the world. Let's confront reality, let's conceal nothing. Let's acknowledge the context – what we can afford and what we can expect. Let's not hide behind appearances and illusions. Let's focus on the actual facts, not on would-be facts, not on wish-to-be facts.

---

rhetoric in Athens and presided over it for the next fifty years. He made a fortune of it and he also developed lasting curriculum for education. He was greatly renowned and influential, many of his students went on to become major figures of the era. Isocrates was one of the ten Attic orators.

[18] Ephorus of Cyme (c. 400 – 330 BC) was an ancient Greek historian. He authored a great universal history in 29 books, reaching up until around 340 BC. He was a pupil of Isocrates. In his early years he tried his hand in rhetoric, but without much success. According to the tradition it was Isocrates himself who suggested to Ephorus to switch crafts.

Fragment II

Some affairs also are not so important in themselves as they are prolific and lead to much more business, which employments, as they involve us in new and various forms of work, ought to be refused. Neither should you engage in anything from which you are not free to retreat. Apply yourself to something which you can finish, or at any rate can hope to finish. You had better not meddle with those operations which grow in importance, while they are being transacted, and which will not stop where you intended them to stop.

Seneca, *Of Peace of Mind*, 6.4

Commentary: Once we set our mind on what to do, we have to decide how to do it. Let's recall the division into things within and not within our power. The better our choice of activity is, the more control we have over the course of action and over our progress down the path. The poorer our choice, the looser our grip. In particular, we should beware of things which tend to shackle us down and then bring us somewhere else then intended. We should always have a safe out, we should always avoid endeavors which tend to spiral out of control. A Stoic likes to keep her hand firmly on the helm. She despises being chained up in the cargo hold while unpredictable forces steer her ship to unknown destinations.

One may argue, however, that we aren't always at liberty to choose. Not everything we do is a matter of our own choice. Sometimes, perhaps reprehensibly often, we are obliged to take part in projects and commitments over which we have no control. This is a fact. So let's be more precise: we should devote no more time and energy than it is absolutely necessary to the inevitable activities which we have little influence over. Let's not engage excessively or carelessly in these kinds of things. Let's do our minimum duty and let's just get those things over with. For example, a Stoic obviously pays taxes and thus she must spend some time filing them. Handling the paperwork may be toilsome and time-consuming (even in the digital age), but she strives not to waste a minute more than necessary. If she decides, someday, that dealing with taxes herself shatters the meaning of her life, then she might think of hiring an accountant. But would she, on the other hand, start a legal battle against the IRS demanding that she be exempt from paying taxes based on the fact that she doesn't like paying them? Obviously, that one is an absurd.

Fragment III

It is above all things necessary to form a true estimate of oneself, because as a rule we think that we can do more than we are able. Someone is led too far through confidence in their eloquence, someone demands more from their estate than it can produce, someone burdens a weakly body with some toilsome duty.

Seneca, *Of Peace of Mind*, 6.2

Commentary: Our next step is to analyze what means and assets we have at hand. If our goal is to become public speakers, then we need to know our eloquence. If addressing a crowd is not our strong suit, maybe it would be advisable to delegate this duty on someone else. But what if we have no choice and we must speak in person? If this happens, we mustn't forget that we are dealing with our weak spot and we must prepare accordingly. We mustn't plan the speech to be an ad-lib performance, but rather craft it in advance. Rehearse in front of a mirror. Look up on the Internet how to overcome stage freight. In a word, we must disregard neither the skills we have nor the skills we lack.

The very same idea holds for managing financial matters and for dealing with our physical fitness. We will lose if we bid more than we can afford. Overtraining is just as much a mistake as undertraining. Cooling down and taking rest periods are crucial for the intelligent use of our physical, mental and spiritual resources. It is our duty to know how much we have left. And it is our duty to plan our actions accordingly so that we don't overburden "a weakly body with some toilsome duty."

This sounds trivial, yet it begs a non-trivial question. The question is this: does Stoicism dissuade us from accepting difficult challenges and from shooting at things that are beyond our reach? Does it forbid us from thinking big and dreaming beyond the circumstances? Does it ask to cut our coat according to our cloth? On one hand, the requirement to honestly appraise our assets and abilities seems to remove the hardest tasks from the equation. On the other hand, we must keep in mind that Stoicism guides us on *how* to act and not on *what* to do.

So, would a Stoic fight a losing battle? There is no clear-cut answer here. It's not true that a Stoic always prefers the high moral ground over an actual win and that she always desperately defends a lost cause. On the other hand, it isn't the case that she, as a rule, refrains from fighting a losing battle. Why? We mustn't forget that the accounts of loss and profit are usually much more complicated than they appear. Such calculations must always take place at a few different levels and they always abound with not-so-explicit variables. A

Stoic won't carry out a doomed-to-fail attack in order to win (because that would mean desiring an impossible thing), but why shouldn't she give it a try if she knew that pinning some enemy forces is essential to relieve another, strategically vital section of the battlefront? In planning deliberate actions, we must calculate many variables at once.

Fragment IV

In every act consider what precedes and what follows, and then proceed to the act. If you do not consider, you will at first begin with spirit, since you have not thought at all of the things which follow, but afterwards when some consequences have shown themselves, you will basely desist [...] [If you don't consider this] you will behave like children who at one time play as wrestlers, then as gladiators, then blow a trumpet, then act a tragedy, when they have seen and admired such things. So you also do: you are at one time a wrestler, then a gladiator, then a philosopher, then a rhetorician, but with your whole soul you are nothing.

Epictetus, Discourses, III.15.1-6

Commentary: Before launching any action, we must go over the possible outcomes and we must do it squarely and impartially. We must cave in neither to overt optimism nor to doom-saying. What will turn out if this happens? What will we do if that scenario unfolds? Every possible ramification must be considered beforehand, rationally, thoroughly and honestly. We must anticipate nonobvious results and clandestine determinants. It happens all the time that factors that seem insignificant at the outset turn into game-changers. Thus, let's mull over the conceivable consequences first, then let's double-check for the ones we've passed over and only then let's act.

This protocol secures us not only against non-deliberate, useless or wrongful course of action, but it also exempts us from the pressure to make decisions *during* action. Let's imagine a typical impromptu, on-the-fly decision. Conditions are seldom comfortable, time to think and available willpower are usually limited, and we are often under duress. A calm head is a luxury. So, it doesn't defy reason to assume that thinking before taking action is always *easier* than thinking in the midst of it. It is always better to plan and think through an action beforehand – this is also a part of Stoic rationality.

Fragment V

We are often [...] guilty of error, because we generally deliberate on the parts of life, without taking in, and reflecting upon the whole. Someone, who lets fly an arrow to any purpose, must first know the mark they aim at, and accordingly direct and guide it with a skillful hand. To one, ignorant of what port they are steering to, [no wind is favorable].

Seneca, *Epistles*, 71.2-3

Commentary: Getting things done, dealing with errands, facing challenges – all of this makes us focus on a narrow slice of life. If we do something attentively, then it tends to crave our absolute and undivided attention. We shouldn't oppose this (see chapter "Live the present day"), but we should remember that our concentration on detail shouldn't obscure the big picture. Only the broad frame of reference allows us to see our purpose clearly. For no specifics are given to us without a context.

Our actions need a purposeful structure. They should be aligned with our values and they should serve our goals. Seneca uses an example of an archer here. An arrow aims at something and it is our duty to remember that we can choose the aim. We have both the right to choose the target and the obligation to exercise this right. When we place the arrow on the bowstring, when we draw back, we must remember that we do all these things not for the sake of themselves, but because they serve the purpose of hitting our target.

In a word, we must never forget how our actions fit into the larger plan. We cannot let any detail preoccupy us as if it was the goal itself. Our every action is a tool we use to reach our goal and it should be treated as such. No more, no less.

Fragment VI

The next point will be to take care that we do not labor for what is vain, or labor in vain [...] In other words, that our labor may not be without result, and that the result may not be unworthy of our labor. [...] We must limit the running to and fro which most people practice, rambling about houses, theatres, and marketplaces. They mind business of others, and always seem as though they themselves had something to do. If you ask one of them as they come out of their own door, "Whither are you going?" they will answer, "By Hercules, I do not know: but I shall see some people and do something." They wander purposelessly seeking for something to do, and do not what they have made up their minds to do, but what has casually fallen in their way. They move uselessly and without any plan, just like ants crawling over bushes, which creep up to the top and then down to the bottom again without gaining anything. Many people spend their lives in exactly the same fashion, which one

> *may call a state of restless indolence. [...] Let all your work, therefore, have some purpose, and keep some object in view.*
>
> Seneca, *Of Peace of Mind*, 12.1-5

Commentary: Every moment of our life must be accounted for. Let's hold on to Seneca and let's imagine that someone comes up to us and asks: "What are you actually doing right now? What are you doing it for?" We must *always* be able to answer these questions. Not having an answer is a clear sign that we are living purposelessly, that we aren't acting deliberately and that we don't care about our values and goals (or maybe that we don't even know what they are). It indicates that we enjoy being carried away by circumstances and that we like when things not within our power walk all over us.

Instead, whenever we do something, and whatever we do, we should have the set of our values and the list of our goals right before our eyes. In every single minute, we must cherish some value and pursue some goal – and we must be aware of what we cherish and what we pursue. No one likes suddenly finding their wallet empty, not knowing how they blew the money. We should feel just as guilty and embarrassed when we catch ourselves not knowing what we have done with our time.

This all sounds like a workaholic's manifesto, so three comments are necessary. First, Stoicism doesn't tell us what external goals to aim at and what values to uphold. Stoicism never obliges us specifically to practice state craft, to live a quiet family life, to make big money, strive for power, help children in Africa, write poetry or indulge in *dolce far niente*. This is our choice and ours only. Second, Stoicism is not about organizing all our activity towards a single end. Pluralism of goals and values is necessary. There is no rule as to how many of them we should adopt and what they should be. What the Stoics prompt us towards is simply that there should always be more than one goal and one value, that they should be well-thought-out and that every minute should be accounted for. It is vital that we know what we spend our time on and it is vital that we control what we do. It is *us* who decide the content of every instant of time. Third but not least: no one says that all the projects we commit to need to be work-related only. *Rest* is a necessity and decent time needs to be allocated for it.

Fragment VII

> *"Well then, do you wish me to pay court to a certain person? To go to their doors?" If reason requires this to be done [...] why should you not go? You are not ashamed to go to the doors of a shoemaker, when you are in want of shoes, nor to the door of a gardener, when you want lettuces, and you*

are ashamed to go to the doors of the rich when you want any thing? [...] You go to buy lettuces: they cost an obolus, but not a talent. So it is here also. The matter is worth going for to the door of the rich? Well, I will go. It is worth talking about. Let it be so, I will talk with them.

Epictetus, Discourses, III.24.44-49

Commentary: Stoicism not only reprehends non-deliberate actions, but it also demands a particular type of deliberation. Deliberation must include the long-term frame of reference. We also need to take into account the ambiguity as well as multidimensionality of the issues we deal with.

The first one is quite self-evident: one is doomed to fail if one considers only the most immediate consequences of one's actions. Let's imagine that we are dealing with some pioneering infrastructure project. For example, we are about to build a system of interstate highways. We can do it cheaply by skimping on materials, labor and quality, or we can use more expensive components and make sure that the whole project is built to last. In the short-term, the former method seems to be advantageous simply because it is cheaper. But a long-term calculation yields an opposite evaluation: yes, initially we will spend less, but soon we will have to spend much more on repairs and reconstructions. Once we adopt the long-term perspective, it is clear that it is not only better but also cheaper to build once and for good. Let's remember that turning a blind eye to the big picture is short-sighted and that it's sure-proof to mislead us.

Next, we mustn't consider anything one-dimensionally. Let's follow Epictetus' example: it's clear that someone who regards honor as a priceless and indisputable value might regard "going to the door of the rich" something disgraceful and impermissible. They might think the following way: "Honor weighs more than money. If I ask the rich to help me out, I will lose my honor. The net output is negative, so I shouldn't go to the door of the rich." And yet this is a painfully one-sided reasoning since it accounts for one variable only (the price of "honor") while there may be other, likely uncountable, values at play. For example, money may be badly needed to help someone's loved one who requires a costly medical treatment. A warped understanding of "honor" might be deadly in this case. Particularly in reformed Stoicism, we need to be highly cautious of being prideful. In a word, our actions have not only long-term but also multi-sided consequences which can easily be missed if one doggedly sticks to just one point of view.

The tale of Epictetus going to the door of the rich reminds us that Stoicism has nothing to do with cheap pseudo-heroism (contrary to what some may claim). Stoicism doesn't value "honor" above all else and doesn't praise blind obedience to exorbitant principles. Honor is indeed important, but it has a price – a high but a measurable one. There are many values in the world and it's us who have to choose which of them we adopt as our own. Stoicism doesn't tell us which value should be sacrificed for the sake of which one. It highlights that the days of our lives are usually ambiguous and that certain situations may evolve rapidly in response to the drumbeat of capricious circumstances. There is no single, ultimate and universal value which guarantees a happy and fulfilling life[19] (if this was the case, life would be easy and philosophy would be useless). Sometimes it is advisable for us to refuse to go to the door of the rich, but sometimes the more advisable (and the harder) thing to do would be the opposite: to swallow our pride and to ask the powerful for help. But, either way, we must act deliberately.

Fragment VIII

> *The wise people never change their plans while the conditions under which they formed them remain the same. Therefore they never feel regret, because at the time nothing better than what they did could have been done, nor could any better decision have been arrived at.*

Seneca, *On Benefits*, IV.34.4

Commentary: Proper scrutiny before making a decision not only makes our action more deliberate and more efficient but it also makes us immune to regretting the decision after it's been made. This sounds controversial because it happens all the time that we regret having done one thing rather than another. But what is the source of this regret? It may be that we've missed something in our hasty decision-making, it may be that the circumstances have changed, or it may be that something new has come to light, something we had no prior knowledge of. We have already discussed the first case and the Stoic prescription is clear: we need to avoid making decisions in a rush. We must think deeply about which bank to choose before we put our savings into the account. But what if bank A offers a better deal than bank B so we trust bank A with our money and then, out of the blue, bank A goes bankrupt?

This example shows what happens when circumstances abruptly change as well as when new facts come to light (as it happens sadly often, when the whole thing comes down it comes out that a group of insiders knew all along

---

[19] Except for virtue, of course. Such an answer would be too easy though and it wouldn't explain much. Thus, throughout this book I stick to a slightly different understanding of "value."

what was going to happen but kept it a secret). But Stoicism teaches us that we still have no reason for regret. Why? Because every decision we make is based on specific knowledge in specific circumstances. If we don't shrink from gathering proper information, if we don't neglect thinking it through, if we don't refrain from employing long-term thinking with multi-points-of-view, then the decision we make is the best decision available, all-things-considered. The only thing that might have changed later on is the circumstance, but that is not within our power. Thus, we have nothing to regret. We did our part and secured everything within our power.

A Stoic adheres to a decision once made not because of stubbornness, honor or inertia, but because of the careful reasoning that preceded the decision. It wouldn't be smart to promptly reverse a decision in which we had put a great deal of thought. In other words, the firmness of a resolution is not a value in itself. Any resolution is worth only as much as the reasoning it is based on. This reasoning is its warranty.[20]

Fragment IX

> *We ought to [...] not become over fond of the lot which fate has assigned to us, but transfer ourselves to whatever other condition chance may lead us to, and fear no alteration, either in our purposes or our position in life.*
>
> Seneca, *Of Peace of Mind*, 14.1

Commentary: If circumstances don't change, a Stoic won't change her mind – but it follows from prior reasoning, not from dogma. Accordingly, if circumstances do change, a Stoic may revise her judgment. The point is that after we make up our mind, we shouldn't forget the whole decision-making process and we shouldn't let go of the arguments we've considered. We should keep them handy and we must be ready to re-evaluate them if necessity strikes. It is better to pull a 180 and back out in time than to ignore new and game-changing information. The rationality of every commitment must be constantly re-thought, just as in business where no amount of money already invested in something absolves us of the responsibility to monitor its current effectiveness. Since even if we had invested an awful lot in some venture it may turn out that it makes more business sense to withdraw now than to continue. Let's beware of the sunk costs fallacy!

---

[20] For more on this see chapter "Beware of Treacherous Constancy."

In brief, we must remember that the world is perpetually in motion, that circumstances change all the time, and that we should persist with a decision only so far as it is a rational decision. We have to constantly upgrade our evaluation of the situation and our assessment of possible scenarios. We must remember that the conditions on the battlefield change constantly and we should not be the generals who are best prepared for the previous war.

Chapter 6

Live the present day

There is no [greater] *obstacle to true living as waiting, which loses today while it is depending on the morrow.*

Seneca, *Of the Shortness of Life*, 9.1

In a nutshell: We need to live today. We shouldn't be tantalized by the past and we shouldn't be worried about the future. The past is gone – it is not within our power. We cannot change it. The only way we can use it is by employing yesterday's experience to live the present better. The future follows suit – it hasn't come yet, so we needn't worry in advance. When it comes to preparing for tomorrow, the only thing within our power is to focus on the present day. If we live the present day, then the useless sorrow about yesterday will evaporate and our outlook on tomorrow will improve. Life is a series of perpetual todays – this is how we need to see it.

***

We should live the present day because it's too late to live yesterday and too early to live tomorrow (fragment I). Only in the present day we can make wise use of our time, because only the present day is at our disposal (II). We need to treat every present day as a distinct whole (III). By living the present day, we will be able to prepare for tomorrow and – to an extent – to cut yesterday loose (IV). Unless a vital reason occurs, we shouldn't postpone things till tomorrow (V). Tomorrow, just as yesterday, is not within our power, while only today is within our power (VI). No day leaves us in the lurch – every day lands us an opportunity to do something valuable (VII). The present day is also the best available opportunity to try to improve our life (VIII).

Fragment I

Everyone lives the present time only, and loses only this.

Marcus Aurelius, *Meditations*, 12.26

Commentary: The present day is all we have. The past, whatever it was like, is something we cannot go back to and it's something we cannot alter. It's already gone, it doesn't exist. The future, in turn, doesn't exist *yet*. Our influence on the future is also incomparably weaker than our influence on the present. What is about to happen depends not only on our will and conduct, but also on other factors of which we may still be unaware.

We are responsible only for the present day. Only the present day can be well used or pointlessly lost. No sloth can make us lose the past, because it is already lost, and no sloth can make us lose the future, because it is not here yet. Of the entire axis of time, only the present day belongs to us.

Fragment II

> *If one should suddenly ask "What do you have now in your thoughts?," with perfect openness you might immediately answer, "This or that."*
>
> Marcus Aurelius, *Meditations*, 3.4

Commentary: The present day is the apple of our eye. It's our sacred duty to use it wisely. It's our obligation to avoid wasting the time we have and to put it to smart use instead.

Of course, we mustn't be foolishly zealous about it. Imagine a specific goal we want to achieve, say, that we intend to write a book about Stoicism. It's a clear sign of a misguided Stoic to translate the idea of "not wasting time" into a restless treadmill of eighteen-hour workdays. Stoicism doesn't demand that we forget or bypass our human limits. Stoicism takes into account that humans have finite energies and that our capabilities are not inexhaustible. Stoicism requires no impossible things. Writing a book requires a specific regimen: not only periods of intense thinking and writing, but also breaks, rest periods and days off. Making smart and rational use of our time means not overburdening ourselves, for that sets us on a straight path to depression and failure. We need to plan for proper recharging. The Stoic way to stop wasting time is to seal every passing moment: this one is devoted to business, that one is devoted to rest. No moment is allowed to pass by without such a seal. No moment is allowed to slip into that cursed gray area of not-really-business and not-really-rest. That deplorable domain is nothing else but time thrown to the wind.

Fragment III

> *Therefore, my Lucilius, make haste to live, and think every day a life.*
>
> Seneca, *Epistles*, 101.10

Live the present day

Commentary: Let's treat the present day as a whole life. This trick helps us make better use of the time we've got... but it's actually two different tricks rolled into one.

The first point is that we often tend to perceive the entirety of our life as something far-flung or abstract. It's the 21st century (with greetings here to those who read future reprints of this book!) and our life usually spans a time frame of several decades. It seems to us that the whole of it is inaccessible within the scope of a single day. But it's a misconception and actually the opposite is true: our life is available to us *only* through the present day. The present day is the only vista we have on our life and the only way we can project our influence on it. No other moment will offer us anything more and it's in vain to wait for some day to come and somehow "open" our life to us. The present day is our only plug-in to life.

Second, Seneca reminds us that we need to treat every day as a separate event. Yesterday and tomorrow are separated from each other, they have nothing in common. The chasm between the two is unbridgeable. The present day is within our power but yesterday is already lost in the abyss of things not within our power. Every new day is a new world. Whatever progress we want to make, we can start over on the new day. Nothing is more absurd than to neglect something today *because* we had neglected it yesterday. Yet this is an all-too-common occurrence! It happens all the time that if something went wrong yesterday, it makes us feel discouraged today. We didn't fulfill our plan yesterday – we feel even less up to it today. There is nothing more wrong than that! Yesterday is gone, it doesn't exist. What we did yesterday is not within our power *today*. Within our power is only what we intend to do today. We need to care only about that, and only for the present day, we will be held accountable.

The same pertains to tomorrow. Tomorrow doesn't influence the present. Tomorrow is still ahead, we still haven't caught up with it. When it comes to yesterday, we at least know what happened. When it comes to tomorrow, we don't know even that. What's the point then in neglecting the present day for the sake of tomorrow?

There are two important asides here. First, "live the present day" mustn't be understood as "live and act as if the present day was your last day." This would be a dead end. Such a misreading would immediately bring about total chaos. If followed dutifully, it would ban all planning beyond the narrow horizon of 24 hours and forbid all undertakings that are too extensive to be completed in a single day. This is downright absurd. Stoicism is not about living as if there was no tomorrow, but rather about living as if everything hinged on what we do today. We need to live as if all of our lives depended on the present day. More than that: we need to live and act as if the entire world depended on our conduct today. That's the proper mindset. The entire universe will collapse unless we do today what we ought to do today. *Everything* rests on how we get on with the present day.

Second, Seneca's words "think every day a life" mustn't be understood as a call for desperate hedonism. Obviously! Stoicism doesn't tell us to jump into a whirl of wild nights, it doesn't make us seek oblivion in a binge of pleasures. It's insane to read Stoicism this way. Living the present day doesn't entail abdication of responsibility. Quite the contrary: since we count every day as a separate entity, we bear total responsibility for it.

Fragment IV

The stronger hold you have on today, the less will be your dependence on tomorrow.

Seneca, *Epistles*, 1.2

Commentary: Seneca spells out one more argument, possibly the strongest of all. Smart and fruitful use of the present day not only enables us not to worry about tomorrow, but also extinguishes the reasons to worry. Let's take the textbook example: imagine we have an important meeting tomorrow. It's a ground rule to prepare well and in advance, but alas, for some reason, we didn't prepare yesterday, because of laziness or other business. Yet, yesterday and all other things are already gone. Today it's better to make up for yesterday's negligence than to lament yesterday's folly. Today is neither the time to think about yesterday's errors, nor the time to be anxious about tomorrow. The only day at hand is the present day. We must sweep all other things aside, we mustn't get distracted by trifles (including the worst of them, that is those trifles that want to distract us *right now* – I got distracted before completing this very sentence) and we must get ready for the meeting. When we use the present day to get ourselves ready, we automatically cease to misuse our time fretting about yesterday. We instead amplify the chances of everything turning out well tomorrow and thus we no longer need to worry.

The arithmetic is as simple as this. If today we are anxious about tomorrow, then both today and tomorrow are in the red. But if today we stop thinking about tomorrow and we do well what we are to do today, then we not only do not lose the present day, we also improve our standing tomorrow. Both days are in the green and the difference in the net output is manifest.

Fragment V

You will hear many people say, "After my fiftieth year I will give myself up to leisure. My sixtieth shall be my last year of public office." And what guarantee have you that your life will last any longer? Who will let all this go on just as you have arranged it? Are you not ashamed to reserve only the leavings of your life for yourself, and appoint for the enjoyment of your own right mind only that time which you cannot devote to any business? How late it is to begin life just when we have to be leaving it!

Seneca, Of the Shortness of Life, 3.5

Commentary: Postponing is not always procrastination. Rescheduling is often purposeful and done in good faith, just as in Seneca's example. It appears logical or even necessary that some things cannot be done until after a certain point in time. Of course, it doesn't always pertain to age: often times it's simply about waiting until conditions improve. If we can't do something today, why not wait until conditions become more favorable?

In Stoicism, thinking this way is even worse than having our time devoured by slackness. Slacking is simply negligence, but deliberately postponing important matters amounts to ill intent. If we slack, we lose the battle. If we postpone, we don't even make it to the field. We must remember that only *we* are responsible for what happens in our life. Circumstances never get the right to vote. The decisions are always ours and ours only. Thus, nothing and nobody can forbid us to live well today. A life postponed is not a life – it is mere survival.

Putting off important things until later is like planning to quit smoking tomorrow. Thinking this way equals signing our death sentence for ourselves. We never know how many years we have left yet, and we have no idea whether a promising afternoon indeed lies in wait for us. Furthermore, even if it so happens that in 24 hours (or years) we are still alive, the circumstances may be far less welcoming. We can lose the capability or the willingness to do so-and-so. We can use the present day whatever way we want, while we may lose the future in a million ways. To postpone life is to cut a very poor deal: for the uncertainty about whether things will be done tomorrow, we pay with the certainty that they won't be done today.

Fragment VI

If you separate, I say, from this ruling faculty [...] the things of time to come and of time that is past, and [...] if you strive to live only what is really your life, that is, the present, then you will be able to pass that portion of life which remains for you up to the time of your death free from perturbations, nobly, and obedient.

Marcus Aurelius, *Meditations*, 12.3

Commentary: The concept here is to apply what we discussed in the chapters on things within and outside our power to the axis of time itself. What will turn out? Obviously, the past is not within our power. In a way, it's even more not-within-our-power than the examples discussed earlier. While our reputation isn't within our power because other people have control over it, no human has any control of the past. The past is gone, closed, irrevocably inaccessible. To be bothered by the past is, for a Stoic, more irrational than to be bothered about sunspots.

Yet, it isn't irrational to evoke or analyze the past in order to make wise use of it. As long as past experiences are read as case studies which can help improve the present day, there is nothing nonstoic in rethinking them. As long as the past is a lesson that can be learned, it should be learned. Productive and informed analysis of past events is a great baseline of a better present. The caveat here is that we mustn't let the past devolve into a black hole where we dump our mental resources that could be used better today. In Stoicism, we refuse to treat past as an excuse from dealing with the present.

Tomorrow is also not within our power. The angle here is slightly different, since, unlike the past, the future isn't defined and closed. To the contrary, it's still unspecified, it's still vibrant with possibilities. We can still try to shape it according to our needs and dreams. But, just as in the case of health and wealth, our future is also influenced by a myriad of factors other than our sheer willpower. Our control over tomorrow isn't absolute. A Stoic asks: where do you see yourself five years from now? Someone replies: "I will become a lawyer unless some obstacle comes up and stands in my way." Alas, there is quite an infinity of possible obstacles. Hence, in Stoicism, we need to focus less on envisioning our bright future and concentrate instead on the actual work in the present day. Particularly, if our job for today is to study in order to get into law school.

Fragment VII

[The present] *is always a material for virtue, both rational and political, and, in a word, for the exercise of art, which belongs to man or God.*

Marcus Aurelius, *Meditations*, 7.68

Live the present day

Commentary: The present day always gives us some material that we can work with fruitfully. The present day never confronts us with a void, it never makes it impossible for us to do something to advance our values and goals. It never happens, even in the most unfortunate and adverse circumstances.

Obviously, it will happen frequently that on a given day we won't be able to do the one specific thing planned for that specific day. We wanted to get some work done, but the Internet connection goes down. We planned to work out a little, but an old injury flares up. Life has its stark rules, which we need to remember and abide by. But Stoicism doesn't feed us illusions, it doesn't demand that we dismiss the realities in which we live. Not every value can be upheld every day. To some things we can devote ourselves only once in a while (like getting face time with friends who live overseas) and in regard to other things, well, we can't even predict when we will be able to tend to them. We may yearn to do something courageous but we might never get an opportunity. To bravely defend an assaulted elderly citizen is no daily occurrence even for police officers. Thus, we need to remember that life is not one-dimensional. It offers us a plurality of tasks instead. It happens often that on a given day, we can't catch up with our friends or defend an abused senior, but it never happens that the present day is empty and offers no opportunity to do something useful and valuable.

Our life cannot aim at just one goal and it cannot be organized around one value only. We need to perform a mental check often and constantly examine our priorities. What is it that we actually want to achieve? What values do we wish to uphold? If we don't neglect this and if we take an unbiased look at the present day, we will see that it seldom deprives us of the opportunity to work on *one* of our values. Certainly, it's perfectly possible that circumstances don't allow us to do the single thing that seems most important to us. But why then, not use this time to work on the second most important thing or the third most important thing? We must be flexible, we must remember what and why we intend to do. We must be quick to scan in our mind the set of our values and the hierarchy of our goals. If we don't fail to do so, we will see that very rarely the state of affairs leaves us no possibility to work on *something* important.

But *rarely* isn't *never*. We can get seriously sick, or we can get locked up. What then? In such a scenario, we have to redo our list of goals and values. But isn't it, one may ask, a failure of the concept described earlier? Only seemingly so. Note that our goals and values are *always* constructed and defined in a certain situation and in a certain context. So why don't we simply qualify sickness or prison sentence as a new context in which we make our decisions? After all, nothing in Stoicism impels our values and goals to be immutable.

In Stoicism, we don't believe in the blind illusion that reality never forces us to revise our list of goals and values. We assert though, that it happens much less frequently than we usually think. And above all, we do claim that we are never doomed to waste a single day unless we decide to do so. No state of affairs can make us abandon the idea of living the present day. Also, the present day cannot make us wallow in the past or worry about the future. In a word, every day and in all circumstances, there will be something valuable to do.

Fragment VIII

> *How plain does it appear that there is not another condition of life so well suited for philosophizing as this in which you now happen to be.*
>
> Marcus Aurelius, Meditations, 11.7

Commentary: There is one thing that we particularly mustn't put off till tomorrow. It's the one thing that we particularly mustn't avoid today because we avoided it yesterday. This one thing is our work on self-improvement.

Marcus' "philosophizing" doesn't mean empty and idle investigations of abstract issues which are detached from daily life. To the contrary, he means the most specific and the most practical thing under the sun, that is, the improvement of oneself. "To practice philosophy" doesn't translate into "read obscure treatises" but rather into "figure out how to live better and figure it out now." There is no better moment to begin to live better than the moment in which you read these *italicized words*.

This notion lends itself to some doubts. For instance, someone may say that they are in a situation which makes them think that something else needs to be done prior to any work on self-improvement. "I have to help my significant other and I have to earn a living before I can actually sit down to Stoicism!" Yet, this is a very misguided approach. Why? For two reasons.

First of all, doing so means attending to things not within our power first. Importantly, it's not – as one may claim – just egoism, since Stoicism never obliges us to put our own interest before all else. It claims though, that things within our power must always be the first order of business. They need to be tended to first. The whole allure of Stoicism consists in the fact, that once we deal well with what is within our power, we will – in passing and offhand – become happy.

Furthermore, we can provide proper help to our significant other and we can secure an adequate income if and only if we put our narratives in order. Dealing with other people and dealing with our job before dealing with our narratives will undermine the value of any relationship and will downgrade productivity in every job. First of all, we need to understand and employ the Stoic principles, and only then we ought to take on other things. Care for our mind and spirit isn't a whim or fancy. It's not a superfluous addendum or bonus. Instead, it's a requisite condition for doing anything else properly. We aren't a good partner and we can't do our job well if we are being torn apart by contradictory narratives.

Another problem is this: what if we simply cannot try to improve now? What if the situation not just deflects us from being better but makes it impossible?

The Stoic answer is plain and simple: the harder the situation is, the more suitable it is to try to become better! The bigger the problems we face, the more useful Stoicism is. Let's think for a second about the kind of situation that is likely to spark the doubt that "this is not the right time for being a Stoic." Supposedly, it would be something along the lines of "I can't live stoically right now, because I am sick." Or: "I have no time for Stoicism now, I have a business to run." Both cases make no sense though. First off, sickness is not a waiver from Stoicism, but rather its testing ground. A malady doesn't render Stoicism useless, it renders it necessary. Let's keep it firmly in mind that Stoicism is about nothing else than being happy, which includes being happy despite adversity. Thus, sickness (or any other misfortune) is a perfect moment to stick to Stoicism, not to abandon it. After all, it makes no sense to throw a medicine out of the window just when it's expected to take effect. It's absurd to flinch at the flu pill just when we got the flu. And it's even more absurd to persuade ourselves that we cannot take the flu pill *because* we have the flu.

How about the case in which some greater necessity – like a looming war – calls upon us and leaves us no time to read this book and learn Stoicism? The Stoic reply is this: if somebody finds themselves in such-and-such situation, and if they are obliged to do so-and-so, and if they do it without hesitation and without consulting this book – they are Stoics in thought and in deed, even if they don't realize it. We don't argue with such individuals, we follow them. We need to remember that Stoicism is about actually *living* a good life and not about merely talking in circles about certain principles. Whoever applies the principles and puts them in motion – is a Stoic.

Stoicism isn't a philosophy of a bygone yesterday and it isn't a philosophy of an uncertain tomorrow. Stoicism is about dealing with the present day, the only one which is available to us. Yesterday isn't a good time to practice Stoicism, simply because it's no more. Tomorrow is also not a good time to practice Stoicism, simply because it hasn't come yet. The best – and the only possible – moment to start practicing the Stoic way of life is today. And specifically, dear reader, it is the very moment when you finish reading *this sentence*.

Chapter 7

Focus on the present action

Do not disturb yourself by thinking of the whole of your life. Let not your thoughts at once embrace all the various troubles which you may expect to befall you.

Marcus Aurelius, *Meditations*, 8.36

In a nutshell: Life is a perpetual today, moreover, it is a perpetual present moment. Life is a string of present moments, coming one after another. They are never available to us collectively, they are always available one at a time. Thus, whatever we do, we need to focus on it entirely. Let there be only this single thing in the scope of our awareness. Let's dedicate ourselves to it one hundred percent. We will thus be able to act efficiently and satisfyingly.

***

Life is a sequence of present moments (fragment I), and in every one of them, we need to focus on just one thing (II). Whatever we do, we must not doubt the purpose of our actions (III and IV). This principle is a universal one (V). The worse the external conditions, the more we need to focus on the specifics (VI). This cannot be undermined (VII). In every present moment, there is something valuable to be done (VIII), and focus on the present moment improves our overall control over our life (IX).

Fragment I

It is your duty to order your life well in every single act.

Marcus Aurelius, *Meditations*, 8.32

Commentary: In this chapter, we will, in a way, apply the idea from the preceding chapter, but on a smaller scale. Our life is available to us only in particular, present and fleeting moments, which we must put to use. All we can achieve in life, we can achieve only through action in the present moment – only through taking action here and now. The present moment is our ultimate and only battlefield. We will never be able to have a broader influence on our life than *via* the present moment. We experience our life only in the present moment, which is going away right *now*.

Life, which we like to frame in general and abstract terms, is, in fact, available to us only as a chain of specific moments and specifics tasks. In this moment we are doing one thing, in another moment we turn another. Never in our life will come a moment when we could experience it as something else than "just" a sequence of specific actions, as a series of goals to aim at and tasks to perform. Thus, we need to put our life together from the tiny bits of the present moments. We need to arrange our actions and endeavors in order like pearls in a necklace, one by one, this comes first, that comes next, and this after that. We need to avoid chaos here and we need to avoid letting particular actions overlap.

Fragment II

> [If we are] *engaged in many various occupations,* [a day] *never passes so happily that no one or no thing* [...] *gives rise to some offence which makes the mind ripe for anger. Just as when one hurries through the crowded parts of the city one cannot help jostling many people, and one cannot help slipping at one place, being hindered at another, and splashed at another, so when one's life is spent in disconnected pursuits and wanderings, one must meet with many troubles and many accusations.*
>
> Seneca, Of Anger, III.6.3-4

Commentary: Focusing on the present action means, first, avoiding multitasking. We need to do (whenever possible) just one thing at a time, instead of many. Second, it means that we need to keep the scope of our awareness limited only to what is directly related to what we are doing. Our thoughts should never wander astray.

In the previous commentary, we compared our actions to pearls in a necklace. And this is what it's all about: pearls in a necklace always come in order, always come one by one. The same holds for our life: we should take on our actions, thoughts and goals one by one, never all at once. Only thus we can avoid disarray and random purposes, only thus we can set our life up as a coherent and round whole (or, at least, aspire to do so). If we do the contrary, that is, if we keep too many irons in the fire, we not only kill all the coherence we may hanker for, but we also slam all efficiency of our doings. An action is always more productive, swifter and more satisfying, if in the present moment it is the only object of our interest.

Yet, it's not enough to just do one thing at a time. We also need to *think* about just one thing at a time. This is the fulcrum of the whole issue. In Stoicism, whatever we do or think about, we need to focus on it totally – the whole rest of the world needs to simply disappear. We need to get rid of all irrelevant thoughts. We need to stop considering anything else. At the present moment, we are doing this: and nothing else. At the present moment we are thinking about this: and nothing else. The train of our thought doesn't get derailed, it doesn't seek any excuse to get stuck or trapped somewhere. Our human ability to think of many things at once and to think one thing while doing another is our curse. It's a terrible disadvantage and we compound it by employing this needless skill not to multitask but to procrastinate. We use it in the worst possible way: to pretend that we are doing something while we are actually thinking about something else. In Stoicism, we are advised to narrow down our focus and to live as if we were incapable of dealing with more than just one thing at once. This way we end up much better off.

There is one more vital point to be highlighted here. When we focus on the present action and when we don't allow ourselves to think about anything but the task at hand, we not only boost our efficiency and the value of the work we do, but we also increase, in passing, our overall contentment. Our happiness surges. It's not only the result of the better job we do. It's also because a full focus on the present task organizes our way of thinking and puts it in order. The more aligned our mental strengths are and the more they are concentrated on a specific goal, the less useless narratives and redundant worries are likely to pop up in our mind. In a word, focusing on the present action not only increases the quality of action itself, but it also boosts the overall quality of our life.

Fragment III

Do not be whirled about, but in every movement have respect to justice, and on the occasion of every impression maintain the faculty of comprehension.

Marcus Aurelius, *Meditations*, 4.22

Commentary: If we fail to put our energies and skills to work to our benefit, we not only lose the benefits, but we also turn those energies and skills into useless narratives, anxieties and doubts. Out of many ways in which the needless narratives may injure us, the most guileful one is when they undermine the meaning and purpose of what we do. Picture this: we are cramming for a midterm. Alas, we don't care enough to focus, we don't demand from ourselves the proper mental discipline. Our one eye, so to speak, pretends to scan the book we are holding before us, but the other eye is staring blankly at the window. What is actually happening right now? Many needless thoughts appear, most of them not even remotely connected with the book and the upcoming midterm. Suddenly and sadly, the present moment strikes us as the best possible one to rethink a thousand other errands, all of which seem to be far more important and more interesting than the book we are reading. What is even worse, we may start to doubt the whole purpose of studying. What's the use of it? Aren't we just wasting our time? Why don't we just take up something else, something new, something refreshing and more promising?

This is a deadly train of thought. It's deadly to the quality of the work we do, it's deadly to our peace of mind, it's deadly to all our efforts to live a Stoic life. Notice that (as discussed in the chapter "Act Deliberately") the careful and continuous reconsideration of the purposes of what we do, the restless calculation of all pros and cons of our actions indicates our Stoic smartness and the proper setup of our narratives. Yet – the crucial point! – we are required to do so only at the stages of decision-making, planning and re-evaluating. When the plan is already in motion, all these ponderings may likely be fatal. After all, it's hard to act if we doubt the meaningfulness of action. Accordingly, it's very hard to follow a plan and simultaneously contest it.

In Stoicism, we learn how to take advantage of this asymmetry. We need to separate sharply the stage of defining strategies and crafting plans from the stage of action itself. During the former, every examination is valuable, every point of view is golden, every possible merit needs to be taken into account. The more aforethought, the better. But once we turn to the second stage all that must stop once and for all. Once we made our final decision, all planning and strategy-crafting must be suspended. They should be denied entry to the domain of action. In the domain of action, there is no place for doubt, there is no place for undermining what we do, and there is no place for empty second thoughts.

Following such a rigorous procedure may seem demanding, but there is a certain trick to help us out. We can split ourselves into two personas, we can separate the commander and the executor. One persona is a commander-in-chief, who is in charge of analyzing, planning and deciding what to do. Second persona is a subordinate who blindly executes all that the commander orders her to do. In other words, we let one "I" think about what should be done and how, evaluate whether a proposed action is purposeful or not and whether it serves our values, goals and interests. Once that is figured out, we pass the baton to the second "I," the silent, diligent and obedient executor. Let there be no more doubts and hesitations – the decision is made, the die is cast. All that is left is to carry out the action itself.

Fragment IV

Nothing so much prevents the recovery of health, as a frequent change of supposed remedies. A wound is not soon healed, when different salves are tried by way of experiment. A plant thrives not, nor can well take root, that is moved from place to place.

Seneca, *Epistles*, 2.3

Commentary: Once we carefully consider our plan and once we make a reasoned-out decision about what to do, we should no longer second-guess our choices. In particular, we should set aside all doubt about whether we decided upon the right *method* of what we try to do. When we set a plan in motion, it must be already thought through and double-checked. Certainly, if something new comes up, or if there occurs a game-changing shift of circumstances, then we need to go back to square one and reconsider. But unless that happens, we have to stick to the original agenda. It's a grave mistake in Stoicism to change the plan in the midst of execution without a really good reason. We don't detour just because something crossed our mind or because someone said something. Let's imagine that we are about to attend a Stoic meeting. Yet, on our way there, we bump into an old acquaintance. We start talking, the conversation spins out of control, and it turns out that we are an hour late for the meeting. Once we finally rush in, it strikes our mind that it would be awesome to not just discuss Stoicism but rather to present it in the form of a monodrama. Sure enough, our Stoic friends will be grateful that we provided them with an opportunity to practice their patience and tolerance, but they have every right to be disappointed with us. We come late, we are performing some stunts instead of getting down to the Stoic business... this was not supposed to be this way!

We need to avoid changing our plans just because some trifle fancies our mood. By allowing minute things to disorganize our life, we greatly decrease our overall capacities and also – over the long sweep of time – we introduce a great evil in our life. What evil? Inconsistency and disorder. We need to be like sailors, who first smell which way the wind is blowing, then set sails, and head for their port. If the wind changes, we need to adjust the sails, but we shouldn't alter our heading. We need to avoid flip-flopping. We need to control our life, we need to control the goals we set up for ourselves, we need to control the values we define for ourselves. Let's not be controlled by winds!

Fragment V

> *– Today I choose to play. – Well then, ought you not to play with attention? – I choose to sing. – What then hinders you from doing so with attention?* [...] *What* [...] *of the things in life is done better by those who do not use attention?*

Epictetus, *Discourses*, IV.12.4-5

Commentary: We have so far discussed dealing with one's business, upholding one's values and fulfilling goals. However, we need to remember that the principle of focusing on the present action holds not only for the earnest and serious things. In life, there is time for business, obligation and duty, but there also needs to be time for other things. We need to focus not only when it comes to the meaningful things that constitute the purpose of our life. Epictetus rightly points this out: whatever we do, it is more satisfying and beneficial if we do it with attention. Or the other way around. It's next to impossible to come up with a single example of something which is better if done light-headedly or absent-mindedly.

Surely, focus on work and focus on leisure are two different issues. In the former case, we concentrate to perform better, which means doing our job more adroitly and efficiently. On the other hand, the notion of "efficiency" can hardly be applied to activities we take up for fun or entertainment. It is, after all, the very purpose of leisure that we detach ourselves from the discourse of solemnity and seriousness. Leisure is not about efficiency. It's rather the contrary, it's about relaxing our mind, about relinquishing control, about taking liberty from focus. This is undoubtedly true. Yet, the Stoic principle about focusing on the present action still applies here, because it's not as narrow and single-purposed as it might seem at first blush. This principle doesn't contradict our intuition of leisure as a time "off" or of "letting go," but it reinforces it. In Stoicism, if we get to take rest, we should engage wholeheartedly in taking the rest. If we stroll through the woods, if we play for fun, if we let the Saturday night fever carry us away, we need to immerse ourselves completely. We need to take pleasure in the walk, we need to focus only on what we are playing at the moment, we need to just go with the flow of tequila. We need to forbid our thoughts from wandering anywhere else. Therefore, when we go on vacation, let's go laptopless. Work should be work and work only, and leisure should be leisure and leisure only. Only then it is satisfying, only then it is the rest period which lets us actually reset and recharge.

Fragment VI

[If someone asks you] *how the name Antoninus is written, would you with a straining of the voice utter each letter? What then if they grow angry, will you be angry too? Will you not go on with composure and number every letter? Just so then in this life also remember that every duty is made up of certain parts.*

Marcus Aurelius, *Meditations*, 6.26

Commentary: The problem is this. On the one hand, it's better in every circumstance to think and act with attention, but, but on the other hand, not all circumstances allow us to be focused and attentive. Sometimes we are able to arrange proper conditions to think and act, but all too often, we are not. It's easy and comfortable for a general to plan the battle when she sits in her air-conditioned office. Yet, it might – and it definitely will – happen that she will have to do it in a stifling tent under the enemy fire. Will she be better off if she lets herself be distracted by shelling? Surely not. Tough circumstances don't suspend the principle of focusing on the present action. They make it even more important.

Marcus Aurelius comes up with the following example: if we are to solve some grammar or spelling problems, then we must do it diligently and carefully, no matter the circumstances. If someone is standing over us and rushes us, or if they start being angry at us, should we then write off our diligence? Quite the contrary. We rather have to focus some more, just to withstand the pressure and avoid mistakes.

Moreover, the spelling example serves to illustrate that the principle of focusing on the present action applies to different levels and different scales of our activity. Speech consists of sentences, sentences consist of words, words consist of letters. The same holds here. First off, we should think in the framework of the whole of our life and define the values we want to uphold and goals we want to meet. Then we should translate them into the language of specific actions, we need to split our big plans into specific tasks and duties. Then, again, every single task needs to be split into even smaller points. This approach can be applied in any case. E.g., writing a book on Stoicism is nothing else than writing all of its chapters, writing a chapter is nothing else than writing all of its commentaries, writing a commentary is nothing else than writing all sentences a commentary consists of. Why put this angle on it? Because splitting the task facilitates our focus. It is easier to focus on the specifics. Even more than that. At the end of the day, only with the specifics we can work.

For these reasons, we need to aim at specifics. Every value, even the most abstract one, and every goal, even the most distant one, needs to be translated into the most specific language available. There is no other way. Let's express our purposes in the parlance of concrete tasks and duties, and let's focus on them. The clearer they are defined, the harder it will be to deflect us.

Fragment VII

> *I must die. If now, I am ready to die. If, after a short time, I now dine because it is the dinner-hour. After this I will then die.*
>
> Epictetus, Discourses, I.1.32

Commentary: The principle of focusing on the present action can also be described as follows. Let's imagine again that we have to prepare for a midterm. OK then, let's turn to it, let's not think how little we have done so far, let's not guilt trip over yesterday's laziness and let's not think about how hard we will party to celebrate passing the exam. The present moment must engulf us completely. We mustn't look or even think of what's before or after. Let's not be misled into thinking that past (or future) moments in any way define or determine the present moment. It's rather the contrary. It is the present moment that defines and determines all.

This reasoning might be opposed, for example, in the following way. "Yes, dear Stoics, let it be your way. But note that however precisely I split my time and however diligently I devote myself to every moment of it, it is always possible that something that is not within my power prevents me from focusing on the present action. However carefully I spell the name 'Antoninus,' it is always possible that a sudden disaster strikes and the ceiling comes down on my head. Or that a SWAT team storms my apartment instead of the terrorist's living next door. In either case, my spelling attempts are thwarted. What do you say to that?"

This counterargument though, however spot on, doesn't diminish the validity and utility of the principle we are discussing. It's true that not only anything can happen at any moment, but also that our whole life can take a completely unexpected turn in a heartbeat. Stoicism is the first to remind it. Yet, focusing on the present action is about focusing on the present action, and, as of *now*, nothing has happened yet. You are reading this sentence, dear reader, aren't you? If so, it means that the ceiling hasn't come down yet. Whatever lies in wait for us, it's still a matter of the future. If it's not going to happen, there is no need to abandon what we are doing *now*. If it is going to happen, there is no need either, since it hasn't happened *yet*. Nothing that belongs in the future belongs in the present moment. Whatever future holds in the closet for us, it is not yet the content of the present moment. Come what may. But whatever comes, we must focus on the present action *now*.

Fragment VIII

> *Here is the proof of the thing, here is the test of the philosopher. For this also is a part of life, like walking, like sailing, like journeying by land, so also is fever. Do you read when you are walking? No. Nor do you when you have a fever. But if you walk about well, you have all that belongs to a person who walks. If you bear a fever well, you have all that belongs to a person in a fever. What is it to bear a fever well? Not to blame [anyone], not to be afflicted at that which happens.*
>
> Epictetus, Discourses, III.10.11-13

Commentary: It seems reasonable and pleasant to focus on the present action if this action is of our own choice. It's relatively easy to focus on an action that we ourselves deem appropriate and beneficial to us. But what about situations when we are actually forced to do something that we would never choose of our own? Moreover, what's the purpose of focusing on the present action if we are sick or jailed, with all of our plans wiped out?

Stoicism offers a twofold answer here. First of all, nothing can put a spike in a Stoic's will. A Stoic can never be forced to do something against her own decision. Why? Because, in a word, she is always able to adjust her decision to the pressing necessity. This happens instantly and with no second thoughts. A Stoic never forgets the realities in which she lives. She always remembers that she may get sick, and that even SWAT makes mistakes which can put her in jail or in hospital. A Stoic always takes that into account. A Stoic keeps in mind that events may develop in a disadvantageous way and she always has contingency plans. In other words, events can never force her to *change* her plans. All they can do is make her choose some of the variants she planned over other variants. In this sense, nothing will ever happen contrary to Stoic's decision. She takes everything into account and has a scenario in mind for every possible development. In this vein, whichever scenario is actually carried out, it is not contrary to her will.

Second, the circumstances can make us change our course of action, but they can't prevent us from focusing on the present action. In every moment when we are alive, there will always be something that may be done as it should be done. The object of our action can alter, but the principle holds. We must be focused on whatever we do and whatever we think. We had focused on some business, the business was cut off because we got sick, so now we must fulfill the duties of a sick person. We need to focus on withstanding the discomfort bravely, we need not to worry beyond circumstances, we need to avoid useless narratives. Particularly, we need to diligently and carefully do whatever we can do to restore our health. We need to stay on our pills, get our shots, keep our diet – and it's no infamy if this is all we can focus on. We are also obliged to keep our thoughts in order and not let ourselves think about all that we had to abandon due to our indisposition. When we are working, we shouldn't think about rest, and when we are resting, we shouldn't think about work. Accordingly, when we are sick, we shouldn't think about what the sickness deprived us of. Our present action is to combat the sickness, that's all. We need to – and we can – focus on that. It's not always within our power to choose what to do, but it's always within our power to focus and to strive to do well whatever we do.

The principle of focusing on the present task is not exhausted through the simple bid for efficiency. It is also a crucial Stoic tool for a time of adversity. It happens all too often to all of us that the duties, setbacks and errands try to walk all over us. Quantity and complexity of the things we have to deal with are often overwhelming. In such cases, it is extremely important to always define the particular components of the problems, split them into parts, put them in a right order, and then deal with them one by one. It will often help, it will never harm. No adversity will become worse if we analyze it point by point.

Fragment IX

Secure this present time to yourself.

Marcus Aurelius, *Meditations*, 8.44

Commentary: No one is eager to give their money away to random people. We like to take care of our assets, but we are staggeringly less careful when it comes to something a hundred times more valuable than money, that is our time and our energy. We invest them every day in errands that are not worth them. We spend days and weeks on things that are not worth minutes. Obviously, it's wrong that we do so. But how can we stop doing that?

Focusing on the present action is the Stoic tool for this. Whatever we do, we need to do it with our full attention. One hundred percent of our accessible mental power must be fixed upon whatever is right in front of us and whatever we work up right now. The present moment is the only moment of which we can be sure that if we bestow it upon ourselves – it will actually be ours. The past is already not within our power and the future is not yet within our power. The only slice of time we can utilize to our purpose is the present moment. Only through the present moment leads the way to bliss and to reasonable management of our life.

The principle of being focused at the present moment doesn't, of course, entail that we are forbidden to *ever* think about things which transcend the reality of the moment. Sometimes it is necessary. Often it is inspiring. Yet, we need to take heed that inattention, distraction and procrastination produce a negative output in a threefold way. First, they make us act less effectively and less satisfactorily. Second, not only the current satisfaction is reduced, but also our overall happiness is diminished, because we let the useless narratives get to us. Third, if we aren't focused now, it means that we aren't focused ever. The present moment is the only moment accessible to us. It is the only moment through which we can try to shape reality, impact our life and pursue happiness. To waste the present moment is to waste something that cannot be retrieved. A "now" wasted is a "now" lost.

Chapter 8

Your lifetime will suffice

Life is long enough, if you know how to use it.

Seneca, *Of the Shortness of Life*, 2.1

In a nutshell: We have enough time at our disposal if only we manage it properly. Life is not short but we ourselves are shortening it. We are shortening it by wasting our time on trumpery and trifle. Every lifetime will be long enough if we use it smart, creatively and purposefully, while every lifetime will be too short if we misuse it. Our time is not limited because we have too little but because we squander too much of it. Let's treasure our time, and it will suffice.

***

Our lifetime is not short in itself but we shorten it (fragment I). We do so by devoting our time to useless things (II). We can live well regardless of how long our life is (III). In order to live well, we should keep an exact record of all the expenses of our time, just as we should do with money (IV). We must know what we expect and what we want to achieve (V), we mustn't do too many things at once and we mustn't overthink the future (VI). Life will surely provide us with enough time to master the skill of living well (VII), but this skill is just a tool – it must be applied and it mustn't become another excuse to misuse our time (VIII).

Fragment I

We do not have a very short time assigned to us, but we lose a great deal of it. Life is long enough to carry out the most important projects. Have an ample portion, if we [...] [live] it right, but when it all runs to waste through luxury and carelessness, when it is not devoted to any good purpose, then at the last we are forced to feel that it is all over, although we never noticed how it glided away. Thus it is: we do not receive a short life, but we make it a short one, and we are not poor in days, but wasteful of them. When great and kinglike riches fall into the hands of a bad master, they are dispersed straightway, but even a moderate fortune, when bestowed upon a wise guardian, increases by use. In like manner our life has great opportunities for one who knows how to dispose of it to the best advantage.

Seneca, *Of the Shortness of Life*, 1.3-4

Commentary: We often grumble at having too little time. We complain that a day has only 24 hours and we daydream about one extra day in a week. Time always seems limited to us: we yammer that we don't have enough of it and that we don't have the time to do all the things we would like to do. Stoicism reverses this point of view. Our time is not limited in itself but it is us who make it seem limited. How come? By spending it uselessly and by wasting it needlessly.

When it comes to time, we are not paupers but wastrels. What does it mean?, time, we are not rich, we are not poor, we are not the middle class – none of these concepts applies here. For there is no objective, universal and clear criterion to tell how much time is "little time" and how much is "a lot." We cannot even know in advance how much time we have ahead of us. The only thing we do know and the single thing that is within our power is how we use our time. Water glides by the mill but we will never know how long it sustains. The only thing we can do is to decide how we try to use the present moment.

Fragment II

Let us take one of the elders, and say [...] "We perceive that you have arrived at the extreme limits of human life: you are in your hundredth year, or even older. Come now, reckon up your whole life in black and white. Tell us how much of your time has been spent upon your creditors, how much on your mistress, how much on your king, how much on your clients [...] how much in running up and down the city on business. Add to this the diseases which we bring upon us with our own hands, and the time which has laid idle without any use having been made of it. You will see that you have not lived as many years as you count. Look back in your memory and see how often you have been consistent in your projects, how many days passed as you intended them to do when you were at your own disposal, how often you did not change color and your spirit did not quail, how much work you have done in so long a time, how many people have without your knowledge stolen parts of your life from you, how much you have lost, how large a part has been taken up by useless grief, foolish gladness, greedy desire, or polite conversation, how little of yourself is left to you. You will then perceive that you will die prematurely."

Seneca, *Of the Shortness of Life*, 3.2-3

Commentary: What do we waste our time on? The only way to know this is to examine our conscience. We must honestly admit to ourselves how much time we have spent and on what. We can easily substitute ourselves for that "elder" who scrutinizes life in retrospect. After all, who hasn't devoted too much time to vain love affairs? Who hasn't gotten caught up too much in ridiculous office politics? Whose days have never been over-consumed by bureaucratic and logistic errands? Who hasn't lost tons of time on pointless quarrels and useless arguments? Finally, has anyone ever been blessed with pristine health and never had to abandon their plans due to a medical condition? Honestly, no one ever said that. Our own affinity with Seneca's "elder" is striking.

Such an examination of conscience is always a (very) hard time, but it is also an elevating experience. To admit to ourselves that we indeed waste time, and to get to know how we waste it, it is the first step towards pulling great changes. We will discuss this at length in the commentary to fragment V, but before we get to it, we should address an important doubt that pops up here.

The doubt goes roughly along the following line. "Okay Seneca! Our 'elder' has squandered most of life and I'm indeed on the best way to do the same. But how can I stop it? Some things that I have to waste my time on are simply not within my power. I can loathe the necessity of sleep, but I can do nothing about it. I will always have to blow away at least a quarter of my life – sleeping. I can do nothing about my sickness, about the duty to earn a living and so on. Also, what do you propose in return? If I strip my life of everything you want me to account for, there would be nothing left! Yes, I do spend my time running my errands and I do spend time with all my lovers. But why not? Don't you oblige me to count *everything* I do as a loss of time?"

First of all, it is true that a great many of things we do, we do under the pressure of external necessity. We just have some duties (social, or simply biological) and we have to spend our time on performing them. But the Stoic advice is this: let's define, as clearly as possible, what part of our business actually serves our goals and values and what part of it is a simple response to the obligations of life. Yes, the distinction will always be a little blurred. And no, it will never be easy to draw. But the effort to draw it is worth it, since the more we allow that line to blur the more time we waste.

Many things are only seemingly necessary. It just seems to us that we must or ought to do so-and-so while as a matter of fact we simply lack strength and courage to stand up to circumstances. Let's be honest with ourselves and let's have a bold and fresh look at ourselves. Let's think about what we use our life for. Should we spend our time helping others? Yes, we should be kind to other people, but we should never lose our priorities regarding how and for who we are helpful. Some people indeed need our help while others just await an opportunity to burden us with some of their own duties. The same holds for when we are "running up and down the city on business." Some of these errands are actual duties, that is, relevant issues we are obliged to deal with for our own and for societal sake, but some of them are simply rubbish. We must be aware of this fine line. Let's have the courage to stop it! Let's have the courage to make the call: "I won't do this! I don't have to! It's just a waste of time! Instead, I'll attend to other, more relevant and more important business!" The Stoic point is that nothing else will give us more power to make this call than an honest account of how we spend our time. Once we realize how much unnecessary things cost us, it will be much easier to rebel against them.

Another doubt is this: if Seneca implies that time spent on love, fun, business, family or caring for one's health is time wasted, then this concept of "time wasted" is pointless. Every use of time is counted as time lost! What is the Stoic reply here? The reply is that spending our time with friends, lovers or on entertainment might perfectly serve *our* purpose, but we have to define it as such. If – and only if – we define our purpose as "caring for friends and lovers" or "entertaining ourselves," then the time wasted turns into time invested. Everything can serve our purpose if we define that purpose properly. Whatever we do and whatever we spend our time on, we should do it consciously and of our own will. We shouldn't conceal anything under the guise of alleged necessity. Whatever we want to do, let's do it, but let's do it candidly and avowedly. Let's call a spade a spade and a purpose a purpose. It's a lot like accounting: a big but reasonable expenditure is far less painful than money embezzled by God knows who to God knows what end.

Fragment III

> *Just as one of small stature can be a perfect person, so a life of small compass can be a perfect life. Age ranks among the external things. How long I am to exist is not mine to decide.*
>
> Seneca, *Epistles*, 93.7[vii]

Commentary: There is no denying that the length of our life is not within our power. Certainly, we can avoid parachuting and abusing drugs (and particularly mixing the two), but still, the final word on the date of our death is not ours. It is not within our power to decide *how long* we live; however, it is within our power to decide *how* we live.

Stoicism teaches us that every life can be lived with merit. It doesn't matter if it lasts sixteen or a hundred and sixteen years. Merit and meaning can be imposed upon a life in a plethora of ways, but all of these ways are independent from the life's length. We should care about the quality not quantity of our days, and it's quality not quantity that we should preen on.

Certainly, there are diverse circumstances in different lives. A healthy youngster and an ailing elderly person will assess the merits of life quite differently. If we hope for a few dozen more years, then we plan and define the meaning of life in a different way than if we are under artillery fire and our future counts in minutes. Stoicism assures us, however, that for every life, long or short, there is always a value that can be upheld. The responsibility for choosing this value, however, will always be ours and Stoicism doesn't lift it from our shoulders.

Fragment IV

> *I cannot say "I lose nothing," but I can tell you what I lose, and why, and in what manner.*
>
> Seneca, Epistles, 1.4

Commentary: As discussed in the commentary to fragment II, the first step to improve our time management is to realize our misuse of it. To realize it, we must construct an account of our time. Let's follow this path and let's write down – literally! – all the disbursements of our time, just as we would write down our household budget. Let's put down how many days, hours and minutes we spend on various activities. Things committed to a computer file (or to ordinary paper) become somehow objectified and pleasantly external to us. And it becomes easier for us to assess them honestly and calmly.

No human being has ever been anything but mortified after logging their activities this way. It's unbelievable how much time and energy we waste and it's impossible not to be shocked when one faces it for the first time. However, let's not forget that we do all this not to beat ourselves down but to better ourselves. Once we see in black and white how many hours we've spent on pointless pleasures, how many days we've frittered away simulating useless work, how many nights we've wasted socializing with people we don't even like – we'll sober up. Yes, the realization of how badly we use our time is, to swallow. But once we swallow it, it becomes much easier for us to take the next step, that is, to start planning our time expenditures more ably and more consciously.

Studying the balance of our time management will also help us understand that there is no magic switch that would instantly make our life better. There is no clandestine mechanism to be unearthed, there is no secret knowledge to be acquired. The wise use of our time is something that can only happen *now*. It can be reached only by putting *this* minute to a wise use. There is no secret agenda here, there is no conspiracy, and there is also no shortcut.

Finally, contrary to what we deal with in accounting, in managing our time, there is no income column – there is only spending. We will never get a minute beyond that what has already been conferred upon us. No time will ever be added, and time lost will never be retrieved.

Fragment V

> *Be your own master and such hours as have hitherto been forcibly taken from you, or stolen unawares, or have flipped by inadvertently, recollect. [...] Part of our time we are obliged to sacrifice to office and power, [...] common occurrences steal another part, and another slides away insensibly, but most scandalous is the loss of it when owing to negligence.*
>
> Seneca, *Epistles*, 1.1

Commentary: Keeping strict control over our time-spending is sometimes harder and sometimes easier. Sometimes just one glance will suffice to tell what has happened to our time. For instance, if we break a leg, we have to spend some time in the hospital, getting the X-rays, the cast, all that. It's clear what we did and why we did it. Alas, in most cases, it won't be that easy. Time will pass imperceptibly and it will be tough to name the cause of our loss. It may turn out that we spent ninety minutes doing something we thought was of our own will, while in fact, we were simply fooled by a person or by a situation. A salesman or a peddler of ideas may steal a lot of our time but sometimes it will be someone or something far less evident. One thing is certain: we have to know what we want and what we pursue. Only from this perspective we should assess how we use our time. If we don't set up a clear agenda for ourselves, we invite people and circumstances to manipulate us. We invite them to fool us that this or that is right and beneficial to us while, as a matter of fact, it's not. If we don't know what we want, we open up a disastrous column in our account: time lost to carelessness.

Fragment VI

> *Occupy yourself with few things, says the philosopher, if* [you want to] *be tranquil. [...] Accordingly on every occasion you should ask yourself: "Is this one of the unnecessary things?" [...] You should take away not only unnecessary acts, but also unnecessary thoughts, for thus superfluous acts will not follow after.*
>
> Marcus Aurelius, *Meditations*, 4.24

Commentary: We must keep in mind that putting our time to good use doesn't imply haphazard or desperate attempts to catch up on everything at once. Quite the opposite! We should avoid trying to kill too many birds with one stone. We should rethink the goals we aim for and the errands we deal with. We should cross out all that is not critical and necessary and we should plan the rest as reasonably as possible. We should check all our duties against our hierarchy of values and then work on them according to a set agenda. In doing so, we mustn't lose our heads. If we don't want to waste our time – we must use it efficiently but not frantically.

We must also be aware that it may be really difficult to wrap our heads around how much time we wasted before we turned to Stoicism. This will be really bitter and discouraging. We must expect a great many thoughts like "It makes no sense! It's downright absurd! I've lost so much time! I could have done and achieved so many things had I been more thoughtful! Now it's all too late!" These are very genuine and very painful thoughts indeed, but they are birth pangs. We must withstand them and soldier on. We will recover quickly: no matter how much time we have lost, the only meaningful solution is to start caring for the time that lies in wait for us. We must keep in mind that the past is already closed, and that it is not within our power. To think excessively about the past and to be overtly saddened by it is a direct road to perdition. Yes, we have to go over the accounts of our time. But we do it to pep ourselves up, not to wear ourselves down.

Fragment VII

> *You choose rather to become good tomorrow than to be good today.*
>
> Marcus Aurelius, *Meditations*, 8.22

Commentary: In the commentary to fragment III we mentioned that regardless of how little (or how much) time there is ahead of us, there is always a value to be found, one which is within our grasp, and upholding of which will supply meaning to our life. Surely, there is no ready-made answer, no prescription and no direct guideline. We ourselves have to find or establish that value. And yet, if we have any trouble doing so, there is still one thing that is accessible to everyone and in every circumstance. What is it? In a word: Stoicism. In a sentence: striving to become just a little bit better than one used to be.

Stoicism is designed in such a way that it may be applied everywhere, always and under all conditions. Regardless of how hard a time we are having – we can always try to become better. Regardless of how little time we have left – we can always try to live it stoically. No vortex of circumstances and mishaps, however adverse, can deprive us of this opportunity. No situation is so dire that it wouldn't be improved if approached stoically.

Fragment VIII

Your days will always be few if you count them.

Seneca, *On Benefits*, V.17.5

Commentary: We won't live well if we keep wasting our time. Accordingly, we won't be happy if we keep counting days, trying to determine whether we have received due amount. There is no "due." There is no universal measure. We only have so much time as we have and we must focus on not wasting what we have. In particular, we should not waste time on lamenting that time is limited.

The more we think about the swiftness of time, the swifter it is. If we feel that time is running away, if it seems to us that we can't keep up, if we can't catch up on all we want to pursue, it would be absurd to compound the situation by actively worrying about it and thus quickening the pace. Elapsing days shouldn't be counted but put to use. Our time will always seem too short if we waste it complaining that it's short. The meaning of life is independent from the length of life and the length of life is not within our power. Therefore, let's not be troubled. Instead, let's busy ourselves with that which is within our power and let's attempt to make the most of the time we have at our disposal.

Chapter 9

Define proper alternatives

Do nothing in a depressed mood, nor as one afflicted, nor as thinking that you are in misery, for no one compels you to that. Is there smoke in the chamber? If the smoke is moderate, I will stay. If it is excessive, I go out.

Epictetus, Discourses, I.25.17

In a nutshell:[21] If we face a problem, we should always define a proper alternative. Either we deem it necessary to solve it and we take action to do so, or we accept the situation as it is and we stop seeing it as an issue. One variant is forbidden: we mustn't concurrently worry about something and do nothing to change it.

***

Any problem can be compared to leaving the theater in the middle of a boring movie: we either decide to watch it until the closing credits and we don't complain, or we stand up, leave and we're not bored anymore (fragment I). Before we make the call, we must weigh all the pros and cons (II). This principle should be applied to the adversities and difficulties we face (III) and to every life situation in general (IV). We can apply it when a fellow human does us a disservice (V), as well as when someone does something wrong with no direct detriment to us (VI). This principle holds for our life as a whole (VII) but also for every single piece of it (VIII). The good-good alternative is a particularly important case (IX).

Fragment I

In sum remember this: the door is open. Be not more timid than little children, but as they say, when the thing does not please them, "I will play no longer," so do you, when things seem to you of such a kind, say "I will no longer play," and be gone. But if you stay, do not complain.

Epictetus, Discourses, I.24.20

---

[21] This chapter is based on a suggestion made to me by Dr. Michał Dobrzański.

Commentary: We have all experienced this: a movie drags on endlessly, we are bored, there is no hope for any bracing development, but we sit still and watch on until the final scene. This happens in theaters all over the world and this happens in all walks of life. And this is an error that Stoicism encourages us to avoid. We must remember that we can always stand up and leave. No one forces us to sit and suffer. We are tormented by our own accord – and this is the craziness that Stoicism wants us to get rid of.

But how? By defining a proper alternative. It is either that the movie is so annoying that we leave *right now*, or, to the contrary, it's not that bad and premature jostling toward the exit (along with the thoughts of having wasted the ticket money) will be a greater nuisance than watching till the end. Once we comprehend the situation this way, it will greatly facilitate making the right decision because it automatically writes off the worst option. It crosses out the excruciating path where we first make up our mind that the movie is dull and then we patiently tolerate it, sitting through the rest of it just to wallow in our misery. Defining a proper alternative is quite simple. Either something is so bad that we take appropriate action to counter it, or we do nothing and get on with the situation with no pain and no regrets.

Importantly, this alternative is never a one-off deal. Think of it this way: a movie is not a point in time, but rather a stretch of time and, accordingly, our assessment of it should be a continuous process. Every evaluation is subject and prone to change. A decision once made, for example, after an intriguing first scene, doesn't in any way oblige us to last until the end. The stay-or-leave decision must be remade over and over again.

Fragment II

> *If you were about to journey to Syracuse, and some one were to say: "Learn beforehand all the discomforts, and all the pleasures of your coming voyage, and then set sail. [...] You have now heard all that can attract you thither, all that can deter you from going. Now, then, either set sail or remain at home!" If, after this declaration, anybody were to say that he wished to go to Syracuse, they could blame no one but themselves for what befell them there, because they would not stumble upon it unknowingly, but would have gone thither fully aware of what was before them. To everyone Nature says: "I do not deceive any person."*
>
> Seneca, *Of Consolation. To Marcia*, 17.2-6

Commentary: Let's now turn to an example from travelling. Notice, that the metaphor is broader here, as it's not limited to a case of temporary discomfort. Instead, it refers to the future and includes scenarios that are

Define proper alternatives

dependent on the decisions we make. For example, we want to visit Syracuse, start a business or a family, or write a book. Each of these endeavors allures us with certain benefits but each is also bound with some costs and risks. We should weigh all the pros and cons and make as informed decision as possible. And there are only two ways to go: we either assess that the pros outweigh the cons and we set sail to Syracuse (write the business-plan, buy the engagement ring, etc.), or that the cons outweigh the pros and that all the perks fade in the face of troubles lying in wait for us, so we abandon our enterprise altogether. There is no third option. We mustn't think "I'm not going to Syracuse, but I wish I were going" and we mustn't think "OK, I'm going to Syracuse, but it will be a bummer I can't cope with."

The meat of defining proper alternatives consists in crossing out the middle way. Doing something and simultaneously regretting it, or the other way about, not doing something and regretting it, is a no-go here. We have decided to set on a journey, to stay put, to get married, to flee from the altar, to start a business or to not start a business. It was our decision and ours only. It was made because we established that the other option would cause more inconvenience. Thus, no need for regrets.

Properly defined alternative also sheds some light on one more misconception about Stoicism. Some people claim that the entire Stoic teaching can be summed up in a single formula of "accept the fate" (i.e., "contentedly accept the course of events whatever happens"). Sure, it sounds catchy, but once we scrutinize it, it's confusing. On one hand, it is true that we should accept all that happens (I prefer to say "take facts into account," or *facta sunt servanda*) but, on the other hand, it is intuitively clear that some twists of fortune we accept more readily than others. Moreover, we have some means at our disposal that we can use to boost the likelihood that favorable things happen to us and reduce the likelihood that unfavorable things happen. In other words, the formula "accept the fate" provides no guidelines as to what to do specifically. Only the properly defined alternative lends us a hand here. Let's take another example: should we travel by plane if we are afraid of flying? The answer is that there are two (and only two) possibilities. Either our fear takes the upper hand and we don't board the plane and we don't worry anymore or we decide to take the chance and go. In the former case, "accepting fate" takes the form of "I have to suffer two days chugging along on a train" but I can't do anything about it – planes are so dangerous and environmentally unsounds!," in the latter: "Come what may! I'm gonna lean back, enjoy the flight and if we crash... huh, it's not within my power!"

Therefore, accepting fate doesn't entail waiving our right to influence it. *First* we determine what is within our power (by defining the proper alternatives) and *then* we gladly accept that which is not within our power.

Fragment III

Everything which happens either happens in such wise as you are formed [...] to bear it, or as you are not formed [...] to bear it. If, then, it happens to you in such way as you are formed [...] to bear it, do not complain, but bear it as you are formed [...] to bear it. But if it happens in such wise as you are not formed [...] to bear it, do not complain, for it will perish after it has consumed you.

Marcus Aurelius, *Meditations*, X.3

Commentary: The present example deals with how our principle of defining proper alternatives should be applied to the adversities we encounter and mishaps we suffer. Let's imagine that we are planning a very exciting trip. The tickets have been bought, the passport is in our pocket, we are almost heading out to the airport, but in the very last moment, a sickness strikes. Instead of boarding the plane, we need to wrap ourselves in blankets and stay in bed for a week. What then?

We should define a proper alternative: we either have enough vigor to go and enjoy the trip despite the medical condition, or the illness is too serious and we have to postpone the journey and stick to being sick. The decision must be made as reasonably as possible and as many factors as possible must be taken into account. We have to speak to our doctor: where exactly do we stand on our health? What's the problem? What's the prognosis? Also, we must mull over how important the trip is. Can it be rescheduled? What happens if we cancel? What consequences do we face? We have to make an honest decision, all-things-considered: do we resign or do we go despite? The decision must be as sincere as possible. We must appeal to all rationality and all the self-awareness we are capable of. There mustn't be any doom-mongering and there mustn't be any grumbling. Specifically, we must remember that the past is bygone and closed. Today's decision about tomorrow must be based on today and today only. Yesterday doesn't count anymore. We must make our decision relying on the facts, conditions and circumstances that are in place *right now*, and not those which were in place yesterday. We have to stick to this even if yesterday's facts were a hundred times more advantageous and alluring.

The burden of responsibility for making this choice is on our shoulders and it won't be lifted. In particular, Stoicism will never free us from this onus. The last thing it intends is to provide us with ready-made answers about what to do.²² All it urges us is to remove the "third way" as a possibility. It urges us to not even entertain the ideas of travelling despite a debilitating illness and of cancelling the trip without a solid reason. Both cases always lead us to misery: either in irritation because the whole trip makes no sense since we are too ill to enjoy it, or, on the contrary, in remorse because we backed out too easily. It's an either-or situation. Either the sickness is not serious enough to make us change our plans, or we cancel everything and we switch from "travelling" mode to "sick & recovering" mode." If we want to be happy: we must choose between these two – and only these two! – options.

Fragment IV

When you have been well filled today, you sit down and lament about the morrow, how you shall get something to eat. Wretch, if you have it, you will have it; if you have it not, you will depart from life. The door is open. Why do you grieve?

Epictetus, *Discourses*, I.9.19

Commentary: The principle of defining proper alternatives holds for everything including – as Epictetus points out – the practical and financial aspect of our life. Let's imagine: we have so-and-so much money at our disposal and our income is such-and-such. Often times we will be dissatisfied by it, often times we will be inclined to think that we would be better off if we earned more. If this is the case, we must ask ourselves a simple question: is our deficit palpable enough to outweigh the toil of working overtime or seeking a better-paid job? Or maybe we would prefer to settle down with the income we already have and spare ourselves the extra effort? We have to answer this question – seriously, sincerely, straightforwardly – and then act according to our answer. And either we happily enjoy what we have or we go out there and seek bigger bucks.

A properly defined alternative eradicates the middle road, one which is most disadvantageous to us but alas not less travelled. It is not unusual for us to complain about having too little money while, at the same time, doing nothing to alter this condition. Many people not only enter this treacherous

---

²² The principle of defining proper alternatives is, in a way, a tool which facilitates clear expression of the problem at hand, so that our choice is easier to make. But the Stoicism – to use the old adage – prefers to teach us to fish than to give us fish. It doesn't make our decisions for us. Stoicism never says "do so-and-so," instead, it says "define a proper alternative before you decide what to do."

path but also brag about doing so or even mock those who try to avoid it. But to do so is as nonstoic as it gets. If the Stoics were to call anything an explicit madness, this would be a great contender.

Fragment V

> *For if you can, correct that which is the cause, but if you can not do this, correct at least the thing itself. But if you can not do even this, of what use is it to you to find fault?*
>
> Marcus Aurelius, *Meditations*, 8.17

Commentary: A particular kind of hardships we deal with in our life are the hardships associated with our dear fellow humans, or even caused by them. The Stoic way of dealing with this is, of course, by defining proper alternatives. Let's imagine that someone offended us with an insulting word. What would a Stoic do?

Insulting others is a clear sign that something is awry in the soul of an individual. If we care for their welfare and sanity, then we may want to try to somehow help them. If someone curses, we may try to calm them down by asking what's wrong and by trying to figure out what useless narratives are the root of their anxiety. If they are angry, we may try to put them at ease. If they are embittered, we may try to cheer them up. Yet, it may happen that they don't even listen to us. Some will always prefer to fortify in their soreness. Sometimes we can be of help but sometimes we can't. And if we cannot help, or if we, for some reason, don't want to help, then we should treat the intricacies and confusions of the soul of the other as something which is not within our power.[23]

Thus, we get to the second option mentioned by Marcus Aurelius: we set the perpetrator aside and we only deal with the offence itself. It's a plain fact that someone said a certain word. How should we deal with it? Let's define a proper alternative: we can either react (throw a punch, demand an apology, sue for slander), or we can deem the whole game not worth the candle and just ignore it. "Fault-finding" in itself does us no good because neither the offender nor the offence are within our power.

---

[23] See also the chapter "To Each Their Own Mistakes."

Fragment VI

If you are able, correct by teaching those who do wrong, but if you can not, remember that [kindness] is given to you for this purpose.

Marcus Aurelius, Meditations, 9.11

Commentary: The conduct of other people can hurt us even if they don't inflict any direct harm on us. For instance, we get to know that one of our friends is a gossip. We don't admire such behavior and we don't approve of it, even though, let's assume, they aren't badmouthing us directly. What should we do?

We should define a proper alternative. We either talk to that person and make it clear to them why we consider such conduct inappropriate, or we say nothing and move on. If gossiping doesn't actually hurt us that much or if we have no hope that our intervention makes any difference – "kindness is given to you for this purpose." But if we choose not to act, then we must also choose not to think about it anymore. We must simply accept that people are what they are and that some of them are and will be telltales. We have to close this topic once and for all as a topic which is not within our power. We must give no second thought to it.

Fragment VII

There is one reason why we should not complain of life: it detains no one against their will. Human affairs are in such a happy situation, that no one needs be wretched but by choice. Do you like to be wretched? Live. Do you like it not? It is in your power to return from whence you came.

Seneca, Epistles, 70.15

Commentary: We have said that the proper alternatives should be applied to hardships and setbacks that come up in our life. But what if a grave disaster strikes and we confront a situation which is both unbearable and irreparable: we can't endure it but we can't do anything either. What then? An appropriate example for this, one sadly well known in contemporary life, is a medical situation: an irreversible and very painful or onerous one. We cannot recover and the suffering is agonizing. What would a Stoic do?

The proper alternative is the following: either the pain is so great that it is easier for us to overcome our life instinct and commit suicide rather than withstand the pain any longer, or it is better to embrace the remainder of life which we have left and enjoy it despite the pain. In other words, our life as a whole is also subjected to a proper alternative. No circumstances force us to live on. We can always say "no!" and exit life. This is the root of the sharp disjunction in the proper alternative. Situations in which it is necessary for us to both live and bear unbearable suffering are very rare. Simply, we should either die or enjoy life as it is. To snark at life and not to commit suicide – it's a height of absurdity.

It's a brutal lesson, of course. But let's not overlook an interesting fact. While thinking up an alternative in which suicide is an option doesn't constitute an obligation or even a suggestion that we should kill ourselves, it is still a very bracing and fortifying thought. Let's imagine that we find ourselves in an extremely difficult life situation. Who can prevent us from approaching it in the following way? "Yes, we are in dire straits, but there is still an out: we either come to terms with the situation or we put ourselves to death." Just reminding ourselves that the latter option *always* exists can restore our spirits. For we always have a way of escape. There is always an out, an emergency exit we can use, no matter how hard we are pressed and no matter what corner we are backed into. We are never hopeless, we are never left without options. Just being aware of this is a great helping thought in itself. Just picturing an equation in which suicide is a part gives us the power to combat adversity. There is great magic in contemplating suicide: just the very possibility of it comforts us.

And there is still more than that. Once we define a proper alternative, we not only see that no trap is without exit but we are also reminded that in whatever distress we are, it is so because of our own choice. At first blush, it might seem a paradoxical thought. At the second blush, it may seem deeply saddening. But at the third blush: it turns out greatly soothing. There is a bitter but great power in realizing that all that we suffer we suffer of our own consent.

Fragment VIII

Well, but you say to me: "Do not live in Nicopolis!" I will not live there. "Nor in Athens!" I will not live in Athens. "Nor in Rome." I will not live in Rome. "Live in Gyarus."[24] *I will live in Gyarus. But [if] it seems like a great smoke to live in Gyarus [then] I depart to the place where no man will hinder me from living,*

Epictetus, Discourses, I.25.19-20

---

[24] Gyarus or Gyara, currently known as Gyaros, is a small (approximately 9 sq. miles), rocky and arid island in the northern Cyclades in the Aegean Sea. In antiquity Gyaros, although located just 60 miles to SE from Athens, had a reputation for desolateness and harsh conditions. It was a common place of exile during the Roman Empire. The island served as a detention place also in the 20th century, for the last time as late as 1967-1974 during Greek junta. Later on (until 2000) it was used by the Greek Navy as a testing range.

Define proper alternatives

Commentary: Life is all about choices – it's a very Stoic truth. All that comes up, all that we intend to do, and all that we confront we have to perceive as a succession of alternatives, as a life-long sequence of decisions to make. Let's keep to the example drawn by Epictetus: a law has been imposed that forces us to leave our place of residence. Such a law is a thing not within our power: we are in no position to repeal it or to exempt ourselves from it and, of course, it would be pointless to be angry at the lawmakers. We have to define a proper alternative: either exile would be such a ball and chain to us that we prefer to stay, break the new law and face the possible penalty, or the lesser evil for us is to take off voluntarily. We have to decide between the two: there is no third way to go. We either prefer to live by the law and leave or we prefer to stay put and face possible prosecution.

This choice from two options is ours and ours alone. We have to apply this scheme to every issue that life throws at us. We have to see our life as a sequence of such choices to make. A proper alternative is the only right way to describe our problems. Only a proper alternative doesn't tantalize us with an illusion of a third way, comfortable in appearances but disastrous in fact. To stay and to worry that we stay is equal to simultaneously maintaining that it's better to stay *and* that it's better not to stay. Similarly, to leave and to worry that we leave is equal to simultaneously maintaining that it's better to leave *and* that it's better not to leave. And this is nonsense.

If we yearn for our homeland lost, we yearn for two things specifically: for a certain place on the map and for the right to freely reside there. But the latter part is already gone: it exists no more, it disappeared. There is a new law in place, one which to the beauty or our Nicopolis, Rome or Athens adds a prohibition on our residence there. These two sides of the coin are now inseparable. We mustn't think of one of them and ignore the other.

Throughout our life, we will encounter plenty of such alternatives. Epictetus says that we may be banished from various cities one after another, and that we can be continually forced to change our way of life. Finally, the circumstances may put us into a situation which is totally intolerable: the island of Gyara is a symbol of this condition. What then? If it comes to such a pass, we must go back to fragment VII and call forth the ultimate meaning of a proper alternative, that is the choice between life and death. As always, it is our choice and ours only. We have the right to choose but we also have the obligation to not regret a decision once made. If we decide to die, we must die without contrition. After all, the life we are exiting is not a great life but a life on Gyara. It is so miserable that we actually prefer to quit it than to live it. And we do so of our own will, so what is there to regret?

Part three.
Do not be afraid!

How to overcome fear, anger and sorrow

Chapter 10

Anticipate mishap

The mind is strong enough to bear those evils for which it is prepared.

Seneca, *Of Anger*, III.37.3

In a nutshell: We need to imagine mishaps in advance, we need to think through and get accustomed to all adversity that may possibly happen to us. If we do so, no mishap will be a surprise. If a crunch time actually comes, it will be like a visit of an old friend. We will know what to serve and how to behave. We need to stay vigilant – both about dangers that we know are looming and about those which did not have the courtesy of giving an advance notice. In either case, we need to anticipate mishap.

***

We should always have the worst possible scenario in mind (fragment I). If we are honest with ourselves, we can predict every stroke of fortune (II). We need to anticipate both crushing blows as well as mere setbacks and we should visualize them all and well in advance. In doing this, we should not fool ourselves and we should not go the easy way (III). We should anticipate mishap, because it's all about narratives (IV), and because we don't want to be caught off guard (V). Anticipating mishap is not "pessimism" and it doesn't mean courting disaster to happen (VI and VII). Anticipating mishap is not equal to a simple assumption that a misfortune must happen (VIII). In order to be able to do this properly, we need to pay attention to the world and we need to put our imagination to work (IX).

Fragment I

All things therefore are to be reflected on, and the mind strengthened against whatever accident may possibly happen. Think upon exile, war, torture, diseases, shipwrecks. [...] The whole state of human affairs must be placed before our eyes. [...] Fortune must be considered in all her mischiefs.

Seneca, *Epistles*, 91.7-8

Commentary: These words of Seneca capture the most of the principle of anticipating mishap. We need to foresee all calamities and hindrances which may happen to us, *we need to always anticipate the worst of possible scenarios*. Every problem we may possibly face will lose its ominous power if we defuse it in our mind by preparing in advance.

There are two possible cases here, which we should discuss separately. One case regards the frequent position, such as when the situation may develop in multiple ways, but these ways are clear and well defined. We don't know what course the events will take, but we know what the options are. For example, there is a legal action pending against us and we will be either convicted or acquitted. Or, we made a bet and we are going to either win or lose. We don't know in advance what will happen, but we know what the possibilities are.

What will anticipating mishap mean in this case? It will mean preparing in advance for the development that is most disadvantageous. We need to imagine that we are already there, that *it* already happened. And we need to rethink and rehearse our reaction. What will it feel like? What will we think? What will we want to do? We have to think about how we will respond and react to the situation. We need a dry run, we need to try the whole situation out. We are awaiting a verdict in court? We need to imagine that we are already hearing the "guilty" formula. We need to defuse the worst, deescalate it preemptively, so that we may be safe and sound whatever happens.

The readers with mathematically-bent minds may be interested in the following type of an argument for this. A situation will either turn out to our benefit or to our detriment. If we assume that the more advantageous scenario happens, then we get either a mere confirmation of our assumptions or we get hit by disappointment (we get a zero or a minus). If, instead, we set ourselves up for disadvantage, then we get either a mere confirmation of our assumptions or we get pleasantly surprised (we get a zero or a plus). It's clear that the latter way of thinking provides a far higher net sum of expected happiness.

The court verdict and the betting scenario both belong to a type of a circumstance where there are just two possible ways for the situation to develop. Sure enough, there may be more of them. For example, we may take part in a game that can result in a win, a defeat or a draw. Regardless of whether there are two, three or more possible outcomes, we should always accustom ourselves with the worst one.

But what if we don't know all the possible ways in which the situation may develop? What if we don't see them, what if no one can see, predict or outline them? Most mishaps may seem difficult or even impossible to predict. How, then, should such things be anticipated? For an answer to this, we need to turn back to Seneca.

Fragment II

Disease, captivity, disaster, conflagration, are none of them unexpected: I always knew with what disorderly company Nature had associated me. The dead have often been wailed for in my neighborhood. The torch and taper have often been borne past my door before the bier of one who has died before their time. The crash of falling buildings has often resounded by my side. Night has snatched away many of those with whom I have become intimate [...] Ought I to be surprised if the dangers which have always been circling around me at last assail me? How large a part of human kind never thinks of storms when about to set sail?

Seneca, Of Peace of Mind, 11.6-7

Commentary: The reality is that we are never really ignorant about what kind of adversity awaits us. We just mustn't be blind, we need to observe life and the world we happen to live in. We must get to know and we need to honestly acknowledge the diversity of misfortunes that happen to people. We must be aware that we can become sick or get killed at every instant of our life. We must be aware that a fire can strike at any moment and that a storm or a war may break out at every instant. The world has tons of surprises up its sleeve, but they are neither infinite in number nor in diversity. If we take a closer look at history and at the lives of our fellow humans, we will quickly acquire a pretty good comprehension of what may await us. We simply need to remember that whatever happens to others may – at some point – happen to us.

We need to make sure that no mishap and no adversity come as a surprise. In order to ensure that, we need to visualize from time to time that this, that or the other mischance hits us. And we need to preempt it, we need to hit first. Once we launch a preemptive strike, we will get the upper hand over fortune. Let's go on the offensive, let attack be our defense! We thus gain additional points in this combat, the points that belong to the attacking side. Let's take nothing in our life for granted, let's din in ourselves that nothing is definite, let's keep in mind that we are entitled to nothing. Let's remember how rapidly and in how many ways our situation may deteriorate. Let's keep this constantly in mind. Doing this will make us happy and grateful that – at the end of the day – most of these bad things don't actually happen.

Yet, a doubt may come up here. "Sounds great, dear Stoics, but we are never able to conjure in mind *all* disasters and distresses that may happen to us. Even if possible in theory, in practice, this would consume too much of our time and energy. We'll always have to skip and omit something, and this will give the fate a chance to take us by surprise. Aren't we back to square one then?" No, we aren't. It's clear that we are unable to actively anticipate all possible bad things. We have to cherry-pick – but how?

We need to consider the probability and painfulness of possible misfortunes. The more probable something is and the more painful it is, all the more reason to anticipate it. It is worth to pause for a moment to visualize another quarrel with our coworkers, which is not a deadly turn of events, but a quite probable one. And it is worth to pause for a moment to visualize having caner, which is a painful blow, but rather infrequent.

Fragment III

> *If you are going to bathe, place before yourself what happens in the bath: some splashing the water, others pushing against one another, others abusing one another, and some stealing.*
>
> Epictetus, Encheiridion, 4

Commentary: The principle of anticipating mishap holds for wars, sinking ships, grave illnesses and other big-time occurrences, but also for the minor setbacks and obstacles that our life abounds with. Epictetus explains this with an example of a public bathhouse: whoever thinks that they will be able to just relax in peace, will be greatly disenchanted. A much smarter and thoughtful move would be to foresee all the mayhem and just assume in the first place that all will go awry. We should expect in advance that the public bath will be an overcrowded beehive, that it will be a dirty, rowdy and noisy place. Of course, reality is always at liberty to surprise us, but if we make proper assumptions, it will be nothing but a positive surprise.

In imagining the possible future adversities, we need to make sure that we don't miss any standard rule of a good visualization: it needs to be realistic, specific, personal and pertaining to our emotions. We must visualize the possible bad scenario specifically, accurately and in detail. Anticipating mishap is not about merely making a mental note that "bad things may happen." No. We mustn't stop at the level of words, we mustn't do it superficially. If we want anticipating mishap to really work for us, we need to actually make ourselves see and *feel* the bad scenario. People are jostling around us, f-words hovering in mid-air, someone is changing baby's diaper, pickpockets are lurking. We need to try hard to really feel as if we were already there. There is no point in cheating while doing this, because we would only fool ourselves. The harder we work with our imagination, the more efficient anticipating mishap will be.

Another way is to actually plan for the bad course of events, that is to sit down and specifically set up contingency plans and procedures for misfortunes. What are we going to do if we get stuck in that crowd? How much noise are we willing to withstand? Where will we go when it becomes unbearable? The same thing holds for our health: let's imagine how we will react if we are diagnosed with inoperable cancer. What will we set our mind to in the first place? How will we want to proceed? Anticipating mishap is not about generic and abstract rumination about bad things happening. It's about drawing up specific narratives and making concrete contingency plans.

That being said, we should discuss one more thing. Let's imagine again, that we underwent a medical exam and that we are about to hear the diagnosis. We anticipate mishap and we picture in mind that this most definitely is nothing short of cancer – stage four, a death warrant. Then we hear the diagnosis: stomach ulcer. Yet... instead of relieved, we are saddened. Why? What went wrong? Where is the rub?

It seems that we closely followed the principle: we visualized the worst-case scenario, one which dwarfs the seriousness of all other scenarios. Yet, it turns out that we *overdid* it. In depicting cancer, we overstated the case because it was not the cancer that we feared most. Deep down, we realized that this scenario, despite being the grimmest one of all, is still too improbable to care about right now. We slipped into an easy route: we anticipated something that was not hard to anticipate, because we didn't really believe in it. The point is simple: in anticipating mishap, we must rely on our own fear and anxiety as the most trustworthy indicators. We must nail down, as honestly and as accurately as possible, what we fear most. And we need to focus on anticipating exactly that what incites our greatest fear.

Fragment IV

Nothing is more bitter than long uncertainty.

Seneca, *On Benefits*, II.5.1

Commentary: Let's now think about *why*, after all, anticipating mishaps works. How is that even possible that we are capable of defusing an adversity by merely thinking of it in advance and preparing beforehand?

Let's start this way: as it was discussed at length in the first chapter, our life is all about narratives and nothing else. It is the narratives, not facts, things and events, that define us and determine whether we are happy or not. As with the previous example: when we are awaiting the decision of a jury in court it is not the verdict itself that makes us anxious (we don't know the verdict yet), but it's our narrative of what it may be. "Long uncertainty," the anxiety of waiting is the time when all our narratives go astray and awry, when our imagination goes bonkers and gets allured by whatever seems bleak and depressive. Our narratives run around like headless chickens just trying to catch upon something that may bring us down. The waiting itself is the worst. This is a truth confirmed by numerous testimonies of tortured POWs, sailors waiting for a forecasted storm and athletes who competed at the top level.

Anticipating mishap helps us cut through this imbroglio. If the anxiety of uncertainty is the most miserable part of the process, we can put it to an end by simply assuming that the worst possible thing has already happened. Thus, life will be in no position to surprise us any more – we will have taken away all its trump cards. The most that life can do to us now is to confirm our assumptions (which won't be anything unexpected anymore) or positively surprise us. Either way, we won't take any new hit. This is how anticipating mishap helps us tame the maze of our haphazard narratives.

Fragment V

> [Fortune] *is only terrible to those whom she catches unawares. One who is always looking out for her assault, easily sustains it. For so also an invasion of the enemy overthrows those by whom it is unexpected, but those who have prepared themselves for the coming war before it broke out, stand in their ranks fully equipped and repel with ease the first [...] onset.*
>
> <div align="right">Seneca, <i>Of Consolation. To Helvia</i>, 5.3</div>

Commentary: The logic of anticipating mishap may be set forth using military language. Let's assume for a moment that our life is constant combat (which is not a unusual concept in Stoicism) and we'll see how useful in it some basic notions from strategy textbook may be. First of all, there is the age-old truth that a surprise attack doubles the strength of the attacker. Thus, we should take care to not get surprised. We should never let our guard down. We should be constantly prepared for an attack, we must be on DEFCON 1 around the clock.

But how can this be done? There are two major policies here: a passive one and an active one. The passive policy involves staying vigilant and being aware that an attack can come at any moment and from every direction. We mustn't neglect anything, we mustn't fool ourselves that we are safe. We mustn't delude ourselves that bad fortunes turned away from us. The strike can come at any moment. A war make break out at any moment, we may have an accident at every single instant of our life. We may fall prey to foul play the very moment we finish reading this sentence. It's an eternal open season, now and always. Every bad luck that is possible may come at any moment. Thus, it'd be foolish for us to not be on alert.

The active policy, on the other hand, entails, first of all, that we regularly play war games in our mind and that we frequently carry out simulation of specific bad case scenarios. We should proactively and well in advance prepare plans and procedures for various emergencies. We should test and exercise our spirit and mind (and our body too!), we need to try them out to see how they behave if this or that happens. The well-known rule applies here: the more we sweat in training, the less we bleed in combat. The better we prepare for setbacks, problems and adversities, the less miserable and overwhelmed we will be when they hit us. Notice the similarity to the pre-flight safety demonstrations the flight attendants give in planes – whoever pays attention to them will have a great advantage should a real emergency occur.[25]

Another element of this "active policy" is to launch preemptive attacks. There is no denying that often times we do in fact know what kind of mishap to expect. If this is the case, we may – instead of just staying put in the trenches – go on the offensive. We may strike and wipe out the fortune's most powerful weapon of mass destruction, i.e., the element of surprise. If we know that something is afoot and looming (like death, like rubbing shoulders with people we dislike, like a defeat of our beloved but inept sports team) – why sit on our hands? Let's make a move, let's imagine what happens when death, distress and disappointment come around. Let's think about how we should and how we are able to react. In this fashion, when they come for real, we won't be rookies anymore. Instead, we'll have valuable experience under our belt. When we are challenged in reality, we'll just have to merely *repeat* what we already did in mind. And this is a true game-changer.

Fragment VI

> *You write, Lucilius, that you are greatly embarrassed, concerning the event of a process with which you are threatened by an implacable enemy. And you expect, I suppose, that I should persuade you to think better, and to acquiesce in the pleasing hope. [...] But I shall lead you another way to rest in security. In order to get rid of (or at least to alleviate) your present anxiety, I would advise you to suppose, whatever*

---

[25] The comparison with the pre-flight safety briefing was suggested to me by Dr. Michał Dobrzański.

> *you are afraid will happen, really to happen, and whatever the misfortune may be, weigh it well with yourself and tax your fear.*
>
> Seneca, Epistles, 24.1-2

Commentary: These words of Seneca lay out what is possibly the greatest problem and the most serious doubt one may have here. It amounts to a simple question: doesn't anticipating mishap equal to pessimism and doom-saying?

This is a fair question. The meat of anticipating mishap is, after all, to conjure all the worst possible circumstances and to actively pre-think all imaginable disasters. But isn't visualizing a calamity a calamity in itself? Isn't it embracing the very misery Stoicism promises to save us from? In other words, don't the pains of anticipating mishap outweigh its gains?

In order to quash this objection, we need to carefully outline the distinction between the ordinary gloom that poisons the mind of a nonstoic scaremonger and the actual anticipating mishap that the Stoic training includes. There are three main differences here.

The first one is the *purpose*. In Stoicism, we visualize catastrophes and we train ourselves in grim scenarios not in order to depress, harass and torment ourselves, but in order to "domesticate" adversities and make them our allies. To the contrary, ordinary pessimists rather dispirit themselves for the sake of dispiriting itself. For a pessimist, contemplation of bad scenarios serves to deepen their sadness and reinforce despair. For a Stoic, such contemplation serves as an insurance policy, to secure good life regardless of scenarios and circumstances.

The second difference is the *control* that a Stoic wields over narratives. Anticipating mishap is purposive and informed: it is *us* who poke and examine the possible hardships, not the other way around. We are the commander-in-chief, we are the one who authorizes and supervises the whole war game. We have the upper hand over the facts, things and events we consider. The position of aforethought allows us to remain in charge, allows us to put grim scenarios to work to our benefit. Such a proactive and preemptive effort has nothing to do with pessimism. There is a world of difference between this attitude and mere doom-saying, for the latter ignores all logic, reason and is clearly out of control.

Third, anticipating mishap differs from pessimism in regard to the time frame. Studying adverse scenarios and contemplation of calamities is not to take up all of our time. Quite the contrary. Even though we must make it a habit to stay vigilant, we still need to arrange it in such a fashion that only a portion of our time and portion of our mental capacity are occupied.

Anticipating mishap is not meant to pollute and cripple our life. Instead, it is meant to be a bitter flavor on the palate which improves the taste of the meal.

This point is particularly important to us. Pessimism tends to put us on a downward spiral and the bleak outlook on life, once adopted, turns itself into a vicious cycle of glum narratives. One vista of disaster and one meltdown are not enough? So, they swiftly yield another one. And yet another one. These are still not enough to beat us down? No worries, enemy narratives have an exorbitant birth rate. There will be no stop to them, unless, of course, we shake them off or somebody shakes us.

Anticipating mishap works exactly the other way around. Once we start practicing it, we will get immune to downward spirals. Instead, we will acquire a self-propelling device for erasing the influence of possible hazards. Also, we may expect a well-defined moment at which the preparatory work will be done and all the mechanisms will be ready. Once we get there, we will be able to cut ourselves some slack and diminish the frequency of contemplating adverse scenarios. The whole mechanism, once properly set in motion, will revolve on its own for prolonged periods of time, allowing us to get back to our regular thoughts and activities. This is just poles apart from pessimism, which does the exact opposite job.

Fragment VII

> *– Further, at the times when you are delighted with a thing, place before yourself the contrary appearances* [i.e. narratives] [...] *– But these are words of bad omen. – And some incantations also are of bad omen, but because they are useful, I don't care for this. Only let them be useful.*
>
> Epictetus, *Discourses*, III.24.88-89

Commentary: Another doubt that comes our way is this: doesn't anticipating mishap actually mean courting mishap? If we think about hardships in advance, don't we actually bring them about? Don't we invite them? Isn't it better to just avoid this ominous thinking?

The Stoic reply is that this is a completely groundless doubt, because there is no causal link here. Imagine the battlefield. Preparing a contingency plan for a retreat in case we are defeated doesn't undermine our chances of victory. In fact, it's rather the contrary. It boosts our odds because it is easier to fight when we know that there is a backup plan in case something goes wrong. This reasoning holds also in other cases. For instance, talking about a possible rainstorm doesn't influence the weather, does it? If we think that it does, we think magically and irrationally, we ignore strong empirical evidence, and we subject ourselves to that very fear that Stoicism intends to liberate us from.

"Think ahead – Stoicism prompts us – and predict the unfavorable course of events in advance. It neither enhances nor squashes the chances that the situation unfolds that way. Yet, in either case it will be to our benefit."

Fragment VIII

> *Whatever may happen, we must think will happen.*
>
> Seneca, *Epistles*, 24.15

Commentary: It's easy to misread these words of Seneca. How? For example, as follows. "We assume that whatever adverse thing may happen, it will most definitely happen. But if so, then it ensues that there is no point in making any long-term plans (let aside working on becoming better Stoics), because we will certainly get hit by a car tomorrow or the climate change will wipe us all out very soon (it may happen, so we assume it *will* happen). All that is left to do is crawl under a rock and die."

Needless to say, this is a caricature interpretation. Why? Because nowhere in anticipating mishap we are coerced to abandon common sense. Let's imagine that we are facing some important situation in our life, and we are not sure how it will turn out. Yet, we realize that, give or take, there is a 95 percent probability that a beneficial A will come about, and around 5 percent probability that an adverse B will hit. If this is so, we then need to organize our plans and decisions according to this breakdown of possibility. We must acknowledge the real but slim likelihood of B, but we mustn't overreact and jump the gun. We need to think about it in advance and draw up some procedures for this case, but a mere 5 percent chance of an adverse scenario can't *limit* our planning just to this worst-case possibility. We need to predict and plan for the worst, but we mustn't fool ourselves and forget about the 95 percent scenario. We need to approach the situation reasonably, with just the right amount of aforethought exactly where and when it is required. Not too much, not too little.

In other words, we need to deliberately impose double standards. There are odds of one to twenty that something disadvantageous happens. In the realm of thought, this is more than enough to visualize, think through and prepare for such a course of events. But in the realm of external actions and our daily conduct, the ramifications are much smaller. We need not to turn our life upside down just because of a 5 percent probability. Anticipating mishap must never be an excuse for resignation from our plans, it must never be a pretext for embracing a withdrawn, low-profile life. We need to remember that we may not live long enough to see today's sundown, but we can't waste our life on choosing a casket.

Fragment IX

"I never thought it would happen!" How can you think that anything will not happen, when you know that it may happen to many [...], and has happened to many?

Seneca, Of Consolation. To Marcia, 9.5

Commentary: This is a temptation faced by all Stoics in training. We diligently practice anticipating mishap, and then we are struck with something adverse but unforeseen. Easy it is at such an instance to let the guard down and start lamenting that the whole principle doesn't work because this particular twist of fate was impossible to predict (for who will deny that the more unpredictable an event is, the more likely it seems to happen?).

We can sympathize with this objection, but it doesn't hold. Diversity of available pains is not unlimited (we discuss it in the commentary to fragment II in this chapter and Marcus Aurelius mulls it over and over in his *Meditations*). The gamut of possible calamities is not broad enough to overwhelm our imagination. We just need to realize what the potential disasters are and we need to conceive a roadmap of them. Once we do so, we will be able to quickly refresh them in mind whenever the need strikes.

But how can we get to know the arsenal of weapons that fortune has stocked against us? Nothing easier under the sun! We just need to observe the world we live in, and we need to be open to what we see. We mustn't turn a blind eye to the bad things that happen to people all the time. Daily experience and common knowledge school us directly in this regard, while history, literature and news from all over the planet give us the indirect knowledge. Let's not play dumb on this. In Stoicism, the phrase "it has happened to others" doesn't mean "well, it didn't happen to me," but rather "it may also happen to me." Wherever, whenever and to whomever something happens, a Stoic always tries it on for size on herself.

Let's remember that our imagination is a mighty weapon, and let's make proper use of it. Our imagination tends to be our adversary, since it likes nothing better than to make up sugarcoated mirages and illusory pictures of utmost prosperity. But for us, this is a direct road to perdition. So we need to override our imagination! Let's force our imagination to work not on its own terms, but on ours and to our benefit. Let's urge it to visualize not sweet pipe dreams but rather let's have it present to us the hardships and calamities that other people deal with today and that we may be forced to deal with tomorrow. What will we feel if a doctor says that we will be dead by the end of this month? What will we do if a tsunami strikes in half an hour? What will we do if our phone dies on us today? These are the questions our imagination should toil at! This is the way to use it wisely and to our advantage. This way, we'll be far better off than if we continue to lure ourselves with the bed-of-roses images.

Chapter 11

Don't dwell on counterfactual scenarios

It is never possible for happiness and desire of what is not present to come together.

Epictetus, *Discourses*, III.24.17

In a nutshell: This is a complement to the principle of anticipating mishaps: let's not think about facts, things and events that might have happened, but didn't happen. In particular, let's not dwell on the benefits and advantages that didn't come our way. Let's not think about how the present moment could be better than it is. Let's not think of any prosperity that could have been endowed on us but wasn't. Let's not mull it over, let's not dwell on scenarios which didn't and don't take place. In particular, let's not daydream about scenarios which seem more alluring than the reality of our actual life.

***

We all like to think more of what we could have than of what we actually have (fragment I). This harmful tendency is at the root of a lot of useless suffering and sorrow (II). We need to avoid this (III), because this line of thinking leads nowhere (IV). Above all, we need to live the life we live, rather than vex and irk ourselves with narratives of something nonexistent (V). We shouldn't think about things we don't possess as if we had them (VI), and we should constantly keep in mind that having something now doesn't entail having it forever (VII). We also need not to disturb ourselves with comparisons to other people (VIII).

Fragment I

True, human nature is so constituted as to love nothing so much as what it has lost, and our yearning after those who have been taken from us makes us judge unfairly of those who are left to us.

Seneca, *Of Consolation. To Marcia*, 16.8

Commentary: Seneca's diagnosis is simple. We, humans, have a disturbing and self-destructive inclination to neglect what is there and to focus on what is not there. We overthink nonexistent things instead of thinking about what is in front of us right now. We love to chew the cud over things that we don't have, things that we lost, and things that we missed. There must be something oddly alluring in nonexistence, for whatever is counterfactual, it draws our attention with great and mysterious strength. Instead of enjoying what's happening now (or at least dealing with it), we prefer to grieve over things that didn't happen.

Let's take a simple example. Most of you, dear readers, live in lodgings of some kind. It may be a home or a flat, it may be an apartment or a hotel, it may be your own or shared, it may be owned or rented, it may be luxurious or basic, it may be comfortable or it may be a nightmare. Specifics don't matter here. What matters is the amazing facility in how our mind sooner or later takes living in a given place for granted. With great ease, we get used to what we have. With great ease, we turn to think about it as something obvious, something that just "is there," something that we are in some sense "entitled to." Or, in other words, with great ease, we turn to actually *not thinking about it*. We start to perceive this lodging of ours as something so evident and elemental that it is not even worth a thought. Consequently, the place we live in inescapably starts to be the point of reference for all comparison. Easy it is for us to think that it would be great to actually have a roomier, better-located lodgings with nicer furniture. Far more difficult it is for us to actually appreciate and enjoy the lodging we do have. And this is exactly what Stoicism wants us to learn to change. This bent of our mind is something we must get straighten up, this weird tendency is something we need to combat.

Surely, these examples are just examples. The principle of not dwelling on counterfactual scenarios is an over-arching one and it holds for everything. It holds for all that pertains to the material and non-material things, to our social standing and to our family relationships, to our way of life and to all our capacities and capabilities. The very same simple rule recurs everywhere. We swiftly and smoothly get used to whatever we have, we forget how great a bliss it comprises, and we start to crave for something more or something else instead.

Fragment II

> *Do you ask what it is that makes us forgetful of a benefit received? The desire of still receiving more. We reflect not upon what we have obtained, but upon what we still hope to obtain.*

Seneca, *Epistles*, 81.28

Commentary: This is how counterfactual scenarios yield misery. Let's imagine that we come to a banquet or any other kind of a formal social event. We take the assigned seat at the table and we start to look around. We often don't sit where we would like to be seated. The best, most prominent places, next to VIPs, are usually reserved for people above our paygrade. What do we do then? Instead of taking advantage of the seats we have and instead of enjoying that we even have them (remember: we might well have been among those who haven't been honored with an invitation to the party), we covet the better seats. It seems to us that we not only desire but we also deserve those seats. It seems to us that only there we would find a company of our peers, and that only there we would be able to fully savor and benefit from the event. Of course, nothing of this is true. And yet, the point is always the same: instead of being satisfied with where we sit, we are dissatisfied with where we don't sit.

This is an absurd and Stoicism is there to save us from it. Dwelling on counterfactual scenarios – in one form or another – is one of the greatest factors contributing to the net value of our misery. Who wants to live well and happily mustn't let their mind covet those better seats. It's impossible to be happy and, at the same time, to yearn for the things we don't have. This is how the Stoic diagnosis goes – in the remaining part of the chapter, we will turn to the treatment.

Fragment III

> *If you be in Gyara,[26] do not imagine the mode of living at Rome, and how many pleasures there were for one who lived there and how many there would be for one who returned to Rome, but fix your mind on this matter, how someone who lives in Gyara ought to live in Gyara [...]. And if you be in Rome, do not imagine what the life in Athens is, but think only of the life in Rome.*
>
> Epictetus, Discourses, III.24.109

Commentary: Our major concern (and our core strategy) needs to be this: let's not use the thought about *what is not there* to ruin for us *what is there*. Epictetus' example is a basic one: if we are somewhere now, let's not imagine being somewhere else.

It is common wisdom that none of us – magicians and conjurors may skip this passage – is endowed with the gift of bilocation. No one is ever able to be located in two distinct places at the same time. If we are somewhere in a given moment, it follows unavoidably that we are not anywhere else. Even if we plan to get elsewhere – in a minute, in an hour, in a week – it still holds that *at this*

---

[26] See footnote to fragment VIII in the chapter "Define Proper Alternatives."

very moment we are just here and nowhere else. In this given second, we are assigned to our current location, location, location. We are here. We are not anywhere else. Moreover, it's not just a coincidence that we are not anywhere else – it is fundamentally impossible for us to by anywhere else. To consider it is to consider not only something counterfactual, but something logically impossible. Why, then, would anyone want to do something like that? In particular, why would anyone think up a thing that is not just impossible, but impossible *and* sorrow-yielding to boot?

Stoicism teaches that whenever we daydream about being somewhere else than we actually are, we do it for the simple purpose of frustrating, saddening and sabotaging ourselves. Doing so means that we are unable to hold on to the thoughts that make us happy and, thus, that we are unable to be content with ourselves. When we are at Gyara, we imagine that it would be far better to pleasantly spend time in Rome, and when we are in Rome, we dream of a life in Athens. But we don't have to think that way! Nobody and nothing forces us to do so! We are perfectly capable of setting our mind on what is happening right now, with us and in front of us. No one can thwart us here, if we don't thwart ourselves.

The first step on this way is to realize that (as always in Stoicism), thinking about something doesn't just "happen" to us. It is always our own sovereign decision to choose this line of thought or another. No one can force us to think anything we don't want to think. Our freedom in this regard is absolute. It is only up to us whether we mindfully focus on what is there, or if we let our thoughts flee towards delusive and vicious mirages.

The second step is this. We must acknowledge the stark truth that a mental escape doesn't benefit us at all. For what good does it do to us if, while sweltering in the sun at inhospitable Gyara, we picture ourselves strolling in the shadow of the columns of the Roman Forum? It will bring about nothing but sorrow. We don't really expect such a thought to be a teleportation machine capable of transferring us to Rome in an instant, do we? And yet, we somehow subconsciously wait for this miracle to happen. It is necessary, then, to nail down this yearning and to sweep it away.

The third step is to purposefully avoid visualizing that Rome. As often happens in life, not the abstract and generic thought about being in Rome poses the greatest danger to us. The greatest danger consists in the nostalgia about our medium decaf latte at Piazza Navona. The devil is in the detail, and misery is in particulars. The particulars set our imagination in motion and fuel it. It is the particulars that push our imagination where we wouldn't like it to go.

Our imagination has very unfortunate default settings: it is inclined to drift away toward unreal places, bygone times and lost loves. We need to change these settings, we need to face the instability of our imagination with all our vigor, strength and resolve. No, we don't want it to be this way! We don't want useless narratives to shatter our happiness. We want bliss in the circumstances and conditions we actually experience. Thus, we need to override our imagination and force it to depict what *we* want, not what it wants. This is doable –Stoicism reassures us. This is desirable – whispers the common sense. Thus, let's cut it once and for good. Let's drop all these darned suggestions that it would be so great and so cool to be in Rome right now. Let's abandon the *would-have-beens*, let's stop confronting this imagined and aggrandized Rome with the actuality of Gyaros we live at.

If there is one rock-solid way to inflict misery upon ourselves – it is to admire the allegedly greener grass on the other side. Doing so guarantees to prevent us from feeling well in the life we have, and to deny all the bliss that we hope to achieve. What's even worse, we very easily end up in a free-fall here. Given that we are staying at Gyara right now, Rome is surely not the only place where we don't dwell right now. There is always an infinite number of places where we aren't. Let's not fight against infinity, since it is a tough fight to win. If we are challenged by infinity, then the only reasonable tactics are to *not* stand up to fight.

Fragment IV

If you should once say, "When shall one go to Athens?" you are undone. [...] Give up then all these things. – Athens is a good place. – But happiness is much better.

Epictetus, *Discourses*, IV.4.35-36

Commentary: Importantly, Stoicism doesn't persuade us that other places, other ways of life, distant cities and people we will never befriend are unworthy just because. Stoicism doesn't want us to lie to ourselves that Athens is not wonderful. Sure, they are. The simple point is that the wonders of Athens are detached from us, unattainable at the moment, and available only in our narratives and through our imagination. Thus, they are less important than the beauty of a good and happy life that we are able to live right now. No thing tempting yet remote is on a par with the present content of our life. The actual and present happiness in the hand is much more valuable to the Stoics than any hypothetical and distant happiness in the bush.

Why is that? First of all, Stoicism finds it impossible to be happy and simultaneously dream of a greater happiness. True happiness is inherently a self-satisfying, self-reliant and independent notion. It doesn't allow the idea of craving more. A supposed better life is indeed an enemy of a good life. Living well and happily forbids us to speculate whether we would live better and happier in other circumstances. Happiness is its own superlative degree.

The second reason for not dwelling on counterfactual scenarios is that such scenarios are unverifiable. We can adequately evaluate only that which is present to us. Only that which actually happens to us we can analyze in detail. Only that we can think and taste through and through. All other scenarios we know as indirectly as it gets: through hypothesis and would-have-beens. We will never know what something is *really* like unless it *really* happens to us. In particular, downsides tend to be hidden from our eyes: all the costs, disadvantages and shortcomings of the counterfactual. Alternate histories are always alluring. All the *other* courses of events (other than our own, of course) appear to be nicer, more colorful, more tempting and, all told, more attractive than that what actually happens. All the hidden costs and problems tend to show only after a given scenario comes to pass. In other words, we are inherently prone to a systematic misoverestimation of counterfactual scenarios. The grass is always greener on the other side, the job of the other always pays more, the not-ours enterprise is always more glamorous. Besides, it usually happens that a distant happiness melts in the air right at the very moment when we try to grasp it. Thus we land ourselves with nothing else but the cost of that grasping attempt – which is usually quite a huge one.

This argument may be well challenged by an imminent question, one which comes naturally to someone who is not easily satisfied with little. This question is this: why can't we have both? Why can't we be happy and still agree at the same moment that in some other circumstances we would be even happier? This is a fair idea, but it looks good only on paper. It will always fail us in practice. Experience teaches us that the very instant we start thinking about a hypothetical, greater happiness which is beyond our reach, the present happiness disappears mysteriously but infallibly. A single thought about the grass on the other side of the fence turns our side into a wasteland. Another point consists in the comparison itself. Even if the pursuit of greater happiness wouldn't necessarily negate embracing the present happiness, it always dwarfs it. Any present bliss – no matter how shining and thorough – will fade in the shadow of that allegedly greater, hypothetical bliss. This is a valid problem, because the Stoics don't want to offer us bleak bliss. They are interested in nothing short of the utmost, absolute and autonomous happiness.

Fragment V

> *No wrong has been done you by the loss of so noble a brother, but [...] you have received a benefit by having been permitted for so long a time to enjoy his affection. [...] There is nothing more inconsistent than that*

> *one should grieve that so good a brother was not long enough with them, and should not rejoice that he nevertheless has been with them.*
>
> Seneca, *Of Consolation. To Polybius*, X.1-4

Commentary: We are now entering a very important, yet still untouched territory. The central question here is quite simple: how does the principle of not dwelling on counterfactual scenarios relate to the axis of time?

The prime idea is clear. We ought to build our good life and happiness from that which is available to us at the present moment. This is our raw, input material to work with. We have hitherto discussed the scenarios that theoretically could be happening right now, but are not happening. Let's now turn to the case of something that could have happened in the past but didn't. Seneca provides an example of losing a brother, but we can discuss a less traumatic story. Imagine it is Sunday, January 3, 1993. We are a football fan, rooting for Houston Oilers in their playoff game against Buffalo Bills. Also, we had made a bet of 100$ that our team wins. Our money seems safe, as the Oilers have a 28-3 halftime lead and then an overwhelming lead of 35-3. But then the miracle happens and the Bills pull off the greatest comeback of all time, erasing this huge deficit and then winning 41-38 in overtime. We lose the bet. Should we start thinking like "Huh, I should have predicted that this will happen! I should have betted otherwise!"? No, we shouldn't. Such a line of thinking is not only ludicrous, but it also undermines the logic at the center of sports betting, which rests on the assumption that the result of every game is definite and that you can't retroactively change your bet. The thought that Oilers could have brought their advantage home serves nothing else but our self-inflicted misery.

Not dwelling on counterfactual scenarios may salvage not only our happiness and good life, but even our life itself. Let's imagine that after surviving a shipwreck or a plane crash, we get stranded on a desert island. We face a major struggle just to stay alive. As every survival handbook will assure us a hundred times, the key to survival is our mental attitude. We desperately need to concentrate on the present moment. Our only concern should be what is happening right now and whatever problem we have to deal with at the present. We must avoid any thoughts about the fact that no earlier than yesterday we slept wrapped in fresh sheets in a comfortable bed, while today we shiver in a rough-hewn DIY shelter, racking our brains for the last bits of knowledge form *Robinson Crusoe*. Accounts by people who have lived through extreme circumstances confirm that not dwelling on counterfactual scenarios turns out a necessary condition for survival. The castaway and the sports fan have something in common: if they invoke a counterfactual scenario, it is only to disempower themselves. Our attention gets scattered on a counterfactual scenario, it gets dispersed on it. Paying attention to counterfactual courses of events drives it away from where it belongs and where it is really needed. And where is our attention needed? Where is it badly required? In the state of affairs that is at hand, right in front of our eyes. This is where a shipwrecked person's struggle takes place, this is where all human struggle takes place.

The course of our life here on earth is just one of the (infinitely) many branches of variants. Some of them come to fruition, some of them don't. In this crooked timber of possible scenarios, we need not to go back to the withered variants which could have been more beneficial to us, but didn't play out. The game could have concluded otherwise, and our ship could have made it safely to its destination. But whatever could have been, it is not relevant anymore. It simply doesn't count. We cannot turn the clock back and we mustn't think as if we could. The final score and the shipwreck are facts.

Fragment VI

Think not [...] of what you have not, as of what you have.

Marcus Aurelius, *Meditations*, 7.27

Commentary: Our mind is wired in such a way that it is difficult for us to think indifferently of some distant good. It is difficult for us to just disinterestedly imagine that somewhere out there – in different places, different times, different circumstances – we would have been happier than we are right now. We have just two ways to go. We either don't think about it at all, or we do think and we dampen our mood in the process.

Obviously, Stoicism squarely suggests choosing the former path. If we don't heed this advice, we immediately find ourselves in a downward spiral of madness. Instead of being happy with what we have, we start thinking that we might have been born better, in a better country, with better health and better perspectives. At this point, of course, we have already abdicated all right to call ourselves happy. As mentioned, happiness is quite an exacting tenant of the soul. In particular, it doesn't tolerate cohabitation with a yearning for something which is not present. Once we allow such yearning to check in to our thoughts, happiness will check out unnoticed.

Alas, this doesn't even mean that the situation can't get worse. Surely it can. The next step on the way to perdition is to start thinking about some imagined benefit (money, fame, glamorous job, etc.), as about something we are certain to achieve soon, or, even worse, as something we are entitled to. The latter is one of the most despair-producing positions of all. Yes, we may well fool and delude ourselves that in some just and fortunate universe, we would be endowed with these things. But this line of thinking doesn't even lead to misery – it *is* misery. It is the gravest cemetery of all happiness and the ultimate death sentence on all good life. We cannot feel happy, if we feel wronged.

Thus, if we want to be happy and if we want to live well, we mustn't think of things that are not ours as if they were ours. Stoicism adds one more argument here, one based on the asymmetry of the situation. Let's notice: we can always be happy with what we have, because we always (well, in most cases) have *something*. What we have is always a limited and countable set of things. What we don't have is something completely different. The set of things we don't possess is the gross, uncountable infinity. If we decide to use it as a means to drown ourselves in sorrow, we will always do it with ease. The only lifeline here, the only way of saving ourselves is to simply *not want* to drown. The abyss of things beyond our reach is always greater than us, incomprehensible, impenetrable. We can't get to the bottom of it. The only coherent attitude to it is to stay clear of it.

Fragment VII

Of the things which you have select the best, and then reflect how eagerly they would have been sought, if you had them not.

Marcus Aurelius, *Meditations*, 7.27

Commentary: These words of Marcus Aurelius complement the previous case. We discussed earlier the mental attitude we should avoid, let's now talk the ways of thinking Stoicism encourages us to employ. There is a lot of symmetry here. Not only we ought to not think about things which we don't have as if we had them, but we also ought to think about the things we have as if we hadn't them. Do we live in an apartment? Fact. So, instead of wondering about having more footage or a better location, let's think about how many people don't have this magnificent opportunity of having a place to live. In particular, let's think about ourselves: oh, how much would we miss our humble abode if we didn't have it! Let's remember how great comfort it is to actually have somewhere to live. Let's imagine that because of a war, fire or bankruptcy we *lose* this very apartment we actually live in. Wouldn't it be painful? And is it not climactically blissful to *not* feel that pain right now? Let's view it the following way: losing our lodging is a piercing blow of fortune... which happens quite rarely. But we may reverse this rarity! A singular but infrequent pain can be transformed into an almost perpetual happiness of *not* experiencing it over and over.

In other words, the best way to actually appreciate our apartment is to constantly keep in mind how many advantageous turns of fortune have been necessary for us to enjoy it. Also, we need to remember how numerous and diverse are the possible ways of losing it in the future. All told, we need to direct our mind in the exact opposite way to what was discussed in the previous commentary. We needn't give in to the dangerous easiness with which we tend to quietly and quickly assume rights to things we don't have, but instead, we need to think about all we have as if it was given to us as a result of a highly favorable and implausible twist of fortune. This is the Stoic way to learn to appreciate what we have.

There is a nicely paradoxical tinge in this approach, since it is just the opposite of what the common sense suggests. The common sense suggests that the thought "it might have been better" entails a promise, or at least a possibility, of some great, although distant happiness. Yet, and to our daily disappointment, once we try reaching for it, we are immediately dissatisfied. Illusion of a greater happiness negates happiness in the present. Thus, we need to reverse our thinking. Stoicism proposes that we use certain grim thoughts as tools to secure our present happiness. In this way, we can employ unpleasant thoughts to work for our benefit.

Fragment VIII

> *Our rival was favored more than we were? Then let us enjoy what we have without making any comparisons. One will never be well off to whom it is a torture to see any one better off [...]. Have I less than I hoped for? Well, perhaps I hoped for more than I ought.*
>
> Seneca, Of Anger, III.30.3

Commentary: The gist of this passage is simple: let's not compare to other people. This advice is both timeless and timely (particularly in the time of social media). Let's not compare and let's not torment ourselves with the fact that certain fellow humans are better off in this domain or another. Comparing to others is plainly counter-effective: it will never bring any happiness, but it will always bring misery instead. But why does it work that way?

First of all, to compare oneself to other people is to use a wrong point of reference. Let's imagine some gruesome turn of events: e.g., we are in an accident and we have a leg amputated. It is a severe trauma and an extreme experience, which deprives us of many capabilities and opportunities. No matter how great a prosthesis we may get, we will never be as agile as able-bodied people are. If we have a leg amputated, it strikes us so painfully that "normal" people have exactly two legs, no more and no less, and that they can walk, run, come up the stairs and do all the things that the healthy majority does, for whom bicycles, stairs and pedals in cars have been designed. And if things turned out so unfortunately that we have only one leg – we are wronged, we are aggrieved, our position is worse than the position of others.

Yet, there is no logical necessity in comparing ourselves to those who have two healthy legs. We are by no means obliged to compare ourselves to healthy people and thus depress and debilitate ourselves. We are perfectly capable of not doing it. Besides, we are free to compare ourselves with whomever we want. In the eyes of the Stoics, someone who has one leg and grieves that they don't have two legs is on a par with someone who has two legs but moans that they don't have wings. A leg won't grow back just the same as we won't ever grow a pair of wings. Why be concerned about either?

It is within our power to adopt any frame of reference we want, to compare ourselves with anyone we want, and to view ourselves against whatever background we want. No frame of reference is obligatory. No viewpoint is forcibly imposed upon us. It is all our own doing and our own choice. Nobody and nothing mandates us to compare ourselves with bipedal people just as nobody and nothing mandates us to compare ourselves to winged angels. This is our own, autonomous and unrestrained choice. We are at liberty to avoid comparisons which are useless, detrimental or painful to us.

Moreover, in all essentials and in the longer run, *every* comparison to others will make us miserable. Every time we compare ourselves to others, we do nothing else but dwell on a certain counterfactual scenario, which – as we have been trying to demonstrate in this chapter – is exactly what we need to avoid. In sum, a good and happy life is not about dreaming of wings we will never have. Instead, it is about focusing on using what is available to us – using it in the most able, aware and creative way.

Chapter 12

Don't desire acclaim

Look at the [...] emptiness of applause.

Marcus Aurelius, *Meditations*, 4.3

In a nutshell: Let's not desire and let's not pursue acclaim. Let's not do things in order to gain recognition and praise. Let's trust our own opinions, judgments and evaluations, let's not rely overly on the respect or disrespect of others. Let's not count on the former, let's not be afraid of the latter. Let's quit the madness of the never-ending social recognition game.[viii] Let's *just do* what we need to do and what we can do. Whether we receive acclaim and accolades for this – it is not up to us. If we receive them, fair enough. If not, no harm will be done.

***

All which is important and valuable is important and valuable inherently – only in and of itself and not because of any outside opinion (fragment I). We shouldn't excessively rely on others, we need to know ourselves what it means to live well (II). We must be vigilant: the desire to be recognized and acclaimed can sneak into our hearts in a very cunning way (III). Acclaim is not desirable because all human praise is volatile (IV), because opinion of people who can't come to terms with themselves is not worth much (V), because human judgments are incoherent, which makes acclaim impossible to earn (VI), and because all judgments change over time (VII). All acclaim is transient (VIII), and it passed over many people who deserved it much more than we do (IX). Nonetheless, if we are not acclaimed today, it doesn't mean that we won't be acclaimed in the future (X).

Fragment I

Everything which is in any way beautiful is beautiful in itself, and terminates in itself, not having praise as part of itself. Neither worse then nor better is a thing made by being praised. [...] Is such a thing as an emerald made worse than it was, if it is not praised? Or gold, ivory, purple, a lyre, a little knife, a flower, a shrub?

Marcus Aurelius, *Meditations*, 4.20

Commentary: Everything that we deem good, beautiful or otherwise valuable, is always good, beautiful and valuable in itself, because of itself and for its own sake. No external evaluation and no outside validation is required in the department of values. Marcus' emerald is beautiful not because Marcus issued an imperial decree about its beauty. Instead, its beauty is an intrinsic quality. All outside assessments, all outside regard (or disregard) of its beauty is secondary and subordinate to that beauty itself. They are merely a reflected light, which has nothing to do with the essence of beauty.

This may be expressed in the seemingly tautological formula that "only the subject of evaluation is subject to evaluation." In other words, the qualities like "good," "bad," "just," "right," or "wrong" can be attributed only to what we assess. We need to disregard the social proof. It should be disregarded, because it relies too much on the merely biological fact that *homo sapiens* is a gregarious species. The intrinsic value of something and how it is assessed by people are two independent variables which don't affect each other in any necessary way. They may dovetail and they may diverge. All possibilities are in play. Valuable things may be praised or scorned, while worthless things may be either condemned or acclaimed. All options are open here and what we need to remember is that there is no logically necessary link here.

All praise and all criticism is essentially a derivative. An emerald doesn't get any more beautiful if someone praises it, nor does it get any uglier if it goes completely unnoticed. Everything that is important and valuable is inherently important and valuable – not because of some external validation. We need to think and act well and properly for the sake of thinking and acting well and properly, not for the sake of other people's approval. We are our own and only jury. And we are also the only ones responsible. It depends only on our decisions and thoughts whether these decisions and thoughts are informed, relevant and productive, or whether they are ignorant, pointless and useless.

Fragment II

> *As the sun does not wait for prayers and incantations to be induced to rise, but immediately shines and is saluted by all: so do you also not wait for clappings of hands, and shouts and praise to be induced to do good.*
>
> Epictetus, from dispersed fragments[ix]

Commentary: A clear guideline for conduct follows from what we said before. In our whole life, in all what we think, do and choose to pursue, we need to be the sun that Epictetus speaks about. We need to do what we need to do, no matter if other people like and praise it or not.[27] The sun radiates in all directions and it's not concerned if anyone appreciates its light. Has anyone ever seen the sun wait with rising until some tribute is paid to it first? Not once. Such detours just don't happen to our daily star and they surely shouldn't happen to us.

Above all, we need to avoid doing things which amount to nothing more than milking for applause, acclaim and acknowledgment. Yes, it's true that in all our decisions and choices we take many factors into account. Yes, it's true that conscious or subconscious desire to be acclaimed (or at least accepted) by others is usually one of these factors. The Stoic line here is unequivocal: the smaller bearing this desire has on our decision-making, the better. Of course, in an ideal situation, it would have no impact at all. We would be best off if we didn't at all let the opinion of others guide our train of thought. This is the ideal we should fix our eyes on. On the other hand, the anti-ideal is a situation where the desire to be praised and applauded becomes the main, or, even worse, the only motive actuating our decisions, activities and life. This is the *modus operandi* we need to avoid as much as we can. This is the negative chakra, this is the pole of the magnet which we should get repelled from.

Stoicism wants us to shine with our own bright light. It wants us to not be satisfied with pale, cast-back light, and with the empty glory reflected in the eyes of others. We need to do what needs to be done simply because it needs to be done – not for the sake of being rewarded. We need not to avoid fame and recognition but we also need not to seek them. Acclaim is just a thing not within our power, hence we should be indifferent to it. We ought to do our job and we ought not to care whether other people appreciate the outcome of our Stoic toil. The sun doesn't care what basks in its light, be it wastelands or flourishing cities. Its job is to shine and it is the job of those who inhabit the earth to use this light adequately.

Fragment III

> *Flattery, according to our quality, plays the fool with us and congratulates us upon our abilities.*

Seneca, *Epistles*, 59.13

---

[27] The entire chapter "Be Autonomous" is devoted to the ability of not relying overly on the opinion of others.

Commentary: Liberation from the yoke of praise and acclaim isn't an easy task. If it were easy, if it were achievable without toil, then this entire chapter would be quite useless. Alas, all too often we stick to the flypaper of sweet words that somebody utters. One of the reasons for this very strong pull that flatteries have on us is that they don't approach all of us in a single one-size-fits-all way. Sycophancies always infallibly know where everyone's weak spots are. Some of us are particularly touchy about their appearances, others about their intelligence, others have a particularly hard time resisting the flirty tricks and sexual overtones. However, we are all in the same boat. We all can be sure that we are always hit where our weakness is. Fortunately, this doesn't mean that we stand no fighting chance. Quite the contrary, once we know where the strike may come from, we aren't surprised anymore. If we examine ourselves carefully and if we find our vulnerabilities, we will know where the mental reinforcements are required.

Stoicism has nothing to do with blind faith in one's strength. It doesn't want us to assume – over-optimistically and groundlessly – that our willpower is infinite, that our resolve is adamant and that we will be always rock-solid in the face of temptations. The Stoic way to overcome our weaknesses is not by negating them, but by acknowledging them. Our road to strength is paved with self-knowledge. We need to know which wing is covered worse, so that we can immediately beef up our forces there and start strategic work over long-term improvement. Self-awareness is a starting point for all meaningful progress and all reasonable action. Is there any military commander worth her salt that wouldn't like to know what is the manpower, the morale and the munitions of the unit they command? The same rationale holds here. If we know well that we are particularly sensible to flattery coming from handsome eighteen-year-olds or from gray-haired professors (cross out the inapplicable), then we shouldn't naively and counterfactually assume that we are immune to them. Let's put it straight that this is our soft spot and let's act accordingly. If we don't want to get into the lion's den, we need to know where it is in the first place.

Fragment IV

> *And the things which are much valued in life are empty and rotten and trilling, and like little dogs biting one another, and little children quarrelling, laughing, and then straightway weeping. [...] To have good repute amid such a world as this is an empty thing.*

Marcus Aurelius, *Meditations*, 5.33

Commentary: Let's now have a closer look at human community, the society, the crowd, which is the source and dispenser of acclaim. Acclaim is – almost by definition – something that is doled out by a group of people. We don't say that someone is "acclaimed" or "famous," if they are acknowledged by a single individual or by a small circle of friends. A substantial number of people is essential here. Yet, being acknowledged, acclaimed and applauded by a vast pool of people isn't and can't be any relevant criterion. Why is that?

Because any collective acclaim is always volatile, illogical, and irrational. It is not governed by any comprehensible principle, it governs itself through contingency and chaos, through a short-lived amazement and even swifter oblivion. Its only rule is the absence of any rule. There is no pattern and no regularity. There is no reasonable prediction about who will be acclaimed and who will be given no attention. Every case is possible. People may acclaim and adore a brilliant writer, but also a tyrant or an abbreviated piece of nothing. This hierarchy may also be reversed in an instant and someone who yesterday was scorned by people today may be loved by them, while someone who is praised today may be held in contempt tomorrow. A collective judgment is neither reasonable nor justified. Also, it can be redone at any moment and in any fashion. There is no way to appeal against it, there is no supreme court, there is no arbitral tribunal. Once we deem "acclaim" something dear to us, we once and for all put the reins in the hands of things not within our power.

A group of people can't be a fair administrator of acclaim for one more reason. It simply doesn't care about being fair. People, when taken not as individuals but collectively, exhibit a strong tendency to flatten everything out and to understand everything as simple as it gets. Alas, people, taken collectively, are frequently reluctant – not to say hostile – to individuals who focus on higher purposes and aspire to greater things. The crowd usually applauds someone who is the embodiment of ordinary and low-key dreams and aims of the crowd. On the other hand, someone who is fixed and fixated on their own way of doing things is usually be stomped by the crowd. To chase acclaim, to think and to act in order to be acknowledged – this is how we get on the leash of unpredictable whims of the fickle crowd. These whims are, of course, impossible to satisfy. For this reason, Stoicism has unambiguous solution for us. We need to know ourselves what is important and valuable to us. Acclaim and lack of acclaim cannot be any guidelines for this matter.

Fragment V

> [A Stoic] *does not value at all the praise which comes from* [...] [people who] *are not even satisfied with themselves.*
>
> Marcus Aurelius, Meditations, 3.4

Commentary: Praise and acclaim are irrelevant unless they come from knowledgeable people. We follow this rule everyday: if we have a sore throat, we prefer to go to see a G.P. instead of a charlatan. If we need legal advice, we go to a lawyer, instead of asking a burnout whose former brother-in-law dropped out of law school a decade ago. Why should we make an exception when it comes to the most important skill of all, the skill of living well? This would be an unforgivable incoherence and inconsequence.

Everyone who desires praise and strives to be acclaimed tacitly admits that they are guided by people who are misinformed about what they are about to judge. Why misinformed? First off, because acclaim by definition means "acclaim by many" and it is unreasonable to expect that many people will be knowledgeable about the same subject at once. A large assembly of people is neither a good expert nor a proper authority. Second, at whatever trade we toil, we may be statistically sure that most other people have less expertise than we do in this field. As a consequence, why on earth should we care about the praises of people who know less than we do? Is a composer satisfied when her music is appreciated by folks whose musical knowledge is exhausted by the ability to tell loud music from quiet? Third, those who try to master their skills of living well (and particularly by following the Stoic principles) are always in minority. This is the final argument here, since it is impossible to live well while craving acclaim of those who don't live well.

In short: if we want to live well and happily, we can't heed the opinion of those who live as if they didn't care. Let's not have our life governed by people who are unable to govern their own lives. They have no interest in helping us, and they don't know how to help us.

One possible objection to this line of reasoning is this: the whole thing rests on a false premise, to wit, on a very negative assessment of human community. True, recognition and praise are volatile and they are rarely coherent or justified. Yet, there is often some kernel of truth in what people say and we shouldn't definitively turn deaf ears to that. It's likely that this way we'll get to know something about ourselves that we wouldn't get to know on our own. Finally, if we were to be on principle immune to the opinions of others, we would never be able to listen to what the Stoics say, would we?

There is merit to this counterargument, but this merit is off the mark. Stoicism doesn't demand that we be *completely* impervious to the influence of others and that we *never* listen to what others say. There is no denying that there are individuals out there who are capable, smart and worthy of following (the chapter "Follow Good Examples" is founded on that), but still, they are *individuals*. A *group* of people will never be able to become a role model for us. A large assemble will never prompt a solution good for us, because informed voices will always drown in mediocrity.

Fragment VI

Not even here do all agree.

Marcus Aurelius, *Meditations*, 8.21

Commentary: Crowd, society, an assembly of people are polyphonic entities. Their opinions are voiced by many throats and it is impossible for them to be coherent. A crowd never speaks in unison. Thus, desiring acclaim is – apart of all else – desiring something unachievable. But here is where the nonstoics may revolt again. "What is that supposed to mean? Such thing as *acclaim* exists undeniably, and there are people who won acclaim. How can acclaim be 'unachievable'? What's your point here?"

It is true that acclaim exists and that there are people who have been acclaimed and acknowledged. However, since a large assembly of people never articulates a single, specific and coherent voice, the very expression "to desire acclaim" gets drained of its meaning. For what does it mean that we want to be acclaimed by a large pool of people? It is certain that we will never be acclaimed by *everyone*. The full ride is always beyond our reach. But if it is so, if all we can reasonably dream of is being acclaimed by just a subset of people, there arises a question of *which* particular subset we are interested in. Do we prefer to be adored by young, pimple-faced fans, or by elderly critics? Furthermore, how many people do we need to appreciate us? If we can't have them all, how many is enough? Being adored by the half of our audience? Or do we need three-quarters of it? Do we mean being recognized in our hometown? Or maybe is it about statewide, nationwide, or worldwide recognition? Does "acclaim" convey the idea of thousands of groupies across the globe, or just a small circle of devoted fans?

Such questions are clearly absurd and they prove by contraposition that "to desire acclaim" is a very vague term at best (not to say self-contradictory). Regardless of whether we are private citizens, a life and soul of the party, rock stars or political leaders, we will never know if we already got "there." We will never know whether this particular acclaim we have already gotten is the one we longed for. In a word, to desire acclaim is to chase something that can never be caught, because there is no definition of "catching" it. It is to pursue a goal which we can never even know whether we have achieved it or not. In this sense, "acclaim" is impossible to earn.

Fragment VII

Consider [...] how they who, perhaps, now are praising you will very soon blame you.

Marcus Aurelius, *Meditations*, 9.30

Commentary: Human acclaim is not only illogical, irrational, unpredictable and incoherent, but it is also unstable and fleeting. Acclaim, once won, is only too happy to evaporate. From this fact originates the likely most famous and most often invoked argument for the worthlessness of acclaim.

Being praised by other people is very fickle and volatile matter. Acclaim, once granted, may be rescinded in an instant, without any reason, justification or right of defense. Acclaim is never definite. It is never to be taken for granted, it is never forever. Fortune can be reversed in an instant and favors can be unmade in a heartbeat. We may shoot to stardom from the abyss of anonymity, and we may just as swiftly be toppled. There is no rule here, there is no regularity, there is no order. Literature abounds with stories of people who rose to fame only to be immediately deprived of it and hung out to dry. History is full of such five-minute fads and each of us could provide an example from his or her own experience.

Acclaim cannot be secured once and for good. If we decide to desire it, we will never be satisfied because whatever we get, it will never be definite. Acclaim will always scream for additional confirmation, it will need to be won over and over again. Even if we get acclaimed, acknowledged and adored by other people, we will never feel safe about it. We will still have to strive to preserve it and the struggle for simply maintaining acclaim will be no different from the struggle to earn it. We will get ourselves into a vicious circle, which rolls us far from good and happy life.

Fragment VIII

The words which were formerly familiar are now antiquated so also the names of those who were famed of old, are now in a manner antiquated. Camillus,[28] Caeso,[29] Volesus,[30] Dentatus,[31] and a little after also Scipio[32]

---

[28] Marcus Furius Camillus (c. 445 – 365 BC) was a Roman military leader and statesman. He earned a great reputation in the wars against the Etruscans, the Volsci and the Aequi. He saved the Roman state during the Gaul invasion. As a result, he was dubbed "the second founder of Rome."

and Cato,³³ then Augustus,³⁴ then also Hadrianus³⁵ and Antoninus.³⁶ For all things soon pass away and become a mere tale, and complete oblivion soon buries them.

Marcus Aurelius, Meditations, 4.33

Commentary: No fame is eternal. Quite the contrary, even the greatest and most widespread fame will always seem just a brief and narrow effusion of interest, if put in perspective and seen in retrospect. Human memory is too flawed a material to build anything eternal. Over time new celebrities and famous figures will claim their share of the common imagination, and whoever is famous today will have to concede to them sooner or later. The heroes of the first war are replaced by the heroes of the second, after artists

---

²⁹ Presumably Caeso Fabius Vibulanus, Roman commander and three-time consul in 484, 481, and 479 BC.

³⁰ Volesus, born probably early in the 8th century BC, was a Roman warrior and ancestor of one of the eminent patrician houses.

³¹ Manius Curius Dentatus (died 270 BC) was a prominent Roman military commander and politician. He defeated the Samnites and the Sabines in 290 BC, he also led the Roman army during the Battle of Beneventum against forces of Pyrrhus of Epirus in 275 BC. Dentatus was famous for his modesty and simple lifestyle, while his nickname ("Toothy") originated from the legend that he was – allegedly – born with teeth.

³² Publius Cornelius Scipio Africanus (236 –183 BC), aka Scipio Africanus the Elder aka Scipio the Great, was one of the greatest Roman generals of all time. He was the commander during the Second Punic War, but also a great authority figure in politics and ethics. He conquered Spain and yoked it to Rome, he also defeated Hannibal at the Battle of Zama in 202 BC.

³³ Cato the Younger (95 – 46 BC) was another legend of Rome. He was a statesman, an orator, and a Stoic. His name became a symbol of moral perfection and integrity. He was an opponent of Julius Caesar and he committed suicide after the lost Battle of Tapsus, unwilling to witness the downfall of the Roman republic. According to the legend (and to Plutarch), having realized that his self-inflicted sword wound is not yet fatal – he tore his intestines open with his bare hands.

³⁴ Augustus (63 BC – 14 AD) was the first Roman emperor, ruling from 27 BC to 14 AD. He was the *de facto* founder of the Roman Empire, and he was posthumously proclaimed a god.

³⁵ Hadrian (76 – 138 CE) was a Roman emperor who ruled from 117 to 138. He was the third of the "Five Good Emperors" and a foster grandfather of Marcus Aurelius (late in his life Hadrian adopted Antoninus Pius and tapped him to be his successor, while he also demanded Antoninus to do the same with Marcus Aurelius).

³⁶ Antoninus Pius (86 – 161 CE) was a Roman emperor who ruled from 138 to 161. He was the fourth of the "Five Good Emperors," a foster child to Hadrian and a foster father to Marcus Aurelius.

and philosophers of one age, come artists and philosophers of another. Not only human memory passes, but also humans themselves pass. Those who praise disappear, and new generations take over. New generations who will have their own heroes to praise and their own legends to repeat. All acclaim and praise fade with time.

We may now propose a simple experiment for anyone who wants to see for their own how swiftly everything is forgotten. The probing factor will be your own memory, dear reader, and the whole experiment amounts to this. Sit comfortably, get a sheet of paper, and something to write with. A smartphone doesn't count – you need to be off the internet. Now, start putting down, in a column, names of all people who were born in the 20th century, and about whom you have heard for any reason and whose name you know. There is no other criterion than the century of birth and that someone's name rings a bell. They may be our family members, acquaintances, authors, scientists, political or religious leaders, people who are dead or still alive, anyone, no difference. Certainly, with the 20th century the list will mushroom in size and it will soon get too long to actually write it down. Point taken. Let's start another column in turn, for people who we know by name and who were born in the 19th century. Needless to say, this one will be much shorter. Let's then move back to the 18th and then to the 17th century. The specific result of how many names we fetch in each column is of course irrelevant and it depends on our background and historical education. Yet, the overall picture is an illustration of one undeniable message: the number of names we can draw from our memory drops dramatically as we advance into the past. It is enough to go just a dozen centuries back and the problem of finding enough paper for writing down all the names will soon be replaced with the problem of producing a single name. And if, dear reader, you don't agree with that, then be challenged to come up – without using Google of course – with a name of one person who was born in the 9th century of the common era. That's a hard one, right?[37]

---

[37] The wonder of Wikipedia allows us to make some back-of-the-envelope estimations. As of November 6, 2019, the English Wikipedia listed 5,640 people in the "2000 deaths" category (people who died in the year 2000). In the category "1900 deaths" it listed 1,759 people, and then 423 in "1800 deaths," 235 in "1700 deaths," 184 in "1600 deaths," 81 in "1500 deaths," 72 in "1400 deaths" and 38 in "1300 deaths". The numbers are clearly dwindling the further into the past we reach. Yet, it doesn't account for the global population change. Factoring that in (using population data from www.worldometers.info, accessed November 6, 2019) we arrive at an opposite conclusion: the further we reach back in history the *easier* it was to be "notable enough" to deserve a death mention in the 2019 Wikipedia. In other words, we, modern people are even less likely to be

This insight serves not only as a reminder about transience of all acclaim, but it also undermines one basic hope (or illusion) that people usually associate with fame. Fame is frequently treated as a prosthesis of eternity, and as an ersatz of infinity. We are all mortal and we will all pass away, but the memory of us, of our deeds, works and achievements may – at least theoretically – last forever. Except it can't. Acclaim has nothing to do with infinity, it gets nowhere near eternity. Instead, it is fleeting and transient. It doesn't last more than a human life, and it doesn't "make the name last."

That being said, we must point out, however, that we don't insist on this point just for the sake of musing on vanity. Moreover, we don't employ the "vanity argument" here. We don't argue that all earthly activity is futile and that thus we need to withdraw from it. This would be as nonstoic a conclusion as it gets. As always in Stoicism, a grim or seemingly pessimistic line of thinking serves as a stepping stone on our way to happiness and it is employed as a tool to overcome suffering and sorrow. In Stoicism, transience of all acclaim proves a positive point. The point is this. Since acclaim doesn't meet the expectations we have of it, why bother about it? If there is no gain in it, why take pains to earn it? There is no need in spoiling our good life with acclaim-oriented thoughts and endeavors. Once we understand and embrace that, we will have taken a giant leap on our way toward happiness.

Fragment IX

It is very possible to be a divine person and to be recognized as such by no one.

Marcus Aurelius, *Meditations*, 7.67

---

remembered because there is so many of us. For the year 2000 the mentioned 5,640 "notable deaths" and a global population of 6.143 billion turn out one person per 918,000. For the year 1900 we get one person per 1,099,000; for the year 1800 – one per 423,000; for the year 1700 – one per 385,000; for the year 1600 – one per 368,000; for the year 1500 – one per 180,000; for the year 1400 – one per 206,000; for the year 1300 – one per 110,000. This calculation goes through Late Middle Ages, but it collapses obviously once we reach far enough in the past that the numerator (number of "famous people remembered") drops to zero. The earliest historical person known by name (and whose existence is to some reasonable degree confirmed by modern science) was a pre-dynastic pharaoh Iry-Hor (or Ro), who ruled the Upper Egypt around 3200 BCE. Whoever came before him, whatever deeds were done, whatever acclaim was gained, it is, as Marcus Aurelius puts it, "smoke and ash and a tale, or not even a tale" (*Meditations*, XII.27).

Commentary: Many humans greater than us have been passed over in the lottery of acclaim. People who deserve all the kudos and recognition in the world receive nothing, while those who deserve nothing, soar time and again to the pinnacles of fame. How many heroic deeds have been perpetrated, how many wonderful ideas were conceived and didn't come to fruition, how many great books came and went unnoticed? Some sank into oblivion simply because there wasn't enough room for them on the pedestal of a given culture and they just didn't fit into the system of prestige distribution. Others were forgotten together with their whole worlds that have passed. We need to always keep in mind that earthly acclaim is not unfair only to us. We are all in this together.

In the chapter "You Are Never Alone" we will discuss in detail the idea that in every misfortune we are accompanied by fellow humans who suffer just the same. The same holds for acclaim: we are not the only ones left unrecognized. We may say even more than that: our desire of acclaim equals desiring injustice! It means that we demand that we be acclaimed while so many better than us have been disregarded. Thus, it is nothing short of chipping in our own two cents to the universal injustice of the world.

Fragment X

> *How long was Democritus[38] taken for a madman? Fame scarce took any notice of Socrates.[39] How long was it ere Rome knew the value of Cato.[40] She even rejected him and knew him not, till she had lost him. [...] How many are there, whose merit was never published, till after they decease!*
>
> Seneca, Epistles, 79.14

Commentary: There is a silver lining to the irrationality and illogic of acclaim. From the fact that we remain unrecognized today it doesn't follow that we won't be recognized in the future. There is no need to let our heart sink because everything is possibly still ahead of us. Maybe the day of our great breakthrough is yet to come. Moreover, this day may well come long after our death and we won't be there to witness it.

This last case happens all the time. Democritus, the first human of record to have come up with the idea that the world is made of atoms, was regarded a

---

[38] Democritus (c. 460 – c. 370 BC) was a major Greek philosopher of the pre-Socratic period. Together with Leucippus he advanced the first atomic theory in the history of European philosophy.

[39] See footnote to fragment VI in the chapter "It's All About The Narratives."

[40] See footnote to fragment VIII in the present chapter.

madman in his own time. Socrates, now acknowledged as the father of the entire Western philosophy, was sentenced to death in his hometown. All too many great people weren't recognized in their own lifetime (a modern era example: Johannes Vermeer, today widely considered one of the greatest painters in history, but obscure until more than two centuries after his death). Thus, if the most talented and remarkable humans faced misapprehension for such a long time, on what grounds do we expect to be recognized today? Isn't it an excess of pride?

We need to reverse our thinking in this regard. Instead of grieving that we are not recognized, we need to embrace and enjoy our splendid company. We find ourselves on the same bench with so many amazing people! And besides that, let's remember Democritus and Vermeer and let's keep in mind that die is not yet cast. It is, so to speak, forever not yet cast. The fortunes can change, even long after we die. We can't force people to acclaim us today, but we also can't predict whether they will acclaim us in the future. It is not within our power to secure acclaim, thus our best possible attitude to it is not to focus on it. We need not to desire it, not to demand it, not to dream of it. We need not to view the world through the lens of acclaim. None of our values should be defined in terms of acclaim, none of our goals should pertain to it, none of our endeavors should be driven by the desire to get it.

Finally, let's remember that not being focused on earning acclaim is a necessary condition for actually earning it.[41] If there is any acclaim in the world that is worth something, it is only the acclaim that wasn't pursued directly and for its own sake. Why? Because acclaim isn't a value in itself – it isn't really of much value at all. It is, at best, a reward that other people confer on us in recognition of our perseverance in pursuing our own values and goals (importantly, they need to be values and goals other than just "earn acclaim"). If any recognition by our fellow humans is worth anything, it is the recognition for something that was *not* done for the sake of being recognized. It shouldn't (hopefully!) surprise you, dear reader, that "don't desire acclaim" is not tantamount to "avoid acclaim." Stoicism doesn't compel us to stick to a low-key and low profile life, but it reminds us not to do things just for the sake of being adored by others.

---

[41] See commentary to fragment V in the chapter "Focus On Things Within Your Power."

Chapter 13

Adversities are challenges

[You should hold] *all misfortunes to be trials of your own firmness.*

Seneca, *Of Providence*, 2.2

In a nutshell: We need to perceive, approach and negotiate all stumbling blocks that life puts in our way as nothing else but challenges. Let's think of all evil as of a rival, who we need to defeat. In the face of a rising tide of difficulty and calamity let's not be like those who grieve and go down, but rather like surfers who take on the wave and get away unscathed. Or like soldiers, who stand up to the enemy and prevail. Fate is up to no good? Let our hearts react not with resignation and despair but with ambition and willingness to fight. And let our mind see in it not a proof of the ungratefulness of the world, but an exercise to solve.

***

We need to treat every adversity that we face as a challenge, or like a competition during a sports event (fragment I). There are deep similarities between these two situations (II). Adversities need to be handled as exercises to solve (III). Only the adversity which actually meets us right now is the relevant one (IV) and no adversity is a dishonor to us (V). Wrongdoings of other people may be a great drill for our character (VI), particularly when this wrongdoing impacts us (VII). Various earthly temptations are also akin to challenges and need to be dealt with as such (VIII). The proof of the Stoic way of life is the life itself (IX), which is why we shouldn't give up too easily in the face of a hardship (X).

Fragment I

[In every difficulty] *choose to make use of it as an athlete would deal with a* [sparring partner].

Epictetus, *Discourses*, I.24.2

Commentary: We need to take all crunches, difficulties, hard times and mishaps as challenges we are required to respond to. Every time something adverse happens, let's see it as a gauntlet thrown down by fate. Let's not assume (as we do so often) that it is a proof that the world is alien and evil to us and that a human being is powerless (and particularly that *we*, personally, are powerless). Nothing of this kind. Instead, let's regard it as a call to arms. Behold and be brave: fate defies us to put up a fight. We are boxers in a ring and when we cross gloves with our opponent, we are not meant to throw in the towel right away. We can take the field – and we may prevail.

"Adversity" serves as a blanket term here. It covers everything that may seem a mishap to someone, great tragedies as well as the little coarseness of the prose of life. The same principle which allows us to get over a life-threatening illness, might be just as well used to alleviate our fear of spiders (if we happen to fear them). It doesn't matter what the adversity is – all that matters is how we deal with it.

Fragment II

> [Athletes'] *strength and courage droop without an antagonist. They can only prove how great and how mighty it is by proving how much they can endure. You should know that* [Stoics] *ought to act in like manner, so as not to fear troubles and difficulties, nor to lament their hard fate,* [but] *to take in good part whatever befalls them, and force it to become a blessing to them. It does not matter what you bear, but how you bear it.*
>
> Seneca, *Of Providence*, II.4

Commentary: Dealing with adversities has a lot in common with sport competition. On the pitch or the track, we contend for victory, while in life, we contend for our good life. A pain we feel is like a fellow judoka who wants to bring us down. Disheartedness and sorrow are nothing else then weariness which comes down on a runner. An unexpected loss is just a goal scored by the opposing team. Do we really want to cave in? Do we want to get knocked down, do we want to not finish the race? Do we want to assume that having a one-goal deficit means losing the whole game? Such attitude is a big no-no in every sport and every coach would berate us on the spot. Do we want, then, to give up in life?

A disease takes us out. Unfairness of others makes us feel utterly alone. Brutal ways of the world rob us of what is dear to us. Injustice makes us disfavored. Low spirits dawn upon us, discouragement sinks in. All of these are nothing else but a question we are asked: can we deal with it or not? Will we let this break us? Will we curl up in a corner, weeping and wailing, or will we engage? The same hearty gumption which drives us in a fight against a live opponent should also fuel us here. But the stakes are much higher! We are not fighting merely for winning a point in a sports contest, but instead, we are fighting for our own good life.

Let's also note that every time we approach adversities as challenges the consequences of doing so reach far beyond the particular situation. There is a double gain in every instance. Every time we call ourselves to arms to confront ill fate, we also reinforce our capabilities to withstand any future confrontation. Every present struggle is also a training for a future challenge. The universal rule holds here: the more we sweat in training, the less we bleed in the field. The more we toil today, the easier the task will be tomorrow. This added benefit is a very important one, since (unfortunately!) no adversity is so great that it cannot be succeeded by a still greater one.

Fragment III

"Unhappy am I, because this has happened to me." Not so.

Marcus Aurelius, *Meditations*, 4.49

Commentary: The principle of treating adversities as challenges seems smooth on paper, but it may suddenly turn quite demanding when we try to put it to action in real life. We, humans, have the irritating inclination towards giving up instead of mobilizing in the face of hardships. Easy and painless it is for us to get to feel overwhelmed and lie down. There is something oddly pleasant to resignation. The state of mind of someone who is lost, defeated or withdrawn is quite simple, comprehensible and tempting. Paradoxically and subconsciously, we are more afraid of the effort twinned with a fight than of the suffering which is knit together with defeat. And this is precisely what we need to override. We need to create a habit and a reflex of making a stand against adversities. We need to kill our propensity for flying the white flag.

There is a trick which can be particularly helpful here. What is it? It is commonly referred to as "task-oriented thinking," which may be set forth as follows. Regardless of how difficult our situation is, we always need to think of it as an exercise to be solved and a task to be fulfilled. No matter what has happened, no matter how great or gross a mishap has befallen us, no matter how crushing the blow of fortune may seem, we need to perceive it as nothing else but a *job* to do. No matter our situation, no matter its seeming hopelessness, no matter the burden on our shoulders, we mustn't express it in the language of a harm inflicted upon us, but we need to describe it in the problem-and-solution language. There is no denying that this may be hard. When we receive a serious blow it is apparently an "organic" reaction to be shattered, shocked, and disabled. In order to pull ourselves out of this, in order to be able to take a grip on ourselves, we need first thing to translate the situation into a workable, task-oriented framework. The language we use always defines us, but particularly in dire straits it determines whether we are Stoics or nonstoics.

In Stoicism, we try to avoid exclaiming "I'm so unhappy because this happened to me!," "This is so grave a position to be in!," "This is unsolvable!," etc. Instead, we need to think and say things like this. "The situation is such and such, because X has happened. Given what I know, all-things-considered, and as honestly as I can figure it out, I have to choose between A, B and C. The arguments for doing A are this. The pains and gains of doing B are this. The pros and cons of sticking to C are as follows. The advantages and disadvantages of D are such and such. For these reasons, it appears most prudent and advisable to opt for…"

If anything adverse happens, e.g., if we get robbed, we need to overcome our primal urge to lament, and we need to jump to the simple question: what's next? Do we stand any chance of getting our stuff back? May we count on the police catching the culprits, or are they in the wind for good? Is insurance part of the equation? Can we do anything to prevent it from happening again?

Notice, that even if our property is irrevocably lost in the crime, even if the police don't move a finger, even if our insurance rips us off, all told, even if all our options are pretty grim, we still have a lot to win by asking ourselves the proper questions. There is great merit in stating the problem in the proposed way. Once we do so, we automatically and almost by default stop complaining and grieving. We get to think productively instead. It puts us in a position where our mental effort is channeled not towards grumbling and groaning but towards framing the situation in a constructive way, enabling us to cope with the problem and move on. Just this change of framework makes it all worth the candle.

Obviously, some circumstances may be so hard or tragic that the very idea of imposing upon ourselves the task-oriented thinking may seem meaningless, futile or even rude. But we should not be disheartened. Adversities, calamities and mishaps all share the same purpose, all aim at the same thing. They seek to disable us, they seek to disempower us, they seek to take us down. They are out there to knock us out from our active status and to snatch away our control over ourselves. We may say that they wish to undermine our confidence in our power over things within our power. Obviously, we need to resist this and one of the best strategies is to embrace the task-oriented thinking. Once we do so, we will force our minds into action. We will stop being a punching bag and we will again become quarterback in the game of our life.

Fragment IV

To my way of thinking no one has got a finer difficulty than the one which you have got.

Epictetus, *Discourses*, I.24.2

Commentary: The principle of holding adversities as challenges is worthy only inasmuch as we are willing to put it to practical use. In particular, we need to apply this principle *every time* we face a hardship and not just when it is convenient to us. This principle is tailored to combat the adversities which come to pass *here and now*. A good life requires us to deal with the problems which actually happen to us, not with problems which are easy to deal with.

Therefore, we mustn't think "Oh, why is it financial problems that hit me! I wasn't prepared for that! If I were to go to war and become a hero, huh, that would be a different story! That would be a whole different ball game! There I could shine! But poverty? This is not for me!" Or, "Why did I get piles? This is so disgraceful an ailment! If only I could have some other condition, preferably something more dramatic, or at least photogenic! Then I would show people what it means to bravely withstand a malady! But hemorrhoids? No amount of Instagram filters makes this look noble!" This is exactly the way of thinking we need to abhor.

That is proper to us which has happened to us. This is the sole criterion. There is no universal scale or generic norm that defines what kind of a bummer applies to whom. The only objective measure which ties people and their mishaps is reality itself. Whatever happens to us, it is ours, and there is no need and no way to appeal it. We have a right to remain silent in the face of hardship, but we don't have a right to pick and choose which hardship we prefer to struggle with.

There is no difference whether we just surrender in the face of adversity, or whether we surrender *and* think that we wouldn't have to surrender if the attack came in a different way. The only strike of fortune that matters, the only bad luck that is important, the only problem that is relevant is the one which actually comes upon us. Only this one is the real measure of our ability to live well. This is the only struggle we will ever be accounted for. No one will ever ask anything else. This is all that matters. It is a lunacy to complain that we were struck by a different kind of misfortune than we would prefer. If we say that, we prove to ourselves that we were partially and selectively prepared – which means not prepared at all.

We need to handle all adversities as challenges regardless of what these adversities specifically are, regardless of how, when they came to us and in what circumstances. Our readiness to stand up to them is worth nothing less or more than how much strength we are able to muster up right now. Our laptop dies on us and we lose some portion of the work we've been doing? Great. At least it means that all other, potentially greater disasters are at arm's length for the time being. All that matters now is to deal with the effing computer and try to retrieve or redo our work. All other problems are at bay, for now.

Moreover, fate is perverse and kinky. It loves to surprise us and it loves to hit us exactly where we are weak and when we are least prepared. Someone would withstand solitude hands down, but it turns out they have a loving and doting family, yet they have to deal with bodily ailments. Another would be tough in the face of physical illness, but their health is pristine yet their partner cheats on them. There is no rule here, except for that at the end of the day, we will always face what we want to avoid most. Everyone deals with the particular (d)evil they fear most.

Fragment V

> *"My nose runs." For what purpose then [...] have you hands? Is it not that you may wipe your nose?*
>
> Epictetus, Discourses, I.6.30

Commentary: As remarked in the case of hemorrhoids, *all* adversities are challenges, not only those that can be easily latched up to heroism, and surely not only those that are great and noble. We shouldn't hair-split and indulge in taxonomy of mishaps, though. We shouldn't waste our time on labeling them as elated or humiliating. All adversities are created equal. We need to treat them all alike, we need to treat them all as challenges, we need to stand up to them all.

We need to be particularly careful, however, when it comes to adversities that are small and ordinary. Misfortunes which seem mere bumps on the road, may be just as dangerous as the big ones. Why is that so? Our mind requires motivation and it is sometimes easier to rise to occasion when the bar is set inspirationally high. If a great calamity hits us – we react appropriately to the stimulus. This opens a disturbingly easy way towards negligence in the department of petty but frequent adversities. Truth be told, these small ball mishaps may have even a greater overall impact on the net output of our life than the problems that are great yet rare. Giving up on the fight against the things which poison us slowly and softly may be more deadly than being crushed on the spot by a singular big-time tragedy.

We need to make a stand not only against splendid adversities, but also against the mundane ones. Yes, it is glorious and clickable to win a top-stakes battle, to beat cancer, or to save a child from a fire. Yet, this is just half of the truth, and possibly the lesser half. Just as brave and just as laudable is to serve on the home front – to struggle with stomach ulcer, or to help a child with their homework. Not the hue of adversity but how we deal with adversity testifies to who we are. There is zero difference whether we slay a dragon in the public eye and to the applause of the world, or if we are adamantly cutting off its growing-back heads in a daily, anonymous toil. No adversity dishonors us – only resignation in the face of adversity may dishonor us. Nothing is disgraceful, if it is bravely dealt with.

Fragment VI

If someone exercises me in keeping my temper, do they not do me good?

Epictetus, *Discourses*, III.20.11

Commentary: Let's imagine that we have a burdensome neighbor, who turned his apartment into a drinking den, sold his furniture for booze and spends evenings by candlelight drinking moonshine with a company of his peers. Stoicism encourages us to regard him not as a pebble in our shoe, or a curse, but rather as a summon to contest. The same holds for unwanted guests, for unsolicited advice, and those fellow humans beings who pointlessly honk at us in a traffic jam.

Our goal is simple: to not lose our cool and not to send them all to hell. Our purpose is to not throw a counter-cluster of f-words at our neighbor, to not start yelling at our guests, and to not honk on everyone around us. But that's not all. Just not doing it is not enough. What is also needed is that we approach these situations as exercises – as a testing ground for our willpower, restraint and patience. Our troubled neighbor is thus useful to us. He is useful because he provides a great opportunity to rehearse our Stoic strengths and capabilities. The next time we overhear party noise from behind the wall, let's perceive it as a free coupon to our mental gym of Stoicism. Let's turn this miserable neighbor from a millstone into a stepping stone. He and his drunkard comrades are our sparring partner, which we may use at will, free of charge and without even them noticing. Let's not miss out on this opportunity!

Fragment VII

Wherein does a person who exercises before the combat profit the athlete? Very greatly. They become my exerciser before the combat: they exercise me in endurance, in keeping my temper, in mildness.

Epictetus, *Discourses*, III.20.9

Commentary: The infamous and irritating neighbor is surely a troublemaker, but his booze-fueled activities are not a barb aimed at us intentionally. He drinks because that pleases him or because that is what his addiction requires him to do. He doesn't mean to harm us (at least not yet). He becomes a trouble in passing and offhand. Alas, this is not the worse possible case. It may happen (and sooner or later it will happen to us, unless we are hermits or live on a desert island) that our dear fellow humans will act with the clear intent of harming us. It may be verbal, it may be physical, it may be with smaller or greater malice, but it surely will go down at some point. No one is so lucky that there is no one scheming against them, or at least against their happiness. How, in Stoicism, do we cope with people who intend to harm us?

Obviously, we need to treat every attack launched against us and every disservice done to us as a challenge and as a training session. If a hater trashes us on the Internet, we need not to take their words seriously but we need to hear it as "I, a hater, hereby insult you. Will you be able to turn deaf ears to it? Will you be able to keep your cool? They say that you've been doing some Stoicism, so why don't you prove now what you have learnt?" We need to strive to see nothing else than an exercise ground in every instance of insult, offence or slander. This should be nothing more to us than just another opportunity to work to improve ourselves. We benefit from it – and we can benefit in many ways.

First of all, in many cases, when someone derides us, there is at least a kernel of truth in what they say. Thus, even if just a portion of it is justified, we may learn something new about ourselves. Our opponent has made some effort to cast light on some of our flaws – why not turn their effort to our advantage? Second, slender may be pure slender, completely off the mark and devoid of any constructive criticism. Yet, the influx of insults and spiteful remarks is still a perfect occasion to take a close look at ourselves and to try to figure out where the chinks in our armor are. Whatever hurts us not only makes us stronger but also makes us smarter because it teaches us what we are sensitive about. Once we get to know what we are touchy about, we will be able to try to immunize ourselves to it. Third and not least, just as every other adversity, human viciousness is a great opportunity to exercise ourselves, it is a testing ground for our Stoic skills and strength. This is where we can really get to try how patient, calm and restrained we are. In these three important ways, we may say that whoever mocks us is our ally. They are our ally in our effort to make us better.[42]

Fragment VIII

> *If a lover is willing, and gives signs, and sends messages, and if they also fondle me and come close to me, and I should abstain [...] that would be a sophism beyond that which is named "The Liar," and "The Quiescent."*[43] *Over such a victory as this one may justly be proud.*

Epictetus, Discourses, II.18.18

Commentary: Hardship and debacles are not the only problems we need to treat as challenges. The same holds for the temptations which pose a treat to our values and goals. Not only an apparent evil can endanger our good life but also an illusory suggestion of some apparent good. The world and the humans populating it will frequently attempt to try to talk us into certain things, for example, that it is impossible to live well unless we live in a posh apartment, or that having an affair with so-and-so is necessary for happiness. Everybody is tempted according to their own taste, so if these examples don't suit you, dear reader, you may substitute for them the particular temptations which you are highly sensitive to. But whatever these temptations specifically are, whatever our weak spot they play on, it will always be easier to overcome them (if we want to overcome them!) if we approach them as challenges. So, let's not think "Dear God! I'd just love to be that popular on social media! Should I start some pointless shitstorm just to get some more following? Or at least post some more cat pictures?" Instead, let's think as follows. "Whoa! Let's try ourselves a little, shall we? Let's see who prevails, I or the temptation? Let's figure out who is stronger here!"

---

[42] We will speak more on the specific Stoic techniques for dealing with insults and other offences in the chapter "Be Autonomous," particularly in commentaries to fragments IX, X and XI.

[43] Epictetus refers to the liar paradox (if someone says "I lie" – do they say the truth or do they lie?) and the sorites paradox (if removing a single grain doesn't make a heap of sand a non-heap, then we may repeat the process enough times to "prove" that a single grain of sand still constitutes a heap). Ancient Stoics derided sophisms and paradoxes. They maintained that pondering them is pointless and that it doesn't contribute to the skill of living a good life.

Let's not sample the flavors we don't want to. Let our thoughts not be on a prowl for the apparent pleasure which the temptations fool us with. Let's not allow them to plant a hook in us. Instead of just caving in, let's think about it as of another opponent or rival we are to contend with. Instead of mindlessly indulging in the allure of temptation, let's appeal to our ambition. After all, we don't want to give up that easily, do we?

Fragment IX

You can judge of a pilot in a storm, of a soldier in a battle.

Seneca, *Of Providence*, 4.5

Commentary: You learn to know a pilot in a storm, and you learn to know a Stoic in an adversity. Stoicism is a system for living well and happily, from now, ever after. It is always important, but it is particularly important when a disaster, mishap, or a setback pop up in our way. An adversity is the best beta test for our ability to live well.

Stoicism is a philosophy of good life. It is a system for institutionalized happiness and it is an organized body of guidelines for proper management of whatever life brings. Thus, the only proper test of Stoicism is life itself. We shall know the Stoics by their deeds. We recognize and respect the Stoics based on the way they behave and what and how they do. Life is the only material in which we can get our Stoic skills to work and where we can test them. It doesn't matter whether one talks about the Stoic principles or not. What matters is whether one follows them. As Epictetus points out in his remarkable style: "[it is like] if I were talking to an athlete [and said], 'Show me your shoulders!' And then he might say, 'Here are my Halteres!' [training equipment]. 'You and your Halteres look to that!' I should reply. 'I wish to see the effect of the Halteres!'"[x]

We learn to know a pilot after the way she is able to steer a ship in heavy weather, not after her knowledge of theoretical complexities of navigation theory. In the same vein, we learn to know someone who tries to live well after their actual life, and not after their ability to eloquently preach on living well. Adversity is a particularly meaningful test. Someone who talks about living well is topped by someone who knows how to live well. Someone who knows how to live well is topped by someone who actually lives well. Someone who lives well when fate is kind to them is topped by someone who lives well despite adversity.

Fragment X

[Abandoning Stoic principles when presented with a difficulty] is just as if someone after receiving blows should give up the Pancratium.[44] [...] What then should one say on the occasion of each painful thing? It was for this that I exercised myself, for this I disciplined myself.

Epictetus, Discourses, III.10.5-8

Commentary: We need to keep firmly in mind that the whole point of Stoicism and the whole point of this book is to figure out how to live well in whatever circumstances we find ourselves in. Therefore, when an actual misfortune strikes, the last thing Stoicism expects from us is that we forget what we have learned. There is no point in studying Stoicism and not trying to apply it. It just makes no sense, it is a contradiction in terms. In particular, it is absurd to abandon Stoicism when it is most needed, i.e., when it comes to a test. Stoicism will never be to our detriment. Stoicism has a treatment ready for every human ailment, but it is up to us whether we want to administer it to ourselves or not.

The Stoic principles are the universal key to happiness. They help us navigate every possible worldly obstacle. They never let us down. Rather, we can let them down by not wanting to try them out. The fact is, every conceivable situation gets easier if approached stoically.

We mustn't surrender too easily in trying to follow the Stoic precepts. There is an untold power in what Stoicism teaches us, we just need to try it for ourselves. Yet, nowhere is it granted that this power is easy to learn and wield. Nobody is perfect: neither in Stoicism, nor anywhere else. It is always possible that we "receive blows," just as Epictetus describes it. Stoicism doesn't claim that the hits we take aren't going to be painful, discouraging or, sometimes, devastating. Surely, they may be and they will be, because this is the way of the world. These are the measures that the world takes to try to take us out. It is not within our power to ensure we will not receive these blows. Stoicism makes a powerful point though, that all of our good life, happiness and overall well-being hinge not on the raw fact that we receive these blows, but on the within-our-power decision about what we want to do after we receive them. It is our own autonomous choice whether we surrender and head-down clump towards our corner, or whether we raise our guard again and get back to fight.

---

[44] Pancratium or Pankration was a sporting event in the ancient Olympic Games. It was a blend of boxing and wrestling, one may say it was the ancient version of MMA.

This is the decisive point. This moment defines all. The decision how we react to difficulty is ours and ours only. No blow of fortune is strong enough to wipe out our right to decide for ourselves. Also, we need to remember that this is what we have trained for. We trained in order to be able to stand up to adversity and view it as a challenge. Do we really want all that effort to be in vain? The time to find out is *now*. The game time is now. There will never be any other test of Stoicism.

Chapter 14

Beware of treacherous constancy

Discordant feelings end by feeding upon their own bitterness, until the unhappy mind takes a sort of morbid delight in grief.

Seneca, *Of Consolation. To Marcia*, 1.7

In a nutshell: Constancy is not always a virtue and it is never an end in itself. The rationale behind every decision needs to be reevaluated every time the circumstances change and whenever new arguments emerge. We are not required to adhere to something pointless or painful just for the sake of mere constancy. It is better to change course – in us, in our thoughts, in our life – than to hold on to misery with asinine perseverance. A coherent narrative about ourselves is important, but a good life is even more important. When necessary, let's not hesitate to change the story we narrate about ourselves. Let's not be like the Japanese holdouts on remote Pacific islands, who refused to accept that the war was over, and continued fighting, some of them into the 1970s.

***

Treacherous constancy occurs when we embrace unwanted emotions or when we stick to useless activities just to prove to ourselves that we weren't misguided to turn to them in the first place (fragment I). Treacherous constancy also refers to a situation when we grow excessively accustomed to suffering (II), or when we acquire a pervert taste for it (III). We need to adjust to new conditions and environments (IV), but not to failures and defeats (V). It is not disgraceful and it is not a dishonor to reverse a decision if its parameters altered significantly (VI). Constancy may indeed be a virtue, but only when it is constancy about a reasonable resolve (VII).

Fragment I

We obey our first impulse, and then, although we may prove to have been excited about mere trifles, yet we continue to be angry, lest we should seem to have begun to be angry without cause. And, most unjust of all, the injustice of our anger makes us persist in it all the more, for we nurse it and inflame it, as though to be violently angry proved our anger to be just.

Seneca, *Of Anger*, III.29.2

Commentary: What Seneca says about anger holds for every passion, every sentiment, every emotion and every mood that rolls upon us, clings to us, and becomes hard to let go of. We find this mechanism in many cases and in many instances of life. It starts off with some external impulse, with a stimulus of some kind, which triggers our anger, sorrow, envy or any other kind of negative sentiment. Certainly, it would be best for us to not to embrace them in the first place, but we need to remember that until we become perfect Stoics (i.e., until never), the errors and blunders will be happening to us. Stoicism highlights that missteps are dime a dozen in all walks of life, and that there is no need to deny them. They are just a part of being human and they happen to us all. Our task and the Stoic challenge isn't to entertain some kind of a magical belief that they will spare us, but rather to learn how to deal with them stoically.

The point about negative emotions and evil sentiments is that we tend to remain in an unsettled state of mind even when the initial impulse is long gone. Furthermore, it doesn't happen merely because of our mental inertia. There is a deeper cause here. There is our *choice* at the outset of every prolonged period of bad emotional state. There is a specific decision that we made, wittingly or unwittingly. We decided that it would be more beneficial to us to last in misery than to withdraw from it. What's the rationale for that decision, if any at all? It's simple: we cling to a bad emotion because it seems to us that letting go of it would be the same as admitting that we didn't have to give in to it in the first place. It would mean admitting that we misjudged the whole situation and that we fell prey to impulses which weren't that meaningful after all. In other words, we persist in misery because it seems to us that pulling ourselves out of it would prove that we had given in to it too easily. This is precisely the deadly gridlock of treacherous constancy.

Stoicism condemns such a line of thinking as a lunacy and downright absurd. Since what is more loony than to remain angry just to prove to ourselves that anger is justified? It's as if we didn't want to recover just to convince the world that we are really sick. This is treacherous constancy at its worst, this is the calamitous need for continuity which costs us more than we can imagine. Someone did a disservice to us: offended us or cheated on us. We didn't keep our Stoic cool and we got swept away with anger, or drowned in despair. Fair enough, that happens to us all. But the game is not over. Indeed, the Stoic game is never over. We got mad, we got down in the dumps, yes, but this is past, which is not within our power and which is now irrelevant. Everything depends on what we do *now*, everything stands on the course of action we take now. Do we decide to persist in the mental letdown, or do we decide to try to get a grip on ourselves? The crucial first step on the path to recovery is to admit that we got seduced and trapped by treacherous constancy. We need to honestly admit that the reason we are stuck in a certain bad emotion is that deep at heart (or sometimes openly!) we agreed to it and we found it easier to suffer from it than to get rid of it. To confess that this is the case – this is the starting point for any Stoic improvement.

Fragment II

> *The weary and exhausted eyes,* [...] *to tell you the truth, are weeping more from habit than from sorrow.*
>
> <div align="right">Seneca, <i>Of Consolation. To Marcia</i>, I.5</div>

Commentary: Let's get back to that initial impulse which triggers our anger, envy, or – to keep to Seneca's example – sorrow. Notice, that usually our reaction is not only long-standing but also too strong, given the magnitude of the starting impulse. We are all pros at bringing ourselves to misery and then at letting misery fuel itself. What we are dealing with here is kind of an escalation of error, or a spiral of self-reinforcing, ill-informed narratives. This is what Stoicism wants us to escape from. But what is the lifeline it offers?

As mentioned, the first waypoint is to honestly admit what has happened. We don't get anywhere, we don't move on unless we acknowledge that this vicious mechanism governs us. We need to accept that it is there, in us. We need to accept that we persist in misery because we decided that to last in it is easier than to recover. Next, we need to face the fact that to stop weeping doesn't mean that we wept needlessly. To end mourning is neither an insult to whom we mourned nor a declaration that they weren't dear to us.

We need to adopt another way of thinking, one similar to the laws of classical Newtonian dynamics. Keep in mind: the default state of each body is straightforward motion at constant pace. Only exertion of an external force can knock a body out of this state. Just the same law should bind us: our normal and default state should be thorough and lasting bliss. Stoicism hands over two dozen principles for securing this bliss, and for making it immune to any external mishap. If we slip and let ourselves get knocked out of this constant happiness, these principles will swiftly bring us back to the initial happy state.

Fragment III

> *We ought to lay* [grief and sorrow] *aside as soon as possible, and restore the tone of our minds after their indulgence in that vain solace and the bitter luxury of woe.*
>
> <div align="right">Seneca, <i>Of Consolation. To Polybius</i>, 4.1</div>

Commentary: Here is the rub – there is certain *pleasure* that we take in misery. Certainly, this is not something we like to brag about and usually it's not something we would easily admit even to ourselves. But it would be a major dishonesty to deny that there is a twisted pleasure in being miserable.

Let's pull up from our memory a prolonged time of sorrow, which came after a loss of someone or something. Let's be honest: wasn't it the case that at some point we felt at home in our sorrow? Didn't it become convenient to us? Didn't misery transfigure itself into our new comfort zone? If we procrastinate misery long enough, we get to know it all too well – and there is a lot of truth to the saying that we like what we are accustomed to. An attempt to shake off the misery, to put it to end and to move on seems an insurmountable effort to us. Kinky as it sounds, an attempt to put a stop to misery appears to be more painful than misery itself! It would be like leaving a pleasantly shaded room and going right into the midst of a sunny and bustling street. We fear the confrontation with the magnificent, manifold and motley world. Misery becomes an excuse, good resting ground and a comfortable perspective for never-ending standing by. Misery pleasantly tickles our faculty of laziness – we withdraw. We get unburdened from a great deal of responsibility: we don't have to care about our relationship with the world, we don't even have to maintain it. We just stick to our guns of defense, we feel safe in the withdrawn and seemingly cozy misery.

This is why the tinge of "bitter luxury" is present in every sorrow. There are also other reasons, individual and custom-tailored to everyone (and usually known only to them), but the ramification is universal and binding for us all. Suffering may attract us. Misery may well wield a mysterious, mesmerizing and magnetic power over us. What we need to do is stop denying it. Once we admit this capability of our adversary, it will be easier to prevail.

Fragment IV

Someone comes and laments that they shall no longer drink the water of Dirce.[45] *– Is the Marcian*[46] *water worse than that of Dirce? – But I was used to the water of Dirce. – And you in turn will be used to the other.*

Epictetus, *Discourses*, II.16.30-31

---

[45] The Dirce spring was a spring in Thebes in ancient Greece.
[46] Marcian aqueduct, or Aqua Marcia, was the longest (57 miles) and the most important of the aqueducts that supplied ancient Rome with drinking water. It was known for its cool and pure water, which was called *aqua Martia* or *Martius liquor*. It was built in the years 144 – 140 BC by Quintus Marcius Rex (hence the name). At the end of the 1st century CE its daily supply was estimated to be around – in today's units – 50 million US gallons.

Commentary: These words of Epictetus clearly depict what treacherous constancy is and how senseless it is. Picture this. We were for some reason compelled to relocate from Thebes, where we used to hydrate ourselves with water from the so-called "Dirce spring," to Rome, where we may indulge in drinking water from the Marcian aqueduct. Clearly, such a transition may bring about a strong nostalgia for Thebes. We may stroll down the Roman streets and flog ourselves with narratives of how much better off we would be in Thebes. We face a simple alternative: we either change ourselves and our thinking, that is, we adapt to the new situation and strive to make the best of it, or we constantly think of bygones and we continuously suffer from being shackled to past habits. The latter option amounts to nothing else than useless, deceitful and treacherous constancy. This is how we pointlessly and harmfully cling to outworn narratives, which have originated in the past and were – possibly – useful at some point in the past, but now they are nothing else then ball and chain. Let's put it flat out: yearning and longing for facts of the past, for bygone things and events to which we cannot return is proof that we prefer misery over living well. It means that even the relatively modest price of accommodating ourselves to a new place of residence is one we are unwilling to pay for being happy. Isn't it, then, a sign that we disregard our own happiness?

Changing the source of our daily water holds of course in the literal sense (since people move all the time, as do expats, migrants and travelers), but it also has a figurative meaning. The ancient Stoics (and Marcus Aurelius in particular) would be eager to say that our whole life is nothing short of a perpetual transformation. Consequently, there will always be something to cry over, because there will always be something that we put behind us, be it location, a job, a way of life, or – just maybe – a discarded version of ourselves.

The last point is really important here. In reformed Stoicism, we desperately and definitely need to be flexible.[47] We need to be capable and willing to swiftly and painlessly adjust our self-narrative in response to the pace of changing circumstances. We need to be able to get in tune with them without losing a beat. We don't want to be miserable, in particular, we don't want to be miserable because our narratives can't keep up with the facts. Thus, if we can't change the facts, let's not hesitate to change the narratives (the narratives about facts, *and about ourselves*).

Let's give ourselves all the leeway in rearranging and realigning the narratives in whatever way we want. Let's not falter to start anew the story we tell about ourselves to ourselves. Have the circumstances changed? We are at

---

[47] For more on this see: Stankiewicz, *Does Happiness Write Blank Pages?*, 107-114.

liberty to follow suit. We may change our narratives accordingly. We may change *ourselves* accordingly. No one is looking over our shoulder. We are on our own. Let's exercise our right freely. Let's close the misery-yielding gap between narratives and reality.

It is within our own power to decide who we consider ourselves to be, what we expect from ourselves and what we hold ourselves accountable for. It is completely up to us to define this. It is also within our power to change this however and whenever we want. We don't answer to anyone in this regard. If we used to dream of a career of a professional athlete, or an artist, or an astronaut, if we gave it a try, but reality smashed our ambitions, let's not convict ourselves to a life sentence of a heartbreak. Failed ambitions and unfulfilled dreams needn't haunt and envenom us. The world is broad and wide and our former plans and dreams are not the only ones possible. Let's set up new dreams, new goals and new ambitions. Whatever happened in the past, it is not within our power to change it and it doesn't count anymore. Let the bygones be bygones. We can start anew at any time and we may completely redefine what we pursue. Our dreams are up to us, and just as much up to us are the standards against which we hold ourselves accountable. No failed enterprise has the capability of shutting down our highway to happiness – unless, of course, we grant it that power ourselves. It is always better to redesign our set of values and goals than to chew our ear off over not accomplishing something that we have set our mind on in the past. The lack of courage to redefine our values and goals when required – this is the pithy definition of treacherous constancy.

Let's take another example.[48] Let's imagine that a big party is coming up in two days, and that this is all that we had been thinking about for a couple of weeks. Everything looks great to us, we are almost ready to go, but, alas, on the night before we come down with a nasty flu. We lie in bed, we are aching, sweating and swallowing pills, and it's soon clear we are unfit to go. What will treacherous constancy mean in this case? It will mean cementing oneself to the plan of going to the party despite the new health situation. Somebody who lives treacherous constancy is a pro at not acknowledging that circumstances have changed. Someone who espouses treacherous constancy will lay wrapped in their blankets, will shiver or sweat, but they will still hold on to thinking about the party. "Oh, how screwed I am! I'm a fortune's fool! I will miss such a great party! I guess the guests are coming in now! Right now

---

[48] This example outlines also the common denominator between the principle of bewaring of treacherous constancy and the principle of not dwelling on counterfactual scenarios.

they are surely making the first toast! Poor me!" It is abundantly clear that whatever such a miserable person thinks, they will still be bed-ridden and the party will go on without them. It is also clear that the sole outcome of such thoughts will be pure misery. This is the bull's eye of treacherous constancy: refusal to update one's mind, refusal to adjust the narratives.

Adhering to a narrative once conjured, clinging to a decision once made, being adamant in the face of changing circumstances – all of these are neither absolute values nor ends in themselves. Quite the contrary, they are rather tools for upholding our values and achieving our goals, in particular, for achieving our core goal of being happy. Stoicism strongly disapproves – to put it mildly – of a situation in which tools become more important than the purposes they are supposed to serve. In this vein, we may ask what would a Stoic do in a bed-ridden situation like the one described before? The answer is simple: a Stoic will immediately rearrange her wishes. She will stop regretting the missed party and she will start wishing to lay in bed, take rest and recover. This is where the instant and lasting happiness is to be immediately found!

Fragment V

> [Do not have a habit of beginning] *with pleasure, and then like a bad athlete [...] being conquered in all the circuit of the games like quails who have run away.*
>
> Epictetus, *Discourses*, III.25.5-6

Commentary: Let's now turn to a particularly heinous case of treacherous constancy. The nth defeat in a row, a seemingly endless sequence of failures may lead us to assume that we are and always will be losers. We may be tempted to take cover under the dangerous flag of grim fatalism, under a banner which reads "I can't achieve anything, I can't accomplish anything, I will amount to nothing." We start to reject in advance all our ambitions and aspirations. We get to assume the doomed-to-fail roles by default, because they seem most fitting for us. We begin to not only expect defeats and losses, but also to actively *provoke* them, just to confirm our self-defeating narratives. Certainly, with this take any new disappointment does nothing else but it reinforces our doom-and-gloom approach and adds an extra layer of self-debilitation. This is exactly how a downward spiral is established and once we misstep into it, we easily go all the way down. We not only become sure that we never win what we want, but we even start seeing victory as undesirable. It becomes undesirable, because it appears a needless deviation, something which breaks the line, a note sung out of tune. We start cherishing regularity and continuity of our failures, it starts to seem to us that we *owe* our failure to the society and to the world.

Way too frequently we are akin to players who lose their game against a mighty rival because their knees tremble before they even enter the pitch. Furthermore and further-worse, we often don't even know that our flesh trembles! It often *seems* to us that we managed to adopt the winning mentality, it seems to us that we are going to take the world by a storm – while as a matter of fact we dream of a swift and straightforward defeat and going home. Thus, our challenge and duty is twofold. First, we need to avoid the fail-oriented pose *externally*, and second, we need to remove the willingness to fail from our very heart (needless to say, the second part is much tougher to do). The point is simple. It is better to learn with difficulty the role of a winner than to be proficient in the role of a loser.

Fragment VI

> *There is no inconsistency in giving up an intention which we have discovered to be wrong and have condemned to as wrong. We ought candidly to admit, "I thought that it was something different. I have been deceived." [...] There is no disgrace in altering one's plans according to circumstances.*
>
> Seneca, *On Benefits*, IV.38.1-2

Commentary: It should be clear already that a Stoic is *not* obliged to uphold all her decisions forever. In Stoicism, we perceive every decision as a function of certain circumstances and a derivative from a particular batch of empirical data. These circumstances and empirical knowledge are prone to change and our awareness of them may also change. New facts and new rationales may come to light at any moment. It is perfectly licit and stoically legit to change or even reverse a decision, if convincing and appropriate arguments arise. There is no dishonor in our effort to try to keep our resolutions up to date. There is no disgrace in including the latest developments in our judgments. A sincere and thorough reality check is not cowardice. Quite the contrary, it amounts to bravery. It is those who doggedly adhere to incomplete or outdated information that are chicken-hearted.

Let's imagine that we have been tapped for a commander of an army and that we have been assigned the task of keeping our national borders secure. We need to fulfill this task, but it is up to us *how* we do it – we have authority on this. It is at our discretion which infantry division goes where, and which fighter squadron is based on which airfield. Like often in the military and like never in Stoicism, we were told *what* to do, but we weren't told *how* to do it. It is clear that specific decisions depend on circumstances, on the general overview of situation and the intel we collect. We cannot conduct proper deterrence operations if we don't know whereabouts and the firepower of the enemy forces. Our activity needs to be based on that information. Above all, if the enemy shifts tactics, we need to follow suit. If the enemy used to press hard on the southern border, but right now, they are about to launch an attack from the east – we need to react adequately. Picture this: new intelligence comes in and we can see that an enemy offensive from the east is looming. We must regroup our forces, so that they are able to respond to the new threat. Imagine what would happen to us if we neglected this new information and kept our armies in the south. Just imagine us in court-martial. "Yes, I knew that the attack from the east was imminent, but I couldn't have beefed up our eastern defenses *because* a month earlier, I gave the order to allocate forces in the south." It is clear that such an argument wouldn't save us from the gallows. Justly so.

It is clear that such a commander will be immediately recalled, but it should be also clear that an asininely steadfast Stoic isn't worth her salt either. There are deep similarities here, and it is no coincidence that the ancient Stoics had a great penchant for military examples. We must never fail to update our tactics and strategies, as well as our goals and values, in response to the changing situation. In an ideal world, we would be able to adjust them in real time, but in the real world, it may be difficult due to the inherent inertia of reality. It is impossible to reevaluate and redraw all of our resolutions every minute. We need to rely on some *periods* of constancy, in which we temporarily waive our duty to rethink what we do. But this needs to be *temporary*: it cannot devolve into treacherous constancy through sloth or negligence. Also, of course, every time new circumstances strike or when the situation changes significantly, we need to take a step back and reevaluate everything from the scratch. Fetish of steadfastness, praising constancy as a false idol – these are huge obstacles on our way to well-being and they may be a great peril to our happiness. Holding on to a decision once made, yes, it is a valuable thing, but only if that decision is sound. A commander isn't held accountable for whether or not she changed or reversed her orders. The only thing she is held accountable for, and the only question she will be ever asked, is whether she managed to defend the country.

Fragment VII

When some people [hear] *these words, that one ought to be constant* [...] *they suppose that they ought without deviation to abide by every thing which they have determined. But in the first place that which has been determined ought to be sound.*

Epictetus, Discourses, II.15.1-2

Commentary: Every escape into treacherous constancy is also an escape from responsibility. After all, it is always easier to just hold on to the things that have been already decided and defined (by ourselves or by someone else in charge), than to rethink a situation. Yet, this is not the Stoic path. In reformed Stoicism, reason is a greater value than constancy. Sometimes it is good and advisable to alter our decision, sometimes it is good to stick to our guns. However, it is never good to mindlessly cling to something just for the sake of evading the effort of thinking. Constancy is valuable and useful when it is based on a relevant analysis of the situation and when it stands on a justified belief that our decision is right, and not on mere mental passivity. Not to mention that the latter is often nothing else than sloth disguised as perseverance.

The crowning example of this is when we hide behind a resolution once made, and then deliberately turn a deaf ear to any further arguments. Epictetus mentions[xi] an adept of his philosophy, who set his mind to starving himself to death for no apparent reason. It wasn't easy to talk him out of it, because, he argued, a decision once made cannot be reversed. It's hopefully clear already, from all we have hitherto discussed, that such a position is absurd and that it is a gross misreading of Stoicism (this is just the point that Epictetus makes). We need to avoid a situation in which a single failure to properly recognize the circumstances may shackle us to a disadvantageous resolution. We need to remember that we are not omniscient and infallible, and that every decision we make is of necessity precarious, since it is always based on some approximation, on limited, partial and unwarranted knowledge. We mustn't turn a blind eye to the necessity of amending and expanding our knowledge. Accordingly, we need to be always open to revise our past decisions, or even override them if necessary.

It never happens to anyone that a single decision based on a single set of circumstances suffices for the rest of their life. The world just isn't that simple and predictable. Instead, it is extraordinarily complex and highly chaotic. Our job is to not shrink from acknowledging and confronting this and, consequently, our every resolution needs to be subject to a never-ending process or reassessment. We need to drop all the mental sloth and slacking, we need to face the whirl of facts and events bravely and smartly. We need to steer away from the perilous reef of treacherous constancy.

Chapter 15

You are never alone

In everything which happens keep before your eyes those to whom the same things happened.

Marcus Aurelius, *Meditations*, 7.58

In a nutshell: Whatever obstacle fate puts in our way, we will always find footsteps of others already making it around and past it. Whatever happens to us, it has already happened to others. Realizing that and finding them is only a matter of seeing the big picture. Grumbling about loneliness in misery is simply a bias of the narrow view. Let's take a broad and fair look at the world, and we will immediately acknowledge our numerous companions in hardships. And let's not hesitate to take solace in that, for it is indeed great human solidarity. We find it, of all things, in suffering, but it is nonetheless mightily reassuring.

***

We should find relief in not being alone in any distress (fragment I). Whatever misfortune befalls us, it puts us in the honorable company of great people who have wrestled with just the same (II). In order to realize that, we need to take a larger (III) or simply the bird's-eye-view (IV). Also, encouragement comes not only from those who hurt *exactly* the same way we did. Subtle differences don't break the solidarity of sufferers (V). Where can we find these co-sufferers? History (VI) and literature (VII) are the most obvious avenues.

Fragment I

It is, therefore, a great consolation to reflect that what has happened to us has happened to every one before us and will happen to every one after us. In my opinion, nature has made her cruelest acts affect all people alike, in order that the universality of their lot might console them for its hardship.

Seneca, *Of Consolation. To Polybius*, 1.4

Commentary: We begin with a simple observation that the hardest on us are these misfortunes, distresses and adversities which we deal with alone. Why is that so? It's indeed a great topic, surely worth a book of its own. To avoid getting lost in it, we'll limit ourselves to just two points here.

First, this is a simple biological issue. In reformed Stoicism, we fully acknowledge and appreciate science. We don't think that science is *enough* to live a good and happy life, but respecting it is surely necessary for it. Science includes biology and biology says that we are a social species, thus we must accept the fact that we are social. We simply require the company of fellow *homo sapiens*. In this vein, it is no surprise that we appreciate that company especially in distress.

Second, coping with something alone also means coping with it single-handedly. If, on the other hand, we realize and accept that we are never alone, then we can share and get advice from others, we can use their resources and strengths, and we can have their shoulders to rest on. Thus, there is a great amount of soothing comfort in the acknowledgement that we are never alone – even if we don't agree with Seneca that it is *the* greatest comfort of all.

Notice that when we are in hardship or trouble, we – instinctively or magically – tend to close our eyes. We stop looking around, we switch our focus onto ourselves only. It's, of course, nothing surprising, because this is exactly how misery works: it fights us down and narrows down our horizon to our meager selves. One who suffers likes nothing more than to see but her own suffering. Yet this is obviously a trap! If pain keeps our eyes closed, we aren't able to see our pain-mates. Even if the same calamity hits two-thirds of humans, we nonetheless think that we are exceptional. We ourselves trap ourselves in ourselves and in our own misery. The distinctive signs of this pitfall are thoughts and words like "Why has it happened to me?" or "Why doesn't it happen to others?" This is exactly how we put our neck in the masochistic noose. Lament that we are the only ones in mishap makes us only more lone and unhappy.

How can we disencumber of this? The answer is simple: we always need to reach out to our companions in misery. But what does it mean "to reach out to them"?

First of all, there is the literal sense. If we get a serious medical condition we need to (after seeing a doctor, of course!) take to an online support group, talk to others who are down with the same, discuss the details, share thoughts, exchange opinions on the medicines and so on. It is deeply unstoic to think that we are obliged to suffer alone. Instead, we need to patiently build our safety net and then use it whenever needed. If our friend also suffers from a nasty flu, we need to call her and lift each other's spirits. We need to trade jokes over the unpleasantness of our shared malady and we need to complain together (a little). But we also need to think bigger than that. It's not necessary for us to personally know the human whose company is our solace. We don't need to know their name and social security number. The very awareness that they are out there may well be enough. It's reassuring to realize that at any given moment, there are scores of fellow people out there who suffer from the same thing. And this is exactly how we break the vicious cycle of it-is-only-us-who-suffer way of thinking. (Or is it really a "way"? It's more of a dead end.)

It is important to always keep in mind that whatever comes to pass, whatever illness we fall to and whatever misadventure we face, it's never true that it's unique to us. It's never "just us." We are alone in nothing. No misery is singular enough to allow that. Whatever happens to us, we can always find or at least think of someone who had to cope with the same. We have partners in every suffering – we just need to be willing to find them.

Fragment II

Fortune has not chosen you as the only one in the world to receive so severe a blow. There is no house in all the earth, and never has been one, that has not something to mourn for. [...] Do you see all these images which fill the hall of the Caesars? There is not one of them who was not [...] either tortured by grief for some of his family or most bitterly mourned for by those whom he left behind. Why need I remind you of Scipio Africanus, who heard the news of his brother's death when he was himself in exile? [49] *[...] Why need I remind you of Scipio Aemilianus, who almost at one and the same time beheld his father's triumph and the funeral of his two brothers?* [50] *[...] Why should I speak of the intimacy of the two Luculli, which was broken only by their death?* [51] *[...] Innumerable instances occur to me of brothers who were separated by death. Indeed [...] we see very few pairs of brothers growing old together. [...] Let no one be surprised at* [Fortune] *committing any act of cruelty or injustice [...] Such has Fortune always been, and such she ever will be in connection with human affairs. She*

---

[49] See footnote to fragment VIII in the chapter "Don't Desire Acclaim."
[50] Scipio Aemilianus (185 – 129 BC), aka Scipio Africanus the Younger, was a Roman politician and general, a consul twice, the commander during the Third Punic War. He was famous for capturing and destroying Carthage in 146 BC. When he was 17, he took part in the Battle of Pydna, won by the Romans led by his father Lucius Aemilius Paullus. Yet, two of his brothers coincidentally died roughly at that time.
[51] Seneca refers to Lucius Licinius Lucullus (118 – 56 BC) Roman politician and general, famous for his victories in the Third Mithridatic War, and his brother, Marcus Terentius Varro Lucullus (c. 116 BC – c. 56 BC).

has never shrunk from attacking anything, and she will never let anything alone. She will rage everywhere terribly.

Seneca, *Of Consolation. To Polybius*, 14.2-15.2 and 16.4

Commentary: Seneca invokes the Caesarian authority in a very curious manner. He points out that it is utterly dumb for us to think that fate may spare us what it doesn't spare even the Caesars. Even those at the heights of earthly power must deal with loss and death – why then think that we, the ordinary ones, will get to avoid that? We shouldn't fool ourselves. Instead, we need to enjoy ourselves in the company of kings and sages who, just like us, have been tormented by the loss of their parents, children, sisters and brothers. In other words: we not only are not alone, but we are in the same boat with many illustrious individuals. If they were able to manage, why can't we manage too?

Just as we said already, the consolation we find in the community of co-sufferers doesn't need to be understood in the strict, literal sense, e.g. when our spirit is restored by a phone talk with a friend who is sick of the same. Our fellow sufferers don't have to share our pain at the very same moment. They might have struggled with it in the past, or, just as well, they may be no longer among us. Shared suffering doesn't have to entail personal relationship, neither it needs to include temporal or spatial proximity. The key here is the involvement in the common fate of all people, past, present and future, the sorority in suffering, the universal togetherness, the global solidarity of us all.

Fragment III

Look down from above on the countless herds of people and their countless solemnities, and the infinitely varied voyagings in storms and calms, and the differences among those who are born, who live together, and die.

Marcus Aurelius, *Meditations*, 9.30

Commentary: If a hardship seems too great for us to bear, we may want to try to look at ourselves from above. Let's imagine (associations with air travel or with out-of-body experiences are welcome) that our eyeballs separate from our body, that they are lifted up high in the air, and that they look around. Let's have them take in the broadest sight possible. Let's observe all that comes to pass daily on the face of the earth. Let's think about all the countries and continents, let's think about billions of people inhabiting them. Let's embolden ourselves to drop the particularity of our point of view, let's look at our problems from above. This very shift of optics will help a great deal to ease our ailments.

We should think about everything that happens to us in the "context of the whole," that is in the context of all of humanity of which we are part. We need to keep that great human solidarity in mind – that huge family, bound together by its universal pains. Let's remember the sheer numbers of people that populate the earth. Once we learn to keep that perspective constantly in mind, we'll see that (if everything else fails to convince us) it's just statistically impossible that something which happens to us happens *only* to us. It would simply defy basic arithmetic. The human world is way too extensive and misadventures just can't help repeating themselves. We will always find a fellow tormented soul... trump that: we will always find a myriad of tormented souls. And when the high heaven collapses, it won't collapse on our head only. For we will have the heads of others just beside ours.

In saying all of this, we need to remember however, that – in reformed Stoicism at least – we don't want to invoke the "broad perspective" argument. What would that be? The "broad perspective" view is that when contrasted with the grand scale of human events, our own personal suffering means plain nothing and thus it needn't be bothered about. "For what mean our little mishaps and inconveniences when compared with the real human tragedies? What means our little flu when compared with cancer that others have to struggle with? What means the death of our dear pet cat when compared to entire families perishing in the war in Syria? Isn't it immoral, isn't it somehow offensive to bother about our trifles while immense calamities happen out there?" Even though this tough stance on ourselves is indeed a noble thing, and even though the "broad perspective" thinking may seem tempting or even effective, we don't want to wander into this territory. Why?

Speaking shortly, because it would be highly doubtful (or even dangerous) to authorize ourselves to try to "objectively" quantify any instance of suffering. Our goal is to combat misfortunes, not to put them on any scale or to measure them. Reformed Stoicism is quite reluctant to any all-embracing scale of anything, including suffering. Pain is highly individual fabric and we believe more – here and everywhere – in our personal judgment and responsibility rather than in a ready-made "objective" recipe which weighs and rates everything. Also, the "broad perspective" argument would be unfair in presenting reformed Stoicism to others, for it would demand telling *them* that *their* own pain means nothing. And this is a line we don't want to cross.

Thus, we needn't confuse "You Are Never Alone" with the "broad perspective" reasoning. The latter is about downplaying human suffering, about appealing to worse problems or to "the first world problems" (as the phrase goes). This is not something we should flirt with in reformed Stoicism. To the contrary, the former concept, "You Are Never Alone," is that looking around and thinking wide helps us find our fellow sisters and brothers in misery. Which is exactly the counsel we should heed.

Fragment IV

If you should suddenly be raised up above the earth, and should look down on human things.

Marcus Aurelius, *Meditations*, 12.24

Commentary: Let's now get back to the idea of looking from above. We already mentioned air travel and it was by no means a coincidence. It's unambiguous in the quoted passage that Marcus Aurelius yearned for such a literal "view from above," or, assuming that "yearning" is a bit unstoical, we may say that he understood the Stoic perks of a bird's-eye-view. Alas, he and the rest of the ancient Stoics were, obviously, deprived of such possibility. In this regard, we are far more privileged than them. Air travel is a commonplace today and we know well that even a single glance from a few miles' altitude confirms Marcus' intuitions perfectly.

Why does it serve our Stoic purposes? First of all, this glance from above means, by definition, looking from a distance; second, it allows us to see further and broader than from the ground perspective. (An important caveat here: in appreciating this we need to remember that, as discussed a moment ago, our problems don't automatically disappear simply because we take a different look. Misery resides in our narratives after all, and no airport security will stop it). The view from a height greater than our usual six feet above ground makes it easier to rip up the noose that anxiety tightens on us. And anxiety is indeed a cunning devil. It knows us well and it knows perfectly that the best way to get under our skin is to block the grand view of the world and to constrict our horizon to our narrow self. And this is exactly what we need to slip away from!

Also, looking wider and further means that we are able to see matters that have so far escaped our attention. There are many things on heaven and earth that we know about... but only in an abstract way. Technically, we know about them, but we don't actively keep them in mind. We rather keep them on the back burner of our brain. The whole plan now is to bring these quasi-forgotten notions and understandings back into the realm of our actual thinking. The point is to broaden our horizon, to raise our awareness. Not to actually learn new things, but to think of and mull over what is already in plain sight.

Let's take a basic example. We all know (the followers of the Flat Earth Society may skip this part) that out there, in other parts of the globe and well beyond the horizon of our everyday experience, there are distant cities, lands and states. And yet, we usually don't remember about them, we don't think every day about billions of people living on other continents. We live after all on the face of a round planet, and the curves of everyday occurrences veil the things that happen in the distance. The closest business blocks the view of the distant matters. It also deceives us. The closest business cries for our attention and it makes us think that proximity and availability makes it important... while in fact it might just be a minute trifle. A glance from above, from a different angle, allows us to escape this illusion. Looking from a distance allows us to rank matters according to their actual importance and not by the blind chance of random perspective. Thus, it allows us to carefully cherry-pick what actually matters to us.

Another vital example is temporal, not spatial, and it refers not to the entire planet but to the scope of our own life. The idea here is that in any instance of adversity or anxiety that we face now, we may want to think back about the problems we dealt with ten or twenty years earlier. Chances are this will immediately provide us with comfort through comparison. Why is that? Because it will – in most cases at least – remind us of the arbitrariness of all our trouble. In other words, we will be confronted with a different scale. We will immediately remember that we have this nasty proclivity to blow the current concerns out of proportion. This is the very specific bias of the present moment: we subconsciously assume that whatever we deal with *now* is quintessentially heavy, difficult and pregnant with consequences. Thinking back to errands and issues we had in our life 10 or 20 years earlier will remove this error from our mind.

Are we slammed at work these days? The deadlines are looming and no potable amount of coffee can make us meet them? Good. This is really a problem and stress. But let us think just for a second, what did we see as a great burden ten years ago? Was it something lighter, or heavier than the work thing today? It could have been either. Ten years ago we might well have been in chemo, fighting for life... or in elementary school, fighting over who is the coolest kid on the block. The nub of the matter is that rewinding the mental tape reminds us how absurd the fixation on our present problem is. The weird tunnel vision makes us overly concerned about minor problems just because they are present problems. The time perspective allows us to get rid of it.

In many cases, the headaches from 10 or 20 years back will seem ridiculous and laughable from today's point of view. And if it doesn't turn out this way, we can always go further back in time to really drive the point home. Let's be honest with ourselves. What was our main worry when we were in our early twenties? What were we concerned about when we were teenagers? These past chagrins will make us smile or even blush now. Yet back then it seemed like the whole world hinged on them! Doesn't the same paradox apply to what is going on *now*? Won't today's problems seem just as silly in a decade or so?[52]

Fragment V

> *Have your servants left you? And is that all? Some have robbed their master [...] some have made an attempt on their master's life by poison, others by a false accusation [...]. These, and all other mischiefs you can imagine, have happened to many, and will happen again.*
>
> Seneca, Epistles, 107.5

Commentary: Let's now get back to the idea of reaching out to our co-sufferers and the idea of community in pain. It's clear what Seneca is getting at here: that fellowship holds despite slight differences. The particulars don't matter much and achieving some kind of high-resolution in defining hardship shouldn't be our matter of concern. It's not our job to affirm a universal cosmic law that no misfortune strikes one person only. Our duty is to find the sense of tender togetherness in shared misfortunes. Let's then reserve a right to imprecision, let's give ourselves a license for deliberate blur and approximation. Let's readily look the other way when little variations come in sight. Common pain is there to unite us, not to divide us. Let's not stand in its way then.

In other words: it is indeed true that for our every misfortune there is a fellow human with the exact same affliction... but we don't have to necessarily search for them. Variations are acceptable and they don't undermine our solidarity. We are the only judges of our own pain, and the others are judges of theirs. Let's learn to accept these small divergences in the patterns of misery, let's get used to them. Our goal is to draw solace from the experience of shared human hardship, not to dwell on the minor discrepancies. Hardship is hardship and pain is pain, after all – no matter the circumstances and scenery.

---

[52] Notice that this approach doesn't conflict with the argument against the "broad perspective" discussed earlier. Why is that so? Because we are not contrasting our own hardships with the hardships of others, but rather with our own past hardships. In a way, our past self becomes our fellow co-sufferer.

Fragment VI

Consider, for example, the times of Vespasian.[53] *You will see all these things, people marrying, bringing up children, sick, dying, warring, feasting, trafficking, cultivating the ground, flattering, obstinately arrogant, suspecting, plotting, wishing for some to die, grumbling about the present, loving, heaping up treasure, desiring consulship, kingly power.*

Marcus Aurelius, Meditations, 4.32

Commentary: There is of course the question of where exactly we can find our fellow sufferers. The basic Stoic answer is pretty easy: wherever we fancy. There is no rule here and anything that works, works well. But in particular we may want to – and need to – look in the past, amid the past events and among those who passed away. The abyss of history behind us is so gargantuan and capacious that we can find in it every conceivable human misfortune, misadventure and misery. Let's just think about the countless crowds of people who came before us, let's just think about the endless continuum of adversities they dealt with. Let's consider for a moment all the libraries full of history books, biographies and memoirs. Isn't it just inane to think that our adversities and miseries are exclusively ours? That we share them with no one? Are we still so eager to say that we are alone in our misery and that it has been inflicted on us and us only? It is indeed an absurd assumption.

Marcus Aurelius advises us to repeatedly think back to the past, to the world that used to be, to the things that came to pass before we were born. Importantly, we need to dry run it regularly, not just turn to it when misfortune strikes. We need to constantly rethink the past – our personal past and the shared human past – to get ready for whatever hardship may lie in wait for us in the future.

Let's do it then. What past era, which century we need to get back to exactly? Whichever we are fond of. It may be the interwar period, it may the industrial revolution, the High or Low Middle Ages, or antiquity, or even the Paleolithic Age. It doesn't matter, we can pick whatever works best for us. We just need to conjure in mind something that we can relate to, something that speaks to us. This is how we overcome our inclination to think that the times and places we

---

[53] Vespasian (9 – 79) was a Roman emperor from 69 to 79 AD. He is famous – if for anything else – for imposing a tax on public toilets in Rome, which have allegedly led to the saying *pecunia non olet*, i.e. "money doesn't stink."

don't live in are fundamentally different than our own. It's quite a commonplace assumption that a hundred or a thousand (or ten thousand) years ago, human concerns must have been entirely different than today. And yet, the Stoic point is that this assumption is very superficial. It's only the scenery and setting, only the ornaments and decorations that change. The passage of time, the innovations of technology and the evolution of society do not alter the core meaning and metaphysics of human life. They don't alter the human condition, which is timeless. The same misfortunes and adversities which have been happening in the past, happen to us today and will happen in the future, regardless of varying historical actualities. We stand by our predecessors whether we want it or not. Just as Marcus Aurelius says – we, humans, always go about the very same human business.

Fragment VII

> *Place before your eyes entire dramas and stages of the same form, whatever you have learned from your experience or from older history [...] for all those were such dramas as we see now, only with different actors.*
>
> Marcus Aurelius, *Meditations*, 10.27

Commentary: Not only the bygone eras are the stockpile of our fellow sufferers – a rich supply of them is also to be found in literature and art. Let's remember this the next time we open a book or start watching a movie. Aside from just enjoying them, let's think about the worlds depicted in them and of the characters populating them. They are a live (even if fictionalized) testimony to what the life of others looks like. Let's follow carefully what happens to them, let's track their hardships and misfortunes. The literary conventions and artistic licenses aside, can we really think that the fates of humans portrayed there are really something else than our own lot? The Stoic answer is clear: no, we can't, and no, it's not. The incalculable value of these "dramas and scenes" is that they show that all the quintessential problems of human life, all the issues we have with ourselves and with the world, all these matters have always been and always will be the same. We are all in this together. We all share the same concerns and carry the same burdens.

Literature, film, theater, all these grand and small human stories are a perfect reminder to us that we are never alone. The ancient Stoics would even promptly say that the inescapable repetitiveness of certain topoi and motifs mirrors the fact that there is nothing new under the sun in our human world and that there was a precedent in the past for every errand we toil at today. A young and ambitious writer sits down to write her great, groundbreaking novel and soon the baffling realization swells up in her that she will never come up with anything radically *new*. And we are all in her shoes. No intrinsically new adversity or misfortune will ever happen to us, because everything has already happened to many. The book of human misery is comprehensive and tragic but it is not indefinitely long. Malignancy of the world and the cunning of fate have already exhausted themselves a while back – they won't be able to brew anything really fresh for us. They won't be able to come up with a truly surprising blow that hasn't already stricken someone. It all recurs, all the same, for all of us. Setbacks, hardships and calamities are all the same, all over the place, all over history. Only we change, the humans, heirs to that misery. We come and go, generation by generation, in a long succession of fellows who wrestled, wrestle and will wrestle with just the same sorrows. Let's accept the handshake from our countless predecessors and inevitable successors. It's a perfect way to both harden and hearten ourselves.[54]

---

[54] There is no denying that a quite conservative overtone rings at least in some passages of this chapter. Yet, beware of reading too much conservatism into Stoicism, even if it may seem tempting every now and then. Reformed Stoicism is quite universal and politically neutral. It can dovetail with a wide range of social and political views. I will speak more of it in the chapter "Whatever the World is Like, Be a Stoic" and also in the "Conclusions and Discussions" section. In short, we need to beware of the conservative misinterpretation of Stoicism. See also: Stankiewicz, *Does Happiness Write Blank Pages?*, 70-83.

Part four.
You in this playground

On our place in the world

Chapter 16

There is no point in flouting the rules of a game

For this is your duty, to act well the part that is given to you.

Epictetus, *Encheiridion*, 17

In a nutshell: Everything we do is participation in a game and every game is (by definition) played according to a certain set of rules. If we play basketball, it is clear that there is no point in kicking the ball and trying to convince others that this is the better way to go. The same holds for all else in life: entering a game is tantamount to accepting its rules. We either play by the rules, or we walk away and go play something else.

***

Everything we do in our life can and should be seen as a game (fragment I) which we play according to its rules (II), or as a role that we perform (III).[55] Our choice is simple: we either play it, or we seek another one (IV). Our task is to play well what we play (V), and every role can be played well (VI), even the role of a sick person (VII). We also need to play consistently and persistently (VIII).

Fragment I

> *This is just what you will see* [in those] [...] *who play at ball skillfully. No one cares about the ball as being good or bad, but about throwing and catching it. In this therefore is the skill, in this the art* [...] *So we should do: we must employ all the care of the players, but show the same indifference about the ball. For we ought by all means to apply our art to some external material, not as valuing the material, but, whatever it may be, showing our art in it. Thus too the weaver does not make wool,*

---

[55] Within this chapter and the next one I basically use the terms "game" and "role" interchangeably.

> *but exercises his art upon such as he receives. [...] When then you have received the material, work on it.*
>
> Epictetus, *Discourses*, II.5.15-23

Commentary: Whatever we do in life, whatever our job is and whatever we toil at, we may and should treat it is *a game*. Let's imagine a dinner at our disliked uncle's or some other mind-numbing family gathering (I guess we've all been there). The situation calls on us to swallow our doubts, put a smile on the face and take on a very specific role. It is a role of a good niece or nephew, who is just over the moon sitting through another dinner, who engages in small talk sincerely and happily, and who – OK, boomer – nods upon hearing for the thousandth time the same creepy-weird "back in the day" anecdote. Such an occasion is a certain convention and it's clear what this convention constrains us to do.

Stoicism tells us that this is how the world works in general. Whatever we do and whatever we get involved in, it's always like entering a certain game. Of course, not all of them are as tedious as that dinner is. In Stoicism, terms like "game," "role" or "convention" don't indicate fake dramas arranged to please our audience. They refer instead to the interface between us and the world, the basic pattern that defines and frames all our activity. "A game" isn't something artificial and imposed upon us. "A game," in the Stoic sense, isn't something that tames and thwarts the spontaneous and exuberant stream of life. A game isn't the opposite of the genuine, candid and organic matters. Instead, "a game" is a category that enables us to navigate reality, to create a roadmap which allows us to get around in our dealings with the world. Concisely, "a game" doesn't stand for "something which is staged and insincere," but rather for "something which is played according to some rules."

We can't avoid being engaged in games and we can't escape playing them – because *everything* is a game of some kind. Dinner at our uncle's is a game, but every other social setting is a game as well, including a good time with our good friends. Dating is a game, of course, and, on the whole, any conceivable communication and interaction with a fellow human being can also be seen as a game. The same holds for every entertainment and every job, for every leisure and every occupation – from a clerk and an accountant, through a businessmen, to a rock star and actor. Any partaking in any human business is a game (like in the elections, in a meeting, in a business venture), and every competition is also a game (like in sports or on the market). Every tradition and every custom is a game. All the Holiday-season-gifts-givings and all the Thanks-givings are games. In short, *all* features of our human reality and all aspects of our life may be described and perceived as a game which is played by a certain set of rules.

Having realized this, *we need to know the rules* of the game. This cannot be stressed strongly enough. We must be aware of the rules according to which human life plays out, we need to have a good grasp of them. This is our core and essential duty of which no one can absolve us. We must comprehend well both the world in general and the particular circumstances we find ourselves in. We must make an effort to get to the bottom of them – even if that effort is odious. We must never keep ourselves in the dark. We mustn't live our life blindfolded. Neither a random path nor a head in the sand is an option for a Stoic. Also, we shouldn't delude ourselves that the rules of the game are easy on us. They aren't. They are often tough, brutal even, and surely difficult to accept. But that's what they are and we need to accept them for what they are. We should accept them with no illusions, no fiction and no false hopes. To recognize the rules of the game as they are – this is the baseline of everything.

The next step is this. We need to understand not only what the rules of the game are, but also that they are totally arbitrary. They are not "objective," they are not "universal," they don't have any external, let alone rational justification. They are defined and decreed by no one. No one supports them, no one imposes them. They just happen to be the way they are and they are their own ground. The Stoic paradox here is that the rules are justified by nothing else but the rules themselves. They are what they are and they neither have nor need any rationale.

Furthermore, it's somewhat odd to demand justification for the rules. Let's think about a basketball match. The question *why* the players shouldn't kick the ball is... surprisingly hard to answer! When a child asks us about it, we feel baffled, because we need to explain to her or him something which is intuitively clear but intrinsically abstract. All the seeming explanations like "you shouldn't kick the ball because this-or-that" miss the point, because what the child is really asking is a deeper truth, namely, that the "the whole merit of a game consist in abiding by its rules." The only "real" answer to the question is that "if we allow kicking the ball, it isn't basketball anymore."[56]

This is also the Stoic merit. There is no point in flouting, contesting or undermining the rules of the game we play. Since there is no outside jury to define and ratify the rules, then there is no one we could appeal to. The twist is that there is no higher authority than the game itself – the game is its own

---

[56] This understanding of "a game" is akin to the concept of language-game in Wittgenstein's thought. A few key similarities are: arbitrariness of the rules, equiponderance of all games (there are no "privileged" games) and the idea that it is impossible to appeal to any external authority. We can reject a given game, but all we have left is just another game.

universum, it is its own and the only point of reference. Outside a given game there is nothing that could compromise the rules of it. Outside a given game... there are only other games!

Theoretically, flouting and disobeying the rules of a game doesn't need to entail any "appeal" to an outside jury in the hopes that they would annul these rules. We can try to take it into our own hands and simply bypass the rules, or try to forcibly change them. And yet, Stoicism reassures us, this would also be in void. Why? Because changing the rules means nothing else but obliteration of the game they define. This statement isn't just a play on words, it's not tautology or a mind trick. Let's picture it this way: a game is nothing but a portion of reality carved out by a certain body of rules. How are we supposed to deal with that? Our deal is *not* to criticize and contest how this space is carved. Instead, we need to decide whether we want to stay inside the part we are now in, or if we prefer to transfer to another one. The former option amounts to playing by the rules as they are, the latter – to switching games.

Fragment II

> *How long then is it fit to observe these precepts [...] and not to break up the play? As long as the play is continued with propriety. In the Saturnalia*[57] *a king is chosen by lot, for it has been the custom to play at this game. The king commands: "You drink! You mix the wine! You sing! You go! You come!" I obey* [so] *that the game may not be broken up through me. But if he says, "Think that you are in evil plight!" I answer, "I do not think so."*
>
> <div align="right">Epictetus, <i>Discourses</i>, I.25.7-9</div>

Commentary: Let's now imagine two teams entering a basketball court. Let's also imagine that it was only on the match day, right there in the locker room, that the coaches broke to the players the big news that the rules of the game are arbitrary. There are two possible reactions to this. Some players may feel free at last, released from restrains, liberated from a great deal of limitations. They may want to violate all possible rules just for show, just to manifest that they can. They may want to kick the ball around, punch each other and yell at the referee. It is plain, though, that such behavior will immediately annihilate the game of basketball. The very basic condition for the game to happen is that the players

---

[57] Saturnalia was a festival in ancient Rome, held annually in mid-December. Just as the name suggests, it was held to honor the god Saturn. An important part of it was a traditional period of heavy drinking and partying.

obey the rules, *even though* they know that these rules are arbitrary. And this is the second possible reaction. They may decide to abide by the rules, despite being fully aware that they are just a convention which makes the game possible. And those who espouse this second way: they are the Stoics!

The Stoics are well aware that the rules of the game are pure convention, but nonetheless, they don't feel compelled to break them. They don't disobey compulsively, the don't violate the rules just for the sheer joy of violation. They don't do it because they know that this would obliterate the game. And they need to have a game to participate in – so they needn't destroy it![58]

Let's consider a few other examples. If the family outings and dinners turn out to be unbearably boring, there is no point in bewailing them. These are just the rules of the game, and if we want to play it – we must follow the rules. If we don't feel like it, if it's too much for us – we need to hit the "abort" button. We need to give them up, we need to stop attending. Also, there is no point in getting churned up about the fact that the hookup culture is a mixture of sweet little lies, light-weight manipulation and a mouthful of cynicism. These are just the rules of this particular game, and if we don't accept them – we don't play it. We set out for a life of monogamy. Similar is the case of the start-up industry. There is no point in whining that it requires some sleazy salesmanship. This is just a rule of this particular game, and if we don't accept it – we don't play it and we take on an ordinary 9-5 job. Politics is also of no surprise. There is no point in grumbling that it requires players to be Underwood-ish a lot. These are just the rules of this particular game, and if we don't accept them – we don't play the game. We scale down our interest in politics to a sporadic newspaper and the occasional Twitter maelstrom.

And finally, the totalitarian example. All the Western guidebooks firmly, sternly and unequivocally warn travelers considering visiting North Korea that at some point of their trip they will be confronted with a necessity of bowing to a statue of the leader. Do as the Koreans do and whoever is not ready to do that, simply shouldn't visit North Korea. When we visit a country, we need to respect the local customs and obey the law – whatever we think of them. And

---

[58] The basketball game metaphor was coined by Dr. Tomasz Mazur. Another point is that the players who feel a compulsive need to break the rules of the game (just to show they can) – these are the Cynic philosophers.

in this particular case, it is painfully explicit why questioning the rules of the game would be utter and dangerous nonsense.⁵⁹

Fragment III

> *Remember that you are an actor in a play, of such a kind as the author may choose. If short, of a short one. If long, of a long one. If the author wishes you to act the part of a poor person, see that you act the part* [well], *if the part of a lame person, of a magistrate, of a private person,* [do the same].

Epictetus, *Encheiridion*, 17

Commentary: If everything we are engaged in can be understood as a game of some sort, the following question comes to mind: how come some of us play this particular game while others play another? In other words, what is the principle for the division of labor, what is the formula for assigning particular roles to various people?

This is where we turn to another great Stoic metaphor. *World and human life are a theater* and we are actors in it, playing certain roles.⁶⁰ All we do in life, all of our activity, every job and every type of entertainment, every social status and every political position – they are roles to be performed. There is an enormous diversity in them. They range from the roles of presidents to roles of everymen, from roles of the beggars to the roles of the choosers, from the roles of the super-healthy to the roles of the sick and dying. There is a colossal variety of possible roles, they cover the entire spectrum of human life, all the individual occupations and collective pursuits. But how are they assigned? Who makes the decision? Where is the deal cut about who plays what?

Not here. Not by us. In most cases, this issue is settled independently of us, well above our paygrade. We don't choose ourselves the roles of the healthy or

---

⁵⁹ For instance, Wikitravel puts it this way: "Most, if not all, tour groups to the [Democratic People's Republic of Korea] are asked to solemnly bow and lay flowers on one or two occasions in front of statues of Kim Il Sung when visiting monuments of national importance. *If you're not prepared to do this, do not even try to enter North Korea."* (Emphasis in the original, http://wikitravel.org/en/North_Korea, accessed March 2, 2017).
⁶⁰ This metaphor sounds of course like utter truism, because it's one of the most widespread cultural motifs. We need to underscore, however, that it seems a platitude *to us* – in the 21st century. Back in antiquity this thought was a refreshing novelty. Furthermore, according to some accounts, it was no one else but the ancient Stoics who actually invented this comparison.

the sick, the roles of the heirs to the throne and the roles of the victims of plane crashes. Who does it for us, then? A curious tenet of reformed Stoicism is that... this question can be painlessly swept aside. Epictetus, spinning out the theater metaphor, remarks that the roles have been provided by "the author" and we are not 100 percent clear how this enigmatic figure should be explained. In the chapter "Whatever The World Is Like, Be A Stoic," we will discuss at length that reformed Stoicism holds however we understand the world, which, in particular, means that we may understand this "author" however we please. It can be "God," fortune, providence or chaos, it can be historical necessity or class warfare, but whatever we think of it – it surely isn't us. Whoever we think the showrunner of the world is – it sure isn't us.

We may simply state that the assignment of the roles is not within our power and treat it accordingly. We shouldn't protest it in vain, we shouldn't complain, we shouldn't groan at unfairness. We shouldn't squander our time whining that the roles are misassigned. Instead, we should focus on what is within our power. And what is within our power? To *acknowledge assignment and act ably*. In other words, it is within our power to strive to do our best within the role we have... or to go find another one, which will work better for us (this second option will be discussed at length in the very next chapter).

Fragment IV

"My brother ought not to have behaved thus to me." No, but he will see to that. And, however he may behave, I will conduct myself towards him as I ought. For this is my own [part].

Epictetus, *Discourses*, III.10.19-20

Commentary: We shouldn't question the components and specific features of the game we are to play. As we will discuss later on, we have a right to switch games, but such a possible switch is an entirely either-or type of situation. We either accept a game fully, with all the responsibilities that come with it, with all the duties, costs and obligations, or we opt out and switch to another one. There are no half-measures and baby steps here. We can't sit on the fence, we can't be in between games. It is also impossible to try to transform or refurbish a game from within, it's impossible to accept *some* portions of it while questioning others. Such a way is a dead end.

Epictetus gives the following example. Let's imagine our brother, a member of our immediate family, who, theoretically, is supposed to have a tight relationship with us, a relationship based on love, patience, respect and mutual support. And let's further imagine that, despite these expectations, the brother turns against us. What can we do? What should we do? Surely, it seems a great injustice and ungratefulness, since brothers are not supposed to behave that way. But what about *us* and our own choices?

Being confronted by a brother, particularly if he confronts us for some minute or ridiculous reason or for no reason whatsoever, appears a lot like an unfair, unjust and undeserved situation. Yet, adopting such narrative is already a mistake. Thinking this way, pondering on how "unfortunate" we are, is useless or even dangerous, because it is nothing short of flouting and contesting the game that the course of events has written for us. If our very own brother throws a crazy tantrum at us, if he gives attitude, if he treats us badly, then *this* is our very game that has been scripted for us. Our game is to deal with a malevolent, ungrateful brother. But importantly, the responsibility for deciding how exactly we should deal with him... is a part of the game itself! Stoicism doesn't provide an exact, off-the-rack answer. It's up to us to decide whether we react patiently, with a big heart and understanding, or if we figure that an open quarrel will get him easier than another round of insincerity.

Stoicism reminds us that every interhuman relationship is a two-way street (it has two handles, as Epictetus says elsewhere[xii]) and our responsibility is to take care of our own end, not of the other's. Our brother is our sibling, true, but we are also a sibling to him! Our duty is to be a good sibling ourselves, even if the other party isn't particularly good in holding up their end. We can do our job and fulfill our duty however he behaves. We shouldn't focus on our brothers' lapses of judgment and wrongdoings, but on our very own duties and commitments.

Life, then, didn't give us lemons, but it gave us a bad brother. What we can and should do in this pickle is being a good sibling *ourselves*. How do we go about that precisely? As remarked already, reformed Stoicism is not about ready-made recipes and it won't bring us an all-set decision on a nice silky pillow. We must choose ourselves. We need to choose between being a tough-love brother or taking a softer, lax attitude. We need to make a choice based on our own intuition and previous experience with this particular brother. Yet, there is no point in denying what has happened or being saddened by it. There is no point in feeling mistreated. It is a stone-cold fact that our brother has been ungrateful to us – and we must deal with just that.

We need to not take offence at the brother, at all other people and the entire world. We needn't bear a grudge, we needn't complain that this particular situation has become our lot. We needn't be vexed that from all the humans on the face of the earth it is us who has been mistreated by a brother. This already belongs to the past and there is no use in arguing that he shouldn't have. He did. We won't annul the assignment of games which already took place, we cannot reject that we were invited to play the game as "a human being who has an ungrateful brother." What we need to do is to play it the best we can.

Fragment V

> [You ought to be] *attentive only to this, how you may fill your place with due regularity, and obediently* [...] [no matter if you are] *a prince or a private citizen, a senator or a common person, a soldier or a general, a teacher or a master of a family.*
>
> Epictetus, Discourses, III.24.96-99

Commentary: Here is the key. Whatever role is our lot and whatever game we play – we need to play it *well*. Our duty and our destiny isn't to whine and complain that this or that should have been better. Our duty and our destiny is to try to thrive within what's available. We don't need to stew about that things could be different, but we need to act and grow in terms of the resources at hand. Let's think about it this way: there is no challenge, there is no glory and there is no gravitas in groaning. It is easy to whine. Everyone can lament that a nicer game could have become their lot. That's the most effortless solution, which, to be honest, isn't a solution at all. What takes real guts is to try to play well the game we are actually in.

The crucial problem is to figure out what it actually means "to play well." As we may expect, reformed Stoicism doesn't provide us with a one-size-fits-all answer. The specifics depend on the current particulars of a given time and place. Every game has rules of its own and these rules are untranslatable into the rules of any other game. The terminology and the concepts that we need to explain what it means to play basketball well are useless in explaining good parenting or good sailing. "Doing a good job" in being a monk has nothing to do with doing a good job being a rock star. In this sense, it is clear that there is no universal code of Stoic behavior and that there is no uniform set of rules valid for everybody and in all games. Stoicism is about playing well, but not about defining the rules – they need to come from somewhere else. We may say that Stoicism is the ethics of playing well, but it is the world itself that sets the rules of the game.

Everyone should be judged only by how they play the game they play. It doesn't matter if it is prestigious or not, it only matters if one plays it well. We judge no one by what game they play and we judge no one by the rules of someone else's game. We never judge a president by how he or she sings rock ballads, and we never judge a president for just *being* a president. We also never judge a professional singer by how he or she conducts international politics, and we never judge a singer for just *being* a singer. We judge a president only on being a *good* president – for this is a presidential duty to be a good president. Just the same for a singer: we judge him or her for nothing else than for being a good singer.

This principle holds for all roles, games and occupations we take up in life. If we are presidents, it is our duty and obligation to be good presidents. We need to preserve, protect and defend the Constitution, we need to well and faithfully discharge the duties of the office on which we have entered. For these are the duties and obligations of the presidency. If we are a rock star, it is our duty and obligation to be good rock stars. We need to perform flamboyantly, we need to provoke scandals, we need to keep it real. For these are the duties and obligations of a rock star. And this is how it goes in any case. If we are teachers, it is our duty to be good teachers. We need to get to the school on time, we need to try to interest our students in what we teach. We need to make the best possible use of our talents and skills to educate our students. We need be a role model for them, we need to be someone they can respect. For these are the duties and obligations of a teacher. Finally, if we are "ordinary citizens" (if that phrase still means anything), it is our duty to be good citizens. We need to be decent and pay taxes, we need to abide by the law, we need to engage in the activities of our local community. In a word, we need to do all that our country and our civil society call us to do. For these are the duties and obligations of ordinary citizens. And if this is the game we play – we need to play it well.

Fragment VI

> *I must die. Must I then die lamenting? I must be put in chains. Must I then also lament? I must go into exile. Does anyone then hinder me from going with smiles and cheerfulness and contentment?*
>
> Epictetus, Discourses, I.1.21-22

Commentary: One point is that we need to play our game well, the other point is that *every game can be played well*. The theater metaphor holds firmly here – not only the leading roles can be played well, but the supporting roles too. Every role gives us just the same floor to dance on.

Epictetus provides three examples here, examples of roles which are apparently invidious and difficult to play. They are the roles of a dying person, of someone arrested and someone exiled. Stoicism asserts that these roles can be played well, just as the roles of healthy, free and respected people. Let's then consider them one by one.

The role of a dying person is just the same test in our skill of living a good life as any other role is.[61] And yet, it is also very particular because we may be certain beyond the shadow of a doubt that this single role will become ours, someday. We are sure that we don't get passed over. Disease, prison, exile and other delights of life may well elude us, but death won't. In this vein, it would be highly short-sighted to allege that it is impossible to cope well with what we will all have to cope with.

But what does it mean "to cope well" in this respect? The standards are in plain sight (which doesn't mean they are easy to uphold). If we are about to die, then we needn't whine, revile and vituperate. We shouldn't berate the world for killing us out. We need to prepare to die in dignity, with our mind in peace and – if possible – with a smile on our face. We are not supposed to overly inconvenience others with our departure, we needn't be pompous, we need to remember that world will still be on its way after we go. Even when we are no longer around, humans will still be born, they will live, love and enjoy themselves. To remember all that and to try to go peacefully – it is to play well the role of a dying person.

If, in turn, we are placed under arrest, it is our duty not to pity ourselves, to try not to break down, not to lose faith in the world, in people and in the department of justice. If we are sent inside the wire, we need to keep ourselves together, stay sharp, and follow the code of conduct. It is our task to accept the temporal loss of freedom and to not revolt needlessly. One thing which is in abundant supply in jail is time, and we need to put it to wise use, doing things which we are allowed to do, like reading, learning, or trying to stay healthy and physically fit. Above all, we need to use it to rethink our life and the circumstances which led us behind bars. We may also cautiously figure out how we can regain our freedom and what we can do to not be sent inside again. To try to do all of this – it is to play well the role of an arrested person.

The case of exile is easier, at least "mathematically" speaking, because being forced to reside *outside* of a given city or country is a milder restriction than being forced to reside *inside* the perimeter of a jail. Clearly, in today's penal system exile doesn't enjoy the same prominent position it did in ancient Greece and Rome, but let's just keep in mind that we may be compelled to relocate not only by high court's sentence but by a host of other reasons. These reasons can vary from economy and international politics to family

---

[61] Or even better. It was a commonplace saying in antiquity that philosophy is nothing else than an exercise in dying. To be able to die well is – in a way – the ultimate test of our ability to live well.

matters. What then, ought we do if we must change our place of residence, for one cause or another?

We need to see it more as an opportunity than as a loss. We need to focus on the new possibilities and new options that the move made available to us. While we may, of course, keep in touch with people and matters we left behind, we need to carefully avoid ankle-grabbing and clinging to them too much. Tender and sentimental thoughts about our previous homeland shouldn't cast a shadow on the advantages and promises of the new homeland. We need to immerse ourselves in the new life, we need to meet new people and adopt new customs. We needn't be afraid of changing a great deal in what we do and how we live. Our new homeland is a place to live just as the previous one was. Moreover, if we chose it voluntarily, it's fairly probable that it is actually a *better* place to live. And whatever it is like, if we can live well, then we will be able to live well regardless of where we live.

Fragment VII

> *But your disease, you say, will not permit you do anything: it prevents all manner of benefits. [...] Do you think you are doing nothing if you are temperate in your sickness? You [...] show that your distemper may be conquered, or at least* [endured] *with patience. Believe me, Lucilius, virtue finds a place even in the sick-bed. Not only arms and battles give testimony of a valiant mind [...]. The brave person is alike seen under their coverlet. You have still wherewithal to employ you: contend strenuously with your disease.*
>
> <div align="right">Seneca, <i>Epistles</i>, 78.20-21</div>

Commentary: The statement that every playable game can be played well is so crucial to Stoicism that we will take to one more example to discuss it. Let's consider sickness. It's an example which serves well to nail certain doubts and then remove them from the equation.

To begin with, Stoicism asks us to completely abandon the idea that the role of a sick person is in any way less charming or elated than other roles. This commonplace notion is a quintessentially mistaken point of view. Whoever holds on to it, definitely loses it even before they get sick. Someone who complains that they are sick propels oneself onto a higher level of misery. Not to mention those unfortunates who try to prove (to themselves and to others) that their sickness is the worst of all – this is a surefire highway to perdition. The prime duty of a sick person is to avoid thinking that way.

Sickness is unpleasant to us not only because of what it makes us go through, but also because of what it takes away from us. In other words, sickness is painful also (mostly!) because it prevents us from attending to business we would otherwise happily attend to. In more Stoic terms, we may say that sickness can greatly limit the choice of what we can play. A mere flu is powerful enough to keep us in bed barring us from hitting a concert, while even a minute defect of our physical condition is enough to scratch a career of a professional athlete or of an astronaut. It is painfully plain: our health puts heavy restrictions on what we are able to do.

The reality is, however, that even though we love to grumble that illness throws a wrench in our plans, it is very rarely potent enough to scrap literally *all* of our plans. A broken leg from a skiing accident impedes us from running and playing football, but it surely doesn't shut us out from playing chess or video games. The flu can indeed obstruct our outings, but it's not a contraindication for reading a book. Even a serious sickness, one which makes us bedbound for quite a time, doesn't thwart our ability to catch up with the latest TV shows. In a word: we need to clearly define what specifically our malady hinders and what it doesn't hinder. And then, without a second thought, we should abandon the former, while from the latter we can pick and choose at will.

The core rule to remember here is that we must avoid fixation on any single narrative. The world is broad and wide and it is open for us to explore. We, as reformed Stoics, are not supposed to cry over any single cause which is lost or removed from us. If our health keeps us from going on a strenuous mountaineering trip to the Andes, it is still possible that it allows us to enjoy mild and pleasant hiking in New Mexico. If a contagious infection prevents us from visiting friends, it still leaves open the possibility to talk to them over the phone. We just need to bear in mind that despite restrictions on our physical mobility and despite the forced modification of our plans, we are still able to do valuable and advantageous things.

We need to take care to keep the table of our values and the list of our goals long enough so that we always have a backup option. Or plenty of backups, to be precise. Contingency values and secondary goals are a must for a Stoic. Some overabundance in what we want to do is necessary in our Stoic life. It's our insurance policy against the unpredictability of the outside world. If we simultaneously uphold many values and keep multiple possible goals in our scope, then no single turn of events (sickness included) will render us useless. If we plan in advance, if we carefully and broadly craft the list of matters that we are interested in, then no circumstance ever will shut us out of all of them at once. No twist of fate will leave us in the lurch.

"Nice to hear all that," a skeptical mind prompts at this moment, "but there is always a possibility that we get into a situation so grave that it precludes us from doing anything at all. We can always contract a sickness so severe that it pins us down completely, which closes us in exitless suffering, in which no activity whatsoever is on the table. What then?" Then, the Stoic reply goes, the very *act* of being sick will remain our sole role to play. To be a gravely sick human being is a role of its own and, just as all other roles, it may be played well. And it's always within our power to strive to play it well.

We may try to be patient in our suffering. We may try not to complain beyond necessity. We may try to look to the future with neither a gloom glance, nor with unjustified optimism. This is the role of a seriously sick person to play. If we are unable to do anything else, we may at least strive to do well in our wrestling-match with sickness. Simply not getting beaten down by our ailment *is already a lot*, for it means that we have successfully beaten down our own weakness.

Fragment VIII

> *When Vespasian*[62] *[...] commanded* [Helvidius Priscus][63] *not to go into the senate, he replied, "It is in your power not to allow me to be a member of the senate, but so long as I am, I must go in." Well, go in then, says the emperor, but say nothing. "Do not ask my opinion, and I will be silent." But I must ask your opinion. "And I must say what I think* [is] *right." But if you do, I shall put you to death. "When then did I tell you that I am immortal? You will do your part, and I will do mine. It is your part to kill, it is mine to die. But not in fear. Your* [part is] *to banish me, mine to depart without sorrow."*

Epictetus, Discourses, I.2.19-22

Commentary: Finally, we need to play our role not only well, but also consistently and persistently. What does it mean? Let's take a look at Helvidius Priscus. The emperor tried to prevent Priscus from performing his duties as a senator, but he resisted. He didn't accept the ban from the senate. He didn't let the emperor shut his mouth. He didn't let the words coming out of his month

---

[62] See footnote to fragment VI in the chapter "You Are Never Alone."
[63] Helvidius Priscus was a Roman politician of the 1st century AD and a follower of Stoic philosophy. He was famous for his fervent republicanism and for his adamant character. He had a turbulent life, he held high offices in Rome but also was banished twice. He was executed by the order of Vespasian.

defy his own principles just in order to please the emperor's ears. He was consistent and persistent in his role of a senator.

When it comes to the roles we play, there are no half-measures and in-betweens. The roles define who we are and we can't just play a role part-time. We can't play a part of it and neglect the other part. What would that even look like? Would it mean playing ordinary basketball on our side of the court, and then kicking the ball freely the moment we cross the center line? Would it mean that we try to be brave in our malady unless it's flu, hangover or Monday? Would it mean that we are a loving parent to our child, as long as he or she doesn't get sick? This just makes no sense. We have covered this already: disobeying the rules annihilates the game. Thus, whatever game we agree to play – we need to play it to the fullest. In Stoicism, everything needs to be a full investment. We have latitude in the choice of what we play, but once we start to play – we must be all-in.

The same goes for the theater metaphor. What would we think of an actor who suddenly exits the stage in the middle of the show? Or of an actor who breaks the character without warning and starts complaining about how difficult her role is to play? This is just unimaginable: it violates in spades all that we know about being an actor. A complaint that the role we play turned out harder than we expected (than *what* exactly? than we predicted? than we hoped for? than we were told in kindergarten? one excuse sounds lamer than the other) is no excuse at all. It's even less than a no-excuse. It is after all (or rather: *before* all) our very own duty to read the script before we start playing. And let's remember Helvidius Priscus. He – rightly! – held that it was impossible for him to be a senator and not enter the senate, to be a senator and to remain silent, to be a senator and to not say the exact things that – in his opinion – the national interest compelled him to say. Since these were the senatorial duties, which he vowed to discharge.

Helvidius Priscus knew the risk of angering the emperor and accepted it, but we shouldn't be deceived by the ancients' fondness for the tough and dangerous situations. No one will behead us for playing our game today. It's important to understand that reformed Stoicism doesn't pressure us to unconditionally fixate on what we play. It doesn't want us to make the ultimate sacrifice at the soonest available occasion. Playing consistently and persistently has nothing to do with mindless stubbornness. We don't need to overdo what we do, but we must keep in mind that it's always an either-or alternative. We either accept the whole package of the senatorial duties and responsibilities, including the burdens and dangers that come with it, or we resign and seek another occupation.

The one thing we can't do is sit on the fence. We can't fulfill our duties halfway, we can't perform some of them and neglect others. We can't just take advantages of being a senator and bask in the dim glory of it, without working the senatorial job and taking the senatorial risks. If we have decided on a given role, then we are obliged to play it fully and all the way to the end. "The end" doesn't mean "until we are executed by a crazy dictator," but rather "until we resign from the role." We are not obliged to perish heroically defending a long-forgotten post. We are obliged, however, to play consistently and persistently the role we play – as long as we play it.

Chapter 17

There are other games to play

[A Stoic is like] *a good actor, who, if called upon to take the part of a Thersites[64] or of an Agamemnon,[65] will impersonate them both becomingly.[xiii]*

Diogenes Laertius, *Lives of Eminent Philosophers*, VII.160

In a nutshell: We are never sentenced to play just one, single game. We can always resign and walk away. Where to? To other games, which are always in abundant supply. There is always plenty of them and we should keep an eye on them. We switch games at any moment, but once we do it – there is no going back. If we switch games, we must engage in the new game fully, we must dive into it and mustn't pass a second thought about what we used to play before. We don't switch games to cry over the abandoned one.

***

There are other games to play, so we don't have to limit ourselves to the game we are playing right now (fragment I). We should use other games to draft contingency scenarios (II). We need to be genuinely open to the other games and be authentically ready to switch, should the need arise at any moment. We mustn't fixate on a single game just because we got used to playing it (III). When we switch games, we need to clean forget the game we leave behind (IV). Yet, the switch needs to be carefully thought-out (V). Whatever our position in life and whatever our circumstances, there is always something that we can play well (VI).

---

[64] In Greek mythology Thersites was the ugliest, most wicked and most cowardly Greek soldier in the Trojan War. Yet, according to some interpreters, he should be viewed more as a wise fool or even a social critic.

[65] Agamemnon was one of the key figures in Greek mythology. He was the son of Atreus (the king of Mycenae), the husband of Clytemnestra, the father of Electra, Iphigenia, Chrysothemis and Orestes and the commander-in-chief of the Greek forces during the Trojan War.

Fragment I

> *Phidias[66] could make a statute not only of ivory, but [also] of brass. Was you to give him marble, or some viler stuff, he would yet form as complete a statue as could be made of it. So you need to display yourself, if you may, in the management of wealth, if not, in poverty, in your own country, if you can, if not, in banishment, as a general, if such your appointment, if not, as a common soldier, as a sound and hale person, if such your constitution, if not, as weak infirm. Whatever your condition of life may be, you will do something notable.*
>
> Seneca, Epistles, 85.38-40

Commentary: We should be like Phidias. Obviously, we are not supposed to try to outflank him in artistry, but we should match his versatility. An experienced sculptor always has their favorite material to work with, but even if they largely prefer wood, they will still be able to do meaningful work with bronze, stone or plaster. What matters is not the material, but the craft itself. A skillful sculptor will produce fine work with any stuff, while a bad one won't produce anything, ever.

Just the same holds with life and anything in it. If we learn how to live well, if we follow the Stoic precepts, then no game will scare us. Every game will be playable and every imaginable circumstance will be favorable to us. The stream of life, the chain of events, whatever comes our way, we need to treat all this just as the sculptor treats marble or bronze, that is as *material*, as substrate, as the input substance for the meaningful process we carry out on our own. The quality of our work, that is, the quality and value of our life isn't defined by what comes into our hands, but by what leaves them. It's not important what material we receive, but whether we can form it into something valuable.

Once we adopt this viewpoint, no change, novelty or twist of fate will be an existential threat to us. Our task and our goal is to take whatever is accessible at the present moment and turn it into a good life. Thus, so to speak, it's fine if we have what we have, but it's also fine if it alters. We'll get on and work up

---

[66] Phidias (c. 480 – 430 BC) was the most famous sculptor of ancient Greece. He created, among other works, the statue of Zeus at Olympia, deemed one of the wonders of the ancient world, the statue of Athena Promachos, which stood on the Acropolis of Athens, the statue of Athena Parthenos, housed in the Parthenon, on the very same Acropolis, as well as the sculptural decoration of the Parthenon itself.

whatever material we get our hands on. Once we learn how to live a good, Stoic life, we will be able to pull off any role that comes our way.

Whatever game we are playing right now and whatever role we perform, we need to keep firmly in mind that there is an entire universe of other games and roles beyond the present one. If we are OK on money, then we have not only the possibility but also a duty to use it wisely. But, on the other hand, if we ever run into financial trouble, then we will deal with that ably and adroitly. If we live in a country we want to live in, then all's well. But it won't be to our detriment if some day, for some reason, we relocate. We'll be well off as expats too. In yet another manner, if we decide to serve this or another country as soldiers, then we must take the oath and perform our duties with gallantry and professionalism. If we rise in the ranks and become a general, then all's well, we will gladly accept that responsibility. But, on the other hand, if our career doesn't develop that swiftly, if we get busted down or simply passed-over with promotions, then we will be able to serve just as well, although as mere privates. In a word: we need to remember, that there are plenty of roles on the market, and whatever we play right now, we might still be able to play something else even better.

Fragment II

You are not able to serve in the army: then become a candidate for civic honors. Must you live in a private station? Then be an advocate. Are you condemned to keep silence? Then help your countrymen with silent counsel. Is it dangerous for you even to enter the forum? Then prove yourself a good comrade, a faithful friend, a sober guest in people's houses, at public shows, and at wine-parties. Suppose that you have lost the status of a citizen. Then exercise that of a human being. Our reason for magnanimously refusing to confine ourselves within the walls of one city, for having gone forth to enjoy intercourse with all lands and for professing ourselves to be citizens of the world, is that we may thus obtain a wider theater on which to display our virtue. Is the bench of judges closed to you, are you forbidden to address the people from the hustings, or to be a candidate at elections? Then turn your eyes away from Rome, and see what a wide extent of territory, what a number of nations present themselves before you. Thus, it is never possible for so many outlets to be closed against your ambition that more will not remain open to it.

Seneca, *Of Peace of Mind*, 4.3-4

Commentary: We need to remember that there are other games to play, particularly when for some reason our favorite game of choice becomes inaccessible to us. But the general awareness, the purely mental reflection that there are other games out there is not enough for us. It's not enough for us to know abstractly that we could be, theoretically, doing something else. We need to raise our eyes from the doldrums of the current work, we need to actually look around for other games and actively try them on. On a daily basis we need to imagine that we were already forced to give up our current game (remember the chapter "Anticipate Mishap") and that we turned to do something else. On this note, let's ask ourselves: what would that be exactly? What's our backup option? What's our plan B? At any given moment we must have a solid reserve, we need to have a number of outs secured, a bunch of contingency games we can switch to if our current endeavor fails. If a major change happens, in the world itself, or, worse yet, in our mind, then we must be quick to switch. Swiftly and painlessly.

A good general always has an auxiliary plan in her mind (not only in mind: on paper too!), a plan which is called into action should the original battle plan not survive the first contact with the enemy (what usually happens). The same holds for a skipper of a sailboat, who has an alternate plan in mind in case a maneuver doesn't go as planned. The same for a politician, who knows what to do in case a campaign doesn't play out as advertised or if a publicity stunt backfires. And just the same in Stoicism. We always need to have an alternate scenario, an abort plan, another fish to fry. Moreover, it shouldn't be just one single plan. We need a number of diversified workarounds for various obstacles that fate can place on our way. We always need to know an escape route, and we need to have a secure position to back off to.

Let's suppose, for instance, that we've always dreamt about being famous writers. Alas, we've run out of inspiration pretty early, or, as it happens all the time, no one wanted to publish (or read) our books. What then? No worries – we may do just as well as literary critics, or teaching literature at a university. Or let's suppose that we've decided to serve our country in uniform, and we've set our eyes on a nice career in the military. Nothing came of his? No worries – we may do just as well in the civil service. Or let's suppose that we hoped to become big in international trade and to become rich that way. Alas, import tariffs and exports quotas changed to our disadvantage. What then? No worries – maybe the tech industry will be our gateway to success? Possibilities are endless, not only in the economic sense, but life-wise. And they are not just possibilities. They are also obligations. It is our duty to keep track of them and to take them into account. Regardless of what we do right now, and no matter how confident we are in the game we play now – we must always have a few backup games in mind.

There are other games to play

At any given moment, we need to have many of them in sight and in mind. We need to always have planned for emergencies and sudden tricks of fate. Whatever we do, whatever game we play, we need to play it ably, persistently and full-time, but this *doesn't* mean that this game is the only pebble on the beach. A Stoic's love with the world is by definition promiscuous. We must always remember that our game is just one of many, and if it fails us, bores us, or becomes unavailable for any reason, then we can switch games in a blink of an eye. We didn't make it in one game – we will in another. Such an attitude guarantees that no circumstances will ever stop us. Nothing will hinder us, because we can circumvent any setback by simply switching to another game. We'll never have time to sit and wail. We won't have time for it because as soon as one game becomes obsolete, we will need to attend to another. Whenever we fail or get blocked in any domain, we simply move on to another goal and next value from our list.

Stoicism italicizes that this constant openness to other games *doesn't diminish* the value and importance of the present game. A glance at another game isn't tantamount to treason. It's not a slander to the game we play now, just as a glance on another human isn't synonymous with cheating on our partner. Suppose for instance, that we are well-off and satisfied members of the top 1% of society. We work in the financial sector, we enjoy the earthly prestige and we enjoy the money. And yet, we look not without fascination at anarchists and squatters, who oppose The System and who peddle universal equality and free love. Moreover, we are aware that under some conceivable circumstances (like a financial crisis and losing our job, or a midlife crisis and losing the meaning of life), we might be willing to enter their game and find contentment in it. But this awareness doesn't signify that we don't appreciate our present position! And the same goes the other way around. If we happen to live in an off-the-grid hippie commune, we may still well respect and understand the exact opposite role, that is the role of an affluent, top-tier banker. Moreover, we may be well aware that under certain conceivable circumstances we too might be forced to reach some kind of a compromise with the system (or, for instance, our long-forgotten grand-aunt may pass away and leave a considerable inheritance to us). And yet, being aware of these possibilities doesn't mean that our anarchist beliefs are in any measure insincere.

Fragment III

> *What kind of solitude then remains? What want? Why do we make ourselves worse than children? And what do children do when they are left alone? They take up shells and ashes, and they build something, then pull it down, and build something else, and so they never want the*

> *means of passing the time. [...] Children do what they do through deficiency in knowledge, and we through knowledge are unhappy.*
>
> Epictetus, *Discourses*, III.13.18-19

Commentary: We should be like children with their keen interest and curiosity about the world. We should be like them regarding the openness to the world and the lack of prejudice. Children are an important point of reference because, apparently, they are free of one particular trait that is so toxic to us, adults. Children don't get fixated on one single game or role to the extent that it erases their interest in all else. (Or, if they do get fixated, it passes relatively quickly for them, and they easily refocus their interest on new errands). Children are admirably unpretentious in their freedom of bias which makes our adult minds narrow, and which bars the candid lookout for the games and roles to play.

Children seem to always know how to spend their time. As Epictetus points out: if only they have a moment to spare, it's enough for them to start their exploration. Why don't I go that way? Why shouldn't I turn over this stool? Maybe I try putting this blue toy in my mouth? And what about tying my kitty's tail to that table leg? Everything is possible, everything is promising! Children don't particularly care about restrictions imposed upon them. Yes, they may respect what's forced on them but – here is the key thing – they don't become miserable (for long) just because we told them not to put their fingers in the power socket. The world is too broad and too riveting to be concerned with one silly taboo. After all, even if experiments with electricity are off-limits, how about ripping off a teddy bear's head to find out what's inside of it?

Where is this coming from? What's the source of this liberty, this sincere, unspoiled and unlimited interest in the world? And how can it be of advantage to us? We may assume that children, who are very new to the world and to whom the world is very new, simply haven't yet taken in all the patterns and practices that are the backseat drivers of our life. Children are just not yet in the ruts, not yet in the claws of routine which fences us in a single game and shuts out of others. From the children's point of view, all the options are equal and still on the table. All that the world has to offer is just as accessible and thrilling, all the chances are tempting and all the opportunities still present themselves. To a kid, no single game is exceptional enough to write the rest of the world off. And no game is crossed out. Each and every game is worth at least trying it – and here is where we should emulate the kids' behavior.

Each of us was a child one day. We have all been there, we've all lived it, we've all experienced that unbounded openness to the world, uninhibited by scruples. Each of us used to know how to be interested in all available games, each of us used to have an unbiased view, used to be able to swiftly switch from one game to another. So why not go back? Isn't it an acute absurd that growing up we grow blind and one-sided, jailed in a single game, stuck in it like in mud, unable and unwilling to go through? Isn't it ludicrous that if a single game is for some reason off-limits to us, then we cry as if we lost the entire world?

Fragment IV

> *Then, I ask you, are you unwilling to live in Rome and desire to live in Greece? And when you must die, will you then also fill us with your lamentations, because you will not see Athens* [again] *nor walk about in the Lyceion?*[67]
>
> Epictetus, Discourses, III.24.77

Commentary: Let's now talk about *how* we ought to switch from one game to another. The first order of business is that no regrets are allowed in Stoicism. And no excuses, either. We mustn't feel sorry about the change we make, we mustn't miss the abandoned game. We need to engage in the new game completely, we must adapt fully to our new role. The previous role shouldn't be mulled over, it shouldn't be regretted. The best we can do about it – is forget it. This is where not dwelling on counterfactual scenarios kicks in big time, for nothing is more counterproductive than sweating over a role we already decided to step out from. If we do so, the only possible outcome is clearly negative: for sure nothing good will come of this, and for sure our new walk of life will be spoiled. The role we abandoned is already past, closed, nonexistent, like it was never there. Remember that the past is not within our power and that we should treat it accordingly.

Having said this, we may jump back to the examples discussed earlier. Once we decide to quit the sweet-payday world of global banking and join a hippie commune, we need to cut the cord once and for all. We need to do it without looking back and without a second thought. We need to stop considering luxury cars and vacations in the Bahamas. We mustn't ponder and we mustn't think back, for this would be the simplest way to make sure that we never verse in the new role. We will never feel fully at home in the new game if we

---

[67] Lyceum was a temple of Apollo Lyceus in Athens, in ancient Greece. Aristotle's school was located in the vicinity of it, and thus the name "lyceum" passed into many educational systems of the modern era.

keep mentally replaying the old one. And the same, of course, holds the other way. If we come to a decision to bring an end to our adventure with the counterculture, we mustn't rue any single thing that we leave behind. We need to put it to bed. We need to put a full stop to entertaining the hippie trail, flower power and pot unlimited. All's well that ends well – and it *did* end. Stoic eyes always look ahead and it is our duty to focus on what we are starting to play now, not on what we played in the past.

This principle holds anywhere and anytime. Once we have decided that due to health concerns we don't go mountaineering in the Andes, and we chose hiking in New Mexico instead, then we must immediately, fully and irreversibly convert our thinking. We need to stop daydreaming about ascending the snow-clad mountains. Thinking about it would be only self-inflicted suffering. Pointless suffering to boot, for there is no need to deliberate on this anymore. Instead, let's think about visiting Walter White's house at Negra Arroyo Lane in ABQ, about some mild hiking in the Land of Enchantment and watching a sunset over Tohajiilee. This is the game we took on to play and only the rules of this game matter. To think back of the rules of a previous, abandoned game, to be concerned about the restrictions of a game which is no longer ours – this is an utterly useless, nonstoic matter.

Fragment V

> *If you have assumed* [a role] *above your strength, you have both acted in this matter in an unbecoming way, and you have neglected that* [role] *which you might have fulfilled.*
>
> Epictetus, *Encheiridion*, 37

Commentary: Regardless of why we switched games, we confront the major task of choosing the new game.[68] And it's not merely a task. *It's our duty to choose the new game well.* But what does it even mean?

First off, we need to accept that this is *our* choice and *our* duty. We shouldn't leave it to chance, we shouldn't lay it on our fellow humans. We shouldn't draw lots and we shouldn't choose blindly. We shouldn't devolve into passivity, we

---

[68] On the other hand, choosing a new game only *after* we had abandoned the previous one is already a mistake. In the light of what we have discussed already (in the commentary to fragment II), we should never allow a situation in which, having quit a game, we face void and nullity, not knowing what to play and what to do. We need to design a backup plan *beforehand*.

shouldn't pretend that there is no choice. Nothing is further from reformed Stoicism than escape from responsibility.

Second, in the quoted fragment Epictetus writes that we shouldn't pick a role which is beyond our powers. True! But this is not the only criterion for choice. The role we intend to play needs to cohere with our talents and skills, and – to the extent possible – with our predilections and preferences. We need to use our best knowledge, we need to take into account all the data and facts that we know of. We are obliged to make the most informed decision we can. In short, we need to call into action the procedure discussed in detail in the chapter "Act Deliberately."

Third, we need to be especially cautious and self-aware when it comes to what we can play well and what we cannot. The commonplace wisdom is that it's better to be a happy McDonald employee than a miserable mogul. This example – exaggerated as it is – illustrates a vital point, namely, that we are better off playing well the role we can play well, than playing poorly a role we can play only poorly. In particular, we need to weigh in the opportunity cost which Epictetus highlights. If we make a mistake in choosing the new role for us, then not only we will have to play something we are unfit for, but we'll also miss the opportunity to play something we are really good at. It's somber to be a frustrated, failing politician, if we could have become an eminent poet. And it's just as somber to be a fourth-rate poet, if we could have had a stellar career in politics.

In reformed Stoicism, we are never allowed to choose carelessly and then grouch that we ended up playing something we didn't want to play. This is indeed a cornerstone issue. It basically works as a trade-off. We invest thought and effort in wise selection of the game, and the profit we get is the peace of mind and contentment in playing it. Ergo, no prudency and careful consideration is too much when it comes to decision-making. And no honesty with ourselves and sober self-estimation is too much when it comes to cutting the coat according to our cloth.

Fragment VI

> *One is never so out off from all pursuits as to find no room left for honorable action.*
>
> Seneca, *Of Peace of Mind*, 4.8

Commentary: In the commentary to fragment I we discussed the idea that a capable sculptor is a fine role model for us, because it is a vital Stoic skill to be able to turn every conceivable input material into valuable output.

Interestingly, this parallel can be stretched even further: we should be able to create valuable things starting from nothing at all. In Stoicism, even nothingness itself can be transformed into something positive. So we need to be even more effective than Phidias was! We need to be able to thrive even if we have no promising material at hand. How is that possible?

In every situation in life and in every supposable circumstance, there is *always* an available role for us that we may play well. There is always something we can excel at and shine, there is always something that can be done well. Hopelessness doesn't stand in Stoicism. There is always something to be done, and it can be done well.

Importantly though, Stoicism doesn't say "you can do something about every situation". In particular, it doesn't boast that it has a solution to every possible problem. This would be something well above the Stoic paygrade. Stoicism doesn't promise an easy solution to every possible plight – that would be highly misleading. Stoicism isn't about false hopes. Stoicism doesn't say that if we are locked in a supermax prison, awaiting execution the following morning, then we can still "do something about it," say, flee, save ourselves, or at least get the sentence commuted. This would be a deceitful assurance. What Stoicism really promises is something much simpler (which doesn't make it less soothing). It is this: even when we face the gallows, there is still time and place for a task that can be done well. Even if it is limited, basically, to coping with the situation well. To play ably and bravely the role of a person sentenced to death is not nothing. Accepting the shared verdict of the court and fate, keeping our peace of mind, bidding proper farewells is a perfectly viable game – possibly one of the most honorable of all.

Part five.
Others in this playground

On the attitude towards other people

Chapter 18

Be autonomous

How much trouble one avoids who does not look to see what their neighbor says or does or thinks, but only to what they do themselves, that it may be just and pure.

Marcus Aurelius, Meditations, 4.18

In a nutshell: Let's not be concerned too much about what other people think and do. We ought to look at ourselves with our own eyes, not with the eyes of others. The principles of our thought and the rules of our conduct, the criteria according to which we measure and organize ourselves, should be all our own. We alone need to decide what matters to us and what's dear to us. Leaving this to other people is nothing short of handing out the keys to our happiness to them.

***

We should be self-sufficient and intellectually independent (fragment I). There is no Stoicism without this (II). Why is that? Since no one knows our guts and instincts better than we do (III), since others often yearn for things which are irrelevant to us (IV), and since we'll never satisfy the desires of others (V). How can we learn to be autonomous? We need to remember that the root of grudge is in us, not in others (VI). We are responsible for the choice of our values and goals (VII), and we shouldn't excessively rely on others because it amounts to seeking misery and trouble (VIII). If someone insults us, we needn't show that it hurts us (IX). If someone criticizes us, we need to criticize ourselves even more (X). If someone laughs at us, we need to laugh with them (XI). Yet, in all this, we shouldn't forget that we ought to have a big heart for other people and that we shouldn't be mean to them (XII).

Fragment I

I have often wondered how it is that everyone loves themselves more than all the rest of people, but yet sets less value on their own opinion of themselves than on the opinion of others.

Marcus Aurelius, Meditations, 12.4

Commentary: In the opening lines of his famous *Discourse on the Method* Descartes remarks, somewhat tongue-in-cheek, that reason is the most equally distributed commodity in the world, since no one ever complains about its shortage. With a similar twist comes the quoted passage from Marcus Aurelius. We love to think highly of ourselves, we love to think that we know it all. (Or, at least, we tend to assume that when it comes to judgments, we are in a better position than others.) And yet, when it comes to this one particular issue, we are farcically dependent on the opinion of others. We trust ourselves with judging everyone and everything, but when it comes to judging *us* – we trust other people more than ourselves. Isn't it ludicrous?

We are usually quite confident in our reason, experience and judgment – after all, we base all of our daily life on it. We even tend to take the next step and shamelessly think that our opinion should be decisive, that others are less smart and less reliable than we are. And yet again, when it comes to examining and evaluating ourselves, all of that self-reliance suddenly vanishes into thin air. We are the first to be judgmental about others, but when we need to properly assess ourselves – we desperately need backup. A flirtatious smile, an appreciating nod, or a flash of acceptance in someone's eyes become far more important to us than our own view. How is that even possible? Isn't it the sharpest paradox of all?

Let's start with square one. There is no doubt that vain pride and empty self-inflation of our perspective is a deplorable thing (in Stoicism at least). We shouldn't let ourselves believe that we are omniscient arbiters, the ultimate gauges of right and wrong, who are entitled to pass definitive verdicts on everything. Clearly, this way of thinking is a trap. Just as dangerous a trap however, lurks on the other side of the spectrum. The name of this trap is simply: unrestrained self-doubt. It's dangerous because it generates treacherous reliance on others. It makes us seek approval in others and makes us vulnerable to their opinions. In a word, it compromises our autonomy.

Fragment II

> *If you wish to seem* [...] *to any person to be* [a Stoic], *appear so to yourself, and you will be able to do this.*
>
> Epictetus, *Encheiridion*, 23

Commentary: An important element of the Stoic life is the firm belief that we made the right choice choosing it. This conviction needs to be self-supportive and unconstrained, it needs to be *ours*, it needs to hinge on us alone and on no one else. Our own assurance needs to be enough for us. Stoicism needn't be a solitary endeavor, but it surely is a self-addressed one. And we can't have it both ways. We can't both rely on Stoicism and depend on support from others. Stoicism requires self-sufficiency and intellectual self-rule. As Stoics, we cannot wait for outside approval or authorization. The only confirmation that matters is the one which comes from within.

A Stoic should be like an independent state, whereas the decision-making powers are located within, not outside of it. In Stoicism, such independence is both an end in itself and it is also a means. It's an end because, as mentioned before, it's impossible to live a good life in the state of mental dependence on something or someone else. But it's also a means because it provides the right environment for us to properly, and calm-headedly deal with various affronts and snubs that others may (and will) hurl on us.

Fragment III

> *When you are surrounded by those who would persuade you that you are miserable, you* [need to] *reflect not upon what you hear, but* [upon] *what you think and feel yourself and* [consult] *with your patience, as you certainly know yourself best.*
>
> Seneca, Epistles, 13.6

Commentary: Why is it our right and our duty to be mentally autonomous? One point to be made is that we are the best to know our own needs, values and goals. We shouldn't be judges in our own cause, but we are an excellent expert witness in it. Our life is lived by us, so to speak, not by anyone else. We need to be in control of it, we need to be responsible for it. There is no other option in Stoicism. We need to know what we need, what we possess and what we lack. And only we know firsthand what is it that we want to accomplish. Other people may have some grasp of that, they can gather a bit, they can make their assumptions, but their knowledge is always piecemeal, always superficial, always indirect. No one has access to our mind, no one truly feels what we feel. It's only our judgment that matters.

Our fellow humans, however, like to pretend it's not the case. It's a fixed point of many interhuman relationships that others feel compelled to press on us what is – according to them – best for us. During our life here on earth, we'll be overflown by an endless stream of unsolicited advice. We'll be flooded with a plethora of admonitions, unwanted suggestions and unwarranted instructions. We'll find ourselves on the receiving end of various mind tricks and we'll be subjected to emotional blackmail by our dear ones. Virtually everyone, regardless of whether they are family or a complete stranger, may declare themselves a self-taught expert on our desires and needs. And they will argue and try to persuade us that they know better what we should wear, where we should go and with whom we should associate. There are plenty of cunning ways in which such suggestions may sneak upon us. They may be avuncular advice or tart preaching. They can be blunt or subtle, sometimes camouflaged to the extent that it's not easy to even realize that we are being pressured. But all these situations have one thing in common: we need to be just as cautious of them all.

Let's keep the right proportions here. In reformed Stoicism we aren't supposed to turn deaf ears by default, we aren't supposed to never hear people out. We need to be very careful instead. In listening to what others have to say we should never assume an inferior position, we should never surmise that their words are the words of an oracle. Among people we are equal among equals. This should be our battle cry in every company and in any social setting, we find ourselves in. It's childish to presume that whatever adults are saying is incontrovertible God's will – and in this respect, we should *not* be like children. We mustn't assume that whatever others say is fixed, immutable and right just because they say it.

Let's now get back to the quoted words of Seneca. He remarks that instigations and incitements by others may be a point-blank attempt to spoil our contentment and ruin our happiness. Others may try to convince us that our happiness is for some reason unauthorized, misinformed or unjustified (whatever that would mean in this context). "You mean you are satisfied with where you are?" they may say, "but just look at you, how much of a loser you are! Who can be happy living in this place?"

This is a bull's-eye, a textbook example of why we need to be impervious to the words of others. This is the defining argument for our case for autonomy. If our goal is to live well and happily, then what's the point of listening to someone who sabotages that? And it's not just this, there is also a logical problem here. For who is a better specialist on our happiness than we are? Literally no one! We are – by definition! – the most knowledgeable about this specific subject. Actually, we are the only human being in the entire world who may have *any* insight into whether we are happy. When it comes to extrasolar planets, we should trust astronomers. When it comes to vaccines, we should trust doctors. When it comes to alcohol's influence on decision-making, we should trust addiction therapists. But we need to trust ourselves when it comes to the assessment of our own happiness. Simply because we have no one else to trust. Upon this one subject, we may be absolutely certain, like truly nowhere else, that we are right and that the opinion of others doesn't matter. We may turn deaf ears and not feel guilty about it at all.

Fragment IV

> *Riches, honors, powers and the like* [...] *have nothing really great in them* [...] *but it is customary to admire them. For, not because they are desirable, are they praised, but because they are praised, they are coveted.*
>
> Seneca, Epistles, 81.27-29

Commentary: Another reason which makes mental autonomy so urgent is that other people (the nonstoics) often praise and cherish things which are utterly useless from our point of view. Let's consider fads. It's a regular occurrence that every now and then it becomes socially important to wear this type of haircut, own that kind of device, or rant on social media about that particular topic. This is serious and this is costly, for it absorbs lots of time and mental effort (and often money). For some people not missing out on these activities is a matter of life and death... or at least of social acceptance, which, apparently, amounts for them to the same. But do we have to follow suit?

Certainly not. Even if our entire social bubble buzzes and turns to follow the latest fad, nothing in it compels us to mimic that. Fortunately, we live neither in a totalitarian state nor in kindergarten, and everyone has their own free will and can decide for themselves. We need to decide on one-by-one basis whether we want to succumb to social pressure or not.

On the other hand, though, the case for autonomy doesn't entail that a Stoic is supposed to wear rags and be completely out-of-date. A Stoic can well be up to date, she can wear the latest gear... and just as well she can be the first among the nonconformists. The one thing that makes her truly and relentlessly exceptional is that she always needs to decide on her own. This is the crux of the matter. Reformed Stoicism is not a direct guide to what clothes to wear and what electronics to possess, but it guides us to make independent and informed decision ourselves. And more than that! It teaches us *why* this mental autonomy is morally important, why it constitutes our happiness, and why it directly affects our ability to live a good life.

Let's think about it. There is nothing intrinsically good, there is nothing *per se* virtuous (or vicious) in wearing baggy trousers, or buying products of the brand X. Nothing in it makes it more noble, more valuable or coveted than wearing tight trousers or buying products of the brand Y. The one and undeniable fact is that we, humans, are a gregarious species, and thus, we have a strong tendency to yield to social pressure and to follow the mob. Reformed Stoicism is happy to embrace this biological approach. Reformed Stoicism highly approves of science, science in turn teaches us that our brains are hard-wired to make us social, and this is a fact we need to take into account. It's as simple as that. In this vein, we need to factor in that if all our folks suddenly get crazy about getting X, we too, as social creatures, may feel pressured to get X. It's just a matter of – to speak tartly and tersely – certain chemical and neural reactions which happen in our brains in response to the behavior of other humans. The point is that, just as Seneca says, such needs and desires, paradoxically, are not intrinsic, but rather *they feed on themselves*. We want things not because we want them, but because others want them.

The Stoic calling is to learn how to break this heinous cause-and-effect chain. The desires and fancies of others cannot be a defining guide for us. They cannot bind us. We don't have to (and we mustn't!) reduce our own will to a mere ctrl-c-ctrl-v of the will of others. We have every right to autonomously decide on what we want and what we don't want.

Fragment V

> *Am I to expect that evil speaking will respect anything, seeing that it respected neither Rutilius[69] nor Cato?[70] Will anyone care about being thought too rich by people for whom Diogenes the Cynic[71] was not poor enough?*
>
> Seneca, *Of a Happy Life*, 18.3

Commentary: Cato and Rutilius were Roman statesmen famous as paragons of virtue and unbendable character. Demetrius the Cynic was a philosopher of ultra-high level of indifference to material things. And yet, as Seneca relates, neither superb integrity nor the extremes of voluntary poverty saved them from human impertinence and insistence. There is never enough for people. If they demand a politician to be upright and high-principled, then no actual

---

[69] Publius Rutilius Rufus (158 BC – 78 BC) was a Roman soldier, statesman and consul, and also a Stoic philosopher, a student of Panaetius. He was deemed a symbol of virtue and moral perfection. In 92 BC he was falsely accused of extorting money and exiled. He spent his final years in Mytilene and Smyrna in Asia Minor where he devoted himself to study. The exile was later rescinded by Sulla and Rutilius was offered to return to Rome but he declined.

[70] See footnote to fragment VIII in the chapter "Don't Desire Acclaim."

[71] This possibly refers not to Diogenes the Cynic, but (as other editions suggest) Demetrius the Cynic, who was a Cynic philosopher of the 1st century AD. He was famous for his life of poverty and extreme contempt for earthly goods. In *On Benefits* (VII.11.1-2) Seneca relates that Demetrius was once offered 200 000 sesterces by the emperor Caligula who tried to corrupt him. Demetrius declined and said that had the emperor been serious about it, he would have offered him the whole empire.

rectitude of real Catos and Rutiliuses will satisfy them. They will always insist on more and more. They will always demand above and beyond the call of reason, and beyond the measure of human capability.

Human desires and expectations are – by definition – insatiable. Stoicism goes even one step further and asserts that they are not even issued in order to be satisfied. What does it mean? Let's think about it this way. A single person may desire a specific thing, like wisdom, wine or wantonness. Acquiring this specific thing may – at least for some time – satisfy that need. We may agree on that. But when we turn from and individual to the collective, when we talk plural, things get different. A definite, full satisfaction of collective desires is out of the question. Plainly impossible. Why? Because they are never well-defined enough and they always lift the bar higher and higher with the infinite drumbeat of "more and more." And this isn't just a random occurrence, this isn't a coincidence. These collective, social expectations are deliberately put out that way. They are crafted like that on purpose so that an individual cannot live up to them and so that an individual can be always pilloried with unmeetable demands. We need to realize that the core purpose of social expectations is about creating a pretext to criticize us. It's not about any specific, justified requirements that could be fulfilled. It's just an excuse for incessant criticism. That's why, as we have seen with Cato and Demetrius the Cynic, even embodiment of virtue will not seem virtuous enough to people, and someone who lives on bread and water won't seem frugal enough to them.

In short, all the demands and expectations that other people confront us with are by definition unquenchable. They are like the escaping ceiling which goes up and up as we try to reach it. The more effort, time and sacrifice we (needlessly!) put in the futile attempts to meet these expectations, the higher they grow. And they can do so infinitely and they can drain our life force for half of forever. There is just one solution: we need to learn to ignore them.

Fragment VI

> *Remember that it is not the person who reviles you or strikes you, that insults you, but it is your opinion about these things as being insulting. When then someone irritates you, you must know that it is your own opinion which has irritated you.*
>
> Epictetus, *Encheiridion*, 20

Commentary: We now know *why* we should keep a healthy distance from the opinion of others. The next step is to figure out *how* to keep it. How can we learn this precious skill? Mental autonomy is neither a self-evident nor an easy state of mind to acquire. It won't be just handed out to us, it's not a free lunch. As mentioned, we are a gregarious species, and we have a strong proclivity for imitating others. And here is where Stoicism comes to rescue, providing us with a set of tools for obtaining autonomy.

The ideas that it's all about the narratives and the division into things within and not within our power are of course a good start. Let's imagine, for instance, that someone hurt our feelings, offended or defamed us. It may seem that the default human reaction is to let it get under our skin and to take it to heart. It may seem that it is an obvious reaction to get angry. It's curious that this assumption is present even in the language we use. Notice, that in everyday, nonstoic speak we will swiftly use the phrases that Epictetus quotes, like "someone insulted us," or "someone irritated us." But beware! Here is where things get difficult. Here is the trap and here is the tacit, but false premise.

The pivotal Stoic point here is that the f-words or accusations thrown at us by our fellow humans aren't the real source of our sorrow, irritation, or wrath. The actual reason, one we can pin down if we are honest with ourselves, is that *we've decided* to get sad, irritated or angry *in response* to these words. But this was never necessary! Whatever we hear from others, whatever they say to us and about us – the choice of how we react is ours. There is no necessity, there is no logical deduction that would bound us to respond in any specific way. It is within our power to decide how we react. It is our own doing. The narrative we create about the whole situation depends solely on us. We create it. We choose our own reactions, even if these choices happen unknowingly. And of course, Stoicism urges us to make these choices consciously and properly.

We are perfectly free and able to decide that we react with nothing but calmness to spiteful words, that we pass them off with a jest, or that we simply say nothing. It's not within the power of another human to make us angry... unless we allow and help them to do so! On the other hand, staying peaceful and indifferent *is* within our power. And this is something we need to remember and hold on to at all times. For this is our prime weapon against inconveniences and maladies coming from other people.

Fragment VII

> "They did not admit me to their house today, although they admitted others." "They either turned haughtily away or openly laughed when I spoke." Or, "They placed me, at dinner, not on the middle couch, but on the lowest one," and other matters of the same sort, which I can call nothing but the whinings of a queasy spirit. [...] Someone [...] who is affected by insult shows that they possesses neither sense nor trustfulness. [...] [A Stoic] *is scorned by no one.*
>
> Seneca, *On the Firmness of the Wise Man*, 10.2-3

Commentary: Excessive sensitivity to the words and thoughts of others can also be rooted in what we conveniently deem "low self-esteem." Clearly, it is something we need to get rid of, since a Stoic, just as Seneca says, knows their own valor. But how, in Stoicism, do we learn to place faith in ourselves and hold ourselves in high regard?

This isn't something that can be built in a day. This is not something we can magically conjure up in a split-second epiphany. Self-esteem is more like a muscle that we need to work hard to strengthen. We become more self-aware and reliant only through patient and persistent practice. This practice starts off with an honest self-inquiry, an inquiry into what our values and goals really are. We must mull it over, we must define what we want, we must define what is dear and important to us. This needs to cover the entire range of the time scale: we need to know what we want in terms of days, but also in our life in general. As long as we are lost, as long as we float one idea and then another, as long we have nothing concrete to hold on to and work with – we will be faltering and we will be dangerously open to influence and manipulation.

Let's consider an example. Someone trashes our work, spills some online vitriol on us, or says mean words of sheer jealousy or malice. We should be able to be indifferent to that. But if we really want this indifference to come, we need to have something to shield us from these rogue missiles. We can't stop them with our bare hands. We require countermeasures. And the best (and quite possibly the *only*) feasible weapons in this battle are our own narratives. We need our own, independently chosen and carefully defined values, goals and commitments. There is only one thing that can make us immune to the vicious criticism and haters' influence. It is our own, self-aware and robust narrative on who we are, what we care for, and on the world in general.

We need to take time and put a lot of thought into this. Let's take bold and restless effort to define our values clearly and precisely. This is our A-game, this is our best possible reply to the pressure of outside voices and judgments. If we work hard to do this, if we buckle up and keep it tight, we'll not only get more immunity to the derisive outside influences, but we'll also have less time and attention span to even keep track of them. Once we have our own values and commitments to manage, we will easily focus on our own instead of paying this excessive, treacherous attention to what others have to say.

Fragment VIII

Someone who seeks to know what is said about them, who digs up spiteful tales even if they were told in secret, is oneself the destroyer of their own peace of mind.

Seneca, *Of Anger*, III.11.1

Commentary: The next device of autonomy can be neatly summed up the following way: let's not court the malice of others! Let's not meet it halfway, let's hold our line. Let's be once and for all *not* interested in scandal and slander, in the small-ball, low-life gossip, in the second-hand and fifth-mouth hearsay. Let's not invite trouble, let's not open ourselves up to spite and venom.

It is – alas – the stark reality that others will try to shove a handful of bitter pills down our throat. It's just a fact of human life. And yet, a great number of those pills can be easily avoided if we don't seek them voluntarily. We just needn't keep an ear out for blather. We can dodge many bullets simply by not attracting them. Let's grant ourselves a right to a degree of ignorance: to a certain extent, it is better to simply not know what other people say and think.

Stoicism underlines that even though the rule "don't make yourself vulnerable for no reason" sounds reasonable, it's still surprisingly often breached in practice. It's a deeply anchored human trait. It seems as if the clay we're made of is laced with masochism. It happens over and over to all of us that we – consciously or subconsciously, by deeds or by negligence – sit down to absorb the harm that others do. We lend a patient ear to what they have to say, we hinge on their opinions, we scroll the newsfeed, we do all this despite knowing full well that nothing will come of this except for bitterness, disenchantment and pain. That's why Stoicism urges us: let's not expose ourselves to blows and influences. We don't need to know *everything* that comes to pass in the human world. Knowing it all is not a necessary condition to live a good life. Moreover, quite often it's a direct detriment to it! We need to temper our curiosity and we need to keep our cognitive urges at bay. They need to serve us – we mustn't be enslaved to them.

Fragment IX

> What is it to be reviled? Stand by a stone and revile it: and what will you gain? If then a [Stoic] listens like a stone, what profit is there to the reviler?

Epictetus, Discourses, I.25.28-29

Commentary: To the spite and malice that fellow humans point at us we should react just as a stone reacts to whatever happens around it. That is, we should not react at all. We should be impervious like a rock. Whether the sun scorches it, whether it freezes to minus fifty below, whether waves gently lap around it or smash into it with full force, a rock is potent to not care. This is what we should aim at. It is, admittedly, an ambitious move and a noble goal. But how on earth could we get there? How can we guide ourselves there?

Epictetus reviews for us a very curious mechanism which works in the reviler's mind. Why do they revile us? Why are they mean to us in the first place? What's the kick, what's their gain? Humans are very self-oriented creatures and revilers are no exception. Thus, most of them aren't interested in actually harming or crippling us, but simply in finding their very own satisfaction. This is the key point! No one (almost) is so into us that they would actually care about harming us. In most cases, the revilers are much more into their own wicked satisfaction.

Let's just recall the last instance (of many, since we all have a long history with them) when we heard that all our ideas are garbage, that our intellect is limited, not to mention our mother, who... And now let's put our mind to this: the person who says all these things has (usually!) no direct interest in trashing our concepts, mind or parent. What they are keen on is making themselves content – through our discontentment. They don't want to really evaluate us (our intellect, our parent, etc.) They just want to see that their words can be effective, that they succeed in getting under our skin. They want to see that they are able to hurt us – that is their joy! They aren't after our pain itself, but after proving to themselves that they are able to inflict pain. They seek their own self-empowerment in their crooked way – by demonstrating to themselves that they are able to make us hurt.

But if this is so, if the reviler reviles us just to earn their corrupt degree of satisfaction, then shouldn't we just break that loop? Why don't we cut this vicious cause-and-effect chain? Here is how: we need to simply *not let on* that the words of the reviler afflicted us. And let's keep in mind the anecdote about Niels Bohr,[72] according to which he was asked why he, a prominent physicist and a rational man, still keeps a horseshoe in his study. The reply: "Because it brings you luck, whether you believe in it or not." And here is the same: the method we are talking about will work whether or not we feel offended to begin with.

The key step here is that we don't give the "feedback" to the offender. Let's condense our will, let's keep a straight face... and just say nothing. Sucking it up is often the bravest thing to do. And by doing it, we take the wind out of the sails of our offender. Once they don't get their feedback, they don't get their satisfaction. Which in turn renders their effort of offending us useless... and they will leave us alone, going somewhere else, to find an easier target.

---

[72] Niels Bohr (1885 – 1962) was a Danish physicist and a Nobel prize winner. He created the so called Bohr model of atomic structure.

And let's firmly keep Niels Bohr in mind! In our social wrestling with other people, in combating insult and tackling passive-aggression (which is, truly and sadly, the universal currency of our interactions), it is really perception over facts. This is the hard truth of social communication: what we let on is more important than what we feel. But as somber as this remark is, there is a silver lining in it. From the offender's point of view, there is no difference whether we already are stone-cold impervious, or if we play it cool through patient and perseverant sucking it up. Even if we do the latter, we'll soon get to the point where we no longer need it, because either the offender goes away, or we actually become impervious. This is where we take benefit from the fake-it-till-you-make-it scenario. By investing ourselves in non-responding we either make the insulter go away, or we stop noticing their vile activity.[73]

Fragment X

> *If a [...] person speaks ill of you, do not make any defense to what has been told [...], but reply, "The man did not know the rest of my faults, for he would not have mentioned these only."*
>
> Epictetus, Encheiridion, 33

Commentary: We have already underscored the importance of making others believe that their mean words make zero impression on us. But what if they don't just offend or insult us, but rather criticize us? There is a discernible difference, for insults and offences are usually emotional, or at least they appeal to emotions. Criticism, on the other hand, works on the rational level (or at least appeals to it). Insults and offences may come from sheer spitefulness, from the pure will to blemish us. Thus, the insulter doesn't have to care whether their remarks are grounded in facts or not. With criticism it's a different ball game. Criticism doesn't rest on thin air and undistilled malevolence only, but it is substantiated by facts (or alleged facts at least). What do we need to do in this case?

First of all, we need to acknowledge and accept whatever actual shortcoming our critics managed to pin down. If someone tells us that we sing out of tune, that we infer far-fetched conclusions, that we drive too fast, or that we have a drinking problem, and if we know they are right on this, then we can't turn a blind eye and refuse to accept this. We cannot deny our flaws and mistakes. We should rather thank the critics. The critics, after all, do work for us: they poke

---

[73] For more on this topic see the excellent book by William Irvine: *A Slap in the Face: Why Insults Hurt, And Why They Shouldn't*.

around, they evaluate us and they track down our weaknesses. A critic is a cross of a beta tester and a therapist, someone who provides a precious service to us, service which we otherwise would have to pay for. And here we got it for free – the critic does it free of charge, fueled by their own desire to diminish us. Why not embrace it and use it to our advantage?

Justified, evidence-based criticism is one thing... but what about criticism which is neither well-founded nor constructive? What about criticism which is just pure nitpicking? Stoicism has a perfect comeback to it, a comeback which is twisted yet effective. It works like this: if someone drones over our flaws and faults, we don't deny it but we immediately retort that they don't even know the whole story. We say that apparently they know just a tiny slice of our deficiencies and errors, because had they known the whole thing, they wouldn't have limited themselves to what little they mentioned. So, if someone says that we sing out of tune, then we need to reply that they missed that we have no sense of rhythm either. If they say that our conclusions are far-fetched, we add that our premises too rest on shifting sands. If they say that we drive too fast, we sass back that they would be scared to death if they saw how recklessly we maneuver in the parking lot. And so on and so forth. In a word: the safest way to pass through the fiery criticism is to add fuel to the flames ourselves. We just need to chip in some extra bits of information (or misinformation) and it will reduce the power of our enemy's ammunition. The more we add to the mix ourselves, the more watered down their criticism is. It will also baffle our critics, since it will prove to them that we are capable of distancing ourselves from ourselves and our own deficiencies. Such feedback isn't something they expected. Thus, chances are they just will be happy to leave us alone. And the cherry on top is that this method is a bit of a magic bullet – it works all over the board. Everyone can benefit from it. After all, no one is boy scout enough to have nothing in the closet that could be brought to light.

Fragment XI

No one is laughed at who begins by laughing at oneself.

Seneca, On the Firmness of the Wise Man, 17.2

Commentary: Laughter is another type of distress that we can be exposed to in our social interactions. Laughter has its own laws and rules, which are markedly different than vicious insults and criticism, and we need to have a distinct measure of defense against it. We need a counter-weapon that would be appropriate and effective. What would that be?

Laughter differs from criticism since it neither appeals to reason, nor it is substantiated, nor constructive. Thus, arguments – the devices of reason – won't be useful here. Laughter happens on an entirely different level, and if someone already laughs at us then there is no use in trying to reason with them. There is no point in trying to explain or prove that their laughter is groundless. What would that even mean? There is no point in saying that there is nothing to laugh at. If someone laughs at us, they are about joking us down, about diminishing, or even humiliating us. They want to deem us insignificant and not even important enough to be criticized seriously. And this is a move that, by its very logic, can't be countered directly. We just become more of a laughing stock if we, under the pressure of laughter, try to prove that we are "serious." To try to debunk our comicality with a poker face and serious eyes – it just excites more laughter from those who already declared that we are laughable.

How then, should we go about laughter? Stoicism teaches us that the patterns and properties of laugher, as recapped above, provide us with an exceptionally powerful weapon against it. We just need to laugh at ourselves! We can either join those who already laugh at us for whatever reason, or we can be even quicker than they are. The moment we start laughing at ourselves, we pull off a really astounding trick: we take the side of those laughing. And here is the magic of it: it doesn't matter that we are laughing at us! The division is not between those who laugh and those are laughed at, but between those who laugh and those who don't. If we willingly choose to join the laughing camp, we show them all that we have a good sense of humor and, more importantly, that we can take ourselves lightly. Not to mention that by doing this we'll make our laughing company realize that laughing at us is not really a laughable matter... and they will more often than not proceed to laugh at someone else.

Fragment XII

Suppose someone shall despise me. Let them look to that themselves. But I will look to this, that I be not discovered doing or saying anything deserving of contempt. Shall anyone hate me? Let them look to it. But I will be mild and benevolent toward everyone.

Marcus Aurelius, *Meditations*, 11.13

Commentary: Having said all this, we still need to remember that a delicate equilibrium is required in this domain. Reformed Stoicism calls for autonomy, yes, but it doesn't call for egoism, dryness of heart or insensibility. It's a fine line here, and we need to stay on the right side of it. Also, by all accounts, deference to our own mental autonomy and deference to others come hand in hand. If we don't learn to respect ourselves and to cherish our own right do define our own values and goals, then no one will respect us. And we won't be able to respect others. This indeed works both ways: our own proper self-respect is an entry ticket to building any in-depth, true relationship with others. Serious, sincere and meaningful interhuman relationship is possible only between autonomous individuals.

Thus, we should be as generous and magnanimous to others as possible in a given context and situation. Remember: when it comes to the narratives of the others, our Stoic goals is to secure our independence from them, not to fight them. And let's also remember that other people have just the same right (and need) to be mentally independent as we do. And let's also remember that being unfriendly to others is a proof of weakness (and of shortcoming of Stoic skills). Ill-disposition, scorn, or mistreatment of others follow from nothing else than our fickleness and incertitude about our own narratives. For whoever learnt to guard their own autonomy, will easily give others the liberty to do just the same.

Chapter 19

To each their own mistakes

Look not round at the depraved morals of others, but run straight along the line.

Marcus Aurelius, *Meditations*, 4.18

In a nutshell: All mistakes of others and all of their corruption – is on them, not on us. Everything they do goes on their account and stains their conscience, not ours. We need to learn how to deal with our own issues, not with the issues of others. Only our issues are an obstacle preventing us from living well, and the issues of others are not.

***

Misconduct of others incriminates them, not us (fragment I), because we have no authority over their will and behavior (II). It is not within our power to correct others (III). Excessive preoccupation with their mistakes is nothing short of tormenting ourselves (IV), and there are so many of these mistakes that we are not even able to reckon them appropriately (V). We need to be tolerant of the imperfections of others (VI), and this has nothing to do with egoism (VII).

Fragment I

It is not the acts of others which disturb us […] but it is our own opinions [narratives] which disturb us. Take away these opinions then, and resolve to dismiss your judgment about an act as if it were something grievous, and your anger is gone.

Marcus Aurelius, *Meditations*, 11.18

Commentary: In the previous chapter, we have discussed the idea that thoughts and actions of other humans inflict nothing on us, unless we give them green light to do harm. For instance, let's imagine a Peter whose only mission in life is to drink hard, harass people and commit petty thefts. Does it concern us? Does it even touch us, does it burden our shoulders or taint our conscience? No, it doesn't. We just need to create a fitting narrative about all this and we will easily stay out of it. What narrative would that be? Simply, that Peter's decisions and actions are *his* decisions and actions.

Let's now expand this example and let's consider another person: an Abigail. Does Peter's decisions and actions concern Abigail? Do they harm her? If Peter commits any wrongdoing, does it go to Abigail's account? Is it her problem? No. If only, of course, she makes sure that she has a fitting narrative. The same holds for Ellen and for William. No matter how hard Peter tries to shift guilt and responsibility on others, he won't succeed (as long as others will secure proper Stoic narratives for themselves). No moral consequences resulting from Peter's actions will ever fall on Abigail or William, or on anyone else. And since they have to fall *somewhere*, they will fall on the only person that can't weasel out of them – that is on Peter himself.

In short, each and every one of us needs to be solely, totally and exclusively responsible for their own life. It's indeed a simple, stark and trivial truth... but the matter of fact is that it's still way too often neglected. Stoicism firmly reminds us that whatever happens and regardless of everything, no matter what we think and what it seems – we must never neglect this principle. We must always live, act and behave as if it held. Nothing should deflect us from this and no one should fool us. We need to do this because it will always be advantageous to us and simply because there is no other option. This is the way of the world. The faults and fails of another human are incapable of jumping onto our account. "To Each Their Own Mistakes" – this isn't just a description or just a postulate. It is the only logical possibility on the table.

Fragment II

No one has in their power the mind of another.

Epictetus, *Discourses*, IV.5.4

Commentary: Other people, their reason and their mind are not within our power to control. We can force no one to alter their thinking, we can't even peek into another's mind. The thoughts of another human are eternally a sealed riddle to us: more or less puzzling, but always a riddle. We don't have control and we also bear no responsibility, because – whilst a commonplace yet important notion goes – responsibility and control go hand in hand. There is indeed a degree of absurd in demanding responsibility from someone who has no control over a given issue. Thus, since we have no control over Peter's, Abigail's, William's and Ellen's thoughts and behavior, we are also free from responsibility for them. And this is a bold statement: we not only have no control over them, but we also shouldn't have it. Other people are and should remain separate, autonomous individuals.

Clearly, this claim might be immediately countered. The objection is clear. Don't we wash our hands too easily here? One may well say – based on intuition and not without some merit to it – that we may have at least some control over what others think and do. After all, we can talk to them, we can *try* to influence their behavior, we can try to reason with them. So, is that Epictetus' claim really 100 percent accurate? What about discussion and persuasion? What about social pressure and cultural context?

I hope that the basic, primary answer is already clear at this point: there is no in-between, no gray area here. The divide between things within and not within our power is sharp. Everything is either fully in our control, or not at all. And let's now think about our interaction with other people. What can we do? How can we try to persuade them? Indeed, we can try to talk them into certain things or out of them… but at the end of the day, the final decision is always theirs. And this means that their actions *aren't* within our power in the strict Stoic sense. Other people aren't (and shouldn't be!) marionettes which dance at our fingertips. We aren't their masters. We don't have full control of them, which, in Stoicism, means that we have no control at all and that we should treat them accordingly.

Lack of control and the ensuing lack of responsibility is one thing. On the other hand, we aren't responsible for other people simply because we shouldn't be. Us taking upon ourselves the responsibility for others is nothing else than stripping them of this responsibility. And this is what we need to avoid. As discussed in the chapter on autonomy, we need to remember that both we and others need to be fully independent individuals. If we rip someone off responsibility, we unavoidably end up treating them like kids, in a condescending, non-serious manner. Such an approach is the direct opposite of respect, for respect means granting to each their own responsibility.

Fragment III

> [It] *is both impracticable and long, to attempt the very thing which Zeus has not been able to do,* [i.e.] *to convince all people what things are good and bad. Is this power given to you? This only is given to you, to convince yourself.*
>
> Epictetus, *Discourses*, IV.6.5

Commentary: Let's now apply the idea of the proper alternatives here. We are confronted with the fact that other people misbehave – they form wrong judgments and useless narratives, they are mean to us or to themselves, in a word, they conduct themselves poorly. What do we do about that? What can we do? There are two options on the table. First off, we can try to fix them, we can try to get them to be better people. The second option is to accept them as they are, and deal with the fact that people are what they are and that they behave as they behave.

The important point is that – despite various misinterpretations – reformed Stoicism doesn't proclaim ex-cathedra which of these two ways is better. It rather insists that we need to decide on one-by-one basis. (This happens in the mentioned spirit of responsibility: reformed Stoicism doesn't strip us off the responsibility for our choices). Both ways have their merits and demerits and we are the only ones to judge which of them fits better in any given situation.

Yet, we need to remember that chances are that if we choose the first way to go, that is if we decide to try to somehow rectify our fellow humans, we will be burdened. The onus of this task is formidable. The level of difficulty may well go through the roof and may easily surpass the capacity of our will and resolve. We may spend infinite amounts of time, energy and skill on debating and dealing with others... and all in vain. It's likely that despite the effort we put in, they won't change at all. They may be reluctant to do so simply because they trust themselves more than they trust us, or, as it might be, just to spite us. Epictetus remarks that this path is "impracticable and long." And indeed – and contra the Einstein's alleged saying – not only the universe and human stupidity are infinite, but human sloth and mediocrity too. Combating them is like struggling with a hydra, with new heads growing even before we manage to cut anything off. It's extremely hard to beat such an enemy... so maybe it's prudent not to engage?

Fragment IV

If it be your duty, to be angry at base deeds, and to be excited and saddened at crimes, then there is nothing more unhappy than you, for all your life will be spent in anger and grief. What moment will there be at which you will not see something deserving of blame? Whenever you leave your house, you will be obliged to walk among people who are criminals, misers, spendthrifts, profligates, and who are happy in being so.

Seneca, *Of Anger*, II.7.1-3

Commentary: If happiness is the goal of life, then the whole *ars vivendi* is organized around how to live well and happily. And there is no surer and more obvious impediment to that than to shackle our happiness to the thoughts, words and deeds of others. These thoughts and deeds are not within our power, for one. But moreover, the mental dependence on others puts us in the grip of a certain grave asymmetry. What asymmetry is that? It is that others are able to make us unhappy, but fundamentally unable to make us happy.

Such an asymmetrical situation is, of course, deeply nonstoic and highly disadvantageous to us.

Forgetting or forgoing the idea of "To Each Their Own Mistakes" sets up a major hurdle on our track to a good life. Moral autonomy and our exclusive access to our own moral account is a must. Of course, we may try to find some kind of a middle way, we may try to work out some kind of a compromise and admit that the mistakes of others burden us *partially*, just to some extent.... but this is a dead end, which we will inevitably learn if we espouse it. It just won't work. It's plainly impossible to build any kind of workable equilibrium between our individual soul and the corruption of the entire world. We just shouldn't wrestle with infinity. We shouldn't stand up to something which is a billion times more powerful than we are. If we allow such confrontation, our happiness and our peace of mind will be flattened and crushed in the uneven battle. The only livable solution is to draw the boundary: no ill-thought or misconduct of others shall be treated on equal terms with our own thoughts and deeds. Nothing that other people say or do is on a par with the things that are within our power – with our own narratives, our moral character, our values and goals. These are two completely different realms and we need to keep a watchful eye on how and when we let them interact. After all, the goal of all this is to be happy, not to settle for "anger and grief."

Fragment V

> *If you want [...] to be as angry as the atrocity of people's crimes requires, you must not merely be angry, but must go mad.*
>
> Seneca, *Of Anger*, II.9.4

Commentary: Letting the mistakes of others sink in and stain our conscience is not only an act of direct auto-sabotage (because if tarnishes our happiness), it's not only in vain (because it won't change the conduct and character of others), but it's also supremely irrational. Why is it so?

Because the grand total of malevolence and moral mistakes of others is so huge, that it's impossible to wrap our head around it and "be angry at it" consistently and appropriately. It's a logical impossibility to construct an appropriate account of it. Capabilities of a human are limited and so are the capabilities of a Stoic. We have a certain threshold of perception and crossing it makes our mind numb... while the overall level of human corruption exceeds that threshold in spades. In this vein, it's an exercise in futility to take to heart the depravity of others.

But what about being selective of it? Instead of being concerned with all of human vice, why not zoom in on a certain portion of it? Why not allow ourselves to remain sensitive to some of human malice, while being indifferent to the rest of it? As a matter of fact, it's quite a widespread policy, but still, it's very inconsistent and irrational. Why is that? Because if we want to be concerned by some of the errors of other people, then we need to set up a clear border between what we are concerned with and what we are indifferent to. But to do so is impossible! Any such border will be – of necessity – completely arbitrary. We won't be able to ground it in anything solid.

Let's picture a gloomy scenario that a close friend of ours gets killed in a car accident. How will that information affect us? What will we feel? And will we feel the same if the same happens to our elementary school friend, whom we haven't seen in years? There are many possible answers here, and every one of them can be argued for and against. The point is not about the exact trajectory of the line which separates things that concern us and that don't, but that this line is of necessity curvy, malleable and by all means arbitrary. There are no universal, "objective," or rational criteria for drawing it. However we choose to do it, it will always be deeply subjective and it will always be hurtful to whoever is left on the other side. And *some* will always be left there – since it is impossible to embrace everybody and everything.

Stoicism reaches an unambiguous conclusion here. If it is so that all conceivable criteria are arbitrary and every conceivable line of demarcation is unjust to some people, why don't we then abandon this line whatsoever? Why don't we just not draw it? Let's drop it once and for all, let's once and for all become equally just and fair to everybody. Let's imply some solidarity here: let's leave *all* other people on the other side of our mind. And let's keep our side to ourselves. Let's settle that other people think and act on their own account, and that their own mistakes are on them. And that they have no bearing on our happiness whatsoever. This is the only logical and consistent solution – every other way will be random, haphazard and arbitrary.

Fragment VI

> Do [people] *ever cease abusing Caesar? What then? [...] Is not what is said reported to Caesar? What then does he do? He knows that if he punished all who abuse him, he would have nobody to rule over.*
>
> Epictetus, Discourses, III.4.7-9

Commentary: Most of the argument presented in this chapter may easily come across as hardline and egoistic. Let's now look in turn at the above words of Epictetus, the words which are softer and which convey more understanding to others. Importantly, the Stoic position comprises *both* these points of view. We mustn't allow others to shift their blame onto our shoulders, but we also mustn't be needlessly harsh on them. The Stoic stance is lame without both these elements. These two viewpoints shed light on each other and explain each other. We need to embrace them both to fully and properly understand who others are to us in this worldly playground.

Epictetus calls for nothing else than simply *tolerance* for the corruption, villainy and mediocrity of other people. The Caesar Epictetus speaks of is every inch aware that most of his subjects are to an extent reluctant toward him. No one loves the sovereign unconditionally. And yet, the Caesar understands that it would be an utter absurd to persecute them all... because doing so would undermine his own rule. He would "have nobody to rule over" – these words have a twofold meaning. First, if the Caesar makes his mind to be really rigorous, if he wants to punish for the minutest wrongdoing, he may have to execute virtually *all* of his subjects. Second, if he imposes a policy of tough austerity, the citizens may turn on him and he may face a revolt. The laws and ways of politics have changed since antiquity, but this reasoning still applies in our social life. If we are too stringent on other people, we will either become loners, or we will have people turn on us. Or both.

The message is quite simple. If we don't want to launch the hermit protocol, if we want to keep living with and among people, if we want to maintain social relationships and if we want them to be meaningful – we need a great deal of magnanimity. People will always be, to an extent banal and erroneous. Accepting and tolerating this is the price which we need to pay if we want to stay inside society. This is what the proper alternative looks like here: we either accept the rules of the social game (which require us to have warm understanding and genuine tolerance for what others do), or we switch the game and head for a life of seclusion.

Fragment VII

You are not formed [...] to be depressed with others nor to be unhappy with others, but to be happy with them.

Epictetus, *Discourses*, III.24.1-2

Commentary: Reformed Stoicism doesn't compel us to be inhumane and cold-blooded egoists. We have discussed it at length already and I hope that the picture that emerges is clear. Yet, it's an important matter and it's worth throwing in some additional argument. For indeed, it's *not* true that the idea of "To Each Their Own Mistakes" amounts to egoism or self-absorption. Stoicism is not Cynicism and autonomy isn't selfishness.

Stoicism holds that everyone is responsible for their own. It insists that everyone's mistakes are their own lot. This doesn't come from heartlessness, though, or from cruelty, but from the demand for autonomy. It is vital in reformed Stoicism that everyone has the inalienable right to decide on their own and define their own character. We don't ignore or neglect others, but quite the contrary: we empower them. We consider others as fully independent, moral subjects who define their own values, goals and commitments just as we define our own. Their autonomy is on a par with ours. But autonomy entails responsibility and responsibility, in turn, entails that no one shifts consequences onto others. The idea of "To Each Their Own Mistakes" comes not from condescension, but from respect.

Just as Epictetus says, our destiny and our human lot isn't to earn a good life and happiness at the expense of others, but to share it with them. We are all in this together, remember? There is no need to multiply misery by absorbing the outside corruption. Our goal is to bring joy, not sorrow, into this world. And there is only one realm where we can really leave our mark, only one domain where we can really have an actual input – in the things within our power. Only inside and through our own narratives, thoughts, values and goals we can have some imprint on the world. This is our only way to increase the overall sum of happiness. Thoughts, values and goals of others belong to them and constitute their own lot. Only by holding up our end, we can contribute to the overall good fortune. Our side of the social bargain is what we can control and what we own. The side of other people is well beyond our ken.

Being good to others doesn't mean that we drop all our errands and race up to others to serve them and to help them with what they can't be helped with. The best and the most urgent thing that we can do to others is to lead by example. Paradoxically: even if we set "making others happy" as the main and crowning goal of our life, even then our prime duty will be to take care of our own. It is after all impossible to make others happy if we are unhappy ourselves. And beyond a shadow of a doubt: we benefit no one if we don't live well and happily ourselves. It's easy to be miserable, but it is a vain effort. Neither will our misery do anyone any good, nor is our happiness harmful or transferable to anyone else.

Chapter 20

Don't ascribe intent

The wave dashes in vain against a great cliff.

Seneca, *Of Anger*, III.25.3

In a nutshell: All detriment that another human may inflict on us doesn't differ from the inconvenience imposed on us by rain, frost or high water. All the hostility that others express toward us, toward themselves, and toward the world, needs to be treated on a par with unintentional, elemental forces. Someone disturbs us? Let's assume that they didn't mean it. Let's just see their actions as nothing else than vile wind or a summer tempest. Someone troubled us? It's nothing else than an inadvertent foul, or being jostled by a drunkard.

***

We need to regard hindrances generated by other people as nothing else than hindrances generated by meteorological forces (fragment I), because neither is within our power (II). Misconduct of a fellow human is like bad weather (III), like the murmur of flowing water (IV), or like injury in sports (V). We should see others' animosity as behavior of madmen (VI) or of inebriated people. We shouldn't pay back to others (VIII), but we need to remain cordial to one another (IX).

Fragment I

> [The Stoics] *endure everything in the same spirit with which they endure the cold of winter and the severities of climate, fevers, diseases, and other chance accidents.*
>
> Seneca, On the Firmness of the Wise Man, 9.1

Commentary: It's a notion that echoes through the Stoic system that we need to be indifferent to the malice and spite of others. This indifference is indeed necessary and noble, but... not easy to attain. In order to make that easier for us, the Stoics point out that in any case of mistreatment by others it is not the facts on the ground that hurt us most, but the perception of malicious intent. And this is something that we can use to our advantage.

For some reason, we are hard-wired to take intentional actions directed against us as much more painful than random misfortunes. It's easier for us to swallow a rainstorm, which floods the neighborhood, than an online shitstorm against us. A cold wave that messes up our vacation is somehow easier to accept, than malicious gossip that someone spreads against us. The difference is that with the cold wave or rainstorm we by default don't ascribe intent to adversity. We assume no conscious agency working to our disadvantage. Thus, the most painful and bitter element is absent. When we deal with elemental forces, we don't have to wonder why another human being wished to harm us or if we deserved it. We don't have to figure out why this comes about, we don't have to ponder what we did to them. There is no "them" in the situation – there is only the irrational element of chance. We never accuse a hailstorm or a draught of intentional wrongdoing, we never think that they conspire against us. In this sense, it's easier to come to terms with them than with other people. And this is the very attitude we need to take on and expand.

Having recognized that it's not the actual harm but ill intent that hurts us most, we need to turn it to our advantage. We should employ it to our own end and start thinking in the same, "intent-free" way even if intent is present. This is the core idea of this chapter. We need to learn to feel about the problems generated by others the same way we think about the inconveniences of meteorology. Whenever another human speaks or acts against us, we need to handle it just as we do with cold rain which soaks us, or wind which blows in our face.[74]

Fragment II

> *Ask yourself: "Is it possible, then, that shameless people should not be in the world?" It is not possible. Do not, then, require what is impossible. [...] Let the same considerations be present to your mind in the case of [...] everyone who does wrong in any way. For, at the same time, that you remind yourself that it is impossible that such kind of people should not exist, you will become more kindly disposed toward every one individually.*
>
> Marcus Aurelius, Meditations, 9.42

---

[74] Remember that it's the misdeeds of others that we want to treat as impersonal, wild forces, not others themselves. Other people are not our enemy – only their wrongdoings are. This will be explored more in commentary to fragment IV.

Commentary: It's highly useful to put annoyances and vexations brought about by other people on a par with inconveniences brought about by unintentional and irrational forces. But is it licit to do so? Does it hold at the bar of reason?

The main affinity between wild elements and deleterious humans is that we are essentially helpless when we face them. They are not within our power to control, we can't just restrain them with our sheer will. We can't stop the rain from raining and we can't intercept someone's will – the two are much alike in this manner. If we set out to influence someone's behavior, or even just their thought, then no matter how hard we try, we will sooner or later hit a brick wall. We will arrive at the unyielding conclusion that another human is a fully autonomous subject, who is independent from us and our interference (is and should be – remember the chapter on this!). Their decisions are their own and their mistakes are on them. If they make up their mind to harbor ill will against us or anyone else, then there is nothing we can do to combat that. This is this fundamental similarity which allows us to apply one and the same approach to our fellow humans and to hailstorms.

We have zero control over the weather and we have zero control over whether others are benevolent or malicious. Both are external forces, they are forces which we can do nothing about and which both may turn against us. But again, here is the key: the theoretical possibility of harm isn't harmful to us. It's not the actual facts that hurt us, but – remember the first chapter! – our narratives about the facts. And in this particular case, it all comes down to whether or not we assume an intent-free narrative. We are well used to explaining the phenomena of weather in terms of non-intentional occurrences. After all, no sane person thinks of a sudden rainstorm in terms of a conspiracy, even if this storm thwarts their plans. The intent is the most painful component of the whole mix. We instinctively refrain from ascribing it to weather. Why don't we do the same about our conflicts with other humans?

Fragment III

> *So far as some people make themselves obstacles to my proper acts, they become to me one of the things which are indifferent, no less than the sun or wind.*

Marcus Aurelius, *Meditations*, 5.20

Commentary: The number of ways in which others may maltreat us is truly infinite. A single person may strike against us, like when they spread gossip about us, but a whole community just as well, like when it pays attention to it. This may happen in a conscious and premeditated way (like when we are robbed, or our car gets stolen), or it may happen incidentally (like when someone drives recklessly and gives us a fender-bender). Regardless of the exact scenario, the turnout is the same and we are the aggrieved party. How do we go about that? We implement one and the same strategy: we ascribe no intent to the external factors. Whatever or whoever they are.

They just happen all around and all over us: like the roaring elements, like the relentless sun on a hot day, like the restless smashing of sea waves. The wind is blowing, the vicious people gossip, the rainfalls come and go, the drunk drivers pose a threat to us – we need to bracket all these cases together. We need to assume one and the same attitude towards them all, we need to take on all these phenomena as unintentional slips of chance. They just came to pass our way – there was no malignity, no conspiracy included. It all just happened. Such instances are and will be there, beyond our ken and above our paygrade, completely out of our control. Gradients of pressure and the whims of Aeolus will always move the winds around, while human weakness and villainy will always push them into gossip and slander. This is just how it goes, unintentionally, by the very way of the world.

Fragment IV

> *Variety of noise surrounds me on every side: I lodge even over a bath. Suppose now all kinds of sounds that* [I hear] [...] *I assure you, Lucilius, I regard all this noise no more than the ebbing and flowing of the water.*
>
> Seneca, *Epistles*, 56.1-3

Commentary: We have all been there. We all know this feeling way to well. Just picture this and listen how it rings a bell. We are working hard on something, we are trying to concentrate, the deadlines are looming... and then the whole focus bursts away when the clatter of calls and voices breaks in. Or on a different note. We are trying to relax, we open a book and a bottle of wine... and then all of a sudden our laptop chimes and a Skype call comes in, and someone drones on for half an hour on stuff which doesn't concern us. Seneca's words strike indeed a very contemporary tone here. We all live in a flood of information, messages, blips and buzzes. This is the true mark of the early 21st century. It's hard to evade it since we are humans, humans are a social species, and the social dimension will always strain us, trying to break and enter into our life at the weirdest hours. And it's particularly alarming a problem in our very own times, when we are supremely connected but distracted, and when the drumbeat of human news is louder than ever.

One way to avoid this continuous exposure to the din of human affairs is to abandon the social world altogether and choose a life of reclusion, in whatever form that may be. Yet, this is surely a solution for few. Reformed Stoicism doesn't insist on this and it doesn't necessarily encourage any detachment from the society.[75] Quite the contrary: it holds that a good and happy life is perfectly possible inside the social realm. Thus, a viable solution is required, one which allows us to deal with the havoc that people create. The idea of not ascribing intent is just this solution. When it comes to the caprices of weather, we are well used to its unpredictability and we get along with it fairly well. The goal is to get along with people just the same.

Imagine again that we are in the middle of a family dinner and our uncle starts over the same rant we've heard a thousand times already. Or let's imagine that we are in the epicenter of a crazy mob, ready and eager to crucify someone. Or, let's take a more mundane example, i.e. that we can't evade the electronic devices which haunt us and pump tons of useless information into our mind. What can we do about that? It may sound off at first, but let's imagine that all of this is nothing but rain, gently murmuring on the roof of our cozy attic. Or that all this is just a pleasant whoosh of a waterfall. We shouldn't care more for the clangor coming in from throats and loudspeakers than we care for the distant thunders of the departing storm. Deep down they are the same: the primordial, inchoate forces which harbor no intention whatsoever, which cannot be stopped and shouldn't be worried about. In both cases, we need to open the umbrella, instead of ascribing malicious intent.

We are members of a gregarious species, so we tend to journey through our lives in the company of other humans. It's inevitable that they will chatter, that they will criticize or even trash us, that they will always have their own point of view, and that they will have their own demands and expectations. More often than not, this won't be very productive, many a time not even rational or on message. At some point, we will surely encounter humans not interested in having any dialogue with us whatsoever, but only in quarrel, obstruction and spite. What can we do about that? We have no choice but regard the voices of our companions as nothing else as the "ebbing and flowing of the water."

Sounds a bit harsh? Only on the surface! Let's not forget that Stoicism doesn't urge us to treat *people* this way, but only their ill-construed thoughts, words and deeds. Here we have a common denominator with Christianity: we are after sins, not after sinners. And accordingly, let's not forget that we aren't talking about *all* that others think, say and do, but only about the crooked

---

[75] For precision: reformed Stoicism neither requires nor prohibits a life of seclusion. Just as it doesn't require or prohibit any other practical arrangement of life.

parts of it. Stoicism emboldens us to embrace whatever inspiring and noble things our fellow humans do. The whole idea of not ascribing intent comes into play only when others behave in a way which is neither helpful, nor understanding, nor creative. It's only then that we need to consider them as if they were a mere murmur of water passing over the board. After all, if someone is disruptive and non-understanding, if they don't contribute but cumber – how are they different from the swish of running water? We won't change the fact that we share this world with mediocre people and we won't change the fact that waves exist. But it doesn't mean that we are supposed to ascribe intent to them and lament that the ship is rolling.

Fragment V

> *In the gymnastic exercises suppose that someone has torn you with their nails, and by dashing against your head has inflicted a wound. Well, we neither show any signs of vexation, nor are we offended, nor do we suspect him afterward as a treacherous fellow. [...] Something like this let your behavior be in all the other parts of life. Let us overlook many things in those who are like antagonists in the gymnasium.*

Marcus Aurelius, *Meditations*, 6.20

Commentary: Marcus Aurelius employs another metaphor here. The time of our life among other people is compared to a sport which we practice with them. Sport is indeed a very particular activity in which there is no want of chaos and no lack of risk. If we get into it, we may be sure that we at some point get injured or bruised. Let's picture ourselves playing basketball again. The moment we enter the court, we need to be ready that we get fouled up, jostled or hurt. These are just the rules of the game and if we want to live with, among and for other people – we need to factor in that risk. Shiners and injuries are always a possibility.

But still, we usually don't get exasperated by our fellow players. We know that the risk is the name of the game, that bumps and collisions are normal and unavoidable, and that they don't come from malice. They are just a part of the game, a byproduct of sport. If someone misses the ball and hits us instead, or if someone collides with us heavily, do we assume that they are after us and that they hate us? No, we don't. Even if the game is tough and sometimes brutal, we still don't regard our opponents as enemies. Not to mention that – in amateur sports at least – we often play against our friends. And for the sage's sake, if a friend draws a different lot and ends up in the opposite team, it doesn't mean they don't like us anymore. Sport is a good example since it's a custom we are all well versed in. We know well that it requires competition, and that competition may turn into a physical rivalry.[76]

Just the same holds in our life in general. Once we enter the court of societal life, we open ourselves to a range of foul and injury. This one will push us, that one will unknowingly hit us, sometimes we get grappled by someone who plays in our own team. And we need to do exactly what we do in sports. We needn't complain, we needn't get enraged. We needn't stop the game over a trifle. Certain brutality is (alas) embedded in the rules of social life and we need to accept this. The alternative, as mentioned, is seclusion.

As a reminder, let's think for a while about those who start ranting too easily. About those who scream and yell the moment they are pulled by their jersey, or when someone runs into them hard time. Isn't it ludicrous? Isn't it against the very idea of the game? As long as we talk sports, we may at least hope for a referee who may blow the whistle, pause the game and punish the wrongdoers. But what about real life? Is there anyone we can appeal to? Is there any jury, any overseeing authority that ensures that the rules are not breached? No.

It's only us and other people. So, if someone kicks our ankle under the table of the daily jostle, or cheats on us, where do we go to protest? Before whom do we bring our case? Who do we ask to stop the game and put the world on hold? There is no one to do such thing. We are adults already and we need to remember that our parents don't watch from the stands anymore. They won't intervene, they won't save us. We need to take care of our own and we needn't complain too easily. In life, as it goes in life, everyone watches their own omelet, and, as the saying has it, some eggs will inevitably be broken.

Fragment VI

> *What physician is angry with a crazy patient? Who takes to heart the curses of a fever-stricken one who is denied cold water? [The Stoics] retain in their dealings with all people this same habit of mind which the physician adopts in dealing with his patients.*
>
> Seneca, *On the Firmness of the Wise Man*, 13.1-2

Commentary: Seneca draws yet another comparison: to be overly concerned with what others say is as smart as taking to heart the words of wackos. That is, it's not smart at all. What sane person is angry at the deranged? Who trusts

---

[76] Let's also keep in mind that the very existence of a game hinges on following its rules. Thus, if we play a contact sport, we need to accept the possibility of contusions.

them? Imagine someone in the state of acute delirium. They run around like bedlamites, they see pink elephants. Do we rely on them? Do we believe them? Do we call in the de-elephantization crew? No, we don't. Another lunatic tells us dead serious that they are possessed by the devil. Or that we are. Do we buy into that? Do we base our judgments, our decisions, our commitments and our values on the babbling of those who lost the plot? No, we don't. And we shouldn't.

It's a social standard that we are allowed to not take too seriously those who are off their rocker. We don't attach much importance to their words and actions, we don't invest time and energy into analyzing any moonshine they come up with. But importantly: we are not ireful with them and we don't despise them. We don't scorn these poor people and we don't have to automatically deem madness as something uninteresting or deplorable. Our reasoning is much simpler. We need to largely ignore what the nutjobs have to say, because otherwise, we wouldn't be able to live our own lives. Their narratives are too much over the board, too volatile and too irrational. As such, they cannot be in any way incorporated into the kind of life that we aim at living. Nothing solid, nothing enduring can be based on what they say. If we open ourselves up too much to it, we quickly end up being completely inundated in garbage data, incoherent, counter-productive, useless. The daily wisdom goes that with each utterly stupid thing in the world comes someone even more stupid, who takes it seriously. But we shouldn't count ourselves in the ranks of prodigal. Maybe there are folks out there who have enough time and energy on their hands to waste them on dealing with the babbling of the madmen. But it needn't be us. We need to be focused on our own values, goals, and our character. We just don't have enough mental resources to deal with what shrinks and collectors of curiosities deal with.

If you wonder at this point about the relevance of this argument, don't. It doesn't come out of the blue. As a matter of fact, the ancient Stoics considered all nonstoics as slightly cuckoo. Their reasoning was simple: what sane person would reject the golden truth that happiness and good life depend on nothing else than what we think? What healthy human would spurn the idea that the key things like our values and goals, our happiness and peace of mind are within our power and we may just grab them? Renouncing all this seems not only nonsense, more than that, it seems a lunacy. The nonstoics are inherently unable to get along with themselves – and thus it's no surprise that their talk may seem similar to the loonies' talk. And we, in turn, should treat it just like that: like jabber of someone raging with fever and "denied cold water" – which is the worst of all!

Fragment VII

Once, when a guest in his cups bitterly reproached Pisistratus,[77] the despot of Athens, for his cruelty, many of those present offered to lay hands on the traitor [...] [Yet, Pisistratus] bore it coolly, and replied to those who were egging him on, that he was no more angry with the man than he should be with one who ran against him blindfold.

Seneca, Of Anger, III.11.4

Commentary: The Caesar we deliberated about in the previous chapter *tolerated* the offences, i.e. he saw guilt but didn't react. Pisistratus puts another strategy to action: he tries to *not even see the offence*. If someone drunkenly derides him, he takes it as if they run into them in the dark or blindfolded. This trick is a direct attempt to remove intent from the equation. This is exactly what Pisistratus does: even if there is some booze-fueled ill-intent in the wrongdoer, he chooses to behave as if there was none.

Drunk people and those who are blindfolded – visually or morally – have one fundamental thing in common. Their mishaps and misconducts aren't usually produced with malicious aforethought. They rather come from aberration of judgment and from eclipse of reason. As such, they are perfect examples of lack of intent. We are quite used to it already: we indeed attach different weight to what people say when they are mellow and when they are sober. We discriminate between whisky talking and a genuine conversation with another human being. And this is exactly the attitude we need to embrace and expand onto a whole new level. We need to acquire a habit of playing down the delinquencies of others as if they came from people who are drunk out of their minds.

Whenever and whoever becomes a possible source of inconvenience to us, we need to not ascribe malicious intent to their actions. We just need to treat them as if they were blind, drunk, unreasonable. Let's treat them as if they were in the world as bulls in a china shop, just rattling around, unknowing what they want and what they pursue. Should we be angry at them? Never! We just don't have the hours for that. We'd run out of our life soon if we were to lament every slip of each drunken tongue.

---

[77] Pisistratus (died 527 BC) ruled Athens for most of the 561-527 BC timespan. Contrary to the contemporary meaning of the word, he was widely praised as a "popular tyrant," who supported the growth of crafts, trade and expanded the city's infrastructure. He was also fond of arts and a generous sponsor of them.

Fragment VIII

Would anyone think that they are in their perfect mind if they were to return kicks to a mule or bites to a dog?

Seneca, *Of Anger*, III.27.1

Commentary: If everything else fails, we need to resort to our last ditch munition, that is the well-known idea of not paying back to those who do us a disservice. This isn't the same as turning the other cheek (which is a path that we are in reformed Stoicism not necessarily obliged to take, particularly if this path is naively charted). This isn't about a blanket ban on any reaction whatsoever. The point is that we need to take care to avoid escalation, to desist from an unrestrained exchange of blows which, in the long run, always does more harm than good.

It's a quite simple matter actually. If we strike back at someone, what keeps them from striking back at us? Remember that the nonstoics are among us. They are really out there. And if we don't curb ourselves down from retaliation, what will they do? What will they have left besides striking back at us even harder? This is how the spiral of violence takes off and for a Stoic, it's of course unacceptable to get involved in one. It's unacceptable not just because it's a grave misallocation of our precious time and energy. The main reason is that if we engage in such absurd give and take, we will sooner or later get caught up in it and we will lose control of our own narratives. That would be an in-spades violation of all that we have learnt.

Open confrontation with others, getting caught up in the exchange of spiteful repartees, paying them back hard – all of this is deeply nonstoic because it's essentially useless. Whatever offence or insult others may have committed, revenge for the sake of revenge will never make anything square. It will surely worsen our situation instead. No matter what happened, mindless reprisal is never the best option. This is what Seneca means with his straightforward comparison that eye for an eye and evil for evil is tantamount to kicking back a mule or biting back a dog. Indeed, we have just agreed that whoever harms us, harms us unintentionally (by definition, or because we refuse to acknowledge intent in their actions). They harm us (or rather the *try* to harm us) as someone who lost situation awareness and accidentally runs into us, or like a drunk person who trash-talks us. Our chief obligation is to strive to *not* become like them. We will often times get bruised by someone disoriented, or reviled by someone drunk. But it doesn't follow that we are supposed to get lost or drunk ourselves.

Fragment IX

When you are with many, you ought not to call it crowd, nor trouble, nor uneasiness, but festival and assembly, and so accept all contentedly.

Epictetus, *Discourses*, I.12.21

Commentary: We have already underscored time and again that reformed Stoicism has nothing to do with narrow egoism in its common, negative sense, and that it should never be mistaken for such. We aren't supposed to become selfish, to become deaf to the needs and emotions of others. We need to focus on our own good life, but not because others mean nothing to us, but because it just so happens, that our good life is something within our power – while the lives of others aren't. There is no gain in trying to forcibly bring others to happiness. If they don't want to do it on their own, fair enough. What we owe other people is, above all, respect for their autonomy. We must grant them freedom to think and act on their own account. Thus, if someone accuses Stoicism of promoting egoism, there is a ready-made answer to that: "What a crazy suggestion! Don't we do all within our power to happify humanity? We work really hard on that end! And we travel the best route towards there: we don't force anyone to do anything, but instead, we take care of what we can, that is, of our own. The best we can do for others is to lead by example, and the best we can be for them is role models."[78]

Bearing in mind that we need to be autonomous, that to each their own mistakes and that we shouldn't ascribe intent, we ought to remember to avoid being hostile or even unfriendly to others. After all, we are all in this together. Marcus Aurelius urges us to look at our companions in the journey through life as if they were classmates in the same gym session... but it doesn't mean looking down on them! The same goes for Epictetus, who compares being among people to being at a state fair. The message is clear. We should take care to protect our own autonomy, but when it comes to others – we should tread lightly. We shouldn't be heartless, but light-hearted. After all, it is human to err. Let's cling to our own and let's not allow others to spoil what we have worked so hard to achieve. This is our best imaginable contribution to the grand total of happiness in the universe.

---

[78] This pertains to the very definition of *respect* to others and to the essence of healthy relationships with them. If we treat others as autonomous individuals, then it follows that we don't impose anything on them. If in turn we treat ourselves as autonomous individuals, then it follows that we don't allow others to impose anything on us.

Part six.
All else matters

Chapter 21

Whatever the world is like – be a Stoic

Whether Fate, I say, binds us by an inexorable law, or God, the sovereign of the world, disposes all things, or Chance impels and tosses about at random human affairs, still [Stoic] philosophy must be our defense.

Seneca, *Epistles*, 16.5

In a nutshell: Nothing can undermine the legitimacy and usefulness of Stoicism. The Stoic way of life holds whatever the world is like and whatever we think of it. Whatever turns out, whatever comes out, the Stoic advice will always be beneficial. A great range of specific outlooks on the universe can be neatly agreed with Stoicism. It also works the other way. Stoicism doesn't necessarily coerce us to adopt any specific point of view, in particular, any social or political agenda. Stoicism is the mightiest of all, above and beyond all else.

***

Stoicism doesn't require any outside proof or validation (fragment I). We can and need to live stoically no matter what we assert or doubt about the world and no matter what we think of ourselves (II and III). It is also our best choice whatever our religious beliefs are (IV). We can live stoically regardless of where we side on social and political issues (V). Stoicism is independent from any great order of things that might be upon us, because any such order is not within our power (VI).

Fragment I

Either it is a well arranged universe or a chaos huddled together, but still a universe.

Marcus Aurelius, *Meditations*, 4.27

Commentary: Let's start off in a somewhat unusual manner. Let's look back and let's ponder a question. Has the Stoic teaching in this book ever been justified by any theory about the world? Have we argued that Stoicism is sound *because* this or that? Have we ever summoned the authority of a good God, who created the world and made it come to order? Have we tried to infer the legitimacy of Stoicism from any abstract, abstruse or arcane notions, like "nature," "cosmic reason," "Tao," "discourse," "historical necessity," or "class conflict"? Have we maintained that Stoicism works because it reflects the way the universe works? Or that because it's scientifically validated? Has nature – of the world or of a human – ever been our recourse?

No, never. Nothing like this has been mentioned in this book. We have never premised the Stoic ethics on any particular doctrine, be it metaphysical, or scientific. We haven't referred to any doctrine or theory about the world. To be honest, we haven't really talked about the external world at all. This book has been mostly focused on what happens in the human soul.

True. But why is that worth mentioning? Because it's precisely what makes the Stoic way of life universal and valid in every imaginable setting. The house of Stoicism won't collapse and it won't be undermined, because it requires no foundations. It's completely independent of the outside world. We can be Stoics whatever the world is like and however we choose to perceive it. Stoicism doesn't need any support, from us or from the world. It is its own bedrock and its own confirmation.

This powerful idea is the subject matter of this chapter. The starting point is that reformed Stoicism doesn't relate to any physical or metaphysical theory. It doesn't use any such theory to prove its relevance. Reformed Stoicism just professes itself. Keeping that in mind, let's read again the quoted words of Marcus. "Either it is a well arranged universe or a chaos huddled together." It's not the only locus in the *Meditations* where our emperor-philosopher entertains such an alternative. He does so frequently, time and again juxtaposing conflicting views of the world. Well-designed, organized and rational world versus purposeless chaos. Divine harmony versus orgy of chance. Either a universal cosmic principle that governs all things... or there is nothing more out there than just a clueless pulp of gurgling elements. The dilemma is clear. What's not clear is *why* actually Marcus Aurelius needs that mantra of incertitude. What Stoic goal does it serve... if any?

First of all, pondering over such alternatives is a reminder that we, humans, can hardly ever be certain about how the world works. There is no wide consensus about that, there never was, and we may guess there will never be. The pluralism of interpretations, the deeply conflicted theories are not an exception, fluke or aberration of our times. They are the meat of the issue. They are the standard. And yet, here is the beauty of reformed Stoicism: all this just doesn't need to concern us! If we stick to the Stoic way of life, none of these problems will be our problems. They are beyond our scope, they don't pose a threat to us, they aren't an obstacle for us.

Our project of Stoic life is neither a religious enterprise nor a scientific endeavor. Due to the former, it doesn't require any dram of faith and it doesn't rest on a wobbly ground. It doesn't require us to circumvent or override our rational thinking. Due to the latter, it doesn't compel us to construct hypotheses and verify them. We, the reformed Stoics, don't construct theories that can be disproved by another discovery down the road. We are practitioners. We don't want to build our life on any thesis or revelation, be it scientific, religious, political or whatever else. The simple reason for that is we don't want to endanger the precious little domain we have, that is, the set of things that are within our power. We don't want them to rest on a foundation that may sooner or later become unstable. We don't want to shackle ourselves to something that may be toppled or obliterated. We want more. We want a system of life that is completely bullet-proof, universal, viable and effective in every cosmic setting.

Fragment II

> *Either all things proceed from one intelligent source and come together as in one body [...] or there are only atoms, and nothing else than mixture and dispersion.*
>
> Marcus Aurelius, *Meditations*, 9.39

Commentary: Let's now look closer at both views that Marcus juxtaposes. On the one hand, we have the world pictured as "one body," deeply banded together by its "intelligent source." It's quasi-divine, it's present in everything and it knits everything together. In such a world, nothing happens by accident. There is a universal plan, there is a Higher Power which takes care of all that comes to pass. There is an order of all development, there is an order of all worldly comings and goings. This order can be disguised, fact, but with more or less effort it can be – and should be – unveiled and comprehended. Such comprehension can then be utilized to find individual peace and to perpetuate our individual goals. A "general," wide-scope arrangement of the universe is not everything: we may rightly expect that there is also an arrangement waiting specifically for us. We just need to find it.

On the other hand, there is a chaotic, haphazard world, devoid not only of any deliberate plan but of any organization whatsoever. "Nothing else than mixture and dispersion" as Marcus puts it. There is no one and nothing above or below such a world. Nothing is hidden behind the curtain of things and events. This is a world in which we have no one to expect help from, a world in which there is only us, little and likely disoriented. No helping hand is ever coming, there is no path for us to find and follow. Such a world is drastically unpredictable, it doesn't respect any rules, it doesn't yield to an easy explanation. It isn't a shoulder to us, it doesn't provide solace. Marcus Aurelius puts it forward in the language of ancient materialism: there is nothing but atoms and void, nothing but the disorderly dance of particles in the boundless and merciless space.

These were the two main worldviews on the ancient table. Today, in the 21st century, our range of options to choose from is much wider. Some of us believe in God, who made all things and who established the principles. That God warrants the world order and is the ultimate seal of the laws of physics and ethics. Others believe in God, but reject the view that the traditional religions advance. Yet others negate the existence of God and doubt if there is any higher authority overseeing the universe but they still retain the conviction, that there is an inexplicable Mystery of some kind, certain impenetrable and inchoate supernatural element. Yet others will deny any divinity whatsoever and they will steadfastly affirm only the material and tangible matters exist and matter.

There is still a diversity of views in the latter camp. Some of us see matter as the active root of all evil, while some as a harsh indifferent, the unsparing struggle for survival which shies away from no cruelty but pays attention to nothing. Others consider the natural world as something to be carefully scrutinized or even followed, something we need to harmonize with and return to like prodigal children. We also need to remember that our knowledge and understanding of the natural world has enjoyed an exponential growth in recent centuries. At least since the 1600s we have a new, huge and imposing branch of human endeavor which is called *science*. The important part is that this is something the ancient Stoics didn't have a chance to relate to. It simply hadn't existed back then.

What's the relationship between reformed Stoicism and science? It's a delicate matter, but the most honest, concise but precise way to put it is this. We endorse science! We appreciate and embrace whatever science can tell us about the world and about ourselves. To go unscientific – it is to go unstoic. If science says that vaccines work, then we accept they work. If it says that a given chemical substance helps to deal with depression, or that low blood sugar impairs our decision making – this is what we work with. We subsume that info into our all-things-considered life-shaping system of thought and conduct. We never compete with science, we draw heavily from it and we are glad whenever science feeds us with input data we can use. Which is indeed most of the time and plenty.

On the other hand, reformed Stoicism works in an entirely different magisterium. Reformed Stoicism is a fully autonomous and self-reliant narrative about human life. It isn't a cult cargo of anything else, it doesn't depend, let alone hinge, on anything else, science included. Thus, we never seek scientific validation for our ethics. Think back about what we have discussed in this book. We have never boasted or even mentioned that reformed Stoicism works *because* science proves it. Nowhere here have we used strictly scientific language. And nowhere do we expect science to use Stoic language in return. Stoicism and science are like two partners, highly independent and self-confident, who voluntarily choose to cooperate for mutual benefit. Or, at least, we hope it's mutual. It's surely true on our part: we, the reformed Stoics, are glad to use any scientific knowledge we can.

Science aside, there are other more general, philosophical doubts about our human position in the world. Look at it this way: some will be eager to say that humans are basically *good*, and the best we can do and what we ought to do is to offer ways and means for humans to grow and develop on their own. On the other hand, they are those more pessimistically-inclined, who assert that there is indelible evil in us and that the most urgent task is to save us from ourselves. Between the two, there is a vast range of medium stances with varying components of realism and delusion. Whatever combination we settle for, however, it will never be a universal choice. There will always be flocks of others who think differently, on this topic and on other issues. This deep pluralism is one of the defining experiences of modern times.

How do, we, the reformed Stoics, go about that? Our resolution is simple: we stay out of the fray. We don't engage in the intellectual, lest aside rhetorical battles over issues that are not within our power. As long as the wide borders of Stoicism are respected – everyone is free and invited to follow. We, the reformed Stoics, offer a whole new ball game on a entirely different level. We propose a system of life which works fine with all worldviews. This is the most solid, most stable answer, and it is also the most all-embracing one. Reformed Stoicism, in this understanding, holds firm regardless of which particular stance we adhere to.

In other words, we, the reformed Stoics, neither play favorites nor do we have a problem with pluralism. Our philosophy holds in every possible universe, under any government and in any economic system. Reformed Stoicism is agreeable with most theories and beliefs that might be held. We can be Stoics no matter what we believe in (well, to a degree). Reformed Stoicism, as proposed in this book, isn't a danger to any particular religious, political or social belief. We may adopt it and we don't need to worry that it conflicts with any other conviction we hold dear. It is safe to our worldview... but it also keeps *us* safe. In other words, no change of heart about any issue, no scientific discovery or religious epiphany will be ever able to force us out of Stoicism. Stoicism will never become outdated, because it contains no dogma that could wear off over time. It has no foundations that could rot or crumble. And nothing will nullify it – because it needs no credentials and no warranty.

As we will learn in the final chapter, the Stoics aim at attaining a perfect, indelible state of mind, like, as Seneca puts it, the clear heavens above the moon. But the first step to get there mentally is to get there logically – and this is the exact reason why Marcus Aurelius mulls the doubts over and over. By entertaining doubts he wants to shake them off. He deliberately confronts various options and alternatives. He makes up possible setbacks on purpose. He does so to attain the firm and blessed certainty. He proves to himself that Stoicism works no matter what. He doesn't *hesitate*. He rather *rectifies* his Stoicism, by testing it against a variety of possible scenarios.

Fragment III

> *In a word, if there is a god, all is well, and if chance rules, do not you also be governed by it.*
>
> Marcus Aurelius, *Meditations*, 9.28

Commentary: Reformed Stoicism and this book alike are addressed to us all, to all humans who are open-minded and want to improve their lives. The entry threshold to reformed Stoicism is very low, slim to none. There are no admission requirements, no visas required. There are no pre-existing conditions to trouble us. There is no paperwork to be done, there is no intellectual background check. We can be reformed Stoics – to state the obvious – regardless of race, faith, gender, economic privilege, sexual identity or political preferences.[79] Reformed Stoicism is a smooth-running, universal system of living. It is tailored for us all.

This also means that it by no means excludes those who aren't endowed with the grace of doubt. Those whose beliefs are firm and stark can – obviously! – be Stoics too and they will greatly benefit from it. For instance, we can perfectly be Christians and Stoics at the same time – there is indeed a notable tradition of combining the two. Stoicism flies well with all the doubts of the world, but it's also at no loggerheads with any robust belief.

In this light, nothing can *falsify* reformed Stoicism. If we set out on the Stoic path, if we decide to follow the Stoic principles, nothing will deflect us.

---

[79] Importantly, ancient Stoicism was the first true call for egalitarianism in the history of Western philosophy. It granted every human the right to strive towards sagehood, good life and happiness attained through philosophy. Ethnicity, background and social standing were of no importance. This is reflected in the back stories of the Stoic authors. Zeno of Citium, the founder of Stoicism, was from Cyprus and possibly of Phoenician descent. Epictetus was a former slave while Marcus Aurelius was an emperor.

Reformed Stoicism is powerful enough to withstand all intellectual turns we may take in our life and it's firm enough to save us from any meaning-of-life crises. Whatever the world is like, whatever surprises await us, the Stoic armor will always be there for us. Reformed Stoicism is a perfectly universal medicine. It's the most versatile of all human devices. It can be used against all imaginable adversity in every possible world.

Having said that, let's get back to Marcus. He says that either "there is a god," or "chance rules." What does the latter mean? That there is no providential, transcendent force in the universe. It means that the world is governed by nothing else than soul-less laws of physics, statistics and Darwinian evolution. The universe is just a plain battlefield of clueless atoms and brutal forces. But still, does it mean that everything in such a world *needs* to be clueless? No. We must never forget that amid all the chaos of primal elements, there is at least one conscious observer. There is *us*. There is our sharp eye and clear mind. What does it mean from the Stoic perspective? It means that in such a grim universe, we ourselves are the only possible source of organization and principle. However random and irrational the world around us is – *we* cannot give in to it. If there is no meaning in the world, then it's our deal to create it. If we live in the kingdom of chaos, then we need to be the compass needle for ourselves. It's our right to do so, but it's also our duty.

Fragment IV

If the gods have determined about me and about the things which must happen to me, they have determined well. [...] If, however, the gods determine about none of the things which concern us, I am able to determine about myself.

Marcus Aurelius, *Meditations*, 6.44

Commentary: One fascinating thing about reformed Stoicism is that it's a lot like Pascal's wager. Whatever the world around is really like and whatever we believe in, our best choice is to be Stoics. It's the sure-fire option, the wild card that always gives us the best outcome. We need to be that "compass needle," we need to "determine about ourselves" regardless of whether we think that the world is haphazard and unpredictable as discussed before, or whether we believe in some Higher Force, one which controls or at least somehow "oversees" things. This Higher Force can be understood in a myriad of ways, ranging from the traditional God, through some form of cosmic reason, more or less personalized, to a mere mysterious "energy," of which we don't know much more than that it exists. But however it is understood, our best way to go is to hold on to Stoicism.

No belief in any God or other Higher Power undermines Stoicism. And none is at variance with it. It's rather quite the opposite: as a matter of fact, such transcendent faith may be vastly helpful in adhering to our Stoic precepts. How come? Look at it this way. In a chaotic, apparently meaningless universe we have the responsibility to create our own islet of sense and principle. We have to do it on our own and at our own expense, accountable only to ourselves, with no helping hand and no encouragement from anyone. It might be a bit tough. But a Higher Force, if we allow it (and however we choose to understand and call it), is usually on our side. It may help us. We aren't anymore the lonely builders of one brave edifice. Now we are accomplices in a much greater enterprise. Now we go hand in hand with supernatural force, which (who?) is – in most views – the major source and shareholder of what we want to accomplish. We are the coworkers in a great endeavor and it's our obligation to make sure that it doesn't fail because of us. We need to deliver. But *how* do we go about it? Again: Stoicism is the best way. Everything appears better from the Stoic position. Once we adopt the Stoic approach, we maximize the chances to hold up our side of the bargain. And this is important, since we not only get support from the Higher Force, but we also answer to it. It holds us accountable. If we choose to believe in God, Providence, or Cosmic Reason – we mustn't let it down. And again, the Stoic way is the best to not let that happen.

Fragment V

> *The universe is either a confusion, and a mutual involution of things, and a dispersion, or it is unity and order and providence.*
>
> Marcus Aurelius, *Meditations*, 6.10

Commentary: There is one issue Marcus Aurelius doesn't mention, but we need to: it's the social and political consequences. Or, to be precise, the lack thereof. Reformed Stoicism dovetails with a wide range of reasonable political stances and social systems. And there is more than that. In reformed Stoicism, we believe that our philosophy shouldn't be used as a rhetorical device to back up any particular political agenda. We aren't necessarily progressive or conservative, neither Republican, nor Democrat. The party lines neither interest nor matter to us. We will thrive in all political systems, we will flourish in all social orders. Reformed Stoicism neither implies any policy nor it requires one. It works just fine in a range of political, social and economic views.

Yet, importantly, we don't fall for naive indifference. We don't fool ourselves into the delusion of non-partisanship. It's not the case that a Stoic is not allowed to have political views. It's not that a Stoic will bury her head in the sand pettily, if history takes a bad turn. It's not that a Stoic won't be an upstander. She may perfectly be one. As a matter of fact, and just as history teaches us, it's exactly Stoicism that empowers us best for political action and saves us from the banality of evil. The bottom line here is that reformed Stoicism in itself doesn't necessarily push us in any specific political direction. It doesn't require us to embrace any particular brand of politics. The political choices are our own doing.

A question follows: isn't it then an escape from responsibility? It isn't. It's just the most cogent and fair interpretation. To do it otherwise, to try to retroactively sign up the Stoic ideas for one of our contemporary political devices – this just wouldn't stand. This would be plain manipulation. It's much more honest to assert that the Stoic and political ideas are – again – non-overlapping magisteria, two separate domains.

How does it relate to the problem of responsibility? The argument is that it's an unfair move to try to bend the Stoic teaching to make it support our own political views. It's much more honest to agree that Stoicism teaches us a ton ethically and that it perfectly pertains to our *private* life... but it leaves our hands untied in the political realm. We can't tearfully fly to the Stoics' for political protection and advice. Politics is on us. It's our responsibility. Hence, this view doesn't mean that we avoid responsibility. It means we embrace it.

Fragment VI

> [Things] *happen either by chance or according to providence, and you must neither blame chance nor accuse providence.*
>
> Marcus Aurelius, *Meditations*, 12.24

Commentary: Whatever the world is like, its mechanism and principle are not within our power. And when it comes to things not within our power, we just aren't the part of the conversation. We are on neither side, we play no favorites. We need to be focused solely on what is within our power, while the things not within our power take care of themselves. They play out on their own. Whatever governs them, we don't get to worry about that. It may be God, it may be the laws of history, it may be atomic vibrations – for us, in a way, it deeply doesn't matter. Whatever it is, we have no authority over it just the same.

The only area where we need to focus are the things within our power. Whatever we think about the outside world and whatever it is really like, our duty is to define and uphold our values, set up our goals and shoot for them, develop our moral character and keep growing in the direction we want to grow. This is both the starting point and the conclusion of reformed Stoicism. And it holds in every possible world, under every possible government, in every social and economic system.

Chapter 22

Follow good examples

In the writings of the Ephesians there was this precept, constantly to think of some one of the philosophers of former times who practiced virtue.

Marcus Aurelius, *Meditations*, 11.26

In a nutshell: Let's bank on the experience of others! Let's not hesitate to follow their lead. We can benefit from others, both from those who originally designed the Stoic trail and those who simply hit it before us. Let's just imagine we march shoulder to shoulder with them. Let's picture they watch us. The presence of another human (even if in mere visualization), particularly someone who we respect, is a great help and motivation. Let's allow ourselves to be inspired! Let's be inspired by the example of the great people who wrestled with their own challenges, failure and weakness. Let's nurture ourselves by reminding ourselves of them.

***

It's our individual matter to choose who we prefer to follow (fragment I). Such patronage will be helpful both in high and low moments, in the doldrums of daily toil (II), as well as in the moments of breakdown or disgrace (III). We don't necessarily need to support ourselves on a shoulder of a great and famous hero. It may well be someone who we know personally and who we simply trust (IV). For instance, Seneca's own pick was Quintus Sextius (V).[80] In all misery and in every hardship, we can find the company of someone else who has already experienced the same, or even worse (VI). Agrippinus peacefully accepted banishment (VII), while Stilpo maintained his integrity despite the cataclysm of war that ripped through his hometown (VIII). Importantly, we should follow good examples not only in case of external adversity, but also (maybe above all) during our everyday struggle on our internal front (IX).

---

[80] Quintus Sextius was a Roman philosopher of the 1st century BC. Not much is known about his life and works except for the fact that he drew from both Stoicism and Pythagoreanism, and that he was greatly praised by Seneca.

Fragment I

We must fix upon some good person, and have them always before our eye, as a witness of our life and actions. [...] Choose someone, among your acquaintance, whose life and manner of address charm you, and having in view either the understanding or presence of such a one, look upon them, either as your guardian or model.

Seneca, *Epistles*, 11.8-10

Commentary: It's a great solace of the human lot that we are never bound to wrestle with adversity single-handedly. No hardship and no misfortune that befalls us, befalls *only* us – just as we discussed in the chapter "You Are Never Alone." But the source of strength doesn't come solely from the generic awareness that we are never alone. The broad sense of human solidarity is one thing, but here is another: we have every right to pick a specific person, someone who we know by name, and make them our role model. Their example will provide us support and inspiration in the crunch time, in the moment of challenge and in the hour of doubt.

In choosing them, we shouldn't yield to social pressure or to what's fashionable. The only gauge is our own, private preference. The emotional connection to the given person is the key here. We need to think of someone who we admire, but at the same time simply *like*. And then, when we face any challenge or problem, we need to immediately ask ourselves: "what would X do? would they give up?" Of course, this unidentified X will be someone else for each of us. For some, it will be a renowned philosopher. For some, it will be a religious or political leader. Or a subtle writer. Or an athlete. Or even one of our actual friends, someone who we adore, someone who pushes and motivates us. It may be someone who is alive and could, theoretically, drop by some day to actually witness how we are doing, but it may well be someone who is a world away from us in time and space. In brief: we can pick anyone we please. The only thing that matters is that they need to be truly inspirational to us. They need to be someone we look up to, someone who mobilizes us to strive and thrive.

Fragment II

Why should I not keep by me the statues and pictures of great people?

Seneca, *Epistles*, 64.9

Commentary: Does it mean that Seneca encourages us to put someone's photo on the wall? Or a souvenir on the shelf, one that would remind us of our bond with that person? Yes! This may actually be a good starting point. Indeed, besides furniture, books and all other worldly stuff we hoard in our apartments, we also keep items of mostly symbolic value. These include pictures of family and friends, but also of people we don't know in person, but with whom we feel an intellectual or emotional bond of some kind. This may involve virtually anyone from our own late grandfather to Pope Francis, and from 50 Cent to Che Guevara. Once we allow – through mementos or pictures – their symbolic presence in our living room, we also authorize them to oversee our daily actions. More than that: we invite them to do so! We accept being watched and we admit that it's beneficial to us.

This is the key message: we need to constantly imagine that someone is keeping an eye on us and behave accordingly. If putting someone's picture on the wall may help with that, why not go that way? We need to pick someone we trust, someone who is dear and important to us. And then, as schizophrenic as it may sound, we need to visualize that they actually watch over our conduct. The concept is simple: it will be harder for us to fail if we know that we are open to their gaze. It's harder to dissolve into negligence if we know we are in plain sight. It's just how the human mind works. If someone is watching us (particularly if it's someone we look up to), then we immediately feel extra geared-up. "What would X say, if she saw me in this position?" "Huh, Y, he's watching, I gotta push through it!" Let's just substitute this incognito Xs and Ys with actual names of real people we take our hat off to, and we'll land a precise receipt for following good examples. Whatever we do, let's project that we are supervised by those who we would like to be on a par with. Or by those we want to look good to. Or by those whom we simply don't want to let down. This makes for the whole trick.

Furthermore, this applies not only to our *actions* and our factual, external conduct in the world. Following good examples works perfectly in the domain of our *thinking* too. Would we be still OK with what and how we think if we knew that X can peek into our thoughts? Wouldn't we be ashamed to admit to Y what our narratives really are? This may sound a bit 1984-esque, but the same notion that's nightmarish in a social dystopia may well be highly useful in our private life. We usually take it for granted that our thoughts are *ours only* – this is the only way we have ever known the world to work. But let's just change it for a moment in our mind's eye. What if our thoughts and narratives were wide in the open? What if our significant other could read through them? What if we could hide nothing from them? Wouldn't it be easier to keep ourselves together? Wouldn't we be stronger in resisting the tempting ill thoughts? Wouldn't it be simpler to stay stoically sharp? Surely it would. Thus, if we have a hard time collecting ourselves on our own, let's turn for help to someone trusted. We can only gain from that, while they won't pay any price or even know that – since it all happens in our imagination.

In this regard, following good examples may simply amount to keeping constantly in mind a few people we hold dear and look up to. We need to remember about them not only in the glorious moments of great challenges, but also in the bleak, everyday doldrums of daily errands. We may think of the great deeds of venerable heroes when we run into a burning house to save a child trapped inside... but just as well we may summon them to mind when we struggle to get out of bed at 5 AM on a weekday. And actually, this latter case may be much more valid, more relevant and, all-things-considered, it may have more bearing on our overall quality of life. The epic poetry of unfading accomplishment is a rare guest in our life. Most of our life is prose, and we need to take care that it be good prose.

Fragment III

> *The frequent seeing* [of wise people], *the frequent hearing of them little by little sinks into the heart and acquires the force of precepts.*
>
> Seneca, *Epistles*, 94.40[xiv]

Commentary: Let's then meet the wise people and let's allow them to look at us. The salubrious gain will be just the same, regardless of whether we meet sages face to face, glance at the picture of our venerable ancestor, read a book of our dearest writer, or if we simply conjure that our idol accompanies us in our daily struggle.

Furthermore, this is not just a go-to tactic for a rainy day. It's something to be used around the clock, including the most mundane and banal circumstances. In no conditions we should be ashamed of being watched – for this would downright defy the purpose. It's quite a tricky matter, since, on the one hand, this is the exact reason why we push ourselves before the eyes of trusted people. We hope that the fear of being shamed motivates us to be a better version of ourselves. Yet, on the other hand, we can't be ashamed that we allow someone to oversee us. This is why it's convenient to keep it a mental technique, instead of living an open life, actually transparent to others.[81]

Let's now think for a moment *why* exactly we are instinctively afraid of being ashamed. We are usually ashamed of moments of disgrace, breakdown, of

---

[81] This pertains to all the dilemmas of the social media. Seneca, obviously, can't help us with this one. Or can't he?

major failure, or mere banality. We have all been there, we've all had those moments. At a low point of our life, it's hard to live with ourselves, it's hard to even look in the mirror, let alone be scrutinized by someone important to us. Failing engenders fragility. When we go down, we switch on the snail instinct: we curl up, we hide in our shell, trying to disappear from the world. We fold and we shrink, ruminating on our failure, unwilling to snap out of it. And the last thing we want is to even imagine that someone we'd love to impress sees us in this state. The tough Stoic paradox is that this is exactly the very moment when the other pair of eyes is particularly of service.

Let's investigate our usual way of thinking here. The Stoic path is that whatever adversity we wrestle with, we should immediately think what would our role models do. The crux of the matter is that it always seems to us that things which happen to us are somehow "inappropriate" for them. It seems to us that the trifles which haunt us don't match the nobility and elatedness of the paragons. Our own problems appear small, trivial and insignificant. In our twisted perception, the people who we admire and who inspire and embolden us, are magically "above" those little, mundane and banal things. It seems to us that the small ball nastiness of life just doesn't pertain to them... which of course is completely wrong.

The greatness of those who we hold in high esteem, their moral nobility, their grit in the face of adversity come precisely from that they could keep themselves together in *every* occasion. It comes from that they strove to combat every hardship alike, be it tremendous or trifle, and that they managed to find a way up from every comedown. It's not that they wrestled only with the grand challenges that make for a good motivational poster. It's not that they had any more leeway to pick problems than we do. A human who is worth being a role model is one who *always* tries hard to snap out of it, one who *always* strains to stick to the better of the two paths, and one who always fights to get out of the swamp of misery. This is how it works for them and this is where and why we should follow their example. No adversity, no hardship and no misfortune is "inappropriate," "low," or unseemly. As the adage has it, no one ever asks the captain what the winds were. The only question she's asked is whether the ship made it safely to the port of destination. In the Stoic department it works just the same as in the maritime one. We never ask whether someone "deserved" the given stroke of fortune. We never ask whether an instance of bad luck was "dignified" or not. The only question we ask is if and how did they fight back against it. Or, to put it yet differently, it's absurd to imagine that our role models, the paragons of fulfillment, the embodiments of accomplishment, have never fallen. They have. Many times. And we stand in admiration for them *precisely* because they were able to shake it off, get up, and climb back to light.

Fragment IV

Choose therefore Cato.[82] Or, if Cato seems somewhat too rigid, choose Laelius,[83] a man of not so severe a temper.

Seneca, Epistles, 11.10

Commentary: We need to leave imaginary friends to children and we need to come up with an "imaginary observer" instead. This is something truly becoming of a Stoic! That imaginary observer of ours, as mentioned already, doesn't have to be someone famous, someone whom we find in history textbooks and in the top stories in the newspapers. Also, it doesn't have to necessarily be someone who is an apostle of all excellence and an epitome of all possible virtue. It's perfectly understandable that looking up to someone too great may, instead of inspiring us, baffle and dishearten us. If this is the case, let's pick someone who we find less overwhelming. The choice is ours.

If we want to, they may be someone of our own league, someone we feel not inferior to but intimate with. It may be someone who impresses us much, but who we know well enough to be aware of their imperfections. This knowledge guarantees that we are dealing with a real person, not just some out-of-the-book Seneca. A beloved poet, a writer, or an artist is a fine example here, since this is usually someone whose not only works but also biography we know through and through. We know enough details to have a square and honest view of the situation. We not only revere the person's achievements, but we are also well aware of the price. We know all their struggle. Thus, we can't diminish ourselves anymore with the crooked argument that great people are superhuman and that they float above the ordinary problems of human life.

We may also imagine that it's one of our actual friends, real-life friends, who follows our thoughts and traces our steps. It's our own choice how we spin it. Our only goal is to use others to effectively inspire us. Whoever works, works. The thought "what would Peter say if he saw me like this?" may be every inch as inspiring as the thought "what would pope Francis say if he saw through my sins?" Or, "what would Che say if he saw what a spineless revolutionary I am?"

---

[82] See footnote to fragment VIII in chapter "Don't Desire Acclaim."
[83] Seneca probably refers to Gaius Laelius, a Roman statesman form the 2nd century BC.

Fragment V

When I read him [Quintus Sextius the Elder] *I am ready to defy all accidents. [...] I long to have something for cause of triumph, in the exercise of patience. For this excellency likewise has Sextius. He sets before you the* [grandeur] *of a happy life, and gives you hopes of obtaining it.*

Seneca, *Epistles*, 64.4-5

Commentary: This is a perfect example of following good examples. Seneca details his reflections and musings that came from reading works of Quintus Sextius. These readings are undeniably invigorating for him. Zest for Stoicism, life force, the willingness to face up to adversity wells up in him. They even overflow him: having read his favorite philosopher, he feels so confident that he not only wants to fight down his own weakness, but is actually tempted to seek new obstacles he could prevail over. Here is how hugely inspiring a good example may be.

What's in it for us? One lesson is that we need to frequently take the books of our beloved authors off the shelf. Fact. But here is another fact to be borne in mind. Seneca himself is a major Stoic philosopher, a role model for us, one of the three pivotal authors we learn from in this book. And yet this great thinker shamelessly draws tons of support from Quintus Sextius. Her relies on him a great deal, he follows a good example himself. He not only doesn't see a problem with it – he boasts about it. He doesn't see it as a liability or a shortcoming of his moral autonomy. No. Seneca serves as a good example... of following good examples.

Seneca knows well that the only matter that he's accountable for (to himself!) is the Stoic grit in sticking to the right path he has chosen. That's all that matters. Whatever means he uses, whatever support he relies on, and whatever readings he absorbs – he is at liberty to do so. There is no contraindication to learning from the examples of great people who came before us. The only difference between us and them is that they walked down the path a bit earlier than we do. But the path is just the same for us all, and the same are the traps and pitfalls. Seneca, his revered Quintus Sextius and ourselves, as strange as it may sound, we are really in one and the same league, in one and the same contest. Why then not support each other? Why not rest and rely on the shoulders of those who have already gotten there? We have nothing to be ashamed of and no one to be ashamed in front of.

Fragment VI

> *Trials have been overcome by many: fire by Mucius,[84] crucifixion by Regulus,[85] poison by Socrates,[86] exile by Rutilius,[87] and a sword-inflicted death by Cato[88] [...] Let us also, therefore [...] be included among the ideal types of history. [...] That which could be done, can be done.*
>
> Seneca, Epistles, 98.12-14[xv]

Commentary: First off, and just as discussed in the chapter "You Are Never Alone," it is vital to be mindful of that in every misery and hardship we have someone we can bond with. No human experience is singular or new – simply because it's human. That holds because the weaponry of blows and strikes that fate can use against us is quite limited. That's for one. Also, if we look around fairly enough, we will learn that many others have suffered much dourer pains and misfortunes than we do. Whatever befalls us... we may be certain that others were befallen with something far worse. There is – alas! – still way too much fire, iron and poison in this world. Thinking that our own suffering is something exemplary, is ... well, it isn't actually substantiated with facts.

This observation is another, fresh source of major solace. Let's imagine that we are suffering or in pain (sadly, often we don't need to *imagine* that). Is it great or minor? Is it something traumatic, devastating, or something that can be endured? Within reformed Stoicism it is *our* choice to decide that. Pain is

---

[84] Gaius Mucius Scaevola was a semi-legendary Roman soldier who lived around 500 BC. In the year 508 BC, during the siege of Rome in the course of the Roman-Etruscan wars, Mucius was sent to the enemy camp to kill king Porsenna. He successfully sneaked into the Etruscan camp, but failed to fulfill his mission, killing one of the king's aides instead of the king himself. He was captured and brought before Porsenna and then famously stated that he came to kill as a citizen of Rome and he will die as a citizen of Rome. To prove his courage he voluntarily placed his hand in the fire that was prepared for a torture session. Porsenna, amazed by this brave deed, released him and subsequently sent ambassadors to Rome to offer peace.

[85] Marcus Atilius Regulus (ca. 307 BC – 250 BC) was a Roman general and statesman, a consul twice. He was famous as a paragon of virtue, integrity and courage. He was taken POW by the Carthaginians during the First Punic War in 255 BC. He was released to return to Rome to negotiate a peace treaty, under the oath that he would return. Having returned to Rome he advised the Senate to continue the war and then – being bound by the oath – returned to Carthage where he was gruesomely tortured to death.

[86] See footnote to fragment VI in the chapter "It's All About The Narratives."

[87] See footnote to fragment V in the chapter "Be Autonomous."

[88] See footnote to fragment VIII in the chapter "Don't Desire Acclaim."

Follow good examples

ours and no one else's. But here is the train of thought we are invited to. Are we in pain? True, no one can deny that. But... Mucius voluntarily put his hand in the flames. Someone did injustice to us? Fact... but Socrates was unjustly sentenced to death. We feel homesick? No one denies that... but Rutilius suffered exile. Thus, why not use good examples to keep the sense of proportion in mind? There is always someone who underwent much more than we did. There is always someone who successfully combated even greater adversities than we face. Does it mean that we need to condescendingly diminish our own pain? Does it mean that our own misery "doesn't count" or that it is a "first world problem"? No. This is not the route we take in reformed Stoicism. We focus on the inspirational part instead. If *they* managed to deal with *their* problems, why wouldn't *we* deal with *ours*?

Fragment VII

> *When it was reported to [Agrippinus][89] that his trial was on in the Senate, he said, "I hope it may turn out well. But it is the fifth hour of the day," this was the time when he was used to exercise himself and then take the cold bath, "let us go and take our exercise." After he had taken his exercise, one comes and tells him, "You have been condemned." "To banishment," he replies, "or to death?" "To banishment." "What about my property?" "It is not taken from you." "Let us go to Aricia[90] then," he said, "and dine." This it is to have studied what one ought to study.*
>
> Epictetus, *Discourses*, I.1.28-32

Commentary: It's hard to comment on the above in any way other than with a simple "wow!". Or by stating that this is how the misfortunes should be weathered. Agrippinus bravely and without blinking eye accepted the fact that legal actions have been instigated against him. He didn't have any way to stop it – so he didn't. After all, court proceedings are not within our power to control. When the senators were debating his earthly fate, he was doing his usual exercise and light-heartedly enjoyed his bath... because that was what his daily schedule called for. Moreover, when he finally heard the news that he

---

[89] Paconius Agrippinus was a Roman philosopher in the 1st century AD. He stood against despotism of the Caesars, and was banished in 67 AD.
[90] Ariccia is a town in Italy, located around 15 miles SE from Rome. In antiquity it was the casual first stop for travelers leaving Rome and heading south. Today it's a town of roughly 20,000 residents and a part of the Rome metropolitan area.

was sentenced to exile, he rejoiced that at least his property was spared, and... invited the messenger who brought the news to dinner.

Agrippinus surely can be a role model, a good example to us. He not only cleared a bad turn of fate, but he also didn't get derailed in the process. He didn't get beaten down, squashed, torn apart. He remained proactive, he didn't break, he didn't start complaining and grumbling about the apparent injustice of the world. He wasn't pushed to deep defense, he wasn't forced on his knees. He didn't just "survive" the situation – he never ceased to thrive. He still *lived*, fully and actively, despite adversity. The Senate hearing, the conviction, all that happened just as it should, perfectly beyond him, with no detriment to his peace of mind, and no detriment to his attitude to life (and, we may add, with no detriment to his schedule). This is exactly the type of good example we need to follow. Whatever, whenever, and wherever happens to us, whatever challenges we face in the future – let's always remember this peaceful harmony of Agrippinus's soul, his unjaded serenity, his tranquil and unbiased outlook on things. Let's keep that firmly in mind when fate knocks at our gate... and also when it doesn't. A good example is a universal one – it can be followed in every circumstance.

Fragment VIII

> *Stilpo, [...] when his country was taken, [...]* [was] *asked by Demetrius Policrates (so called from him having destroyed many towns) whether he had lost anything. "No," says he, "all the goods I have I carry with me."*
>
> Seneca, Epistles, 9.18-19

Commentary: Agrippinus from the previous commentary was indeed a brave person, but one may point out that although fortune stopped smiling upon him, he still didn't lose everything. After all, he didn't lose his wealth... which is quite crucial when it comes to deciding about the arrangements of one's worldly life. Agrippinus still had money in his pocket to pay for that lunch in Aricia and he had means to start a new life in exile. One may thus say that the hardship he experienced was still short of an ultimate calamity.

If we want to take on ultimate calamity, we need to talk Stilpo. Stilpo lost everything that a human can lose on this earth. He lost his hometown, which was looted and destroyed. He lost his family, which was killed in the process. In a word, he lost all material possessions he had accumulated over his life. He was left standing with just the clothes on his back and the narratives in his mind. We may rightly say that his world literally came down. Agrippinus lost much, but much was still left to him. Stilpo lost everything and had nothing

Follow good examples

left. Nothing except for his biological life, naked existence... and the things within his power he still cherished in his mind.

Despite the catastrophe, despite obliteration of everything he was ever attached to, our philosopher still managed not to lose his Stoic resolve. In this vein, if we – fate forbid! – face such a disaster one day, we will know that it can be survived stoically. Even if we ourselves don't manage to withstand it... we will at least know that it is possible. We'll know that there is a path that can be chosen. And above all, why don't we apply this extreme Stilpo story to the cases which are less tragic? Stilpo didn't crack under tremendous duress, so why don't we try to bear our own burdens, which, as we have already agreed, are usually much milder?

Fragment IX

Do you think Cato[91] would have chosen some pleasant shore for his dwelling-place, that he might count the [...] variety of pinnaces painted with divers colors, or a lake strewed over with flowers, or to have heard the nocturnal revels of jovial songsters?

Seneca, *Epistles*, 51.12

Commentary: Following good examples is not about wars and disasters only. Tragic and life-changing as they are, they are rare occurrences. Our life consists mostly of small-ball dealings and doings, which we have to tackle on a smaller scale, yet systematically and restlessly. Furthermore, an external enemy is not really required here. The most damning and important challenge is often presented to us on the internal front. More than that! According to Stoicism, it's *always* the internal, home and mindful front that matters most. What does it mean specifically?

Examples abound. If we decide that we want to be more healthy, then we need to reduce the intake of junk food. If we decide that we want to climb the ladder of worldly accomplishment, then we need to resist the temptation of scrolling the internet till midnight and then staying in bed till noon. If we decided that we want to study to pass an exam, then we need to pass on the invitations to hang out with friends. If we decided that a life of celibacy is the way to go – then we need to renounce what's necessary for that.

In this guerilla warfare against coarse reality, we ought to follow good examples just as we do in the hinge times. We mustn't be ashamed of our daily

---

[91] See footnote to fragment VIII in the chapter "Don't Desire Acclaim."

struggle, of the toll of renunciation, of the unending and mind-numbing toil. No combat is disgraceful to a human. Particularly if it's a combat against oneself. Regardless of whether we are resisting a temptation or avoiding some unnecessary involvement – there will always be good examples of those who we may follow. We've had Agrippinus who went to exile peacefully, we've had Stilpo's bravery in the horror of war. But we need to complement this picture with Cato, who steadily and steadfastly overcame the bodily temptations. All of them represent Stoic ideals, and all of them may be role models for us. In every domain and discipline of our life we can find good examples – we just need to be open to finding them.

Chapter 23

Practice regularly

[The Stoic] *is always exercising* [the] *mind*[xvi].

Diogenes Laertius, *Lives of Eminent Philosophers*, VII.128

In a nutshell: We will attain no good life and no happiness unless we exercise hard. Stoicism is akin to the Red Queen's race, where we need to run fast just to remain in the same place. We need to regularly practice our Stoic skills and to continuously develop them. If we don't do that, they will fizzle out just as unused muscles deteriorate. We mustn't suppose that Stoicism comes for free and we need to remember that once it's acquired, it requires further effort to sustain it. There are no wild cards here. We need to practice and polish our skills all the time. We need to do it regularly, persistently and properly.

***

If we want to live stoically – we need to practice daily (fragment I). We can practice while we run any other errand (II). Abstract understanding of Stoicism isn't the same as practicing it, just as knowing the recipe isn't tantamount to being a cook (III). The skill of living well will never be magically granted to us. We need to learn and practice it (IV). One way to start is to acquire a habit of recapping and analyzing the events of the day every evening (V). We need to practice even if no danger is looming (VI). We need to be particularly diligent about our weak spots (VII), and our exercise mustn't be just vocal – we need to practice not just regularly, but also fairly and properly (VIII). A degree of austerity and tough stance on ourselves will be useful (IX), yet we ought to be smart about all this. We need to start with easy tasks, and only then turn to the more demanding ones (X).

Fragment I

If you would make any thing a habit, do it. […] So it is with respect to the affections of the soul.

Epictetus, *Discourses*, II.18.4-5

Commentary: Epictetus pretty much says it. This is one universal and incontrovertible rule, which cannot be defied or circumvented. It's exercise, it's the habit, and nothing else, that makes us excel. More than that. It's the habit that makes us – us.

If we want to be good at something, if we want to do it skillfully and with self-confidence, then we need to turn it into a habit. We need to be doing it frequently and with adamant regularity. No chess player is born from sitting down to the board every second Monday in the month. No fitness emerges from jogging once a fortnight. No language acquisition comes about if we run through our vocabulary list once a month. We won't learn how to live according to the Stoic rules if we are not serious about them. Our good life requires permanent attention and constant practice. No pain, no gain. And surely, no effort, no happiness.

Let's get this straight: learning how to live stoically is the same as any other goal. And exactly as with all other goals in life, we need to allocate time and effort to achieve it. If we want to be chess players – we must play chess. If we want to be fit – we must work out. If we want to speak a language – we must learn it. The same goes for life itself. If we want to live well and happily, if we want to be Stoics – we must practice it. We must rehearse the Stoic techniques, we must go over the Stoic methodology again and again. Stoicism is not about waiting for epiphany or for some divine intervention. It's about practice, practice, practice. Let's then dry run the proper alternatives. Let's perfect anticipating mishap. These are skills as any other, and we need to practice them just like any other skill.

Fragment II

> *One ought to know that it is not easy* [...] *to acquire a fixed judgment, unless* [we] *should day by day state and hear the same principles, and at the same time apply them to* [our] *life.*
>
> Epictetus, Fragments, 16[xvii]

Commentary: How about we carve out in our daily agenda a specific time that we could spend solely on cultivating our Stoic skills? It's not a bad idea to begin with! Yet, we will learn soon enough that a "please don't disturb from 8.00 to 8.30 PM since I am working on my Stoicism then" approach is sufficient only for starters. As a matter of fact, as we will soon learn, Stoicism demands much more from us.

First off, we need to bear Stoicism in mind at all times, not just during our evening session. Wherever we are and whatever we do, we need to remember that we aspire to be Stoics. And it's a great, continuous challenge. We mustn't slip just because we are tired or bored. We mustn't lapse into the ordinary. We need to keep our mind fixed on the goal at all times. Stoicism isn't a gym that we attend in the evenings to shake off the cobwebs of a heavy workday. Stoicism is not a checkbox we can tick off and forget. It's just the contrary: it's a standing challenge to transform our whole life. And as such, we must work it up unceasingly and adamantly.

Stoicism needs to be practiced at every occasion and along every duty we perform. It is, in a way, like a program that can run in the background of all what we do. It's possible because Stoicism isn't a distinct and abstract project separated from the life itself. Instead, it's the very practice of life itself. Stoicism is a philosophy of life, a philosophy of a good and happy life – and in order to live it, we must do stoically all that we do. Visiting the promised land of Stoicism from time to time is not enough. We must move there for good. Whatever call we are pulling off for work, whatever jovial pastime with friends we are having, or whatever friend's passing we mourn – we can be stoical in all this. *Everything* is an opportunity to practice Stoicism. And practicing it will not only make us better Stoics, but it will also make us better at whatever we are doing.

Fragment III

> *A bull is not made suddenly, nor a brave person. We must discipline ourselves in the winter for the summer campaign.*[92]
>
> Epictetus, *Discourses*, I.2.32

Commentary: No one is born a Stoic, but everyone who is, became one. And more importantly: everyone who isn't, always has a chance to become one. Our Stoic powers are just like our bodily strength. They come not from some instant of epiphany or transcendent endowment, but from long and sustained practice. Every trait of our moral character, every ability we have and every skill we aspire to, requires incessant practice, constant annealing in the furnace of trials, testing in a range of circumstances and conditions. It necessitates unremitting, effortful exercise, just as physical fitness does. In this regard, the materialism of the ancient Stoics plays well. After all, in their old view, we weren't an incompatible mix of radically different elements of body and spirit, but rather a coherent and harmonious composition of them.

---

[92] The wars of antiquity weren't usually fought during the winter months and armies were temporarily disbanded then. To continue military training during winter was a sign of perseverance and serious commitment.

Both mind and spirit were alike made of matter, and both were governed by the same principles.

The skill of Stoic life is nothing else and nothing more than simply the skill of applying the principles presented in the previous chapters. In other words, living stoically is equivalent to following the rules we have discussed. And there is only one path there and reading this book is just its trailhead, just a gateway. The real meat consists in actual practice.

On the other hand, the Stoic practice entails fair and first hand learning what works for us and what doesn't. To learn how to properly tailor the Stoic training to our individual soul – it's a part of the training itself. A practicing Stoic knows when they need to focus on the present action, when to anticipate mishap and when not to dwell on counterfactual scenarios. And this is something we can and need to learn! We need to scrutinize our own preferences and proclivities. We have the latitude to pick and choose. Reformed Stoicism is not an off the rack, one-size-fits-all endeavor. It offers a selection of possibilities, it may and should be customized. Some of us will be particularly attracted to the idea of defining proper alternatives, and some to not flouting the rules of a game. It's perfectly normal that for one and the same ailment different Stoic solutions will be preferred by various individuals. This is our very own task: we need to try out the Stoic assortment and find out what exactly works best for us. Focusing on the things within our power, or not desiring acclaim? What serves us better when people circulate gossip about us? Or if one of our projects fails? And what if our health fails? No handbook, no philosophical lecture will teach us this. There is only one way to learn: through tough practice.

If we are serious in our Stoic aspirations, if we are thinking solemnly about revamping our life, then reading this book just once will far from enough. If we sleep-walk through it and put it back on the shelf, then we just as well might have spared ourselves the time and money and not have had read it at all. Reading a book on Stoicism, *any* book on Stoicism, is just a pre-run, just learning the ropes, just acquiring the basic *know-how* for our own endeavor. Any description of Stoicism, any introductory volume, any pertaining guidebook is a lot like a recipe. True, we need to know it, because without it we will prepare no meal. But a recipe isn't the same as a ready meal. Furthermore, the ability to read a recipe doesn't make us brilliant cooks. Cooking is something fundamentally different from reading the recipe, and it is cooking that we need to learn. Vain boasting about reading manuals leads us nowhere.

On a different note, a book on Stoicism may also be compared to a musical score. The analogy goes just the same: we need to be able to learn notes if we want to play the piano. But neither the notes themselves, nor reading them is

Practice regularly

tantamount to music itself. To be able to play is much, *much* more than just to understand the notes, because music is much more than what's on the staff. And for Stoicism, accordingly.

Fragment IV

> *Wisdom is not an accidental accomplishment. Riches will sometimes come of themselves, honor will be offered you, favor and dignity will haply be your portion, but virtue is not to be obtained but by great and incessant labor.*
>
> Seneca, Epistles, 76.6

Commentary: There is a funny paradox that if we are lucky enough and if fortune smiles upon us, then a great many of earthly arrangements may come to us randomly and with no effort on our end. It may happen that we become rich totally by chance: we may be born into great financial circumstances, or someone may die and leave us inheritance. Or, at the very least, we can win the lottery. It can also happen that the circumstances kick us up and we land a prestigious position or a great career without really striving for it. In general, if we just happen to be in the right place at the right time – any worldly development is possible. Everything is possible... except for the good and happy life, which will never come to us unearned and uninvited.

Stoicism will never "just happen" to us. We won't inherit it, we won't receive it as a gift. It will never emerge in our mind from nothing. No Higher Forces (however we understand them, or however we *don't* understand them) will deliver it to us on a silver platter with a silky pillow. In this industry, there is radical egalitarianism. There is no illumination for the chosen few. There is no magical pill. There is no sudden realization which endows us with everything within a blessed moment. Stoicism is always something we need to work hard to attain. It's our decision to learn it and it's us – no one else – who need to practice and strain. After all, it's us who want to live well, not anyone else. Why then expect that we may benefit from a practice of another? Why expect that someone else will benefit from our own efforts? This can't be transferred. There is only one way towards Stoicism and this is *our own* path of practice and exercise. There is no shortcut here, there are only many ways to deceive ourselves.

Fragment V

> *It was the custom of Sextius[93] when the day was over, and he had betaken himself to rest, to inquire of his spirit: "What bad habit of yours have you cured today? What vice have you checked? In what respect are you better?" [...] I make use of this privilege, and daily plead my cause before myself. [...] I pass the whole day in review before myself, and repeat all that I have said and done. I conceal nothing from myself, and omit nothing.*
>
> Seneca, Of Anger, III.36.1-3

Commentary: One easy way to begin our adventure with practicing Stoicism is this. Every day at bedtime, at that intimate moment of limbo between wakefulness and sleep, let's take some personal time and let's rewind and reassess everything that happened throughout the day. Let's do a Stoic examination of conscience. Let's get back to everything we did (and thought!) during the day. Now that the rush of the moment is gone, let's analyze where we did a good, Stoic job, and where there is still room for improvement. Where did we bravely hold the Stoic line and where did we yield to nonstoic temptations? Where did we manage to organize ourselves and our endeavors properly, and where did we let ourselves veer astray from the right path? These are the questions we should mull over before sleep creeps in.

Doing it between bedtime and sleep may be a useful strategy, since it affords us at least a small benefit of hindsight. Stoicism is a philosophy of living an active, productive life, and during the business hours, within the stream of errands and events, there may be just not enough time on our hands for a calm and careful meta-analysis. Once we set ourselves on the path towards Stoicism, more often than not, our days will be packed and our calendars will be full of all sorts of activity, practical and spiritual alike. In the buzz of the mid-day, it is a usual occurrence that whenever we wrap up one issue, another one immediately requires our attention. And we don't have the time to think about the previous matter anymore. That's perfectly understandable and normal... but it doesn't make the moment of reflection any less necessary, even if we push it down the road. Thus, the time right before falling asleep is a perfect moment to do that. We need a moment to feel our righteous pride about whatever we did well during the day and we need a moment to peacefully think through whatever we did wrong. Healthy Stoic life requires both.

---

[93] See footnote to the nutshell section in the chapter "Follow Good Examples."

Fragment VI

> *The soldier, in the time of peace, exercises [...], throws up trenches and [...] takes a great deal of pains, to get inured against the time, when it may become necessary.*
>
> Seneca, Epistles, 18.6

Commentary: As we have said, the Stoic practice may essentially accompany whatever we are doing at any moment. Whether we work or work out, whether we are swamped with tasks to perform or we just take some leisure, whether we stroll alone in the rolling charms of May, or if we attend a beehive family meeting – all of it can be done stoically. Whatever we do, it can both enhance our Stoic practice and be itself enhanced by it. In other words, Stoic practice can be performed alongside all other errands of life, because – in a way – it means nothing else than running these errands stoically. We may smell tautology on this, but it's indeed as simple as that.

The other side of the coin is that practicing Stoicism serves as anticipation of a mishap. We need to practice within what's available at the very moment (we have no other option after all) but we also need, at the same time, to be getting ready for the future. Our practice is not only aimed at boosting our Stoic performance at the present moment, not only at increasing our overall Stoic and moral character, but it is also preparation for the future. In the chapter "Anticipate Mishap" we talked about why and how we need to rehearse all possible adversities before they happen. And here it's the same: we are practicing Stoicism not only to flourish at present, but also to get ready for whatever fate has up its sleeve. In this regard, anticipating mishap is an umbrella idea for the whole of Stoicism: whatever happened in the past, we need to exercise our Stoic skill to excel in the present and to be ready for the future.

Seneca draws another military metaphor here. We, the Stoics in training, are just like soldiers in training. We are in the army now, and we have to live up to it. We never know what awaits us tomorrow, we never know whether the sun will rise to cast its light on peaceful or belligerent earth. And if it is to be war that engulfs us, then we never know until the last moment from where exactly the attack comes (and who the enemy is). This is exactly why we need a versatile, all-weather training program. We need to be stoically fit and ready for battle... even in the absence of any signs of danger. We need to practice relentlessly even when it seems that there is no hazard ahead. For there is no truly safe situation ever, there is only unnoticed danger. And this is something we must be ready for, this is something we need to practice for. Again, it's just as the saying goes. The more we sweat in peace, the less we bleed in war.

Fragment VII

We ought to oppose to [a] *habit* [with] *a contrary habit.*

Epictetus, *Discourses*, III.12.7

Commentary: Over the course of our Stoic practice we need to take particular care for our weak spots. They are critical to our success, since they are usually the gateways through which misery lurks into our soul. What does it mean and how do we go about that?

Our weak spots are the particular kinds of things, events, useless narratives and temptations that we are oversensitive to. Everyone has their own weaknesses – to each their own weaknesses – they differ greatly from person to person (which is also a reason why reformed Stoicism doesn't offer one universal solution relevant for everybody and for all problems at once). For some of us, the desire to be famous is particularly difficult to manage. For some, it's the sexual temptations. For some, the plain and simple laziness is the mightiest enemy of all. For others, money, or lack thereof, will be the weak spot. There is no logic in this, and there is no rule – just our very own idiosyncrasy.

The only principle which holds here is that whatever our soft spots are, we must know them. They can't be a surprise for us. We mustn't keep our head in the sand, we are no longer allowed to deny our weakness. Doing so would simply be self-delusion and an act of self-sabotage. Our Stoic powers rely on self-knowledge and are based on honest acknowledgment of our vulnerabilities. We can set out on the path towards improvement only if we find out what our weak spots are and if we nail them down.

Our Stoic training needs to be focused on these Achilles' heels. They need to be covered as the first order of business, because they pose the highest danger to our happiness. They need to be worked up, they require most of our effort. If we are too easily affected by gibes or praises, this is exactly what we need to improve. We need to practice and develop our indifference to it. If we are too easily susceptible to money or praises, then we need to grow our detachment in this regard. If we are overly concerned about what others think, say and comment on Facebook, this is the prime area we need to work on. If our chief problem is laziness, then we definitely need to work to improve our work ethics… or do we? Note, that this last case reflects a greater problem. After all, one may say, practice and toil at improving any single weak spot requires lots of effort and perseverance. But what if our problem is the lack of perseverance itself? What do we do then?

We do just the same. Perseverance, willpower and grit are a very curious thing: strengthening them is within our power. Surely, if we lack the proper genes, education and luck, then no amount of practice will make us another Mozart or Michelangelo. But practice is enough to increase patience! Perseverance can be trained, and willpower is enough to train willpower! In the ultimate sense, no one has an excuse in this regard. Rare endowments are requisite for pulling off some brilliant feats like creating groundbreaking works of art, but there are indeed no special talents and rare gene combinations required for, say, getting up at 4.30 AM to do workout. There is simply no entry, not-within-our-power condition for working hard to improve our perseverance. If we fail to do that – it's solely on us. Our fault, no one else's.

Fragment VIII

Exercise not the tongue, but the mind.

Seneca, *Epistles*, 82.8

Commentary: In all of our Stoic journey, we must never stop on the surface of words and superficial declarations. Practicing Stoicism isn't about practicing Stoic rhetoric. It isn't about the ability to defend Stoicism in an abstract philosophical debate, be it in ancient forum or online. These skills have really not much to do with the actual Stoic life. It may be – and it often happens – that someone living a very Stoic life is unprepared to elaborate on it, while someone who writes a lengthy book on Stoicism is continuously haunted by severely nonstoic problems. Thus, just as Seneca says, Stoicism is not about the words. It's about how we act and what we think.

And this is exactly what we need to exercise. We need to actually try to think and live as Stoicism urges us to. There is no shortcut to that. There is also no point in faking our practice, no point in bashing it out. Stoicism is for us and we have no one to fool but ourselves.

Let's draw examples from other walks of life. If we want to stay fit physically, we need to work out not only regularly but also without cheating. What is the point of jogging daily, if our laziness reduces the pace to 13:00 per mile? What's to be gained from hitting the gym thrice a week if we mostly chat with friends while in there? What's the use of attending a language course if we don't do homework? We won't learn French as long as going to French class remains *going* only. The same holds for Stoicism: not just regularity of our practice counts, but diligence too.

If we really wish to become Stoics, then we need to be serious and sincere about it. Stoicism is no trifle, no toy, and we'll get out of it only as much as we put in it. There is no magic and no free lunch here. All the Stoic skill we'd like to have, we need to practice in and out. Also, we mustn't forget the discussed weak spots. It's more fruitful to run one exercise twice but on something we don't feel well about, than to dry run two things that we already feel quite confident about. Our Stoic capability and confidence grow best in wrestling with real challenges. It's no news after all that athletes lift heavier weights in training than they intend to clear in the contest itself. We need to look all the hardships in the eye – they are not our enemies, they are allies in our battle for a new, better life. We need to tackle head-on the adversities we face, without sugarcoating, without diluting the difficulty. We are not supposed to swift past them, we are not supposed to water them down. We are supposed to overcome them. We must deal with them, in fact and matter, not just verbally. It's no surprise after all that we make a laugh of a bro at the gym who instead of showing how he pumps the iron, just talks in circles about it. Stoicism is not about disguising the problems with a curtain of adroit words, but about facing up to the problems and beating them down in fair combat.

Fragment IX

> *Any road is tolerable to our pack-horses, whose hoofs are hardened [...] by travelling in rough and craggy ways, while such as are fed in soft and marshy pastures are soon fretted and worn out. The hardships of a country life generally make better soldiers than the idle and tender breeding of the city. The hands that are transferred from the plough to the pike refuse no labor.*
>
> Seneca, *Epistles*, 51.10-11

Commentary: We shouldn't be fooled by the smiles of fortune. We shouldn't drop the ball and let our guard down just because things are going smoothly at present. Of course, Stoicism is all about happiness and we need to cherish the moments when fate is kind to us. But here is the catch, here is the tricky part. If everything seems to be on the right track, we may get accustomed to it too easily, and clean forget that sudden derailment is possible at any time. It's dangerous to lose our Stoic vigilance, it's dangerous to go soft on ourselves. It's dangerous to get isolated from the bumps and pains of life. It abates our alertness, it deludes us with a one-sided, biased picture. Stoicism compels us to enter the real contest with actual problems daily, instead of shutting them off or evading them.

But doesn't it translate into courting trouble? Isn't it doomsaying, plain pessimism? Doesn't it wipe out the very happiness we have worked so hard to build? Notice, that this is the same question we already dealt with in the chapter "Anticipate Mishap" (commentary to fragment VI to be precise) and, just as we discussed it there, preparation for adversity has nothing to do with inviting it. If mere mental rehearsing of possible problems doesn't invite them, then surely it's even more OK to practice dealing with it. And this is exactly how it works in Stoicism. The constant awareness that behind the fortune's smile another, treacherous face of it may be concealed, makes us not only immune to adverse surprises, but it also allows us to appreciate more all those favorable twists of fate that we have already experienced.

Just as Seneca puts it: animals which are used to rough ground will endure much more than those who are used to soft pastures only. The same with us, humans. Whoever is used to working hard on improving themselves, will sustain more and live better than someone who is versed in sloth only. Thus, we need to take care to do our workout regularly – not just physically (this part is not mandatory, yet advisable in reformed Stoicism), but mentally. A bit of toughness won't spoil us. It will actually improve a lot. If we want to be good Stoics, if we want to really learn how to live, we can't limit ourselves to the protected and pleasant conditions. After all, when it comes to our life's battles, we don't want to fly a white flag the moment we spot the enemy, do we?

Fragment X

> *We ought to exercise ourselves in small things, and beginning with them proceed to the greater. "I have pain in the head." Do not say, "Alas! I have pain in the ear." Do not say, "Alas!" And I do not say, that you are not allowed to groan, but do not groan inwardly.*
>
> Epictetus, Discourses, I.18.18-19

Commentary: The task of preparing ourselves for adversity, of hardening up and strengthening ourselves is surely not an easy one. Slackness and reluctance of mind are clear and present obstacles for that, just as bodily laziness is for workout. If our lifestyle is persistently sedentary, if our only physical exercise is bar-hopping, and if the very thought of climbing two flights of stairs makes us pant, then we have every moral right to laugh in the face of someone who floats the idea of running 10k daily. If we are only at the beginning of our journey, we shouldn't judge ourselves by the measure of those who are well advanced. Here and everywhere: if we take the opening steps, we should make them baby steps.

Let's think about running. No one becomes a runner at once. If we want to go that route, we need to kick it off easy, we need to start with no more than walking and only later add some trot and only then pick up the pace and boost the volume of our runs. If we are diligent and patient in that – our fitness will gradually improve over time. Rushing things will take us nowhere (except from frustration and discouragement). And just the same works in the Stoic domain.

We need to start easy and then gradually climb the Stoic curve. We needn't force ourselves into challenges we aren't ready for yet. Let's practice and test our skills on the problems from our own league, and then let's gradually work our way up. We will always have time for dealing with heavy-duty challenges. No one, after all, is fortunate enough to be spared them.

There is no Stoicism without practice and continuous exercise. Stoicism is a way of life and – to put a tautology to use – a way of life is useless, unless it's lived. Just *talking* about Stoicism turns it into a scrap of a pervert theory and a bunch of pearls of empty wisdom. Thus, there are just three gateways to Stoicism: practice, practice, practice. This practice needs to be systematic, diligent and intense. But it also needs to be *smart*. And being smart entails that we don't impose the highest standards on us all at once. Doing so wouldn't set us out on any journey, but on the direct track to dispiritedness and abandoning the Stoic endeavor altogether.

In Stoicism, we do aim very high, but we also aren't naive. We take on a long haul and we need to start it by charting the course. No responsible and rational person claims that daydreaming on effortless teleportation is more productive than spreading the map on the table and actually navigating it. And once we plan and put everything on the map, we need to follow the chosen route, shying away from no effort and no difficulty that may haunt us down that road. We need to be self-aware of what Stoic skills we have acquired already and we need to be motivated to climb the ladder even higher. And we need to practice to make that possible, we need to practice smart, hard and on schedule. This is the only path to Stoicism. We need to travel it ourselves, and we may start just today. We may start just now. So, let's go! The clock is ticking.

Chapter 24

Be happy – it's simple

Like a mariner, who has doubled the promontory, you will find calm, everything stable, and a waveless bay.

Marcus Aurelius, *Meditations*, 12.22

In a nutshell: The first, final and foremost goal of the whole Stoic enterprise is to be happy. Stoicism is about good, blissful life. It's about freeing us from all sorrows and distress. The goal of the Stoics is to teach us how to live happily, and the core purpose of this book is to present this case to the contemporary reader. I hope that this pitch was comprehensible and convincing. And that's all. Live stoically, be happy. That's all this is about. That's all there is.

***

Happiness is easy because it depends on a few factors (fragment I). It is our innate ability and human calling (II). Happiness depends on nothing else than what we think (III), and attaining it may appear difficult only to those who haven't tried (IV). Happy life is logically simpler than misery (V). Even if we fall, it's easy to jolt ourselves back into happiness (VI), because the things within our power, that we need to focus on, are always with us (VII). Thus, our happiness is always with us – this empowers us and our relationships with others (VIII). In Stoicism, we surpass gods because all we achieve is our own doing – and that achievement is open to everybody (IX). Stoicism is the ultimate bliss and completion of the human condition (X and XI).

Fragment I

Very little indeed is necessary for living a happy life.

Marcus Aurelius, *Meditations*, 7.67

Commentary: Happiness is simple because it doesn't require much. Truth be told, it requires only one thing: living a good life. This is the core Stoic message: happiness is nothing else than a byproduct of a good life. And another bullet point is that attaining it is simple. We have navigated already through two dozens of chapters on Stoicism and it may seem complex in retrospect. But as a matter of fact – it is not. The bottom line of Stoicism is one of utter and breathtaking simplicity.

Time and time again people will try to convince us that there is a long list of factors and standards that need to be factored in a good life. There is quite a diversity here. Some claim the basics, i.e. that a good life is possible only in a nice home and with a fancy car. Some say (or even believe) that a life is dull unless we travel a lot and spend every weekend in the arms of another casual lover. Others want to get us to believe that life is pointless unless some Higher Power provides us with meaning and solace. Others say that only a life of deed is a life indeed, and that we need to dedicate ourselves to some concrete earthly cause, be it political, social, or whatever. Yet others will insist on a bookworm's life of quiet contemplation. The list spins out on and on. But it is entirely wrong.

All above requirements are false, all mentioned conditions are empty. All these investments, commitments and solaces aren't at all necessary. In fact, more often than not they degenerate into excuses. We use them to exculpate ourselves. We use them to ease ourselves into a failed state of mind. We get stuck in the holding pattern of misery and strive for happiness no longer. And this is the worst iniquity of all. This is the flatness of soul that's plainly unacceptable to Stoicism.

We need to be highly cautious about all these useless narratives. Think about the marketing industry. All it does is pumping a load of artificial needs into us. This surely keeps the economy spin, but it does so at our expense – and we need to be aware of that. The same happens in other aspects of life. Just as we don't necessarily need the latest phone model, we also don't require protection from a benevolent god, we don't need a celebrity status for ourselves or the promise of an afterlife. We don't need to go on a three-week retreat in Thailand to learn meditation from Buddhist monks just the same as we don't need a Ferrari. Superfluous needs are all the same. They are delusional and they lead us astray. Happiness rests on very few conditions and complying with them is very simple.

Few conditions? We can even beat Marcus: happiness actually rests on *one* condition. Namely, on the focus on things within our power. We need to take proper care of them and disregard all else – this is enough to live a good life. All else is excessive and takes care of itself. Our focus and our business need to be centered on our own domain of control, on the sacred realm governed sovereignly by our will and reason. Our path to happiness starts there... and it also leads anywhere else but there.

Happiness is simple and it is to be found within things within our power. The entire Stoic recipe – and this entire book – consists in there. We need to focus on this simplicity instead of coming up with lame excuses and out-of-thin-air reasons which "prove" that good life and happiness are hard to come by. They are not. This is the strength of the Stoic message coming from 2300 years back. We just need to hear it, we need to comprehend it and embrace its radical clarity. Let's develop useful narratives, let's focus on what's within our power... *and that's it!* All else follows.

Fragment II

> *Place before your eyes this facility with which the reason will be carried through all things, as fire upward, as a stone downward, as a cylinder down an inclined surface, and seek for nothing further.*
>
> Marcus Aurelius, Meditations, 10.33

Commentary: Happiness is simple because it is our innate and undeniable capacity. Truly, happiness is our shared human calling. This is what makes us different from the rest of the universe. We, humans, possess the unique capability of making ourselves happy through our own thinking. This is our superpower. And this is what Stoicism is all about. We can transgress any circumstance, we don't have to be enslaved by anything. Through Stoicism, we break free from the tyranny and oppression of external things. This makes us outstanding. Being born into the human race means being born for happiness. This is our true and only calling.

Stoic happiness is at everyone's fingertips, regardless of gender, wealth, race, country of origin and any other quality. It's accessible to every human, whatever one's circumstances. This is the greatest feat, the remarkable potential we all take part in. This is what binds us together.

And just right there, a question arises. If happiness is the true name of the human game, why then so many of us are unhappy? If happiness is simple why doesn't it come effortlessly? Why doesn't it grow organically? Why do we even need Stoicism to tell us all that? If it's all so simple, why then do we need to *learn* it?

That's a fair question and the answer is as follows. We tend to forget that happiness and good life are simple. We have that great endowment, that capacity for bliss... but we often fail to use it. We don't tend to it, we let it wither. We let our daily lazy routines take over. We cave in to the nonstoic societal norms, to outside temptations, to equivocal whispers. We get entangled in useless narratives and we don't cultivate our talent to be happy. And this talent is both like and unlike any other talent. It's like any other because it requires nurturing and development. It's unlike any other because of all our faculties this one is *the* most important and hence it deserves the most attention. After all, what good all other talents do us if we fail to live well and happily?

Our talent for happiness is a great potential, but it's not a magical pill. It won't do the job for us. It won't develop by itself. We mustn't spoil it. If we choose to think and act randomly, if we mindlessly take up any narrative that comes about, if we head downstream instead of toward our goal, if we flip-flop in response to which way the wind is blowing... then we are on the right track to wasteland. We will squander our ability to be happy.

To avoid all this, we need to remember the Stoics. If we forget that happiness is our destiny – they will remind us. If we delude ourselves that a good life is difficult to live – they will restlessly rectify us one more time. They will convince us yet again, that happiness is simpler than what the unhappy think.

Fragment III

> You can pass your life in an equable flow of happiness, if you can go by the right way, and think and act in the right way.
>
> Marcus Aurelius, Meditations, 5.34

Commentary: Happiness is simple because it hinges only on our thinking. It depends on nothing else then on the narratives we adopt, on the values we pick and on the goals we set up for ourselves. All else is irrelevant – we aren't at the mercy of anything external. We make ourselves happy ourselves. It's really that plain and simple.

If we decide that we want to be happy, we may be happy in every circumstance and on every occasion. Whatever happens outside, whatever comes to pass – it won't blur our happiness if we don't let it. No one ever peeks into our head and no one forcibly switches the tracks of our thought. It's impossible to make us think in a way we don't want to think. It's that simple and that undeniable.

In Stoicism our own thinking (our narratives, our values and goals, the way we want to shape our character) is not simply "within our power," but it is also logically the easiest thing to change. Think about it this way: in order to change the way we think, in order to reset our values and redefine goals, we need to move no mountains and we need to spark no revolutions. Neither effort of our muscles, nor backup from other people is required. We don't need to alter fate, we don't need to court the powerful. We just need to rearrange our mind and soul. That – and nothing more!

This surely sounds like a radical position and obviously, there are intellectual currents which take a different position. But Stoicism is firm. Let's think for a moment what would be the case if the opposite were true, that is, if great labor and deep engineering of the outside world were required to make an individual happy. If our good life and happiness were shackled to what happens beyond us, well, we would be hostages. More than that: we would be slaves. We would be slaves of the cruel and unpredictable fate, we would be slaves to a myriad of factors we have zero control of. We would be subordinate to anyone and anything, we would be forever inferior to the whole universe. Such a life would be utterly unliveable. It would be the antipode of happiness, it would just be a deplorable strain of resignation. And here the Stoic promise shines: it's entirely up to us what sort of a life we choose to live. More than that: it is within our power to define the world we live in. Why then don't we choose a world in which good life and happiness are our own doing? Isn't that simpler and better, for us and for the world itself? Sure it is. And this is exactly what Stoicism stands for.

In other words, we don't need to wait for the world to grant us the capacity for happiness. We do that ourselves. We endow ourselves with the greatest power that a human may aspire to. This is how Stoicism works! It creates our own, private and unyielding interface for lasting happiness. It's our own deal and no one else's. We adopt a worldview in which our happiness is on us, the mistakes of others are on them, and the indifference of the world is beyond our concern. This plays on what we discussed in the chapter "Whatever The World Is Like – Be a Stoic." Stoicism doesn't hold *because* it's based on some theory of how the world works. The Stoic principles aren't *inferred* from anything. They are our own device. We establish them by ourselves for ourselves. It is our responsibility, our opportunity, and our duty. This duty can be carried out regardless of the outside world. Whatever the world is like we can, by our own means, set up rules for ourselves. Why don't we then set up rules that procure happiness for us? It's all our own choice. We don't need the world to sign off on anything. Our happiness isn't a property, it isn't any benevolence of the universe. It's the sacred thing of our own.

Fragment IV

"The way by which we are asked to climb is steep and uneven." What then? Can heights be reached by a level path? Yet they are not so sheer and precipitous as some think. It is only the first part that has rocks and cliffs and no apparent outlet, just as many hills seen from a long way off appear abruptly steep and joined together, because the distance deceives our sight, and then, as we draw nearer, those very hills which our mistaken eyes had made into one gradually unfold themselves, those parts which seemed precipitous from afar assume a gently sloping outline.

Seneca, *On the Firmness of the Wise Man*, 1.2

Commentary: One curious fact about the Stoic way is that it may *seem* difficult... but only from a distance. Once we examine it closely, we will always be positively surprised by how simple it really is. Let's second Seneca for a while and let's follow his mountaineering metaphor. True, from far away the trail may seem hard and unconquerable. But when we get closer, when we actually hit it – the illusion disappears. Some obstacles turn out much easier than they seemed and some obstacles turn out to be... not there at all. Once we dig deeper into Stoicism, we see that we can find our way past everything. And this isn't a surprise. After all, scaling a cliff face may appear impossible if we look from a distance. The distance covers details. It masks all the little ledges and crevices that one may grasp and get a foothold. We can see them only if we find the courage to get closer, scratch that, only if we really start to climb. The same logic holds for all the challenges of human life. Including Stoicism, which is both the highest pinnacle and most trustworthy hope of all.

Stoicism is not designed to be just brushed with and then set aside, just as this book shouldn't be barely put on the shelf once it's read. Reading about the Stoic principles is not enough. Learning them is not enough. What we need to do is internalize them. We need to make them our own principles. We need to genuinely start living by them. The Stoic promise is that once we do it, we'll momentarily recognize that they are much easier than what we feared. We will realize that good life and happiness are *really* within our reach. We'll see that we are separated from them by nothing else than mere inadequacies of our thinking. Nothing more than the primordial resistance of our soul. And once we break it, once we push through that gray matter – it will all go on surprisingly smooth. Stoicism, once we grasp its meaning, becomes its own guideline. It will lead us deeper and deeper into its wonderful territory. And it will show us the way itself. We just need to find the courage to take the first step.

Most people who gave Stoicism a try remember one singular experience. There is one point on the Stoic path that gives a very specific, indelible experience of a breakthrough and sudden clarity. It's a point where we break free from our misconceptions and finally wrap our head around the magnitude of the Stoic project. It's when we realize the scope of what Stoicism promises us. It also dawns on us at this point that it's all far easier than we thought before. This is the moment of ultimate liberation. This is the moment when a warm tsunami of happiness engulfs us. We are finally delivered from all affliction, we are once and for all unchained from the evil and uplifted from the dirt. From this moment on we may stay in the fresh, salutary current as long as we want. It's our own decision to go with the divine, Stoic flow – or step out of it.

The practical question now: when exactly should we expect this breakthrough experience? There is no strict rule for that. As we have talked about over and over, Stoicism is plural. There is no one fact sheet for it, there is no universal recipe. Everyone finds their own way. That being said, accounts of many Stoics – myself included – focus on the moment when we get the full grasp of what Stoicism tells us about the narratives. The realization of the full meaning of the first chapter of this book – it's all about the narratives, how deep that idea really goes – is often referred to as the most breathtaking moment of realization. Once we get past that point, we'll never again slip the words "Stoicism is difficult." We will never again be able to fool ourselves.

Fragment V

> *What is more restful than a mind at peace, and what more toilsome than anger? What is more at leisure than clemency, what fuller of business than cruelty? Modesty keeps holiday while vice is overwhelmed with work. In fine, the culture of any of the virtues is easy, while vices require a great expense.*
>
> Seneca, Of Anger, II.13.2

Commentary: Let's pose a simple question: what's simpler, a happy life or a miserable life? What takes less pain and toil? What has fewer requirements and rests on a shorter list of conditions? Surely, the Stoic answer isn't a surprise here. Happiness is simpler than misery.

Let's recall some miserable moment of our life (i.e. from our pre-stoic period). Let's try to examine what that low state of mind was like. Was it simple? Did the anguish just happen to us, did it play out on its own? Let's be honest. *Staying* in misery – wasn't it our own doing? Hasn't it cost us a lot of wit and resolve to remain down there? Some people say tongue-in-cheek that it takes a lot of grit to be sick, that is, to deal with the doctors, hospitals, all that (not to mention the medical bills). The same holds here. A weak person wouldn't have the necessary stamina to be constantly unhappy! It's just too great an effort. It takes a lot of willpower to keep making oneself unhappy. How draining, how exhausting is that continuous quest to find new reasons for sorrow! How great is that wicked work we do to undermine ourselves! It takes a lot of blood, toil, tears and sweat to keep the bleak glasses constantly on. The point is clear: misery is toilsome. We pay for it in the currency of dispiritedness and exhaustion. Misery comes in package with resignation, bitterness and erosion of spirit. It makes our life wither, it makes it scale down to a sheer negative and resentful vegetation. This is a very high price. And we need to think twice and hard whether we want to pay it.

We don't have to, once we espouse Stoicism. This is exactly what Stoicism says: we need to be happy for the sake of logic, sanity and self-preservation. The Stoic life, the good life of happiness is much simpler than persistence in misery. It costs less, it's easier, and it's also logically simpler. It requires us to abide by a much shorter list of rules. It requires less strain, less mental maneuvering. Think of it this way: this book contains 24 chapters and it may seem difficult to swallow them all in one big gulp. But think about the alternative costs. The funny thing is that *not* following the Stoic principles takes much more out of us than following them. Being a happy Stoic is easier than being a miserable nonstoic. Whoever opts for the latter way, faces far greater and graver problems.

Let's stick to the simplest but still most significant example. The first Stoic principle reads: it's all about narratives. No fact, no event, no outside circumstance concerns us – only our narratives do. It's quite a plain idea. Now, let's imagine what an opposite principle might look like? "All facts concern us"? Or just *some* facts? Probably some. If so, which exactly? What (or who) tells us what concerns us and what doesn't? How would we even know that? The point is: even phrasing a nonstoic principle is difficult. How difficult, then, following it would be?

Fragment VI

> *To someone who is penetrated by true principles even the briefest precept is sufficient [...] to remind them that they should be free from grief and fear.*
>
> Marcus Aurelius, *Meditations*, 10.34

Commentary: Simplicity of happiness entails that if we accidentally lapse out of it, we may return to it very easily. Of course, the ideal is to no never disconnect from the Stoic bliss. But it is human to trip. And, as stated already, Stoicism is not for those who haven't fallen. It's for those who want to get up. How do we get up?

Marcus Aurelius points out that reading just one Stoic passage may be enough to put us back on track. In my experience, it might be even simpler than that. Just opening a Stoic book, or even having a glimpse at its cover may be enough to pep us up. This is exactly why Marcus' *Meditations* were written. His work was meant to do what a QRH – or Quick Reference Handbook – does in aviation. It's a lifeline to grasp, a guideline to consult in a moment of crisis. We may take additional solace in the fact that Marcus himself felt the urge to have such a safety device. If he, such a great Stoic, craved such support, aren't we entitled to it even more?

On its own modest scale, this book is meant to serve the same purpose. I have carefully chosen the most powerful and articulate passages from the ancients, I have commented on them and designed this book to be a manual easily accessible for instant support. Such support is needed particularly in the moments of letdown or doubt, which are, by definition, moments when we need Stoicism most.

Stoicism is about lasting bliss which surpasses all and cannot be barred or denied. The logical simplicity of that bliss, our autonomy in it and independence from external factors make it boundless and timeless, make it transcend any particular circumstance and condition. And yet, our human fallibility makes us fall time and again. Fortunately, a one-off failure is not an overall disaster. The sequence of falls and subsequent recoveries is the meat of Stoicism. Some will even say that entire Stoicism consists in the perseverance to get back to it once we have fallen. In this regard, it's akin to mediation. No one will ever be able to focus their attention on the breath and keep their mind clear forever (or even for a minute). Needless thoughts will always pop up and the mind will drift away. And that's OK. The whole secret is to realize this and get back to one's breath. A meditation guru isn't someone whose thought doesn't drift, but someone who is adamant in trying again. The same with Stoicism. Stoic happiness is a simple either-or situation, but we, its mere adepts (no one is actually more than an adept), will lapse out of it time and again. And it's neither shameful of us, nor does it disqualify us. It's just how things work. It's all about the unrelenting "getting back" motion. Stoicism is measured by nothing else than by our adamancy in getting back to it. Or simpler: adamancy in getting back to Stoicism *is* Stoicism itself.

Fragment VII

> [A Stoic] *is one who full of joy, lives as happy [...] as the gods [...], ever cheerful, placid and unshaken. [...] The effect of wisdom is constant joy. Such is the mind of* [a Stoic] *as is the region above the moon, perpetually fair and serene. This is therefore a sufficient inducement to study wisdom: because it is never without joy, that joy which ever springs from a consciousness of virtue.*
>
> <div align="right">Seneca, <i>Epistles</i>, 59.14-16</div>

Commentary: Simplicity of the Stoic system makes it a perfect philosophy for living a good life. It's, in a word, a philosophy of joy. It's a philosophy designed to make us happy here and now, every day and no matter what. With no rain check, no parole, and regardless of things not within our power. In Stoicism, we are joyful and grateful no matter where we dwell, what we do and what's our position in life. Happiness can't be taken away from us because it's not a "thing" – it's our way of being.

This book presents this way of being at length. But how about a concise version? The succinct recap is this. In Stoicism, happiness follows from a good life, and a good life is lived by virtue. The notion of virtue is a bit abstract and hence I refrained from using it in this book (in a way, "living virtuously" equals "living according to the principles set forth in this book). But virtue may be translated into a more mundane concept of agency. Virtue – following Lawrence Becker's line here[xviii] – can be interpreted as maximized or even perfect agency. And what about agency? If we agree on that working term, we may shortly say that *Stoicism is all about continuous employment and enjoyment of one's agency.* And happiness follows from it.

Whatever our condition and position in life, no matter what happens, no matter what, we may still develop virtue. Is there a circumstance, is there an event that can bar us from trying to be more magnanimous, trustworthy, resilient or patient? No, there isn't. This is how things within our power work. Once we focus our energies and attention on them, nothing will hinder us. Bliss lasts forever.

In more practical terms, Stoic happiness is based on that we can always make the decision which is best under the circumstances. Even if our choices are narrow and all the available options are grim, one of them will always be the best one. And – Stoicism reminds us – we can always opt for it. And that's the point! We need to be focused not on the options themselves (particularly if they are all pretty bleak), but on the fact that we have our sacred right and ability to decide. Retaining that ability, exercising it, and cherishing it – this is Stoicism. This is how it provides overwhelming, undeniable and lasting happiness.

This happiness doesn't originate in the outside world, it doesn't come from a smile of fortune, nor is it granted by any higher force. It doesn't really *come*. It rather *is* our own internal alignment. It is the way we set up our focus and mental power. Hence, nothing and no one can steal it from us. The cosmic power and greatness of Stoicism consist in its simplicity. If one wants to argue for the *beauty* of Stoicism, this is also a good place to start. Stoicism may seem radical to the layman, but it is indeed utterly simple.

Fragment VIII

> *If you choose, you are free. If you choose, you will blame no one, you will charge no one.*
>
> Epictetus, *Discourses*, I.17.28-29

Commentary: This understanding of happiness allows us to have it always with us, always handy. It's a part of our EDC, the Every-Day Carry. Happiness is always with us, it is always *on* us. It isn't some outcome of things external. It doesn't hinge on any outside events. It is our relationship with ourselves and with the world. Thus, it's impossible to lose it... unless, of course, we let it go.

Imagine someone who speaks no foreign language. Their whole universe of expression consists in the mother tongue: they know no other way to speak than to speak English. We don't expect them to suddenly start speaking Mongolian, do we? Or to forget English, right? The same holds for Stoicism. Once we make ourselves at home in the joyful Stoic attitude, we will realize that we can remain there as long as we want. External events and outside forces will have a hard time trying to smoke us out. As the Stoics, we are always under our lucky star. A tortoise or a snail don't need to worry where to find their shelter and they don't have to worry about losing them. A Stoic is just as shelled. We carry our bliss with us.

An important feature of Stoic happiness is that it is achieved *in this world*. And let's be precise about this. "This world" means, first off, the physical, common world of our shared everyday experience. Stoicism is about this life, as opposed to religion which tends to be overly focused on the afterlife. In Stoicism, we don't concern ourselves with any prospect of a life after death, heaven, paradise or any reward on the other side of the grave. It's not our problem. We are interested in happiness here and now. "Here and now" – this is our true domain. Happiness in life, not after death. Happiness in this world, not any other.

In Stoicism, we don't delude ourselves that the world may be any different. We, the Stoics, don't live in a net of illusions and "coulda woulda shoulda." We live well with the world that's really out there. We don't distort reality, we don't deny it. And above all: we don't run away. We don't run away from the world, from people, from the perennial business of life. We live in the world and we neither enter heaven alive, nor do we take refuge on the fringes of the human world. Our soul and our body are firmly in place, no escape route is needed.

Simplicity, autonomy and fullness of Stoic happiness bear deep impact on our relationship with others – both with individuals and with society. As Stoics, we are utterly confident about our own happiness. We are confident because we confide in ourselves. We are free of anxiety and envy. We know that our happiness is our own doing and that no one will ever steal it away. No stranger, no alien, no other person endangers it. No one will ever make us unhappy. It's quite the contrary: we may help others become happy! If they want our help, of course. After all, the wants of others are not within our power.

Fragment IX

> *There is something wherein* [a Stoic] *has the advantage of the gods themselves. They are what they are by nature,* [while a Stoic] [...] *– by own industry. Behold a wonderful thing: to have a weakness of a human and the security of God.*
>
> Seneca, Epistles, 53.11-12

Commentary: Stoicism is a very here-and-now philosophy, preoccupied only with the present, earthly life. Thus, when Seneca mentions gods, it's basically a figure of speech. And we need to cut him some slack. This choice of words is legitimate for a person from the 1st century. He uses the metaphor to express the idea that Stoic happiness is *the* happiness – supreme, ultimate bliss that tops all. You just can't get any higher on the ladder available to humans. In this regard, we are on a par with gods. We are their peers.

However, as Seneca points out, we outflank gods at least in one respect. Think of it this way: we are on a par with gods – but we credit ourselves for that. We've gone all this way on our own. We climbed here ourselves. In most traditional religions, you can't become a god – you can only be born a god. The caste of gods is forever closed to people. And look how utterly non-democratic and discriminating that is! On this view, the highest rank of existence is accessible only to the chosen few. Stoicism, in turn, proposes a vastly more egalitarian, available and, simply, more human take. For no one is ever born a Stoic... but everyone can become one. No one ever came out of their mother's womb with a copy of *Meditations* in their hand. No crying baby in a cradle has ever followed the advice of Epictetus. We are all born nonstoics... but we are also born into this unbelievable opportunity to become one. And this is how we, humans, are supreme to gods. We can make ourselves Stoics. This option is open to absolutely everyone. No birth certificate is needed.

Fragment X

> *"What then? Will there be no one who will try to do an injury to* [a Stoic]*?" Yes, some one will try, but the injury will not reach* [a Stoic] [...]. *Even when powerful men, raised to positions of high authority* [...] *strive to injure* [a Stoic], *all their darts fall as far short* [...] *as those which are shot upwards by bowstrings or catapults, which, although they rise so high as to pass out of sight, yet fall back again without reaching the heavens. Why do you suppose that when that stupid king clouded the daylight with the multitude of his darts, that any arrow of them all went*

into the sun? Or that when he flung his chains into the deep, that he was able to reach Neptune? Just as sacred things escape from the hands of people, and no injury is done to the godhead by those who destroy temples and melt down images, so whoever attempts to treat [a Stoic] *with impertinence, insolence, or scorn, does so in vain.*

Seneca, *On the Firmness of the Wise Man*, IV.1-2

Commentary: Let's be Stoics then! Let's be happy and joyful, let's live a good life. Nothing will harm us, nothing will grieve us, nothing will eclipse the excellence of our bliss. We will be like the sun in the sky, where no concern and no distress can reach it. Or, if we don't like the picture, Seneca offers another one. Let's be Stoics and we will be like the gods of high seas. Our joy will be timeless and tameless like an ocean. Let's be Stoics and nothing will concern us. No earthly misery, nothing that comes to pass under the sun will ever bother us. Even if the sun itself goes out, even if darkness, war and insanity engulf earth, even if the most wicked of human villainy assails us – nothing will trouble us. Once we become Stoics, no fact or event from the outside realm ever hinders us. They don't belong to us anymore. They are not ours. And they will bother us no more.

Fragment XI

[The soul of a Stoic] *avoids all storms* [and] *stands on firm ground in fair daylight, and has brought to perfection its knowledge of all that is useful and essential.*

Seneca, *On Benefits*, VII.1.7

Commentary: There is a lot still ahead of us – many challenges, developments and novelties. Life takes its restless course, old beings fade, while new ones take their place. We connect with new people and we are confronted by yet new facts and circumstances. In all this, Stoicism will always be the clearest source of strength and ultimate empowerment. It will make us tougher and happier than any other system of thought ever dreamt of by human philosophers. It will prepare us to cherish the fortunate developments and to take on the unfortunate twists of fate. It will make a smile never disappear from our face. It will enable us to turn every turn of events to our benefit. Let's be Stoics then. We will know how to live well, we'll find our own in every situation, we'll play out our life on our own terms. We will be as happy as a human being can possibly be.

Let's be Stoics and we will be "like the promontory against which the waves continually break, but it stands firm and tames the fury of the water around it."[xix] Or, in another picture sketched by Marcus, once we become Stoics, we will be "like a mariner, who has doubled the promontory, and finds everything stable, and a waveless bay."[xx] Let the wind blow East, let the wind blow West – we won't get lost in any storm. No bitterness will reach us. We will be safe and satisfied – now and forever. We will always have a smile on our face, serenity in our soul and bliss at heart.

Let's be happy. This is what Stoicism is for. We get an inalienable right at birth: the right to be happy. There is no use in not using it. Let's not let anyone or anybody convince us otherwise. We don't need to be miserable. We can and we should be happy – this is what Stoicism is all about. This is what being human is about – and only Stoicism allows us to exploit this potential fully. This is the core message: the human condition is a condition of bliss. Our position in this universe is unique and remarkable. We are endowed with reason, which, if applied stoically, translates into the capability for perennial happiness. This is what we all share, this is our mightiest capacity. We just need to make use of it.

And let's make it right away. Literally, *now*. There is no time to waste. After all, we have already wasted a lot, haven't we? So, let's hit it now. Let's drop everything that holds us back, let's let go of everything that impedes us. Let's take a deep breath and let's live at last like humans are supposed to live. Let's live stoically. Thus we achieve the greatest bliss possible and the supreme fulfillment of the human condition. It is indeed the proudest boast of our time – of every time – to truly say about ourselves: we, the Stoics.

Conclusions and discussions

We have thus reached the end of our shared journey. We will part ways soon. Before we do that, I'd like to congratulate you, dear reader, for your patience in getting this far. I hope that reading this book was as beneficial to you as writing it was for me.

Getting this far in reading a book on Stoicism is a clear sign that you have found in it something for yourself. Perhaps something of interest, perhaps something for longer. Stoicism is all about "longer." No Stoic progress was ever made without repetition and ever-renewed effort in trying again. It doesn't mean simply reading this book one more time. Reading it – or any other book on Stoicism for this matter – is basically a prep session, just the first step in putting the Stoic ideas in action. The Stoic principles aren't supposed to be read only – they need to be lived. We learn how to do it from a book, but the only testing ground is our own life. Living according to these principles is the ultimate goal of all this.

The presentation of the principles ends here. I have done my best to show what reformed Stoicism is. What we need to do now is to go through a number of meta-comments. I need to briefly lay out the entire framework of this book and elaborate on the concept of *reformed* Stoicism itself. This stuff is a bit more theoretical and not compulsory for everyone. It doesn't belong to the curriculum itself.

The reformed view

This book is an *interpretation* of Stoicism. I don't have any pretense to an ultimate or universal truth. All I do is I put forward an interpretation of Stoicism and I try to convince you of its relevance. Every time I use the phrase "it is so-and-so," what I really mean is, obviously, "in my interpretation it is so-and-so". Other interpretations are perfectly possible and they are out there. I'm in no position to judge whether they are more or less convincing than that of my own.

The difference between discussing Stoicism and discussing modern authors is that in the former case, it's hard to draw a line between "an interpretation" and "the original." Why? Because we have hardly any originals. We don't even have enough of the basic facts to say for sure what the original Stoicism was like in the first place. I organized this book around a number of quotes from the Roman Stoics since some of their complete works are extant. They represent late Stoicism though and their writings aren't clear testimonies to the original doctrine. Seneca, Epictetus and Marcus Aurelius were interpreters themselves – they conveyed the Stoic thought in a selective and twisted way. Each of them added their own bias, to boot. All this is one reason which makes a conversation of ultimate truths about Stoicism impossible. The interpretative approach is not a defect of my book. I indeed propose a specific interpretation, but interpretations is all we've got.

The perennial problem with interpretations is that none has ever pleased all. If we agree to consider interpretations, an indeterminable debate and divergence of opinions will follow. And rightfully so. Dialogue is a source of insight. We get a deeper understanding of matters through the confrontation of distinct points of view, and through constant challenging of the assumptions we make. And certainly, if someone isn't satisfied with this interpretation of the Stoic thought – they are more than welcome to present their own.

The bedrock idea of this book is that it presents a reformed version of Stoicism. 2,300 years have passed since Stoicism was established, 1,840 have elapsed since Marcus Aurelius died. That's quite a stretch of time. Much has happened, a lot has changed. A question arises, first stated by Lawrence Becker in his *A New Stoicism* in 1998,[xxi] what would Stoicism look like today, if it had enjoyed an uninterrupted intellectual and institutional history for the last 23 centuries? Christianity, for one, had the opportunity to evolve continuously for two millennia (and reformed movement emerged at some point). What kind of Stoicism would we have today then, if it had developed without interruption, if it had had the opportunity to respond to all the innovation of mediaeval, modern and contemporary philosophy, if it had had the chance to react to the changing historical, social, political, intellectual and scientific context? This book is an attempt to answer this question. Stoicism is coming back in a big way. But *what* Stoicism? My answers are manifest: we need reformed Stoicism.

If we choose to leave Stoicism to historians, if we regard it as a dusty exhibit in the museum of bygone eras, then we probably don't have to interfere with it. Yet, even the ancient Stoics themselves wouldn't want that! Cold treatment is an insult for them. Handling Stoicism as some kind of a dead artifact would seem utterly absurd for them. Stoicism was – and remains – a philosophy of life, a real and concrete system of thought and conduct. This is exactly why I think that Seneca, Epictetus and Marcus Aurelius would have green-lighted my efforts here. They intended us to *live* according to the Stoic principles. In order to do that, we need to express Stoicism using our own words and concepts.

It is somewhat like the Constitution of the United States. It was written in a time immensely different from our own, but does it mean it's inadequate today? Of course not. The great success of the US as a political project is a testimony to that. Does it mean, however, that this project should be driven by the limited, literal understanding of the Constitution? Of course not. Doing so is impossible even if one wants to, because today we face a vast panorama of issues, matters and challenges that the Constitution doesn't mention simply because they weren't around in the 18th century. The power of the Constitution and of any other well-written legal document of this kind is that even if the wording turns outdated over time, the spirit is timeless.

The *idea* behind the words is just as relevant today as it was when the Constitution – or Stoicism – were first conceived. We just need a proper interpretation. We need to take what the Founding Fathers meant to say, and try to express it using contemporary concepts. They used the language of a bygone world of their own, we need to interpret it into the world of the digital age, space travel and gene therapy. This is exactly what I'm trying to do in this book. Interpretation, adaptation and reformation are both the way to make Stoicism solid, valid and inspiring again, and, at the same time, the proof that it is so.

Farewell to nature

One of the key points where reformed Stoicism departs from the orthodox line is the problem of nature. "Following nature" was one of the core principles of ancient Stoicism. In fact, it was more than just a principle – it was also an identity banner under which the Stoics gathered.

The idea itself was simple (at least at first blush) and has been described in numerous books. In short: nature (or Nature) is intrinsically good and everything that is consistent with nature is also good. "Consistency with nature" acquires ethical dimension, nah, it doesn't *acquire* it – in ancient Stoicism it is the essence of ethics. Ethics, so to speak, consists in consistency with nature. So does the human duty. We need to recognize what nature (universal nature and our own) demands from us and start doing it. In other words, there is a rational and all-encompassing (some may even say divine) order in the universe. It is organized toward a certain end and this organization provides meaning and purpose for everything. What we need to do is to find it (this is what learning Stoicism is for) and adjust ourselves to it. In other words, we need to find the role that has been set up for us in the pre-ordained scheme of things. We need to find it, accept it and find fulfillment in it.

That's the traditional Stoic approach. Does it hold in the 21st century? In my view, it doesn't. We, the reformed Stoics, trying to live our Stoic life in the contemporary world, need to reject the ethical relevance of "nature" and abandon the idea of consistency with it. Obviously, it is a radical step. But we really need to take down this banner. As reformed Stoics, we can and we should unshackle ourselves from "nature." "Nature" has not once been mentioned in this book – this is a proof that this can be done. But why should it be done?

There is a number of reasons and each of them deserves a book-length treatment of its own. I have discussed it already in the Introduction to my previous book on Stoicism, *Does Happiness Write Blank Pages? On Stoicism and Artistic Creativity*.[xxii] Rephrasing that, I will state the following. The general problem we have with "nature" today is that its meaning and status are much more unclear than they were in antiquity, when Stoicism was first conceived. Reading Marcus Aurelius we get the impression that "nature" was an axiom to him. To us, it is not. The two millennia of development of human thought and the exponential accumulation of modern knowledge make "nature" highly doubtful. Both as a self-evident concept and as an ethical guideline.

More specific arguments can be laid out as follows.

(i) The emergence of modern science is one of the critical differences between the present and antiquity. Science and scientifically-based discourses today push any conversation about a pre-ordained order in nature into a much more irrational, or even mystical area than the ancient Stoics intended. Thus, if we espouse their views verbatim – we distort their doctrine. **(ii)** For obvious reasons the idea of rationally organized nature is hard to uphold after Darwin. **(iii)** In the contemporary world – due to our scientific and social progress – "nature" is much more governable and even flexible than it used to be in antiquity **(iv)** The rhetorical power of the "appeal to nature" may be downright dangerous. History teaches us that it tends to be used in support of racist, sexist and nationalist positions – with horrific consequences. **(v)** "Following nature" may degenerate into flight from responsibility and Nuremberg defense. If nature commands us, then we aren't to blame if something goes wrong – nature is. With all the consequences that follow, again, known all-to-well from tragic history.

A more analytical approach lands us the same conclusion: even if we want to "follow nature" today, we don't know what it means exactly. I remarked already that in Marcus Aurelius' *Meditations* "nature" is an unquestioned notion. It seems that its meaning was plain to the author, requiring no explanation. Yet, when we think about "nature" today, we face anything but clarity.

There are interpretations of "following nature" which are basically tautologies, such as when we read "nature" as "everything that comes to pass." On this reading, necessarily, *everything* that happens is consistent with nature. On the other hand, nothing, no real thing, fact or event is contrary to nature. Thus, this interpretation of "nature" is ethically empty – for everything is good and nothing is evil. According to another view "consistency with nature" means "consistency with science," or, more specifically, consistency with the laws of nature that modern science describes. Yet again, this entails that only miracles (suspensions of the laws of nature) are contrary to nature and thus "evil." This, of course, makes little sense as an ethical rule or practical advice. Another interpretation translates "following nature" into "following reason," or, in yet different approach, into "following facts."[xxiii] This is a more sophisticated take, but it, in turn, makes the term "nature" redundant. If "following nature" means "following reason," then there is no need to use the term "nature" itself. As a matter of fact, there is no need to use "reason" either. For we don't need vague terms, we don't need slogans. We need to focus on their content, and we need to put it to action. This entire book does just that.[xxiv]

Narratives of our time

The Stoic school has always had multiple entrances. There are many ways to enter it and historically the presentations of the Stoic doctrine have taken many forms. I believe that in reformed Stoicism, we need to rely primarily on two foundations covered in the first part of this book. It's the narratives and the great divide of things into what is and what isn't in our power. The first of these two ideas, the narratives, requires a larger discussion here.

What I call "narratives" is the modern equivalent of what the ancient Stoics called "conceptions," "impressions," "sense-impressions," "imaginations," or "opinions". I hold that "a narrative," with the little bit of postmodern tinge there and the emphasis on the temporal dimension ("a narrative" has a dynamic that a static "opinion" or "impression" hasn't) is the best term we can settle for today. "Impression" and particularly "opinion" are too abstract, or even detached, while "narrative" is necessarily attached to us. A narrative requires a person who narrates and it empowers that person. One can have "an impression" mistakenly, while "an opinion" can be wrong. A narrative, on the other hand, allows (and calls for!) much more activity and responsibility. A narrative can hardly "just happen" to me – I need to develop it, or at least willingly adopt. It's also much more malleable than a rigid "conception" is. A narrative can be shaped, can be formed and reformed, it can be changed at any time. Finally, narratives may serve as a bridge between reformed Stoicism and other currents of contemporary thought, of Marxist origin and other, which study the influence of outside factors on the narratives a person tends to embrace. Here I extend gratitude again to late professor Becker for reassurance that this bold step makes sense of the Stoic ground.

Having settled on the "narratives" I had to make one more major choice. Basically, there are two interpretations on the table. First of all, we may say that there are true narratives and false narratives and, consequently, we need to embrace the former and let go of the latter. This may look logical – but only on paper. The problem is that the qualities of "true" and "false" don't really apply to narratives. Truth value of an impression, opinion or a concept might be verified by the correspondence theory of truth, i.e. based on how they reflect reality. It's different with a narrative. The very notion of a narrative entails certain autonomy and – let's just say it – a degree of independence from the facts. Truth is just not necessarily the best parameter to evaluate a narrative.

If we insist on true and false narratives, then we need a definition of truth and a procedure to tell true narratives from false ones. Make no mistake: these are quite challenging metaphysical expectations which can't be met without a correspondingly serious metaphysical debate. Such debate, however, is not something that the reformed Stoicism wants to engage in. Once we open ourselves up to such deliberation, we have no time whatsoever to discuss the Stoic life proper. We would be flooded with metaphysics and this book would have to be ten times thicker. But that's not just that. More importantly, we, reformed Stoics, intend to refrain from such debates on principle. The reason is plain: we want to be free from any metaphysical assumptions. We simply don't want to make any. As discussed in the relevant chapter – reformed Stoicism needs to be valid whatever the world is like. However, metaphysics works, whatever theory turns out true, whatever *true* even means – we retain our right to be Stoics. Stoicism is the best possible option for a human, regardless of the outside world. Hence our skepticism towards concrete metaphysical commitments and, accordingly, hence our problem with settling which narratives are "true" and which are "false."

The other possible interpretation calls for a distinction between narratives themselves and the actual "truth of things." On this reading a Stoic would be supposed to discard all narratives whatsoever. In contrast to these mere fleeting and superficial narratives, the "truth of things" stands – solid, ageless, immovable.

Yet, the same problem reemerges here. Any conversation of "the truth of things," of "what things really are" (or however else this reference standard might be framed) requires serious metaphysical assumptions. To begin with, the very idea that such "truth of things" even exists implies some form of essentialism, while the concept that it's cognizable is entangled in a thick net of epistemological issues. In short, we get embroiled with metaphysical matters just as we were in the previous case. The conclusion is the same. Reformed Stoicism aims to avoid such involvements, assumptions and commitments.

How do we achieve that? The bold proposal made in this book is to use yet another distinction: the distinction between useful and useless narratives. Of course, it's a radical step, which can be criticized. The major objections are, first, the pragmatic, or even cynical tinge of such approach and, second, the possibility of relativism. I believe, though, that this concept defends itself. The idea is that usefulness – understood in terms of facilitation of our happiness and well-being – justifies itself. It's its own validation. Focusing on useful (as contrasted to useless) narratives underscores our agency in developing, selecting and adopting them. This approach is empowering: it makes *us* the measure of the narratives. After all, their relevance isn't defined by some abstract yardstick of "truth," but by our own well-being.

The ultimate goal of the entire Stoic philosophy is happiness. Therefore, and in the light of what I already said above (particularly in respect to the modern doubts about the teleological view of nature and universe) it seems logical and legitimate to make usefulness of narratives the chief criterion. Are they conducive to our happiness? Do they make us feel better, or worse? If we embrace a given narrative – will we feel happier, empowered, more proactive, or rather sadder, diminished, degraded? This is the key according to which we need to choose – because happiness is the ultimate goal of it all. And we have every right to stick to it and fight for it.

Some objections to this approach are arranged around the line of "usefulness is not enough," i.e. that it's too subjective and self-centered. "We are not enough," the objection goes, "to decide ourselves. We need some greater, outside validation (like 'truth,' 'facts,' 'scientific proof') – otherwise, we face the danger of relativism." I disagree with that. Certainly, we are flirting with a major philosophical problem here, perhaps one of the most urgent problems of our time. It's not the subject matter of this book however, and this is not a discussion that reformed Stoics are interested in. And we have the right to go down this path. To repeat it once again: our ultimate goal is happiness. This authorizes us to disregard a lot. Make no mistake here: reformed Stoicism is not egoism. We aren't supposed to disregard other people. But if certain metaphysical position is not conducive to our happiness and fulfillment? Why take it? The metaphysical position of reformed Stoicism is not to hold any metaphysical position.

The world-stage of our time

Another point where significant reinterpretation of the original doctrine is required is the world-stage metaphor. The ancient Stoics proposed the following picture: the entire world is a theater in which we, humans, play different parts. We do not decide though, what roles are assigned to us. We don't run the show, we are merely actors. All that is within our power is to try to play the given role the best we can. In short: accept assignment and act ably.

That's the original Stoic view. I'm convinced, however, that such modus operandi is not satisfying to us, reformed Stoics. This interpretation is too simplified. It doesn't cover the whole complexity and multidimensionality of human life. First of all, if we hold on to it, we face the risk of falling for the conservative misinterpretation of Stoicism.[xxv] Overt passivity is the danger here. If we are required to merely accept what's given to us and fulfill our duties, whatever roles we are appointed, then no progress and no change is possible. The examples are plain. On this view, if I'm born a slave, then I need to accept my slavish duties forever and never revolt. If I'm born a woman into patriarchy, then I need to make peace with it and never challenge the system. In this framework, there is zero potential for progress, emancipation and empowerment. Do we really want to go down this path today? The ideas of progress, emancipation and social liberation are a way too vital part of the conversation today – we can't just leave them out. Overall, that's one of the challenges with modernization and reinterpretation. We aren't supposed to twist Stoicism so that it covers the entire panorama of the present thought. But we mustn't ignore the key aspects of it.

This issue is not just political. The problem with passivity and the conservative misinterpretation of Stoicism stands also in our personal life. If we interpret Stoicism in a passive way, we may perceive it as a debilitating advice to basically surrender to the course of events and succumb to fate. This may lead to various forms of withdrawal and resignation. Instead of – to use Epictetus' terms – playing the ball well, we drop it.

This is a major difficulty, for this avenue of interpretation not only leads us in a quite pessimistic and above all *defensive* direction, but it also severely distorts Stoicism. This reading reduces Stoicism to passivity and neglects all it has to say about agency and activity. We get something clearly different from what we were promised.

Another problem with the traditional reading of the world-stage metaphor is that it sometimes is too crude. It's too low-resolution, it misses certain vital aspects of reality. The idea that we *never* have anything to say in the assignments of the roles can be challenged. Of course, we can hold steadfastly to the original view, but such approach turns a bit too mystical if held verbatim today (this is a similar argument to what I mentioned in the section about nature). In real life, on the practical level, we need to admit that even though sometimes indeed assignments are completely not up to us and all we can do is to play the hand we are dealt, sometimes we do have some liberty in selection. This is a very important "but." It's not that rare after all that it's either within our power to choose between the roles, or at the very minimum that we have the room to reject the one we are currently playing. As reformed Stoics, we can't afford to ignore this.

There is also the matter of responsibility. The original approach removes it from our human hands and places it somewhere else (with Nature, Fate, The Playwright, etc.). This is a striking moment, for this is again a flight form responsibility and a gambit that opens the Nuremberg defense. "We are not responsible for the role we are assigned. We must do what we must do, we only carry out our duties, we only follow orders." This approach is at odds

Conclusions and discussions 319

with contemporary sensibility, since after the experiences of the 20th century we can't pretend any more that we don't know where this leads. If we want updated, reformed Stoicism, then we mustn't dispatch responsibility to some inchoate outside powers. Responsibility is always human, it's always ours. And it's more mine than others'. Even if it's just the responsibility to say "no."

That's the rationale for the reinterpretation I offer in this book. Instead of just one principle, namely "accept assignment and act ably," as the ancients proposed, reformed Stoicism puts forward a pair of *two* principles. Two relevant chapters cover this. First, "there is no point in flouting the rules of a game," second, "there are other games to play."xxvi The nub of the matter is *not* about our inability to change the games (or roles) we play. That's a superficial reading. The real point is deeper: it's about the impossibility to change the rules of the game. And here all holds fast. Indeed, it's not within my power – or anyone else's for that matter – to redefine what it means to be a father, a sibling, a soldier or a president of the country. If we accept either of these roles, we need to follow the rules. It's not just ethical absurd, but also a logical impossibility to simultaneously try to be a good father and neglect paternal duties. It is impossible to be a good soldier and disobey the orders. It's impossible to be a good president and not follow the law and regulations. And so on.

Hence, two principles instead of just one. As reformed Stoics, we cannot flout the rules of the game we play. Yet, we don't have to always accept the assignment that is given to us. As I explain in detail in relevant chapters, more often than never, we have the capability to opt out of a given game and try to find a new one. This is the fresh interpretation that reformed Stoicism needs.

Broad perspective and gaslighting

Another area where a reinterpretation – or maybe just a recalibration– is needed is the axis around which the chapter "You Are Never Alone" is organized. The idea is, in a way, "scaled down" to better fit our modern sensibility. The main focus is on the fact that in whatever misery we find ourselves, we are never alone because there always have been and will be other humans, who share the exact same predicament. That's clear and the chapter sets it forth in great detail. But what doesn't it mention?

There is a deliberate omission in this book. I specifically left out the ancient concept that we need to assume "a broad perspective," or a "cosmic point of view" (wording may vary) and thus see that all our problems, miseries and adversities are insignificant. Factually it is a sound argument. We don't mean much in the greater scheme of things and neither do our setbacks and tragedies. Whatever pain I'm in, whatever loss I lament, whatever disappointment descends on me – that's meaningful only to me and a few other humans at best.

For the course of history, for the great struggle of humanity, for the universe as such – this is all nothing. Speck of dust and not much else. The argument is clear and it has been around for millennia. And it is present in the ancient Stoics, particularly in Marcus Aurelius who found beautiful lines to express it.

Reformed Stoicism, however, needs to be restrained about it. We, in reformed Stoicism, are in no position to diminish and trivialize problems that others face. The original "broad perspective" argument does just that: it diminishes and trivializes. I believe there is something deeply outdated in doing so. Modern sensibility shudders when we preach to other people that their problems are insignificant or that they perceive it wrongly. Imagine a mother who lost a child. Imagine if we tell her that "it's not that big a deal," that she is unreasonable if she weeps over such a trifle (after all, she gave birth to a mortal, so a death was always possible, nah, expected), or that death of her child changes nothing in the universe. There is something profoundly unsettling, revolting about this. Epictetus uses such arguments, but should reformed Stoicism include it? My position is that we should refrain from any form of such patronizing, condescension, gaslighting.

The ethical argument is crucial, but not the only one. Our modern sensibility can be – in some respect – described in terms of skepticism towards great, universal and "objective" discourses that describe, include and measure all. In the 21st century, it's hard to image a universal scale, or a protocol, that dictates to people what in their life is important and what's not. Everyone, so to speak, is the measure of their own problems. Everyone decides themselves what is difficult or painful to them. Everyone decides on their own – everyone has the right to do so.

The example with a passing of a child is an obvious one. I assume no sane person will argue to a mother that losing a child is no big a deal. Often times, however, the situation is much more ambiguous. People commonly have issues – at least I do all the time – with things that for the impartial observer may seem trifles, absurdly minute and irrelevant. Not having the favorite teddy bear around might be the mother of all grave problems for a two-year-old. Or even having it, but having it the wrong way – misplaced or paired up with the wrong doll. The original Stoic line is straight here: we shouldn't be like such children. We mustn't be that unreasonable and irrational. We, as adults, need to "know" what is important and what is not, we need to have the "rational" knowledge of that and we need to make reason-based decisions on what we define as a problem. Obviously, teddy bear falls into the category of irrational idiosyncrasies, that only "unwise" people or children get frustrated over.

But we are all such children! We all have our deep idiosyncrasies, irregularities, irrationalities. It's totally outdated to believe in the 21st century that there is one, universal norm of what is and what isn't a "serious," or "real

Conclusions and discussions 321

problem." And it's not just about personal quirks – the whole idea of "rationality," taken in this context, is blurred. The measure with which we judge our issues depends very heavily on who we are. It will be different for a man and a woman, for a millionaire and a member of the working class, for a Norwegian and a Somali, for a white person and a person of color, for a five-generations-in member of the establishment and a newly arrived immigrant, for a cisperson and a transperson, for a straight and a gay person, for a young, single professional, and a working single mom, and so on and so forth. In this context, any aspiration to one great measure and scale of things appears silly.

Finally, it's also much more interesting to learn how to deal with a problem as it is, without discarding or downplaying it. It's more inspiring and more empowering to tackle a problem head-on. We acknowledge it's serious, painful and harmful, and we want to combat it as such. It's a harder, more demanding path but also much more rewarding. It means much more to accept the gravity of a problem and then find a way to wrestle with it, than to play some philosophical tricks to "prove" that it's a minor issue. Reformed Stoicism proposes to try our tools on the problem itself instead of seeking a way around it. That's how we get a much more powerful toolkit.

Inclusion

The quotes used in this book all come from the works of Seneca, Epictetus and Marcus Aurelius. I polished the classic English translations a little bit in terms of punctuation and grammar, since all the "thou hast" forms sound off today. What sounds even more off, however, is the ubiquity of the "he" pronoun and the use of "a man" to denote humans in general. I amended that to redress the inclusivity and gender-neutrality of the Stoic language.

This, obviously, is always a controversial step to take. This problem pertains of course not just to Stoics, but to the works of ancients in general, and truth be told, not only ancients. It's always an open issue as to whether or not we are authorized to interfere with someone's work post factum. I believe in this case it is justified for a number of reasons. First of all, I don't doctor the original Stoic works – I calibrate the translations of them. Every piece of writing is a sign of its own time, but a translation of an ancient work is even more so. Every era imprints its own sensibility on how it chooses to interpret the classics. The translations used in this book – otherwise noble and powerful – indeed seem overly masculine, often more than the original text.

Secondly, it seemed worthwhile to me to skip all those "man"-based structures and "he"-oriented phrasings because the alternative was one big series of misunderstandings. The gender bias would just draw too much attention. After all, placing the ideal of a "wise man" on a pedestal and making him the role model we should look up to is not necessarily the most fortunate language in the 21st century.

And above all: it's something that neither reformed Stoicism wants nor original Stoicism intended. Unfortunate wording in the translation would distort the message gravely. The ancient Stoics were *the* progressives of their time. The crazy liberal idea that women have just the same philosophical capabilities as men and the breathtaking concept that the gates to the philosophical schools should be open to non-Greeks also were both of the Stoic doing. The Stoic idea of the all-permeating, rational-divine Logos laid the ground for radical egalitarianism and thus it was in the Stoic teaching that for the first time in the course of Western thought the idea was floated that all people are essentially equal. Two millennia later the declarations of universal human rights were to build on that. There are books that discuss this at length and with great scholarship – I encourage any reader to learn more about this fascinating aspect of Stoicism. In the 21st century this profoundly egalitarian, empowering aspect of the Stoic thought becomes more and more vital. It would be a great shame and dishonesty to our predecessors to lay this message to waste because of the grammar choices made by the translators a good while ago.

Within our power and not

One of the foundations on which reformed Stoicism and this book are built is the famous "Great Divide" of all things, facts and events into what is within our power and what is not. Here, contrary to what was said earlier about nature, narratives, the world-stage metaphor, etc., no reinterpretation, no new name or framing is needed. It is *the* part of the original doctrine that shines and serves us today in the exact same form as when it was first conceived. The ancients really hit the jackpot thinking this up. Oikeiosis, hegemonikon, Logos, nature – all these concepts are prone to change their meaning over time, get blurred, be questioned. More than that: our understanding of them rests inevitably on the historical, social, economical, political and other constraints of the time. Thus, after two thousand years, we have little insight into their original meaning and more importantly, we don't have much chance to build a relevant ethical theory on them. Any attempt to do so is open to serious criticism.

Things are different with the divide into what's in and outside our power. The logical simplicity of this divide, its irrefutable, quasi-tautological power make it perennial, immune to the passage of time and changing circumstances. This is what makes it great and what makes it timeless (and ever timely). We can see it well once we take a larger view. There is a great debate in the humanities whether one should try to describe a given problem

Conclusions and discussions 323

"objectively," and from the outside, or rather in a critical and an "anthropological" way from the inside. This book is obviously written in the former tradition (I hope, however, that my future works on Stoicism will engage more with the latter). If there is, however, a single idea that may reasonably aspire to the name of truly universal and timeless, then it is, I believe, the Stoic concept to divide things into what's in and what's outside our power. As I have remarked already, the paramount, pristine logical simplicity makes it stand out. If there is anything that stands the test of time unchanged – this is it. Hence my choice to use it as a cornerstone of reformed Stoicism. We shouldn't rely on nature, logos or oikeiosis because these concepts rest on shifting sands. After two millennia, in a totally new conceptual framework we live in today, they are just too uncertain, too equivocal. The division into things in and outside our power is a whole different ball game. If anything stands, this does.

What reformed Stoicism isn't?

We have dug deep under the cornerstones of reinterpretation. I will now try to briefly recap the broader view of reformed Stoicism – interestingly enough, it can be done neatly by pointing out what it is *not* about.

(1) Reformed Stoicism is skeptical of much more than just "nature." It abstains from any major theory that tries to explain all. Reformed Stoicism doesn't aspire to any universal, ultimate truth. It aspires to one thing only: to the fact that it works. To use the language of some recent philosophers: reformed Stoicism doesn't offer any great narrative about the world as such. To use the language of some earlier philosophers: it doesn't proffer any metaphysics. Reformed Stoicism is not set to explain how the world works. All it explains is how to live well and happily. Also, reformed Stoicism doesn't *need* any such metaphysics to rest on. Its usefulness proves itself.

(2) Reformed Stoicism develops only a part of what ancient Stoicism was (the best part of course!). Ancient Stoicism consisted of three parts: logic (i.e., theory of language and knowledge), physics (i.e., cosmology and metaphysics) and ethics (i.e., the practical art of living a good life). All that reformed Stoicism is interested in is the last part. Why? Because the other two aren't in sync with the times we live in. They explained a lot in antiquity, but – given the progress of philosophy, science and human knowledge in general – they don't explain much today.

(3) Reformed Stoicism (and any Stoicism for that matter) isn't tantamount to asceticism. A reformed Stoic doesn't have to refrain from regular worldly pleasures, she doesn't have to give away her possessions and depart into reclusion. Reformed Stoicism isn't all about withdrawal, curbing our needs

and living a life of high frugality. Certainly, this is all an important aspect of the Stoic thought, but it's merely an element of a more comprehensive system. Overt focus on this one element is a distortion of the doctrine. In *Does Happiness Write Blank Pages? On Happiness and Artistic Creativity* I address this problem directly and at length, calling it *the ascetic misinterpretation of Stoicism*.[xxvii] It's a misrepresentation of the Stoic thought and even more than just that. It's a false reduction of its magnificent multidimensionality to just one, doubtful path.

(4) Similarly, reformed Stoicism isn't necessarily conservative. Such an assumption is just another great distortion and misunderstanding of Stoicism. Living a Stoic life entails neither a conservative political position, nor passivity in one's private life. This is likely one of the most important points that reformed Stoicism underscores. A Stoic life is much more open, multifarious and malleable than some tend to think. This is one of the key factors in the adjustment of Stoicism to the present day. Today, after all, the magnitude of our human agency is vastly different than it was in antiquity.

Stoicism promises us a good life and happiness independent from the outside events. It doesn't follow, however, that we must slavishly accept whatever fate brings. Stoicism empowers us to actively seek, create and cherish circumstances that are favorable to us – to the extent possible. The whole point of reformed Stoicism consists in finding a reasonable way to do both: to disregard what's not within our power to change and exercise our agency within the realm of things that are in our power to change. Again, I explain all this in great detail in *Does Happiness Write Blank Pages?* calling this issue the widespread *conservative misinterpretation of Stoicism*.[xxviii]

(5) Contrary to yet another widespread misconception, Stoicism – and reformed Stoicism in particular – is not a "negative" philosophy. Some say that Stoicism merely combats adversities and doesn't do much more. The catchphrase is that Stoicism is a bit like medicine and it's – allegedly – entangled in a similar paradox: it fights with exactly that, what makes it necessary. I believe that I have shown in this book how reformed Stoicism overpowers these doubts. Reformed Stoicism is singularly focused on a good and happy life. The art of overcoming adversity is only auxiliary to that. To prevail over hardship is not the ultimate purpose of Stoicism – it's just a stepping stone by which we pave the way to lasting happiness. It's an important stone, for no life is ever free from adversity. But it's never the end in itself.

(6) Reformed Stoicism withdraws from what I call the "vanity arguments." As you surely have noticed, this book never argues that human matters are short-lived, insubstantial and thus worthless. Many religions preach that and many philosophies preach that – but reformed Stoicism does not. Why?

Conclusions and discussions 325

First of all, such position doesn't yield much in terms of guidelines for the practical life. If everything is vain and meaningless, then there is no difference what I do. Every course of thought and action seems just as okay, because the result is always equally worthless. And also, as Marcus Aurelius would put it, we all will be dead very soon, while the consequences of our actions will evaporate even sooner. Why then strive and toil?

Second, the "vanity argument" is actually two arguments (at least two). One is the "fleetingness argument," well-known since Buddha and Ecclesiastes, i.e. that all things are impermanent and vanish over time. Therefore they are futile and shouldn't concern us much. We have covered this a moment ago. The other line of thought is the "essential worthlessness argument," i.e. one which infers the vanity of things not from their impermanence but from their essence. Marcus gives multiple examples for that, for instance: "[Meat] is the dead body [...] of a bird or of a pig; and again [...] this [wine] is only a little grape juice, and this purple robe some sheep's wool dyed with the blood of a shell-fish."[xxix] What's the problem with this argument? Obviously, it implies that some "essence" of things exists. Sweeping that aside though, we can see the most interesting twist: this reasoning can be reversed. If it is okay to say that a robe is *only* mere wool dyed with blood, then it is logically just as sound to say that mere wool and blood can *wonderfully* turn into a beautiful robe. Needless to say, it holds for everything, not just food, drink and clothes. The argument is symmetrical and thus it doesn't solve anything by itself. Specifically, it doesn't convince us of the worthlessness of things.[xxx]

Third and finally, as argued for already, reformed Stoicism is sound and valid regardless of the world view we espouse. This universal applicability is – from the practical point of view – much more important today than a metaphysical debate of vanity of things. Whatever side we take in the debate outlined above, we still need to live stoically.

(7) On the other hand, for similar reasons, reformed Stoicism doesn't rely on the notion of beauty or harmony of the universe. It doesn't insist that the world we live in is good as such, or that everything in it is purposefully organized towards a rational end. The Stoic way of life is – needs to be – independent from the way the world is organized. More importantly, any idea that the world is inherently good is highly questionable after Auschwitz, Kolyma and Rwanda. The original Stoic argument, that seemingly adverse things turn out to be actually good once we get the bigger picture, is downright unacceptable in this context.

(8) Reformed Stoicism refrains from any overly specific advice about what to do. Whoever looks for a tap on the shoulder and a pointed hand showing "do this," or "don't do that," will be disappointed. And rightfully so. Because this is not what reformed Stoicism is about. It's not a magic box, that we feed with

input data, then punch some buttons and get a ready-made answer like "take this job," or "don't go to the party today." Why? First of all, reformed Stoicism includes a lot of contextualism. This is why this book puts emphasis on the notion that "There Are Other Games To Play" and that we need to "Beware Of Treacherous Constancy." Second, the Stoic way of life is not about the blind following of some preordained rules. Quite the contrary: it is about taking responsibility for our conduct. This point is particularly important today. There is no serious, contemporary conversation about ethics and human duty without acknowledgment of individual responsibility.

(9) Reformed Stoicism doesn't focus on hardcore examples of death, torture, war and the like. The ancient Stoics had an inclination for them, but today we need much more of lighter examples, embedded in daily life and its ordinary issues. This approach is more informative and it not only matches the *Zeitgeist* better but also covers a wider area of real-life scenarios. After all, we aren't all a Roman oligarch or an emperor – enemies scheming to kill us aren't usually our number one problem. We aren't Epictetus, to boot. Thus, as reformed Stoics, we don't really want to whisper in our child's ear that "tomorrow you will die," as he advises.[xxxi] I elaborate on this issue much more in chapter 6 of *Does Happiness Write Blank Pages?*[xxxii]

(10) Continuing with the child example: in this book I specifically chose not to write a separate chapter on death. It's a standard in the Stoic writings that authors (both ancient and present) spend a lot of time and pages to argue the point that our mortality needn't be feared. And indeed, Stoicism provides a number of convincing and colorful arguments in this matter. I skipped all that. Why? Because, in a word, we don't really fear our own death. What we fear is the death of a loved one – a child, a significant other, a parent, a sibling. And that's a whole different ball game.

(11) All that being said, there is no surprise – I suppose – that I haven't organized this exposition of reformed Stoicism around the abstract, "big" concepts like good, evil, virtue and others. The whole deal is not to talk about them but to put them in action. This entire book speaks of how we do just that.

(12) In doing so, it makes manifest – I hope – that the full depth of reformed Stoicism has little to do with the ordinary meaning of the word "stoical" (such as when we speak of "being stoical" about something). As reformed Stoics, we are of course very happy that Stoicism plays in Peoria so well that the name itself became an ordinary adjective. After all, no one ever speaks of being "Spinoza," "Thomas Aquinas-ian," or "Democritean" about something. Popularity comes at a price though. As I have been trying to argue throughout these pages, reformed Stoicism is much more and, truth be told, something else than "being stoical." It's a much wider, more comprehensive, ampler and more fertile school

of thought. Specifically, reformed Stoicism is not tantamount to cold-blooded indifference to others and repression of emotions. Reformed Stoics can live with any blood temperature, so to speak. I assume it is clear at this point that unhealthy and withdrawn relationships with others are not what's proposed here. Also, rooting out all emotions is not the point. The goal is to root out *bad* emotions. The good ones are to be cherished.

(13) Finally, reformed Stoicism is not a "totalizing" system, i.e. it doesn't claim us fully and forever. If we benefit from reading this book, the benefit will be ours regardless of whether we become devoted Stoics or not. Even if our brush with Stoicism is a brief one, it will still be advantageous to us. It's always good to have this Stoic experience under our belt. It is always good to have been exposed to the Stoic ideas and to have at least once peered in the Stoic lens. It'll be valuable to us no matter if we stick to Stoicism of if we set off on another course. Either way, we'll carry with us the insurance policy signed by the Stoics – we'll have somewhere to get back to, should the need arise.

A few more remarks

(1) To the best of my knowledge, I'm the first to use the term "reformed Stoicism." Yet, my view on how to reinterpret and reapply Stoicism today is surely not the only one possible. There are many others and I make no pretense to the absolute Stoic truth – I will happily let others convince me wherever I'm wrong. Openness to debate and multiplicity of mutually interacting interpretations has always been the characteristic of the Stoic school. It should remain so.

(2) I organized this presentation of reformed Stoicism as a string of "techniques," "spiritual exercises," or, as some would say, "lifehacks." There are 24 of them in this book and I was pretty strict about setting forth the entire doctrine in this fashion. Clarity of presentation translates, hopefully, into clarity of application. Of course, neither am I the only author to frame Stoicism this way, nor is this way the only possible one.

(3) More importantly, I also arranged it around solutions, not around problems. This book contains no chapters like "Broken Heart," "Stay in a Hospital," or "Financial Difficulty." Instead, there are chapters "Anticipate Mishap," "Adversities are Challenges," "You Are Never Alone." I don't try to put together a list of maladies and miseries and then assign treatments to them. Instead, I provide a detailed review of the Stoic toolkit. The decision on what to apply when and where — is the reader's.

Why so? The list of possible adverse situations is very long – no book of reasonable length will ever be able to exhaust it. The list of remedies is quite the contrary: we can produce it quite easily. This book does just that.

Moreover, as I've stated a few times already, reformed Stoicism aims to be independent of grand narratives and universal explanations. Hence the reluctance towards any one-size-fits-all protocol that matches a specific tool to a given problem. No ready-made answer will suit everyone. In reformed Stoicism, we go over the toolkit together, but everyone decides for themselves. Everyone determines themselves what kind of treatment is most appropriate for them. Everyone is the judge of their ailments. And of their recovery too.

(4) The obvious fact about the form of the book is that it's structured as a series of commentaries to a selection of fragments from the ancient Stoics. This form allows us to learn from the prowess of the old masters. We enjoy the rhetorical skill of Seneca, the curtness of Epictetus, the poetic mastery of Marcus Aurelius. We don't reject them, we don't deny them. We learn from them, but not blindly. We don't read them on our knees. Instead, we read them wisely. We want to be clear where we remain faithful and where we depart from them. This approach opens up an interpretative space between the old text and its modern sense. This book is a bit of a seminar: writing it was a seminar and I hope reading it also will be one. Shared inquiry into the original becomes a quest for the modern meaning.

(5) Finally: why do I use these three authors and not any others? I wanted to meet two conditions. First, I turned to original, ancient Stoics. Second, I picked those whose works survived relatively intact. The latter condition places the bar quite high – only the big trio of Seneca, Epictetus and Marcus Aurelius is able to pass.[94] It's only from them that we get entire books. From most of other Stoics, including the founders of the school and other representatives of the Old Stoa, we have only dispersed fragments, second-hand references, shreds.

Other philosophies of life

Just as I don't hold that my views on reformed Stoicism are the only true ones, reformed Stoicism itself makes no pretense to be the only and exhaustive truth about us, humans, and our place in the world. It aspires however to be a coherent and autonomous story. I wrote this book to prove that it is such. But why is that important and what does "coherent and autonomous" even mean?

In other philosophies of life, in other religious and intellectual approaches, in other ethical programs we will find similar, at times identical ideas. Passages that ring Stoicism may be found in the Epicureans, in various Christian writers

---

[94] Truth be told Musonius Rufus receives a bit of unfair treatment here. His position however isn't on a par with the mentioned trio.

and certainly in Buddhism. Psychology and psychotherapy commonly give us manifestly Stoic advice. The same holds for the entire wide and multifaceted current of various ways of intentional living, varying from mindfulness to minimalism. Once we get acquainted with them, we immediately see deep affinities with the Stoic doctrines. But does it mean that these schools of thought are stealing from one another? Or that any of them is by definition inferior or less interesting just because it repeats what was said by others in a different context? No. We all scrutinize one and the same human soul, so it is not surprising that we arrive at similar conclusions (even if we take different languages to express it). It's a pleasant and reassuring concord that the Stoics, Christian preachers, hermits of various ilk, masters of Zen, psychotherapists, minimalist bloggers and neuroscientists concur unexpectedly often.

I'm not trying to persuade anyone that reformed Stoicism floats an agenda that no one ever had before. That's next to impossible after the millennia of philosophy and centuries of science. I'm trying to argue, however, that reformed Stoicism is, at the very minimum, a coherent story about us, humans. And I hope that I managed to convince you at least a bit, that it is also colorful, relevant and inspiring.

It's clear in this context why, in discussing Stoicism, I stuck to Stoics only. I made no excursion into other fields, even though it was tempting to seek backup there. Each of the fragments quoted in this book might be cross-checked with other, nonstoic discourses and traditions. For instance, one may say that anticipating mishap is valid *because* modern psychology confirmed it in a peer-reviewed journal. One may say that anticipating mishap is legit because it employs the mechanism of hedonic adaptation. This is exactly what I strove to avoid. Reformed Stoicism values its autonomy. It validates itself and its usefulness proves itself. We, as reformed Stoics, don't require any outside support or guarantees from anywhere else. This point holds for any school of thought that attempts to find a truth of its own.

The revival

I'm not alone in my interest in Stoicism. Quite the contrary: the last quarter of a century has seen an immense upsurge of interest in it. It's not an exaggeration to speak of a "Stoic boom" which echoes all over, not just in the academia. Authors, coaches, scholars, psychotherapists and many others take up Stoicism and preach it as the response to the challenges of our time. Professional athletes, soldiers, business executives, and above all, ordinary people turn to Stoicism and find solace in it. There is no doubt that Stoicism is coming back in a big way.

The list of vital people invested in this way or another in the modern turn to Stoicism is too long to even try it. It testifies to the success of the movement that I need to apologize in advance that I can't mention everyone – which I hereby do. The key person is undeniably late prof. Lawrence C. Becker, a Stoic in spirit and flesh, who published his groundbreaking *A New Stoicism* in 1998.[xxxiii] We are all indebted to him. Another two famous books in the framework were *A Guide to the Good Life: The Ancient Art of Stoic Joy* by William Irvine, first published in 2008,[xxxiv] and *How To Be a Stoic* by Massimo Pigliucci, first published in 2017.[xxxv] But truly, the list of modern Stoic authors and promoters of Stoicism is indeed imposing. It includes Alkistis Agio, Julia Annas, Chuck Chakrapani, Ray Cooper, Christopher Gill, Ryan Holiday, Andrew Holowchak, Ben Kimpel, Christina Kourfali, Sharon Lebell, Anthony Long, Gregory Lopez, Donald Robertson, Gregory Sadler, Keith Seddon, John Sellars, Nancy Sherman, William Stephens, Peter Vernezze and many, many others, myself included. I don't even try anymore to keep track of all the various "Stoic Manual to Living" and "Path to Resilience, or How To Live Stoically" books that Amazon is teeming with. It's a little sub-genre of its own. Maybe not that little really.

Moreover, it's not just individual authors and followers scattered around the globe. People write books on Stoicism, people do workshops on Stoicism, people post and blog about it. There are Stoic groups on Facebook and elsewhere, some of them about to hit the 6-digit mark. Another sign that this is all not just a fad but an established cultural phenomenon is that the revival of Stoicism is taking institutional forms. For instance, there is the Modern Stoicism organization (where I have the opportunity to add my humble two cents) which runs the major modernstoicism.com website, the annual Stoicon (New York City 2016, Toronto 2017, London 2018, Athens 2019 – to be continued) and much more.

The Stoic philosophy is truly on the rise. I hope it's clear at this point that there is no expectation that all these new interpretations and takes on Stoicism will converge in saying the exact same thing. It's quite the contrary: they all differ vastly. As I wrote elsewhere, "it's a major perk of Stoicism that we are aware of the differences and that we don't shoot for any enforced unity. We need a debate, not a monolithic church. Or, at least, this is what I think we need."[xxxvi]

Reformed Stoicism

Debate, however, is one thing. The ultimate question this book faces is different. Can my view on Stoicism – retailored, resuited, reassessed – be even called Stoicism? I propose significant changes and reinterpretations of the original doctrine, some explicitly, some by omission. Some will say that these

Conclusions and discussions

corrections cross the line, and thus the ideas I preach here can't be labeled "Stoicism" anymore.

I disagree. We don't need a dogmatic church and Stoicism has never been one. It has always allowed conceptual latitude. Presumably this openness and propensity to evolve contributed to its success as a vigorous, influential and lasting school of thought. In Stoicism transformation of the doctrine has always been a part of the doctrine itself and thus I do believe the term "Stoic" is broad enough to encompass my reinterpretation too. After all, it is within my power to try to reform my own philosophy.

A new adjective is required though. The new interpretation of Stoicism, as set forth in this book, remains in the broad current of Stoic thought, but it clearly stands out. With no reliance on nature, with the recalibration of the metaphysical positions, with skepticism towards grand discourses and universal answers, with the emphasis on the usefulness instead of truthfulness of narratives, with the term "narratives" used in this context in the first place, with the absence of the vanity argument, with the strong criticism of both conservative and ascetic misinterpretations of Stoicism, with the overall softer and more empathic approach we cannot go under the generic term "Stoicism." Hence the term "reformed." The reform movement has been flourishing in Christianity for five hundred years and in Judaism for two hundred. There is no reason why we, reformed Stoics, shouldn't set off on this path too.

***

Once the book goes to print, I will inevitably remember something more that should have been mentioned here. For the fleeting moment, however, I believe I've covered and commented on all the issues I wanted too. The project of reformed Stoicism is and remains open though – just as it should be.

This book is in great measure based on my book *Sztuka życia według stoików*, a Stoic work I published in Poland (my home country and mother tongue) back in 2014 with G.W.FOKSAL.[xxxvii] But a single book never exhausts the topic, even if we get a chance for a substantial revision. Particularly, this book is designed as an exposition of reformed Stoicism, but not a critical discussion. This conclusion section provides some theoretical justification but it obviously isn't a full-on analysis. I spared it here, for the length concerns – no one wants to read a book of a thousand pages. I also meant to keep this book accessible and easy to read.

Much more of a theoretical insight can be found in my other Stoic book *Does Happiness Write Blank Pages?*[xxxviii] I hope that these two distinct but connected works shed light on each other and that together they form a double voice, providing a better, more thorough inquiry. This book is a positive, practical presentation of what reformed Stoicism is and why it's relevant today. *Does Happiness Write Blank Pages?* is much more critical and focused on the philosophical assumptions that make it all possible. It also discusses the trade-offs that Stoicism makes in order to be relevant in the modern world, as well as the hidden problems it conceals. If all goes according to the plan, it will be all continued and developed in my subsequent books exploring the Stoic sensibility in the 21st century.

I wrapped up *Does Happiness Write Blank Pages?* saying that Stoicism is one of the greatest philosophies ever "conceived by humans, for humans, and of humans."[xxxix] That stands. The above pages are my effort to provide a modern, revised interpretation of it – i.e. reformed Stoicism for our time. "If, however," as Arrian puts it, "the words by themselves do not produce this effect, perhaps I am at fault, or else, perhaps, it cannot be otherwise."[xl]

Endnotes

[i] Lawrence C. Becker, *A New Stoicism* (Princeton: Princeton University Press, 1998), 6.

[ii] Throughout this book I use the following translations of the classic Stoic works (unless explicitly stated otherwise in an individual endnote). (1) All quotes from Seneca's *Of Providence, On the Firmness of the Wise Man, Of Anger, Of Consolation. To Marcia, Of Consolation. To Helvia, Of Consolation. To Polybius, Of a Happy Life, Of Peace of Mind, Of Clemency, Of Leisure* and *Of the Shortness of Life* come from: Lucius Anneus Seneca, *Minor Dialogues Together with the Dialogue on Clemency*, trans. Aubrey Stewart (London: G. Bell and Sons, 1889); (2) All quotes from Seneca's *On Benefits* come from Lucius Anneus Seneca, *On Benefits*, trans. Aubrey Stewart (London: G. Bell and Sons, Ltd., 1912). (3) Lucius Anneus Seneca, *The Epistles of Lucius Annaeus Seneca; With Large Annotations, Wherein, Particularly, the Tenets of the Antient Philosophers Are Contrasted With the Divine Precepts of the Gospel, With Regard to the Moral Duties of Mankind. In Two Volumes. By Thomas Morell, D.D.*, trans. Thomas Morell, vol. I-II (London: W. Woodfall, G.G.J., J. Robinson, 1786); (4) Epictetus, *The Discourses of Epictetus with the Encheiridion and Fragments. Translated with Notes, the Life of Epictetus, and a View of His Philosophy, by George Long*, trans. George Long (London: George Bell and Sons, 1890); (5) Marcus Aurelius, *The Meditations of the Emperor Marcus Aurelius Antoninus. Translated by George Long, M.A. With a Biographical Sketch and a View of the Philosophy of Antoninus by the Translator*, trans. George Long, (New York: A.L. Burt, Publisher, 189?). As discussed in "Conclusions and Discussions" I occasionally modernized grammar and spelling and changed it to American English.

[iii] I borrow the phrase "all-things-considered" from Lawrence C. Becker. See: Becker, *A New Stoicism*, 5.

[iv] Seneca, *Of Consolation. To Helvia*, 8.2.

[v] "Fragment 9" in "Fragments" as published in: Epictetus, *The Discourses*, trans. W. A. Oldfather (Cambridge: Harvard University Press, 1925), vol. II, 451.

[vi] The tennis match example and its analysis are based on the excellent insight by William B. Irvine (see: William B. Irvine, *A Guide to the Good Life. The Ancient Art of Stoic Joy* (New York: Oxford University Press, 2009), 95-96).

[vii] Seneca, *Epistles*, 93.7. In: Seneca, *Epistles*, trans. Richard M. Gummere (Cambridge: Harvard University Press, 1925).

[viii] This formula is borrowed from: William B. Irvine, *A Slap in the Face: Why Insults Hurt, and Why They Shouldn't* (Oxford University Press: New York, 2013) 192, 202-203, 211 and others.

[ix] Quoted from http://www.perseus.tufts.edu/hopper/text?doc=Perseus%3Atext%3A199 9.01.0236%3Atext%3Dfrag%3Abook%3D0, retrieved January 18, 2015. The website refers to *The Discourses of Epictetus, with the Encheiridion and Fragments*, trans. George Long (London: George Bell and Sons, 1890).

[x] Epictetus, *Discourses*, I.4.13.

[xi] Epictetus, *Discourses*, II.15.4-13.

[xii] See: Epictetus, *Encheiridion*, 43.

xiii Diogenes Laertius, *Lives of Eminent Philosophers*, translated by R.D. Hicks, (Cambridge: Harvard University Press, 1942).
xiv Seneca, *Epistles*, 94.40. In: Seneca, *Epistles*, trans. Richard M. Gummere (Cambridge: Harvard University Press, 1925).
xv Seneca, *Epistles*, 98.12-14. In: Seneca, *Epistles*, trans. Richard M. Gummere (Cambridge: Harvard University Press, 1925).
xvi Diogenes Laertius, *Lives of Eminent Philosophers*.
xvii "Fragment 16" in "Fragments" as published in: Epictetus, *The Discourses*, trans. W. A. Oldfather (Cambridge: Harvard University Press, 1925), vol. II, 461.
xviii See: Becker, *A New Stoicism*.
xix Marcus Aurelius, *Meditations*, 4.49.
xx Marcus Aurelius, *Meditations*, 12.22.
xxi Becker, *A New Stoicism*.
xxii Piotr Stankiewicz, *Does Happiness Write Blank Pages? On Stoicism and Artistic Creativity* (Wilmington: Vernon Press, 2018), xvi.
xxiii See: Becker, *A New Stoicism*.
xxiv In these passages I mostly rephrase what I wrote in a corresponding section about nature in: Stankiewicz, *Does Happiness Write Blank Pages?*, xvi.
xxv See: Stankiewicz, *Does Happiness Write Blank Pages?*, 70-83.
xxvi See: ibid.
xxvii See: ibid., 30-41.
xxviii See: ibid., 70-83.
xxix Marcus Aurelius, *Meditations*, 6.13.
xxx The idea that "this reasoning can be reversed" comes from Henryk Elzenberg. See: Henryk Elzenberg, "Marek Aureliusz. Z historii i psychologii etyki," in: Henryk Elzenberg, *Z historii filozofii*, ed., Michał Woroniecki (Kraków: Znak, 1995), 97-213.
xxxi Epictetus, *Discourses*, 3.24.
xxxii Stankiewicz, *Does Happiness Write Blank Pages?*, 30-41.
xxxiii Becker, *A New Stoicism*.
xxxiv Irvine, *A Guide to The Good Life. The Ancient Art of Stoic Joy*.
xxxv Massimo Pigliucci, *How to be a Stoic: Using Ancient Philosophy to Live a Modern Life* (New York: Basic Books, 2017).
xxxvi Piotr Stankiewicz et al., "Symposium: What Is Modern Stoicism", source: https://modernstoicism.com/symposium-what-is-modern-stoicism/, published July 29, 2017, retrieved November 8, 2019.
xxxvii Piotr Stankiewicz, *Sztuka życia według stoików*, (Warszawa: G.W.FOKSAL, 2014).
xxxviii Stankiewicz, *Does Happiness Write Blank Pages?*
xxxix Stankiewicz, *Does Happiness Write Blank Pages?*, 114.
xl Arrian's introduction to the *Discourses* by Epictetus. In: Epictetus, *The Discourses*, trans. W. A. Oldfather (Cambridge: Harvard University Press, 1925), books I-II, 7.

Bibliography

Becker, Lawrence C. *A New Stoicism*. Princeton: Princeton University Press, 1998.

Diogenes Laertius, *Lives of Eminent Philosophers*, trans. R. D. Hicks. Harvard University Press: Cambridge, 1942.

Elzenberg, Henryk. "Marek Aureliusz. Z historii i psychologii etyki." In: Henryk Elzenberg, *Z historii filozofii*, edited by Michał Woroniecki, 97-213. Kraków: Znak, 1995.

Epictetus, *The Discourses of Epictetus with the Encheiridion and Fragments. Translated with Notes, the Life of Epictetus, and a View of His Philosophy, by George Long*, trans. George Long. London: George Bell and Sons, 1890.

Epictetus, *The Discourses*, trans. W. A. Oldfather. Cambridge: Harvard University Press, 1925, books I-II and III-IV (Loeb Classical Library 131 and 218).

Irvine, William B. *A Guide to The Good Life. The Ancient Art of Stoic Joy*. New York: Oxford University Press, 2009.

Irvine, William B. *A Slap in the Face. Why Insults Hurt And Why They Shouldn't*. New York: Oxford University Press, 2013.

Marcus Aurelius, *The Meditations of the Emperor Marcus Aurelius Antoninus. Translated by George Long, M.A. With a Biographical Sketch and a View of the Philosophy of Antoninus by the Translator*, trans. by George Long. New York: A.L. Burt, Publisher, 189?.

Pigliucci, Massimo. *How to be a Stoic: Using Ancient Philosophy to Live a Modern Life*. New York: Basic Books, 2017.

Seneca, *Epistles*, trans. Richard M. Gummere. Cambridge: Harvard University Press, 1925 (Loeb Classical Library 77).

Seneca, Lucius Anneus. *The Epistles of Lucius Annaeus Seneca; With Large Annotations, Wherein, Particularly, the Tenets of the Antient Philosophers Are Contrasted With the Divine Precepts of the Gospel, With Regard to the Moral Duties of Mankind. In Two Volumes. By Thomas Morell, D.D.*, trans. Thomas Morell, vol. I-II. London: W. Woodfall, G.G.J., J. Robinson, 1786.

Seneca, Lucius Anneus. *Minor Dialogues Together with the Dialogue on Clemency*, trans. Aubrey Stewart. London: G. Bell and Sons, 1889.

Seneca, Lucius Anneus. *On Benefits*, trans. Aubrey Stewart. London: G. Bell and Sons, Ltd., 1912.

Stankiewicz, Piotr. *Does Happiness Write Blank Pages? On Stoicism and Artistic Creativity*. Wilmington: Vernon Press, 2018.

Stankiewicz, Piotr. *Sztuka życia według stoików*. Warszawa: G.W.FOKSAL, 2014.

Online resources

http://www.perseus.tufts.edu/hopper/text?doc=Perseus%3Atext%3A1999.01.0236%3Atext%3Dfrag%3Abook%3D0, retrieved January 18, 2015.

Stankiewicz, Piotr *et al.*, "Symposium: What Is Modern Stoicism." Source: https://modernstoicism.com/symposium-what-is-modern-stoicism/, published July 29, 2017, retrieved November 8, 2019.

http://wikitravel.org/en/North_Korea, retrieved March 2, 2017.

https://en.wikipedia.org/wiki/Category:2000_deaths, retrieved November 6, 2019.

https://en.wikipedia.org/wiki/Category:1900_deaths, retrieved November 6, 2019.

https://en.wikipedia.org/wiki/Category:1800_deaths, retrieved November 6, 2019.

https://en.wikipedia.org/wiki/Category:1700_deaths, retrieved November 6, 2019.

https://en.wikipedia.org/wiki/Category:1600_deaths, retrieved November 6, 2019.

https://en.wikipedia.org/wiki/Category:1500_deaths, retrieved November 6, 2019.

https://en.wikipedia.org/wiki/Category:1400_deaths, retrieved November 6, 2019.

https://en.wikipedia.org/wiki/Category:1300_deaths, retrieved November 6, 2019.

www.worldometers.info, retrieved November 6, 2019.

Index

A

acclaim, 59, 147, 149, 150, 151, 152, 153, 154, 156, 157, 158, 159, 288
Act deliberately, 69
Adversities are challenges, 161
adversity, 6, 15, 89, 100, 118, 123, 125, 127, 161, 162, 163, 165, 167, 168, 170, 172, 189, 193, 250, 269, 273, 274, 277, 279, 282, 294, 295, 324
agency, ix, 250, 306, 316, 318, 324
all-things-considered, x, 38, 78, 114, 164, 266, 276, 333
ascetic misinterpretation, 58, 64, 324
autonomy, x, 29, 39, 226, 228, 229, 231, 234, 238, 239, 243, 245, 247, 248, 259, 279, 305, 307, 316, 329

B

Be autonomous, 225
Be happy, 297
Becker, 306, 312, 315, 330, 333, 334, 335

C

conscience, 18, 51, 105, 241, 245, 290
conservative misinterpretation, 56, 193, 317, 318, 324
counterfactual scenarios, 135, 136, 137, 140, 141, 178, 219, 288

D

Darwin, vii, 314
death, 9, 10, 11, 12, 17, 18, 36, 85, 86, 106, 118, 119, 127, 129, 143, 156, 158, 159, 182, 185, 186, 187, 207, 210, 222, 229, 237, 280, 281, 307, 320, 326
Descartes, vii, 226
desire, 27, 36, 37, 40, 42, 45, 48, 49, 61, 104, 135, 136, 137, 147, 149, 153, 154, 158, 159, 219, 231, 237, 292
difficulty, 161, 165, 171, 172, 180, 244, 294, 296, 318
Diogenes Laertius, 213, 285, 334, 335
discomfort, 13, 49, 100, 112
Does Happiness Write Blank Pages?, xi, 56, 58, 177, 193, 314, 324, 326, 331, 332, 334, 335

E

egalitarianism, x, 268, 289, 322
Elzenberg, 334
envy, 3, 24, 174, 175, 307
Epictetus, ix, 9, 10, 13, 15, 17, 18, 21, 23, 24, 25, 27, 28, 29, 31, 32, 33, 34, 36, 37, 38, 39, 40, 43, 44, 47, 48, 50, 52, 54, 55, 57, 58, 60, 63, 73, 76, 96, 98, 99, 111, 115, 118, 119, 126, 131, 135, 137, 139, 148, 149, 161, 165, 166, 167, 169, 170, 171, 176, 177, 179, 181, 182, 197, 198, 200, 202, 203, 204, 205, 206, 210, 218, 219, 220, 221, 226,

231, 232, 234, 235, 236, 242, 243, 244, 246, 247, 248, 259, 268, 281, 285, 286, 287, 292, 295, 306, 308, 311, 312, 318, 320, 321, 326, 328, 333, 334, 335
exercise, xi, 4, 13, 21, 52, 74, 86, 129, 161, 163, 167, 168, 178, 207, 215, 245, 279, 281, 285, 286, 287, 289, 291, 293, 294, 295, 296, 324
external factors, 6, 15, 34, 35, 38, 52, 252, 305

F

facts, 3, 4, 5, 6, 7, 8, 9, 11, 12, 16, 18, 19, 21, 36, 51, 56, 64, 70, 77, 113, 114, 127, 130, 135, 142, 177, 180, 182, 221, 236, 249, 251, 280, 304, 309, 311, 315, 316, 317, 322
fear, 3, 10, 17, 18, 19, 49, 62, 78, 113, 121, 127, 130, 131, 162, 166, 176, 210, 276, 304, 326
focus, 20, 22, 40, 47, 48, 49, 52, 53, 55, 56, 57, 58, 59, 60, 61, 62, 63, 70, 74, 81, 86, 91, 92, 93, 96, 97, 98, 99, 110, 127, 135, 138, 151, 159, 184, 203, 204, 208, 220, 233, 252, 259, 271, 281, 288, 297, 298, 303, 305, 306, 315, 319, 324, 326

G

goals, 19, 29, 31, 36, 37, 39, 45, 49, 53, 56, 58, 59, 65, 69, 74, 75, 87, 92, 94, 95, 96, 97, 105, 109, 159, 169, 178, 179, 181, 209, 225, 227, 233, 238, 239, 245, 248, 256, 265, 271, 286, 300
good examples, 273, 275, 276, 279, 281, 283
good life, 5, 13, 18, 50, 58, 59, 89, 130, 139, 141, 143, 157, 162, 163, 165, 169, 170, 171, 173, 207, 214, 227, 229, 234, 245, 248, 256, 259, 268, 285, 286, 297, 298, 299, 300, 301, 302, 303, 305, 306, 309, 323, 324

H

happiness, ix, x, xi, 3, 13, 24, 27, 28, 29, 31, 42, 47, 48, 49, 50, 56, 58, 63, 93, 101, 124, 135, 139, 140, 141, 142, 143, 144, 157, 168, 169, 170, 171, 175, 177, 178, 179, 181, 193, 228, 229, 244, 245, 246, 248, 256, 259, 268, 285, 286, 292, 294, 297, 298, 299, 300, 301, 302, 303, 304, 305, 306, 307, 308, 310, 314, 316, 317, 324, 326, 331, 332, 334, 335
hardship, 161, 165, 183, 184, 186, 190, 191, 273, 274, 277, 280, 282, 324
hedonic adaptation, 329

I

insult, 168, 175, 232, 236, 258, 312
intent, 42, 85, 168, 249, 250, 251, 252, 253, 254, 257, 258, 259
intentions, 54, 59
Irvine, 236, 330, 333, 334, 335

L

laziness, 21, 25, 84, 98, 176, 292, 293, 295

M

Marcus Aurelius, 3, 5, 6, 12, 18, 42, 59, 81, 82, 86, 88, 91, 93, 97, 100, 108, 109, 114, 116, 117, 133, 142, 143, 147, 150, 151, 153, 154, 155,

Index   339

157, 163, 177, 183, 186, 188, 191, 192, 225, 226, 238, 241, 250, 251, 254, 259, 263, 264, 265, 268, 269, 270, 271, 273, 297, 299, 300, 304, 311, 312, 314, 320, 321, 325, 328, 333, 334, 335

Marx, vii

mishap, xi, 123, 124, 125, 126, 127, 128, 129, 130, 131, 132, 133, 162, 163, 170, 175, 184, 286, 288, 291, 329

mistakes, 53, 97, 99, 236, 241, 245, 246, 248, 251, 259, 301

N

narrative, 3, 4, 5, 6, 7, 9, 10, 11, 12, 13, 14, 15, 16, 17, 18, 19, 20, 21, 23, 24, 25, 26, 27, 29, 45, 65, 128, 173, 177, 179, 204, 232, 233, 241, 242, 251, 266, 300, 315, 316, 317, 323

nature, x, xi, 22, 43, 135, 183, 264, 308, 313, 314, 317, 318, 322, 323, 331, 334

P

pain, 3, 5, 11, 13, 14, 15, 17, 21, 49, 57, 112, 117, 143, 162, 184, 186, 187, 190, 234, 235, 280, 286, 295, 303, 319

painful, 15, 54, 62, 106, 109, 117, 126, 143, 145, 171, 173, 176, 209, 250, 251, 320, 321

patience, 95, 167, 203, 208, 227, 279, 293, 311

perseverance, 29, 159, 173, 182, 287, 292, 293, 305

philosopher, 9, 50, 73, 99, 108, 158, 230, 264, 273, 274, 279, 281, 283

Pigliucci, 330, 334, 335

poverty, 9, 49

practice, ix, x, 70, 74, 75, 88, 89, 95, 125, 133, 140, 233, 234, 254, 285, 286, 287, 288, 289, 291, 292, 293, 295, 296

present action, 91, 92, 93, 96, 97, 98, 99, 100, 288

present day, 74, 81, 82, 83, 84, 85, 86, 87, 88, 89, 324

proper alternative, 111, 112, 114, 115, 116, 117, 118, 119, 247

R

reason, xi, 7, 8, 9, 12, 13, 18, 19, 25, 49, 62, 73, 75, 78, 81, 84, 95, 115, 116, 117, 126, 130, 140, 151, 154, 156, 175, 177, 182, 204, 215, 216, 217, 219, 226, 228, 229, 231, 232, 234, 237, 238, 242, 243, 250, 251, 257, 258, 264, 265, 268, 269, 276, 292, 298, 299, 310, 312, 315, 316, 320, 331

recovery, 55, 95, 174, 328

reformed Stoicism, ix, x, xi, 32, 187, 203, 280, 292, 311, 312, 313, 315, 316, 317, 319, 320, 322, 323, 324, 325, 326, 327, 328, 329, 331, 332

reformed Stoics, ix, 265, 266, 313, 316, 317, 318, 326, 329, 331

rules of a game, 197, 200, 288, 319

S

Seneca, ix, xi, 3, 5, 6, 7, 8, 11, 14, 17, 18, 20, 22, 50, 62, 64, 69, 70, 71, 72, 74, 75, 77, 78, 81, 82, 83, 84, 85, 92, 95, 103, 104, 105, 106, 107, 108, 110, 112, 117, 123, 124, 125, 127, 128, 130, 132, 133, 135, 136, 141, 144, 149, 158, 161, 162, 170, 173, 174, 175, 180, 183, 184,

185, 186, 190, 208, 214, 215, 221, 227, 228, 229, 230, 232, 233, 237, 244, 245, 249, 252, 255, 257, 258, 263, 268, 273, 274, 276, 278, 279, 280, 282, 283, 289, 290, 291, 293, 294, 295, 301, 302, 303, 305, 308, 309, 311, 312, 321, 328, 333, 334, 335

simplicity, 298, 305, 306, 322

sloth, 25, 59, 82, 181, 182, 244, 295

Stankiewicz, xi, 56, 58, 177, 193, 334, 335, 336

T

There are other games, 213

To each their own mistakes, 241

Treacherous constancy, 173

U

useless, 6, 13, 14, 17, 18, 19, 20, 21, 22, 23, 24, 25, 26, 27, 28, 29, 44, 59, 70, 73, 77, 81, 89, 93, 100, 101, 103, 104, 105, 107, 116, 135, 139, 145, 148, 150, 173, 177, 204, 205, 209, 220, 229, 235, 243, 253, 256, 258, 292, 296, 298, 299, 316

V

values, 19, 29, 31, 36, 37, 39, 45, 49, 54, 56, 58, 59, 65, 69, 70, 74, 75, 76, 77, 87, 94, 95, 96, 97, 105, 109, 148, 159, 169, 178, 179, 181, 209, 225, 227, 233, 238, 245, 248, 256, 271, 300, 329

virtue, ix, 86, 173, 208, 215, 230, 231, 273, 278, 280, 289, 305, 306, 326

W

weakness, 150, 210, 239, 252, 273, 279, 292, 308

wealth, 31, 33, 45, 48, 63, 86, 214, 282, 299

Whatever the world is like, 263, 269, 271, 301

within our power, 31, 32, 33, 34, 35, 36, 37, 38, 39, 42, 43, 44, 45, 47, 48, 49, 50, 51, 52, 53, 54, 55, 56, 57, 58, 60, 61, 62, 63, 64, 65, 71, 75, 78, 81, 83, 86, 88, 100, 104, 106, 109, 110, 113, 116, 117, 119, 145, 149, 151, 159, 164, 171, 174, 178, 203, 210, 219, 232, 241, 242, 243, 244, 245, 248, 249, 251, 256, 259, 263, 265, 267, 271, 281, 288, 292, 297, 298, 300, 301, 305, 306, 307, 317, 318, 322, 324

Y

You are never alone, 183

Your lifetime will suffice, 103